THE POSTHUMOUS CAREER OF
EMILIANO ZAPATA

Joe R. and Teresa Lozano Long Series in Latin American and Latino Art and Culture

THE POSTHUMOUS CAREER
OF EMILIANO ZAPATA

Myth, Memory, and Mexico's
Twentieth Century

SAMUEL BRUNK

UNIVERSITY OF TEXAS PRESS
Austin

Requests for permission to reproduce material
from this work should be sent to:
Permissions
University of Texas Press
P.O. Box 7819
Austin, TX 78713-7819
www.utexas.edu/utpress/about/bpermission.html

♾ The paper used in this book meets the minimum requirements of
ANSI/NISO Z39.48-1992 (R1997) (Permanence of Paper).

Library of Congress Cataloging-in-Publication Data

Brunk, Samuel, 1959–
    The posthumous career of Emiliano Zapata : myth, memory, and
Mexico's twentieth century / Samuel Brunk. — 1st ed.
        p. cm. — (Joe R. and Teresa Lozano Long series in Latin
American and Latino art and culture)
    Includes bibliographical references and index.
    ISBN 978-0-292-71780-0 (cloth : alk. paper)
    1. Zapata, Emiliano, 1879–1919—Influence. 2. Mexico—Politics and
government—20th century. 3. Hero worship—Mexico. I. Title.
    F1234.Z37B79 2008
    972.08′1092—dc22
                                                    2008000385

To Phyllis, Anne, and Maddie

CONTENTS

ACKNOWLEDGMENTS ix

INTRODUCTION 1

1. A WAR OF IMAGES 21

2. THE REGIONAL CULT 41

3. FORGING A NATIONAL ZAPATA, 1920–1934 59

4. MAKING ZAPATA OFFICIAL 88

5. A MODERN ZAPATA FOR A GOLDEN AGE, 1940–1968 119

6. PUTTING ZAPATA ON THE MAP, 1920–1968 152

7. RESURRECTING THE REBEL: EMILIANO ZAPATA
AT WORK AND PLAY, 1968–1988 187

8. GOING HOME TO CHIAPAS 220

9. CONCLUSION: OF LEVIATHAN, *LO MEXICANO*,
AND ZAPATA ON THE BORDER 249

NOTES 267

BIBLIOGRAPHY 317

INDEX 341

ACKNOWLEDGMENTS

Books that take as long as this one to complete leave a lot of people to thank. For help on the research end, I offer my appreciation to the employees at the following Mexican institutions: the Archivo General de la Nación; the Archivo Histórico de la Defensa Nacional; the Biblioteca Manuel Orozco y Berra; the Centro de Estudios de Historia de México, Condumex; the Instituto de Investigaciones Sobre la Universidad y la Educación, Archivo Histórico de la UNAM; the Biblioteca Nacional; the Hemeroteca Nacional; the library at the Universidad Panamericana; the Instituto Nacional de Antropología e Historia; and the Instituto de Investigaciones Dr. José María Luis Mora. Thanks are also due to the staffs of the library at the University of Texas, El Paso (UTEP); Love Library at the University of Nebraska; and the Nettie Lee Benson Library at the University of Texas, Austin. I am extremely grateful to Mateo Zapata, Ana María Zapata and her family, the children of Antonio Díaz Soto y Gama—Salvador, Magdalena, and Enriqueta Soto y Ugalde—and others who took the time to grant me interviews. Reginaldo Allec Campos and Javier Flores helped arrange these interviews and contributed insights of their own to my project.

Over many years I have received sage advice and much encouragement from other scholars of Zapatismo, including Laura Espejel, Alicia Olivera, Salvador Rueda, Ruth Arboleyda, Felipe Arturo Avila Espinosa, Francisco Javier Pineda, Carlos Barreto, and Theresa Avila. Two of my UTEP colleagues, Yolanda Leyva and Cheryl Martin, were kind enough to give me materials pertaining to Zapata's myth, and many other scholars, as the endnotes indicate, provided me with important leads. Crucial institutional support for my work came in the form of two summer research fellowships from the University of Nebraska, Lincoln, and a University Research Grant and a Faculty Development Leave from UTEP. UTEP, in particular, with its dynamic scholarly community and exciting border environment, has been the ideal place to bring this book to fruition.

Gabriela Cano, John Lear, and Enrique Ochoa all read the entire manuscript and offered guidance that greatly improved it. Ben Fallaw helped me broaden my thinking about many key issues. The following UTEP graduate students also read the manuscript, whether they wanted to or not: Ron Adams, Miranda Barton, Javier Beltrán, Braulio Cañas, Sheron Caton, Jill Constantin, Aaron Edstrom, Manuel Enciso, Daniel Flores, Nancy González, Luis Herrera, Antonio López, Lisa Miller, Keith Morris, Nohemí Orozco, Guillermina Peña, Adrian Quesada, Gabriel Ramírez, Naipo Robertson, Jorge Rodríguez, Endi Silva, Jamie Starling, Jackie Stroud, and Gabe Valdez. Antonio López offered especially perceptive comments. Thanks to three other UTEP graduate students, Juan Manuel Mendoza Guerrero, Jorge H. Jiménez, and José Mariano Campero, for their help with Mexican colloquialisms. The University of Texas Press, the University of New Mexico Press, and Duke University Press allowed me to include material from, respectively, my edited volume with Ben Fallaw, *Heroes and Hero Cults in Latin America* (Austin: University of Texas Press, 2006); my chapter, "The Mortal Remains of Emiliano Zapata," in Lyman Johnson, ed., *Death, Dismemberment, and Memory: Body Politics in Latin America* (Albuquerque: University of New Mexico Press, 2004); and "Remembering Emiliano Zapata: Three Moments in the Posthumous Career of the Martyr of Chinameca," *Hispanic American Historical Review* 78 (August 1998). I would also like to thank the always encouraging and helpful Theresa May, copy editors Victoria Davis and Marjorie Pannell, and others at the University of Texas Press for all they have done to steer my work toward its final form.

This book is dedicated to my mother, Phyllis Brunk, my wife, Anne Perry, and my daughter, Maddie Brunk. The accomplishment would mean little if I could not share it with them.

THE POSTHUMOUS CAREER OF
EMILIANO ZAPATA

INTRODUCTION

No book could possibly chart the innumerable ways in which people have remembered Emiliano Zapata. In Mexico, streets, *ejidos, colonias,* cities and towns, schools, children, restaurants, hotels, auto repair shops, hospitals, and a subway stop have been named for him.[1] He has been the subject of gossip and rumor, *corridos* and other songs, folktales, newspaper articles, political speeches, works of visual art, novels, plays, and movies.[2] His image has been engraved on coins, immortalized in statues, affixed to a ten-peso note, and marketed on posters, T-shirts, and mouse pads. He has crossed borders, too—in the United States he has been appropriated by a line of frozen Mexican foods, embodied by Marlon Brando, and acclaimed by the band Rage Against the Machine. A recent Google search yielded about 71,500 results. Both in Mexico and elsewhere Zapata has been a statement of purpose, the center of controversy, an object of worship. Because of his very ubiquity, however, it has also been possible to take him for granted. The inhabitants of a given Colonia Emiliano Zapata might know little about him, and the prominent scholar Roger Bartra discounts his importance in Mexico's political culture.[3] In a sense, then, Zapata is—and has been—both everywhere and nowhere in Mexico. He is a bit like the air people breathe, part of what it means to be Mexican, but these are not things people think about every day.

Before Zapata was a memory, of course, he was a man. In early 1911, he and a group of *campesinos* (peasants) from in and around his home village of Anenecuilco, Morelos, joined a broad rebellion against the regime of longtime dictator Porfirio Díaz. For them, taking arms against Díaz meant fighting to stop expanding haciendas from infringing on the land and water rights of their villages. It also meant fighting for local liberties—for the right to make many of their decisions for themselves, decisions that had increasingly been taken out of their hands during Díaz's extended rule. Together, land and liberty were critical to the preservation of the rural culture that Zapata and his collaborators valued. Zapata soon took over the leadership of this movement, and Díaz, surprisingly, soon fell. Zapata then began to discover, however, that land reform was not high on the agenda of leaders of the many other groups that had joined the revolution. In November 1911, this realization prompted him to produce, with the help of local schoolteacher Otilio Montaño, the famous Plan of Ayala, with which he laid out his demands to the nation and struck out on his own revolutionary path. The civil war deepened as one faction battled another, and for nearly a decade Zapata fought for his principles—and tried to implement them— in this conflict that became known as the Mexican Revolution. In the process, he developed a national program and reputation. Then, on April 10, 1919, he was killed in an ambush at the hacienda Chinameca by revolutionaries loyal to Venustiano Carranza, who had been trying since 1915 to consolidate power from Mexico City.

Zapata was far from being a national hero when he died, but his program, and his clarity and consistency with regard to his goals—unrivaled by any of his revolutionary competitors—captured imaginations in what was then a largely rural country. The lasting power of his memory was apparent on the first day of 1994, when the Zapatista Army of National Liberation (Ejército Zapatista de Liberación Nacional, EZLN) rose up in the state of Chiapas against the neoliberal policies of President Carlos Salinas de Gortari. In an attempt to allow market forces freer play in the Mexican economy, in 1991 and 1992 Salinas had taken the controversial step of abandoning provisions in Article 27 of the Constitution of 1917 that called for the redistribution of land and protected communal landholding. Although politicians of the ruling party—the Institutional Revolutionary Party (Partido Revolucionario Institucional, PRI)—had claimed for decades that Zapata's demands were the inspiration for Article 27, the Salinas administration frequently employed the figure of Zapata, both visually and verbally, in pushing its reforms.

But Salinas was not successful in his efforts to steer Zapata's meaning in a new direction. Peasants opposing the changes to Article 27 utilized Zapata in their marches, and the EZLN rallied opposition to the national government around a renewed Zapatismo, often in creative ways. In August 1994, for example, they held a convention in Chiapas. To house this event, they carved a new settlement out of the jungle, which they named Aguascalientes in reference to the site of a military convention that occurred in 1914, in the thick of the revolution. At that original convention, the Zapatistas and the followers of Francisco "Pancho" Villa formed an alliance, which was consolidated when Zapata and Villa met in Mexico City

FIGURE I.1

Zapata with Pancho Villa in Mexico City. (Used by permission of Special Collections,
University of California, Riverside, Libraries, University of California, Riverside.)

in December 1914. There they were memorialized in one of the revolution's
most famous photographs, which pictured Villa sitting in the presidential
chair, Zapata beside him with a giant sombrero on his knee, and a crowd of
hopeful revolutionaries behind them (see Figure I.1). To advertise *its* Convention of Aguascalientes, the EZLN plastered Mexico City with posters that
appropriated this photograph, inserting in place of Zapata the EZLN's most
prominent spokesman, Subcomandante Marcos, wearing his signature ski
mask but also holding the sombrero. Beside him, supplanting Villa, was
urban social activist and former professional wrestler Superbarrio Gómez,
in his customary wrestling garb (see Figure I.2). Salinas answered the EZLN
with political theater of his own. Although he was not ready to surrender
the PRI's claim to Zapata, shortly after the outbreak of the Chiapas insurgency he chose to proclaim amnesty for the rebels and express his desire for
dialogue in front of an image of Carranza—the man ultimately responsible
for Zapata's death. The threat was not lost on Marcos.[4]

Clearly, Mexican politics in the 1990s were about more than just policy.
They were about style, too, about "spin," and for both Salinas and the EZLN
finding the proper spin meant, among other things, deciding how best to
engage in the symbolic battle over Zapata. This was true because Zapata, as

3

FIGURE I.2
EZLN poster, De la Selva de Concreto a la Selva Lacandona, *1994.*

the key spokesman for the revolution's most fundamental social issue, was
a commanding historical personage. But the political need to make something of Zapata probably had less to do with the story of Zapata the man
than with that of his mythical twin—with the way in which memories of
him had developed since his death.

A myth can be defined as a "traditional story of ostensibly historical
events that serves to unfold part of the world view of a people or explain a
practice, belief, or natural phenomenon."[5] This definition does not exclude
the possibility that elements of a myth might be historically accurate. Indeed, it is difficult to separate mythical and historical stories precisely. Both
refer to the past—to "history," that is, in the sense of things that have happened in the past rather than in the sense of what has been *written* about
the past. And both fall short of capturing that past, and thus of expressing
the "truth," most fundamentally because, like all stories, they have to cut
experience down to a thinkable, meaningful size. One difference, though,
lies in the kinds of meaning that myths and histories deliver. The meaning of a myth is communal and popular, with value for the "world view
of a people." Religions are composed of myths. A history, meanwhile, is

4

simply an account of change over time, and is not required by definition to intrude on anyone's worldview. That does not mean that historians never have mythical goals in mind; they have often sought, for instance, to justify a "people's" claim to land, recognition, or authority. But even with such goals their books are unlikely to appeal to enough imaginations to generate myths on their own. Rather, they typically provide raw material that gets swept up in myths, which must ultimately be bigger and broader than histories, based on the contributions of a wide variety of people, to have much impact on a group's view of reality.

A myth, then, is a story from which people can derive a sense of shared identity and community. In his book, *Imagined Communities,* Benedict Anderson has drawn attention to the ways in which myths have helped people imagine—or create—*national* communities in particular, often by envisioning historical unity for a given population based on common cultural roots.[6] Anderson adds that nationalist thought is intensely concerned with the deaths and immortality of those who have sacrificed for the national good, something that can be seen in the tombs of unknown soldiers that exist in many countries. The imagining of a nation, in other words, often includes what can only be called ancestor worship, in which heroic ancestors of a national community represent ostensibly shared cultural characteristics and the historical events that are accepted as being critical to that nation's formation and survival.[7] One of the key functions of such departed heroes is that they help simplify conceptions of nations, which is necessary because national communities are, in reality, far too large and complex to be easily understood and envisioned in themselves. One cannot, for instance, know everyone in a nation as one might in a small town. By serving as shorthand for aspects of nations, heroes can help large numbers of people identify with their national communities and accept their basic principles and laws.[8] Clearly, nationalism and religious thought are strongly interrelated; in fact, nations themselves are mythical creatures.

As symbols of national unity, heroic ancestors are often employed by officials seeking to enhance state power (a "state" being defined as the civil and military bureaucracies of a territory and the officials, in different branches and at various levels, who run those bureaucracies).[9] State authorities can benefit from the national identity that heroes help produce because a population of people who feel themselves to be part of a single community may be less fractious—and thus more easily governed—than a population that does not. In addition, political leaders often invoke heroes in an effort to bolster their own legitimacy through association with admired predecessors, and in the hope of making citizens more virtuous and productive by giving them models to follow. Ideally, heads of state want to encourage their constituents not to differentiate between state and nation, so that when a Mexican considers the Mexican nation, she or he automatically thinks of the Mexican president as its embodiment and spokesperson.

Rulers cannot, however, just shape heroic myths and their national contexts according to their own designs. Though specific groups and individuals try to manipulate them, at base myths are social products, made by the many, not the few. In this vein, it is crucial not to take the concept of the nation as an "imagined community" so far as to envision nations as being imagined out of nothing, the purely fictional constructions of elites. A useful caution against any such tendency comes in the work of Anthony D. Smith, who stresses that though nations are relatively modern entities, they are generally built from materials excavated from older traditions.[10] Anderson's reference to ancestor worship, after all, brings to mind images of tribally organized peoples remembering departed elders, and when a national hero is called a founding father it is an evocation both of the family community and of the ancestor cult. The Christian cults of saints that arose during Europe's Middle Ages and traveled to Latin America constitute another type of hero worship in existence long before there were nations, and during the last two centuries leaders of many countries have consciously sought to bolster national identification by adopting heroes with religious vestiges—those who can be understood, as noted above, as having become martyrs for their nations—to capture for their states some of the sense of the sacred at work within religious communities.[11] Those who become heroes of nations, then, often have roots in other, usually smaller communities. These communities are also "imagined," because even in cases where members of a community all know one another, the elements that define and unite it are unlikely to be entirely obvious or natural. At any rate, predating the nation, such communities limit what leaders of modern states can do with the myths they supply.[12] Elite conspirators might seek to avoid those limitations by fabricating myths out of whole cloth, but given their lack of rootedness, such creations would probably not achieve mythical status, and thus be of little use to their makers.

A second critique of the top-down approach to the generation of myth is that we cannot completely separate states from the societies in which they operate. Replete with different branches, levels, ministries, and committees, states are rarely highly unified structures. They are therefore inevitably staffed by people, themselves members of society, who work at cross-purposes from one another on behalf of different constituencies and consequently deliver different and sometimes conflicting messages. Indeed, the signals sent by a particular representative of the state are likely to be intended in part for the consumption of other officials, in the vain hope of getting the state's actors on the same page. All this makes it impossible to draw a hard line between cynical official manipulators of a myth and the gullible masses who accept it.[13] Rather, everyone who employs a myth (except for its hypothetical inventor) has received it first from someone else, and any given member of a political elite may wholeheartedly believe in the mythical constructions he or she disseminates. Everyone, in other words, is to some extent both caught in the "web of significance" spun by his or her society and a participant in its spinning.[14]

Thus, while the building of state power and institutions and the forging of nations *have* been profoundly interconnected because elites have had good reasons to create and manipulate national mythologies and the heroes that are part of them, the creation and use of nations and their heroes is both a collective endeavor and one that can be opposed. Non-state actors can reject the concept of nation altogether and instead use heroes to bolster the identity of local communities, or they can embrace the nation but define it in ways different from those used by members of the state.[15] At a minimum, for heroes and nations to be heroes and nations people have to accept them, and in doing so they also participate in their formation, adapting them to their personal needs or to those of the smaller communities in which they live.

Precisely when myths arose is impossible to ascertain; they do not turn up in archaeological digs. But widespread practices such as the ceremonial burial of the dead and the composing of accounts of creation demonstrate that myth has long been a fundamental facet of human life.[16] The existence of leaders who organized their communities for food collection and production, for warfare, and for religious ritual was also pervasive in early human societies. These leaders were often remembered after their deaths through ancestor worship.[17] An ancestor cult need amount to nothing more than a family coming together around an altar in the home or at a burial site to remember an ancestor who has died. But leaders and—an overlapping category—individuals with charisma have often been of lasting significance for people outside their family circles. Sociologist Max Weber defined charisma as "a certain quality of an individual personality by virtue of which he is set apart from ordinary men and treated as endowed with supernatural, superhuman, or at least specifically exceptional powers or qualities." Others have suggested that charisma derives from being near the center of power or important events.[18] Those dead whose value to the living transcended their families came to serve as ancestors of communities—bands, tribes, villages, ethnic groups, and eventually nations—which formed around their memories. Often still conceptualized as heads of families, these sacred, charismatic dead thus became part of the cultural glue that held their societies together.

The first Mexican civilization, that of the Olmec, which began to take shape on the Gulf of Mexico around 1200 BCE, did much to establish core beliefs in central Mexico. The Olmec worshipped the powerful or otherwise impressive animals in their environment, such as the jaguar, the largest predator. They developed a priesthood and began the tradition of human sacrifice and other forms of bloodletting, as well as that of making pilgrimages to sites they considered sacred. Specific kings were often depicted on Olmec monuments, and frequently related to gods and other supernatural forces. Various skills were attributed to the powerful, such as the ability to transform themselves into jaguars. The Olmecs probably had gods associated with rain, earth, and corn—as would later Mesoamericans—and worshipped a feathered serpent, a god subsequent cultures would identify as Quetzalcóatl.[19]

Later cultures elaborated on some Olmec beliefs and added others. Quetzalcóatl reappeared at the city of Teotihuacán, and developed in different societies into a hero with a role in creation. The Aztecs conflated him with a historical figure from the Toltec world, and the city of Cholula, with its massive pyramid, became his pilgrimage site.[20] In these agricultural societies mythical developments were often related to agricultural cycles and the earth. The Mayan concept of the afterlife envisioned death as leading to a journey into the underworld, where one sought to outwit the gods of death. If successful, one appeared thereafter in the sky as a heavenly body. This story of death and regeneration was associated with the life cycle of corn. The Mayan creation myth, in fact, included the idea that humans were made from corn, and the Maya often depicted the god of corn rising from the earth as a growing cornstalk. Other peoples in the region also developed the notion that human beings had originally emerged from the earth, and associated death with renewal and fertility.[21]

Ancestor worship was important throughout the area and, at least once they were dead, most rulers were apparently recognized as divine. Pyramids in the Mayan world often housed tombs that enshrined important ancestors, and Mayan art was full of rulers and their kin offering sacrifices to honor the dead. King Bird Jaguar, from Yaxchilan, depicted his parents in the heavens on his monuments, enclosed within cartouches—outlines—of the sun and moon. Texts on Mayan monuments were both historical and sacred, and representations of Mayan rulers were ambiguous enough that they could be seen as deity impersonators, actual gods, or both at the same time. The Zapotecs of the territory that became the state of Oaxaca, meanwhile, built underground tombs for their renowned dead, decorated with paintings and equipped with pots for food and drink. Zapotec gods were probably idealized ancestors of particularly important lineages. The Aztec Moctezuma, who was present at the time of the Spanish conquest, seems to have lived his life as if divine: his feet never touched the ground, he avoided all eye contact, and no one was permitted to watch him eat.[22]

Profound concern with death, sacrifice, and the afterlife; the worship of important personages in death and sometimes in life; the association of myth with particular places; the lack of any clear distinction between myth and historical record and, sometimes, between humans and gods; the importance of corn and the earth—these were key elements of pre-Columbian belief, many of which would reappear in Zapata's cult. But they did not do so until after the Spanish made their contribution to the history of Mexican myth following the conquest of 1521. That contribution, of course, came in the container of Christianity. Driven by great fervor connected with the fall of the last bastion of Islam in Spain and the simultaneous discovery of a new missionary field in the Americas, the Spanish rooted out and destroyed the "idols" of the indigenous inhabitants, replacing them with their own images—of Jesus Christ, the Virgin Mary, and a wide array of saints. Duplicating practices established in Spain, they developed a network of sanctuaries honoring these figures across Mexico, often at sites that had attracted pilgrims before the conquest.[23] But much as Olmec myth had blended into the traditions of subsequent cultures, so did pre-Columbian religious thought merge with Christianity. Aztec festivals for dead children and dead adults, previously held during separate months, were moved to coincide with Catholic observance of All Saints and All Souls days at the beginning of November, and the Mexican Day of the Dead was born.[24] Through vehicles such as this one, ancestor worship may have remained the key element of religious activity among indigenous populations into the eighteenth century.[25]

The Virgin of Guadalupe, whose tale as patroness of Mexico goes back to 1531, made her famed appearance on a hill associated with the worship of the earth goddess Tonantzin, her dark skin representing the coming together of cultures and peoples. Hers was a foundation myth, a specifically Mexican foundation for church and, ultimately, nation, which helped give Mexicans the status of a chosen people.[26] There was also Santiago (the apostle Saint James), who had since the ninth century enjoyed a pilgrimage site in Spain around what were ostensibly his bones. Over time he had developed into the warrior saint figuratively at the head of the Christian re-conquest of the Iberian Peninsula. In Mexico he manifested himself as pa-tron saint of the conquest and his contributions as warrior were ritualized, particularly in the widely performed Dance of the Christians and Moors. Christianized Indians readily adopted this ritual and in doing so appropri-ated Santiago in various ways, as a defender of their interpretation of the faith, of course, but also often of the specific localities in which they lived. A crucial element in establishing Santiago's sway with the indigenous pop-ulation was his horse, a powerful animal, essential to the conquest effort, that was in some ways comparable to the jaguars and eagles worshipped by pre-Columbian cultures.[27]

After 1810 the movement for independence gathered these mythical predispositions toward the formation of a national myth. Some lower-class participants demonstrated their partial acceptance of messages from the mother country when they pictured the king as a source of justice in a patriarchal world, a messianic figure who would liberate Mexico from the bad rule of Spanish officials.[28] But leaders among the creoles—people of Spanish ancestry born in Mexico—looked instead to the Indian past. They borrowed Aztec resistance leader Cuauhtémoc as a patriotic hero who had struggled against Spanish tyranny, much as independence leaders Miguel Hidalgo and José María Morelos were doing. With Cuauhtémoc's help they argued that a Mexican nation had existed before the conquest, and that it was time to reassert its freedom.[29] They also adopted Quet-zalcóatl. Stretching their theological hypotheses to include the Americas, some early missionaries had contended that Quetzalcóatl was actually the Christian Saint Thomas, who had come long before the Spanish to instruct the Indians in Christianity. It was a perfect notion for indepen-dence leaders seeking to minimize the gifts Mexico had received from its erstwhile mother country. (On the other hand, some indigenous think-ers anxiously awaited Quetzalcóatl's return, not as a proponent of Christi-anity but as a liberator, whom they expected to form an invincible Indian army that would sweep the whites from the land and restore Mexico to its golden age.)[30]

Obviously, all of this was infused with a large dollop of religious fervor. With the Bourbon Reforms of the late 1700s, the Spanish crown ironically distanced itself from the religious ideology that had, since the conquest, played a fundamental role in legitimizing Spanish rule. This enabled both priests, such as Hidalgo and Morelos, and laity to put that ideology to use in justifying their desire to break the colonial relationship.[31] They did so, most strikingly, by drafting the Virgin of Guadalupe, who oversaw the work of the rebels and joined them, on their banners, as they fought. The driving ideological force behind the uprising was thus a form of religious nationalism, and so it was only natural that once independence was achieved, the remains of Morelos, who had been executed in 1815, were moved to the Virgin's shrine outside the capital.[32] In contrast to the universal posture of the founding fathers of the United States, then, Mexican expressions of patriotism at independence were based on Mexican history and religion. Both nations were mythical—if we stick with Anderson's definition—but Mexican national identity could be expressed through a rich and specific body of myth for which there was apparently no equivalent in the United States, where rebels drew instead on the principles of the international Enlightenment.[33]

The leaders of independence had settled a political issue with violence, establishing a habit that was not abandoned once independence was achieved. The ensuing period was characterized by the rule of *caudillos*—men on horseback leading troops loyal largely to them—who rose to compete for power. Seeking to gain legitimacy for the regimes they established, these men patterned themselves on the mythical archetypes of their culture— the Spanish kings, Jesus Christ, Santiago, Cuauhtémoc, Morelos—as they cultivated images as brave and selfless saviors of the nation.[34] For some this worked for a time, but it was hard for caudillos to appear selfless as they subverted the constitutional order, and their hero cults rarely outlasted their deaths.

A far more successful candidate for the new nation's pantheon was Benito Juárez, the Zapotec Indian politician who became a major figure in the Liberal Party's celebrated Reform era of the 1850s. Perhaps most important, in 1867 his forces defeated those of Emperor Maximilian, the Austrian archduke who had been given a Mexican throne by an invading French army. Juárez and the other liberals were no friends of the church, so rather than looking to Santiago or the Virgin of Guadalupe for inspiration and authority, they usually referred to the more recent national and secular past. "We come from the village of Dolores [Hidalgo's parish]," one asserted; "we descend from Hidalgo." Indeed, the identification was strong enough that Juárez would come to be seen by many as the father of a second independence.[35] With the liberal victory came the complete disgrace of the Conservative Party, which had supported the French invasion, and an epoch of liberal control of the presidency that continued—if we define liberalism broadly—virtually uninterrupted until Vicente Fox, representing the avowedly conservative Partido de Acción Nacional (National Action Party, PAN), came to power in the year 2000. Liberalism became identified with the nation, conservatism with its betrayal, and Juárez, some say, became Mexico's most revered ancestor of all.

The second great rider on this liberal wave was Porfirio Díaz (1876–1880, 1884–1911). Díaz took the presidency as a caudillo—by force of arms—and corrupted, thereafter, the democratic provisions of the Reform Constitution of 1857 in order to perpetuate his power. On the other hand, he did preside over the kind of economic growth of which the progress-minded liberals had long dreamed. Like the makers of independence, he mined the Aztec past as he sought to legitimate his rule, centralize power in the capital, enhance national identity, and project a vision of a unique Mexican nation into the international community. Díaz's era was one of monument building. For the first time statues made the concept of nation visible to the populace in many parts of the country, and in the capital, along a fancy new boulevard called the Paseo de la Reforma, the dictator's regime laid out the liberal version of Mexican history in stone and bronze, embracing the foundational Indian past with Cuauhtémoc and the modern, progressive nation with imposing monuments to independence and Juárez.[36]

By the time of the Mexican Revolution, then, Mexico was endowed with a broad and deep tradition of myth in general and ancestor worship in particular. Ancestor worship was performed, in part, on the Day of the Dead, actually the first *two* days of November, when families remembered (and remember) their departed by building colorful altars and feasting in the cemeteries. It was manifested in the saint's day festivities carried out in nearly every Mexican settlement. And it infused Mexico's already sizable pantheon of national heroes. The process through which the body of Mexican myth evolved was one of accrual, in which new beliefs and rituals mingled with those that preceded them, producing new forms, but not fully distinct ones, so that the religious and the secular, the indigenous and the Spanish, became hard to separate one from the other.

What are the implications of this history of myth for the story of Zapata's cult? First, it was on this base that the myth of Zapata would be built, because the leaders of the revolution, despite being revolutionaries, were no more able, in some cases, and no more inclined, in others, to throw out the mythical past than were those who presided over previous periods of change. Second, it demonstrates the persistent need for myth, not because Mexico remained somehow backward and superstitious but because myth is a fundamental, pervasive, indispensable component of human existence. It came more or less with language, or so it would seem, and as long as we use language and remain social creatures it will surely endure, despite modernity—whatever precisely that is—with its supposedly rationalist inclinations. The nature of myth has changed at points in Mexican history, becoming more about nation and less about god during the nineteenth century, but secular attitudes did not stamp it out. Finally, we should note that the indispensability of myth suggests that it cannot be seen as something peripheral to human activities, only symbolic, somehow, in contrast to real, practical action. Rather, it is built in from human beginnings, a part of doing what humans do, and as such is both action in itself and a form that action takes.

Jesús Silva Herzog, a postrevolutionary economist and government official, was not overstating the case by much when he declared, "we Mexicans have two deities: Our Lady the Virgin of Guadalupe and Our Lady the Mexican Revolution."[37] Two noteworthy books have explored the birth of that second goddess. Ilene O'Malley's pathbreaking *The Myth of the Revolution* (1988) describes how, in the years between 1920 and 1940, the new revolutionary rulers distorted history to portray deceased revolutionaries as founding fathers of the new order. As they did so, she contends, they attached to such popular leaders as Zapata messages of nationalism and patriarchalism meant to pacify and otherwise manipulate the inhabitants of Mexico. In particular, they promoted fatalism, rather than revolutionary action, by claiming that they, as rightful heirs of these founding fathers, would see to people's needs. Individuals and groups that resisted such efforts to pull them into the national community the revolution sought to construct were stigmatized as antipatriotic.[38]

Unfortunately, O'Malley's discussion of revolutionary myth is a tale in which the political elite uses it to bludgeon the masses—who apparently do not help create the myth but are merely its victims—into mystified submission. Though she is correct that those at the top of the postrevolutionary heap sought to manipulate symbols to their own advantage, without an examination of the rest of Mexican society she has only part of the picture.[39] A useful corrective to her overemphasis on the role of the state comes in a second broad assessment of revolutionary myth, Thomas Benjamin's *La Revolución: Mexico's Great Revolution as Memory, Myth, and History* (2000). Benjamin argues that through rhetoric, ritual, and symbol, the sundry events and factions of the decade of fighting (1910–1920) were molded into the concept of a single revolution that became absolutely critical to the way in which Mexicans viewed their country. He attributes this mythification process to the efforts of people he calls "*voceros* of the revolution"— "scribblers, journalists, politicians, intellectuals, propagandists, and other insurgent spokesmen and women"—and maintains that the state did not need to manage revolutionary history because "the government's view of the history of *La Revolución* seemed to be the same as that held by society in general."[40] He does not, however, offer an explanation of how this consensus took shape, nor does he explore precisely who his *voceros* were. At base, the problem is that, like O'Malley, Benjamin fails to consider either how the messages he studies might have been received or—beyond discussion of a few corridos—the ways in which the revolution's lower-class participants may have helped shape ideas about it. He does, though, reinforce O'Malley's work in offering solid appraisals of the pace at which memories of the revolution were institutionalized and the role of personalism within revolutionary myth.

Other scholars have focused on memories of Zapata in particular, many of them researching the way he has been used by groups that O'Malley and Benjamin overlook. One historian, for example, has interpreted postrevolutionary peasant mobilizations as elaborations on Zapata's program, and another has traced the vicissitudes of an organization of Zapatista veterans.[41] Some have studied the corridos written about Zapata and his movement, and others have concentrated on visual images, historiography, and textbooks.[42] At least one author has compiled information on commemorations of the day of Zapata's death.[43] Various social scientists have done detailed studies of communities in Morelos, where they have discovered ongoing Zapatista sentiment at the local level.[44] Oral history projects have also recorded lasting identification with Zapata.[45] Salvador Rueda and Laura Espejel have produced a general essay on the mythical Zapata, while others have addressed the uses of Zapata since the 1990s.[46] One work along the latter lines is Lynn Stephen's *Zapata Lives!,* which inspects memories of Zapata in four villages in the states of Oaxaca and Chiapas during the 1930s and the 1990s, thus broaching the subject of the myth's geographical range.[47] Finally, Claudio Lomnitz has used rhetoric about Zapata to examine relationships of culture and power within Morelos and between the state of Morelos and the national government, demonstrating how Zapata's image has both greased the wheels of the political system and supported dissent.[48]

This book is a synthesis in that it draws from the work of these scholars, and also because, unlike some of the publications mentioned above, it considers a wide variety of primary sources. Unlike any of the works mentioned above, it also details the course of revolutionary myth—or at least one more or less manageable strand of that myth—throughout the twentieth century. By taking the long view, I believe, it helps answer one of the fundamental questions about the revolution that scholars have not yet fully resolved. Alan Knight's powerful survey of revolutionary history, *The*

Mexican Revolution (1986), maintains that it was fundamentally a popular, peasant rebellion, but there has been much debate on that point.[49] Those who have argued most strongly against conceptualizing the revolution in this way—historians known as "revisionists" who were active in the 1970s and 1980s—were influenced by the fact that the revolutionary state had increasingly revealed itself to be a corrupt and nondemocratic entity.[50] Especially since 1940, it had not looked very "popular." Moreover, this state had not resolved the problem of peasant poverty. Though it was sometimes only implicit, a key question of the revisionists was whether a truly popular revolution could produce an authoritarian state. A better question is why such revolutions *do* produce such states, for they have done so in a wide variety of world contexts, especially since the beginning of the twentieth century.[51] If Knight is right, the masses of Mexico—workers and, especially, peasants—mobilized in a social revolution that lasted for a decade and profoundly fragmented state structures in the process. In some localities the state disappeared completely. Why, then, in the decades that followed, would this mobilized citizenry permit the pieces to be put back together to produce the kind of state that drew revisionist ire? And what gave the new political arrangements such longevity, producing a single-party system that lasted for the remainder of the century?

There are a number of partial answers to these questions, some of the most obvious and well established focusing on material rewards and organizational accomplishments. Campesinos did receive land in the aftermath of the fighting, especially in the mid-1930s, and in exchange many were willing to pledge their loyalty to the regime, even when that meant the surrender of democracy and other liberties.[52] Beyond policies that were actually carried out, there were also the *promises* of rewards for peasants and workers that had been written into the Constitution of 1917, and the ensuing pronouncements of politicians in postrevolutionary administrations meant to keep people hoping and thus string them along. Then, on the base of those rewards and promises came the construction of the ruling party, ultimately called the PRI, which would control Mexican politics from its creation in 1929 into the 1990s. The main architect of this party was President Lázaro Cárdenas (1934–1940), who made peasants and workers—newly organized into separate, officially recognized confederations—two of its main pillars. While inclusion in this organization surely raised some hopes, as time passed any expectations that party membership would give lower-class groups substantial power faded. Peasants and workers could and did bargain for benefits, but their pull was limited in a party that served more to manage them than to give them voice.[53] Other big pieces of the puzzle may be found in the repression directed against peasants by self-interested army officers, and the ability of the civilian leaders of the postrevolutionary state to slowly subject the military to their command.[54]

While these arguments are valuable, to some extent they beg the question. Why, exactly, were peasants and other groups willing to be demobilized, to accept the promises and pronouncements, to make the concessions and trade-offs? Why, when they realized that material benefits would be limited, did they not again rebel en masse? What was the role of local cultures, the cultures of the people who did the fighting during the revolutionary decade, in conditioning those decisions? And what about the issue of national identity—could loyalty to the idea of a Mexican nation have played a part? The answers to these questions lie in the realm of political culture, which Florencia Mallon has defined as a combination of "beliefs, practices, and debates around the accumulation and contestation of power."[55] As we have seen, O'Malley finds that the state subjugated the people of Mexico with its hero cults, and Benjamin that the new government benefited from a consensus about the revolution's meaning. Looking more closely at both the nature of the political system and its constituents, Lomnitz indicates considerable success on the part of the state, using Zapata, in integrating the people of Morelos into national culture and establishing paths of negotiation between Morelian bureaucrats and peasants. He finds that the state achieved a substantial degree of "cultural hegemony," but not so much that it became impossible for peasants to make claims against it or even reject its authority altogether.[56] Other cultural explanations have been offered as well. Mary Kay Vaughan professes, for example, that the role of education and of discussions, through teachers, about education and other issues ultimately helped produce a "hegemonic consensus" unique to Latin America. This consensus allowed the PRI to rule as it did, but it also helped defend local identities and cultures.[57] Finally, Knight has argued that in terms of cultural transformation, revolutionary programs often failed to overcome behaviors of "recalcitrant people," and that market forces and better communications were more important than revolutionary policy in creating a more homogenous Mexican people with basic loyalty to party, state, and nation.[58]

Taking off from the thought of Italian Marxist Antonio Gramsci, the concept of hegemony that lies at the center of these discussions of political culture has been defined in many ways. At bottom it means legitimacy, but with the understanding that legitimacy does not exist simply because people approve of their government, but rather through the exercise and influence of power, which is unequally distributed within society. It is, in other words, a state of affairs in which the government is accepted by the people it governs because representatives of the state and substantial sectors of society have reached general, often tacit, agreement about the rules and practices of political power. The existence of hegemony means that those who rule do not need to depend solely on force to do so but can complement their use of force, which is always necessary to some degree, with rule by consent.[59]

Two issues related to the idea of hegemony are significant for our purposes. The first concerns the goals of the state. Since it is clearly in the interests of those who seek to govern to be considered legitimate, it may seem predictable that states have cultural projects to persuade or manipulate subjects or citizens into agreeing with their representatives about the basic rules of power. A typical goal of such a project, discussed above, is to instill a sense of national identity in a population while simultaneously trying to associate the nation with the state. Given the size and complexity of most modern states, however, one cannot take the existence of a coherent cultural project for granted.[60] Rather, its existence needs to be demonstrated and its characteristics described.

The second and more thorny issue has to do with the nature of the consent that produces hegemony. One possibility is that people are completely fooled by the state. To continue with the example offered in the previous paragraph, they come, perhaps over generations, to identify themselves above all as members of a national community and to understand their nation as inseparable from, or even the same thing as, their state. They also come to believe that the political culture of their nation is part of the natural order of things rather than a man-made settlement that could therefore be challenged. This degree of consent creates what has been called a "thick" form of hegemony, and those who have internalized and accepted the state's propaganda to this extent are said to be victims of "false consciousness," unable even to perceive their own interests, much less defend them.[61]

Consent can also be understood in a much "thinner" form. People who receive benefits or opportunities from the rules of the political game may agree to those rules out of self-interest rather than the belief that they are good or natural. Others may accept political arrangements they find unfair because they cannot imagine how to do anything about them. At any rate, individuals or groups falling into this thinner category of hegemony are able to see their interests—at least in part—despite the messages generated by the state. Those messages may be important somehow in keeping them from challenging the entire system, but they are not strong enough to prevent them from seeking to reshape that system, whether through direct negotiations, resistance to particular rules or procedures, or illegal activities, such as theft, that lessen the difficulties they face within the hegemonic order. This, then, is "consent" in only a limited sense, and many scholars have emphasized that the creation of hegemonic relations under such conditions must be an ongoing process, with readjustments constantly being made because of the negotiations and resistance. Still, under these conditions hegemony does exist; there is no *fundamental* challenge to the status quo, and state officials have tools other than violence and intimidation that help them keep it that way.

This book seeks to complement the findings of Lomnitz, Vaughan, Knight, and others by using Zapata's myth to explore the degree and nature of the state's legitimacy across twentieth-century Mexican history. Initially, there was no reason to expect that his image would have much to say about the legitimacy of the state. It did become vital to the identity of many people in his home region, but at the national level the adoption of Zapata as a founding father was just a small and unambitious facet of the moderately ambitious cultural project fashioned by the postrevolutionary elite. Zapata's myth turned out to be a remarkable part of that bigger picture, however, because it gradually became, and remained, a creation of substantial value at both national and more local levels. It became a central element of various imagined communities, in other words, and in the tension that resulted lies its lasting power.

During the decade of revolutionary warfare, with its accompanying political disintegration, Zapata had limited national appeal. He earned admiration on his home turf for his advocacy of peasant demands, but much of the rest of Mexico saw him as the enemy—and a bloodthirsty one at that. After his death in 1919, the campesinos of Morelos rewarded what they perceived as his sacrifice by infusing his image with sacred characteristics. Then, in 1920, the fighting—or at least the capture of national power through military force—ended, yielding a new central government that sought to put the country's pieces back together. With the aid of various artists and writers, Mexico's new rulers borrowed memories of Zapata from Morelos much as they found them, with the immediate goal of forging ties between nation and region and thus bringing the Zapatistas back into the national fold. Zapata was also useful in reaching out to a broader constituency as a symbol of the peasant role in the revolution and of the cause of land reform; as, alternately, a *mestizo* (of mixed ethnicity) or an Indian, who in either case embodied messages about Mexican ethnicity that the government was promoting; and as a patriarch who could convey lessons about authority—rather scarce in the wake of the war—to communities as small as families and as large as the nation.[62] Combining honors for Zapata with land reform, national politicians gained substantial peasant support between 1920 and 1940, though their program for the countryside, bestowing land but not liberty, only partially satisfied Zapata's demands.

Between 1940 and 1968, the state put its use of the Zapata myth to the test. National officials took steps to strengthen it—such as continuing the process, begun earlier, of spreading the cult around the country—in the hope that it would work alone, without the support of programs that offered clear benefits to campesinos. The national founding father Zapata proved equal to the challenge. People in Morelos and elsewhere did grumble, openly, about government hypocrisy on anniversaries of Zapata's death, but they either would not or could not formulate a counter-vision of Zapata that would help them confront the rules of the political game directly. As gauged by the myth of Zapata, then, hegemony continued to exist, albeit in only a thin form. Indeed, the government would never produce much false consciousness with Zapata, never achieve the kind of control over how he was remembered needed to create hegemony's thicker manifestation. Famed Mexican poet Octavio Paz put his finger on one reason why when he wrote in the 1950s that "Zapata dies at every popular fair."[63] By disseminating memories of Zapata around Mexico, the state created the conditions in which he could become rooted in new localities. There, like Santiago, for instance, before him, he could represent more local interests and, ultimately, local communities of protest could use him to challenge the government's authority. This became especially possible after the 1960s, when rural rebels in the state of Guerrero, Chicanos in the United States, and leaders of Mexico's student movement made conscious decisions to employ him against governmental forces, paving the way for subsequent organizations, some of them armed, to conceptualize Zapata as a rebel, not a founding father of the state as it was constituted.

Still, until 1994 the state continued to get mileage out of Zapata during a period in which something of a draw developed between officials and protesters about his meaning. This suggests the existence of only the thinnest of hegemonies, but politicians could in some cases still make forceful claims for their policies in Zapata's name, and despite rising instability the fundamental fact of Mexican politics did not change: the PRI controlled the presidency. After 1994, however, with the rise of the EZLN and the circulation of its inventive and resonant message—resonant in good part because Zapata was used to send it—Zapata became a known associate of the opposition. The postrevolutionary state had received magnificent returns on its investment in his myth, but he was now of little use in protecting the political status quo. In the year 2000, after seventy-one years of single-party rule, the election of Fox signaled the advent of new, more democratic political practices and the end of the PRI's monopoly on presidential power. Does that mean that a share of the myth of Zapata was a necessary component of the PRI's power? Surely not—again, his image was just one aspect of a much larger picture. But Zapata's myth does prove to be an effective measuring stick of certain political processes.

Given Zapata's nearly infinite number of manifestations, this book cannot have the final say on its subject; there are probably exceptions to every generalization in these pages. What I hope to offer instead, based on a sampling of Zapata's cult, is a readable story about political culture after the revolution, as well as a survey of the fascinating history of twentieth-century Mexico through the window provided by those who have chosen, for whatever reason, to remember Zapata. The details follow.

ONE

A WAR OF IMAGES

On December 4, 1914, Zapata met Francisco "Pancho" Villa in a school building at Xochimilco in the Federal District to firm up an alliance against the revolutionary faction of Venustiano Carranza. It was one of the pivotal moments of the revolutionary decade, and Zapata had dressed for the occasion. Wearing a black jacket and tight black pants with silver buttons along the outside of each leg, a loosely knotted silk tie—light blue in color—and a lavender shirt, Zapata as *charro* embodied country elegance as it was understood in his south-central Mexican world.[1] His dress reflected success and it was meant to leave an impression. This it certainly did, combined as it was with his dark, penetrating gaze and his long, thick mustache that curled up slightly at the ends.

Zapata and Villa began their conversation by complaining of Carranza, then spoke of the challenge of running the country, something neither of these relatively unschooled men professed the ability to do. Villa had more to say than Zapata on most subjects, but when they came to the issue of land reform, Zapata was less reserved: "They [the villagers of his region] have a great deal of love for the land. They still don't believe it when you tell them: 'This land is yours.' They think it's a dream." The two men talked of their individual struggles, Zapata tracing his rebellion back about seventeen years, to when he was eighteen, and promising to fight for his goals until his death. Indeed, there was plenty of machismo in the air. Zapata bragged about having executed the father of Pascual Orozco, a prominent revolutionary from Chihuahua who had supported the government of Victoriano Huerta that Zapata and Villa had recently helped bring down. "I fulfill a duty," he asserted, "in killing traitors." They also spoke of hat styles, of Zapata's broad sombrero and Villa's pith helmet. Zapata indicated that "he wouldn't be found in a hat other than the kind he wore."[2]

Two days later, riding side by side, these two men, the people's revolutionaries, made their official entry into Mexico City at the head of about fifty thousand troops to establish a national government. Spectators lined the streets and hung from the balconies, throwing confetti and streamers. When the procession arrived at the National Palace, Zapata and Villa posed for the photograph mentioned in the introduction: Villa in the president's chair, overcome by an irrepressible grin; Zapata beside him, staring into the camera, his sombrero on his knee; behind them a pyramid of expectant faces (see Figure I.1). Zapata refused to sit in the chair Villa occupied. Some say he suggested it be burned, "to put an end to ambitions." [3]

These activities of December 1914 did not amount to high political theater on Zapata's part, but he was projecting an image—or, rather, he was projecting two. In the triumphant ride into Mexico City and the photographs that were taken there he was symbolically placing himself, his movement, and his program on the national stage. But Zapata always denied he was a politician. He shared with most of the villagers of Morelos a distrust of politicians, from whom they had learned to expect little but the betrayal of their interests. It is not, therefore, surprising that the declaration of national power in which he was engaged was full of signals that that power would not bewitch him. Though his charro attire surely made some sort of impression on everyone who saw him, it was a sign in particular for his local followers. Like his dark, penetrating gaze and his long, thick mustache, like the general reserve, the discussion of land reform, and the rejection of the president's chair, his clothing demonstrated that he would not forget his core constituency. The limits to the political theater, in other words, were themselves politics, and it was this balancing of the need to compete for national power and to hold local support, to engage in politics without seeming like a politician, that was the biggest challenge of Zapata's revolutionary career. [4]

Precisely when Zapata recognized the need to shape an image for local consumption is uncertain, but the image he eventually molded had deep historical roots that make it seem almost natural. It was generations in the making, developed in part by ancestors who had played noteworthy political and military roles in and around his home village of Anenecuilco at least since Mexicans began to fight for independence in 1810. His family stood out, too, in its small measure of economic success, upon which Zapata built to become one of the area's leading citizens. As a young man, before the revolution, he owned some land and livestock and ran a mule train through the valley south of Cuautla, the most important town in eastern Morelos. [5]

But if Zapata's family background was distinctive in some respects, it was not enough to set him apart from the cultural milieu of rural Morelos. Like most young men of the region he plunged enthusiastically into the events of market days and fiestas—the cockfights and card games and fire-works, the singing and dancing and drinking—that were the best way the villagers knew to break up the monotonous cycle of country life. By all accounts one of the leading horsemen and judges of horses in the state, Zapata also performed in local rodeos, in which he specialized as a bull-roper.[6] This, then, was some of what held the people of Anenecuilco—and other villages like it—together despite their socioeconomic, gender, and merely personal differences. At base these villages were united by their his-tory of collective ownership of the fundamental resource, land, that made this way of life possible and by the common struggle to protect that land against neighboring haciendas. That struggle was coming to a head as Za-pata reached manhood.

Zapata was born in 1879 and raised during the long regime of Porfirio Díaz. During this period, the political turmoil that characterized Mexico's first decades as an independent state gave way to a dictatorship that pro-duced stability at the expense of the republican principles of the Constitu-tion of 1857. That stability permitted policymakers to seize the opportunity for greater integration into the world economy that the technology of the industrial revolution offered. Foreign investment was encouraged; railroads were constructed; mining flourished and industry increased; both interna-tional trade and the domestic market expanded. The sugar planters who dominated the economy of Morelos actively sought to participate in the prosperity. They undertook new irrigation projects and invested in the most modern milling equipment. For them the results were gratifying: between 1905 and 1908 alone they increased production more than fifty percent.

Unfortunately, few campesinos benefited from the boom. To maximize their profits the hacendados sought greater control over land, water, and labor, and through a combination of legal maneuver and brute force they usurped village resources at a great rate. In 1909, twenty-eight haciendas may have covered as much as 77 percent of the state's surface. Many previ-ously self-sufficient peasant farmers were forced to seek day labor on the estates or even to become full-time hacienda peons. Individual insecurity was on the rise, and the uneasy coexistence between hacienda and village that had been established after the Spanish conquest seemed to be breaking down. Many towns and villages stopped growing, and some disappeared entirely. Campesinos who resisted this sort of progress could find them-selves drafted, imprisoned, or carted off to work on the plantations of Oax-aca or Yucatán.[7]

Not surprisingly, then, Zapata's entry into the historical record was re-lated to the issue of land. At the age of seventeen or eighteen, when his personal rebellion reportedly began, that relationship was probably only indirect. Given the tensions of Porfirian arrangements, daily life at the local level was full of potential conflict, and, as one Anenecuilcan later put it, "'Miliano was a brave man who would not take any crap; as a result, already during the time of peace, he was often in trouble." By 1906, though, when we can document Zapata's attendance at a meeting at which Anenecuilco tried to resolve its difficulties with a neighboring hacienda, land was clearly the focal point. He had begun a struggle to defend his village and others like it that would, as he predicted to Villa, end only with his death.[8]

Though Zapata was still little more than a minor troublemaker in the Porfirian scheme, in 1909 he was exactly what Anenecuilco needed when the aging president of the village council resigned. The past activities of his family, his own efforts on behalf of village land, and his reputation as a macho and something of a rebel must all have weighed into the decision of the villagers, who gave him an impressive majority of their votes. What Anenecuilcans got in Zapata was a man who was both one of them and one of their best. He was somewhat taller than the average campesino and of average build. His limited education had left him rather ignorant about things one learned in books, but he understood the world around him. He seemed fair and trustworthy, and he was in control enough not to lose himself in drink as many locals did. At base, his selection was a sign that Anenecuilcans wanted a man of action who could do whatever it took to make sure their village survived Porfirian progress.[9]

Whatever it took did not immediately mean revolt, but the conditions that would make it possible for Zapata to help bring down the Díaz government were evolving. In 1908 Díaz announced in an interview with U.S. journalist James Creelman that, when his current term was up in 1910, he would not again run for the presidency as he had done every four years throughout his reign to give it a veneer of legitimacy. He soon changed his mind, but the hope raised by this interview helped produce an electoral challenge from a Coahuilan hacendado named Francisco Madero. Madero's campaign tapped into rising discontent with Díaz's policies, and Díaz demonstrated that age had taken a toll on his political judgment. In the summer of 1910 he imprisoned an increasingly popular Madero while the election was fixed; after the election, underestimating the threat, he set him free. Madero fled across the border to San Antonio, Texas, where, in the Plan of San Luis Potosí, he proclaimed his intention to fight.

Initially planned for November 20, 1910, Madero's revolt got off to a slow start, and Zapata was one of many potential rebels who were not yet ready for war. Still, guerrilla warfare did begin, especially in the northern state of Chihuahua, and Zapata and those who conspired with him around Anenecuilco saw their opportunity. The broader rebellion would distract the coercive arm of the Porfirian state, making it easier for local uprisings to get started. It might also confer legitimacy on local struggles. In pursuit of that legitimacy, Zapata would increasingly be drawn into a kind of politicking that had not been a part of winning the trust of Anenecuilcans. The first step he and his fellow conspirators took was to send one of their number, Pablo Torres Burgos of Villa de Ayala, to Texas to obtain Madero's recognition of their movement. When Torres Burgos returned with Madero's stamp of approval, there was little to do but get started. They took up arms on March 11, 1911, and sought sanctuary in the mountains of southern Puebla, picking up recruits along the way.[10]

Torres Burgos was the first leader of this revolt, probably due to local support that Madero ratified. His qualifications for political position included a better education than that of Zapata and greater experience in statewide politics. He was not, however, especially qualified to lead a grassroots rebellion, as events soon demonstrated. Less than two weeks after the uprising began, forces led by septuagenarian Gabriel Tepepa briefly took the town of Tlaquiltenango, Morelos, and looted it—against Torres Burgos's orders. When the other leaders of the movement refused to condemn the looting, Torres Burgos quit. He and his two sons were shot the following afternoon, on their way home, by federal troops. That same day an impromptu council of peasant rebels chose Zapata to assume the leadership of their revolt. What they seem to have seen in him was a man who could accept the realities of the conflict because he was immersed in their culture—unlike, perhaps, the more educated sometime schoolteacher, Torres Burgos—but also a man who was steady, who would not let anger cloud his thinking as it did that of Tepepa. It was not much different from the image Anenecuilcans had embraced.[11]

Zapata's leadership of the expanding rebellion was soon confirmed on two separate occasions. On April 4 he came across a former medical student from the city of Puebla named Juan Andreu Almazán. Claiming to be an emissary from Madero, Almazán declared Zapata official head of the revolution in Morelos, status Zapata had already begun to seek by sending a messenger to Maderistas operating in Mexico City almost as soon as he replaced Torres Burgos. Shortly thereafter, at the urging of a Maderista delegate who hoped to coordinate the activities of different *jefes* (leaders of troops), Zapata met with Ambrosio Figueroa, whose revolutionary operations were centered in the neighboring state of Guerrero. The pact they signed gave Zapata sway in Morelos and Figueroa primacy in his home state.[12]

But winning battles, for the time being, was more important for culti-vating a reputation than these politics among revolutionary leaders. Zapata and his followers quickly became adept at guerrilla warfare, fleeing from large concentrations of government troops, focusing their attacks instead on lightly defended villages and haciendas, where they gathered arms and provisions and then moved on before the enemy arrived. When federal forces divided into smaller groups in an effort to track them down, the campesinos ambushed them, putting their intimate knowledge of the ter-rain to good use. To fighters trained in conventional warfare this looked like cowardice, but the tactics worked, and success brought more people to Zapata's side. By early April he led between eight hundred and a thousand men; on May 12 he laid siege to Cuautla with about four thousand troops, and a week later he took it, striking one of the final blows against the now reeling Díaz regime. On May 21 the federal army evacuated the state capi-tal, Cuernavaca, leaving Morelos entirely in rebel hands.[13]

As federal troops vacated Morelos, representatives of the old regime and of Francisco Madero were coming to the agreement—the Treaty of Ciudad Juárez—that ended the fighting of Madero's revolution. Madero's forces had captured the Chihuahuan border city for which the treaty was named on May 10, in the most important battle of the revolution's first stage. It was important because it gave the northern revolutionaries easier access to arms and other critical resources available in the United States. It did not mean that the federal army was defeated, but rather demonstrated that the revolutionaries would not soon be beaten. If the war went on, the disor-der and the damage to the interests of the propertied would continue and probably worsen, and those who were essentially unpropertied—like most of the supporters of Zapata—could continue to exploit the instability to make their demands. Thus it is not surprising that the propertied, who sat on both sides of the negotiating table, found a recipe for peace. Díaz would relinquish the power he had held for so long, there would be elections in the fall—which Madero could expect to win—and in the meantime Díaz's secretary of foreign relations, Francisco León de la Barra, would assume the presidency. The Porfirian government would remain largely intact, as would the army.

Because the fighting ended without having resolved the social and economic issues that motivated many revolutionaries, the conflict would now take other forms. The hacienda owners of Morelos and their allies felt threatened by Zapata's drive for land, and they made certain that their appraisal of local conditions immediately reached the ears of the Maderi-sta leadership. Charges that Zapata could not control his following were

FIGURE I.I

Zapata posing in Cuernavaca, 1911. (Archivo General de la Nación, Mexico City, Archivo Fotográfico Díaz, Delgado y García.)

already in the air in Mexico City on June 8, when Zapata first met Madero. Perhaps that was why Madero focused on the need for order and insisted that Zapata disarm his troops.[14] Toward the end of what was a sometimes heated conversation, Zapata invited Madero to Morelos to observe the situation for himself. But when Madero made that trip, in mid-June, the hacendados orchestrated an effective propaganda campaign; it became a tour of the ravages of Zapata's hordes. Madero was informed, for instance, that when Zapata had taken Cuautla his forces had destroyed homes, stores, factories, and hotels and burned nineteen wounded federal soldiers alive. Zapata himself stood accused of murdering the former secretary of the *jefe político* (the political boss of the district). Madero, who had always hoped for an orderly revolution, could see for himself that Cuautla was in shambles. He avoided openly blaming Zapata for the destruction, but whether he realized that combat, not looting, was responsible for most of the destruction is anyone's guess.[15]

In their effort to fashion an image for Zapata that would destroy his cause, the hacendados could rely on the aid of many of Mexico City's newspapers, whose owners shared their conservative outlook. On June 19, the ironically named *El Imparcial* reported that it was Zapata's negative influence that made Tepepa a menace, and that the young girls of Cuernavaca had fled in terror from Zapata's men, but not before Zapata personally ravaged at least three of them.[16] On the following day, beneath the headline "Zapata Is the Modern Attila," *El Imparcial* claimed there were signs of open rebellion in Morelos. Announcing that "the only government I recognize is my pistols," Zapata had supposedly raided Cuernavaca's armory.[17]

At base it was an appeal to a notion that many Mexicans of urban culture and upper- or middle-class status had come to share, during the nineteenth century, with their counterparts in other Latin American nations: that theirs was a society divided by the forces of civilization and barbarism. The businessmen and planters who dominated the economy of Morelos described themselves, in one document, as "the class that thinks, feels, and loves" and the source of the nation's vitality and hope. They felt threatened and bullied by the "unconscious masses" with their "unruly appetites" that the revolution had awakened.[18] It was the city against the countryside, progress against decadence, whites and mestizos against Indians. The racial dimension was critical in that fears that Indians—a group that included, from the urban perspective, virtually everyone with dark skin who lived in the countryside—would engage in a caste war ran deep in Mexican life.[19] Given such preconceptions, it was easy for many Mexicans to accept that Zapata was nothing more than a blood-soaked bandit.

Whether Zapata really was a bandit depends somewhat on one's perspective. A bandit might be defined as someone who engages in property theft as part of a group, theft that is usually associated with rural areas and with direct confrontation rather than stealth. In that case, the activities of Tepepa at Jojutla might pass as banditry, and they did not constitute an isolated incident. Zapata was implicated, at least indirectly, in that he rose to the leadership of the movement precisely because, unlike Torres Burgos, he had been willing to tolerate a certain amount of looting. In his defense, this looting was undertaken in the context of a rebellion that aimed at the redistribution of resources, a goal that it forwarded in an immediate way. It is also clear that many of the allegations against Zapata and his followers were either exaggerations or complete fabrications.[20]

But in this war of images, the truth of the matter was not as important as what people were persuaded to believe. Zapata tried to defend himself against the accusations, even granting an interview to *El Imparcial* in which he assured that paper's worried readership that he hoped simply to discharge his forces and return to private life.[21] But disarming his followers before they received the land they had fought for would be difficult, given their fundamental distrust of politicians, and the new national regime—divided and inconsistent—did nothing to win their confidence. As the summer wore on, Madero wavered ineffectually between Zapata's interpretation of affairs and that of the hacendados. The interim president, de la Barra, clearly favored the planters over the peasants. The pressure mounted until, on August 9, de la Barra sent an old Indian fighter, General Victoriano Huerta, to Morelos with instructions to finish disarming Zapata's men—by force if necessary. On August 29, Huerta drove Zapata south from Cuautla into the mountains, and the war was on again.[22]

Zapata suddenly had the responsibility of leading his own revolution and of justifying that revolution so that it would not be dismissed as banditry and barbarism. The primary means with which he did that was the Plan of Ayala, which was completed in November 1911.[23] The Plan of Ayala spelled out Zapatista demands for political liberties and land reform, going beyond calling for the restitution of stolen land and water to submit that haciendas were monopolies that should have a third of their land expropriated for the public good. The lands of hacendados who opposed Zapata's rebellion would be nationalized without indemnification. Conceived as a series of reforms of and additions to the Plan of San Luis Potosí, the Plan of Ayala looked to Madero's revolution for legitimacy. In pursuit of personal power, it charged, Madero had betrayed his followers, labeling those who asked that his promises be fulfilled "bandits and rebels" and producing "the most horrible anarchy in recent history." Zapata proposed to put the revolutionary process back on track: "from today on we begin to continue the revolution begun by him."

In seeking to appropriate Madero's revolution, the authors of this plan—Zapata and schoolteacher Otilio Montaño—framed it as an appeal to the Mexican nation. But it also had local and regional applications. The rebellion Zapata now headed had bubbled up out of villages in Morelos and southwestern Puebla in a decentralized fashion. The grievances of campesinos from these diverse villages often centered on land and other basic resources, but there were also differences in local experience and motive that made the cause unclear for some actual or potential participants. The Plan of Ayala thus had a crucial role to play in recruiting and, by shaping group identity, in serving as a centripetal force in a decentralized uprising. It was also, of course, an assertion of Zapata's leadership and of his identification with the issues of land and liberty. In sum, though the movement began to take on Zapata's name already in September, the Plan of Ayala was the birth certificate of Zapatismo.

But the Plan of Ayala was not the only way in which Zapatista identity and Zapata's position within Zapatismo were established and reinforced. Villages like Anenecuilco, as we have seen, were drawn together by cultural practices they shared, and one might argue that the region of south-central Mexico in which Zapata operated also had a cultural unity. The inhabitants of different villages were often related, or connected by the ties of *compadrazgo*—godparenthood. Such periodic activities as religious pilgrimages and regional markets also brought them together. Since this was a mostly illiterate society, oral traditions remained important, and one of the key components of the shared culture was the *corrido*. Indeed, corridos written in Morelos were sung throughout the region that ultimately embraced Zapatismo and can be seen as a critical facet of that region's definition.[24]

Given this regional predilection for corridos from Morelos, the Zapatistas naturally commandeered the vehicle. Marciano Silva emerged as Zapata's official bard with a song about the capture of Cuautla in May 1911. One of the most noteworthy aspects of this corrido is that it explicitly refuted *El Imparcial*, which had reported that the federals won the Cuautla engagement. "If one thus triumphs by running," Silva sang, "I am a hero without doubt." Silva also rejected the charges made by both the hacendados and the press that Zapatista looting had destroyed Cuautla.[25] This corrido thus reflected considerable interaction between the urban culture of the capital and the regional culture of south-central Mexico. By using a medium for which the campesinos of their region were the primary audience to refute the press of Mexico City, the Zapatistas demonstrated their recognition that the newspapers could influence the peasant population.[26]

Another interesting aspect of this cultural dynamic was that the capital did not concede the corrido to the Zapatistas, despite its rural roots. Rather, writers in Mexico City were already producing their own corridos by the summer of 1911, which reiterated the attacks made in the press even as Silva repudiated them. Although these urban corridos were in some respects an effort to meet Zapatista *corridistas* on their own turf, they were probably meant more for the middle- and lower-class population of Mexico City—to which they were available in printed form on inexpensive broadsheets—than for the inhabitants of Morelos.[27]

Zapatista corridos and Mexico City newspaper reports were similar both in their propagandistic intentions and in their efforts to mask those intentions by presenting direct and detailed accounts of events written soon after they took place. Corridos differed from the newspaper articles, however, in their ability to address a particular regional audience in its own vernacular. This gave them greater potential to shape the collective memory of that audience and, through that memory, group identity. Some corridos contributed to that process simply by enhancing the reputation of Zapata, who would, like other revolutionary leaders, symbolize his movement. In a corrido that dealt with Zapata's break with Madero, Silva argued that Zapata was not the coward that some considered him; in fact, the government persecuted him precisely because of his bravery.[28] In late August 1911, when government troops tried to ambush him at the hacienda Chinameca—just south of Cuautla—he had proved that bravery by leading ten Zapatistas against six hundred federal soldiers. Zapata was "calm" under fire and the Zapatistas defended their "great conquests." If the machismo of Zapata's persona was significant, so was his lack of political ambition. "I don't desire the [presidential] chair," Silva had him say as he called his people back into arms, "or a high office."

Other corridos sought to put Zapata and the Zapatistas in historical context. An anonymous corridista used a Zapatista celebration of independence day to link Zapata to two of Mexico's most revered figures. After noting that the business of the day was to consecrate the history of the nation's heroes, this author called Zapata "another Hidalgo." If it were again necessary to drive out the Spanish, he added, "we could count on señor Don Emiliano, / he will go in defense of our flag." The author then evoked Benito Juárez, who, he avowed, had passed "his scepter and crown" to Zapata. The corrido closed with the request that Zapata receive the "laurels and garlands" with which heroes were customarily honored.

Zapata, in short, was the heir of the liberal nation builders of the nineteenth century.[29]

A deeper historical current surfaced in frequent references to Zapata's followers as Indians. In his piece on the battle of Cuautla, for example, Silva alluded to "Zapata's Indians / in *huaraches* [sandals]" and called Porfirio Díaz the protector of the Spanish and the terrible stepfather of the Indians.[30] The use of this label is somewhat perplexing in that there is no mention of Indian ethnicity in the Plan of Ayala, and most of Zapata's followers would probably have called themselves mestizos. What Silva seems to have been doing, at least in part, was turning conventional racial categories against the enemy. To be Indian in Zapatista corridos did not mean to be barbarous, as it did for many urbanites. Rather, it meant having suffered a long history of oppression and having fundamental rights that had long been ignored, a situation with which most Zapatistas, whatever ethnicity they claimed, could identify.[31]

The campaign conducted in both corrido and Plan of Ayala to forge a Zapatista identity as Zapata broke with Madero was a success. Much of the population of Morelos and southwestern Puebla backed Zapata, and his regional base would expand through 1914, until it included parts of the states of Guerrero and Mexico and of the Federal District. One significant stimulus for this growth was the regime established in February 1913 by Huerta, who helped engineer the coup that drove Madero from power and then, apparently, ordered him killed. In northern Mexico this meant the renewal of broad rebellion as the Constitutionalist faction—led by Venustiano Carranza with such figures as Pancho Villa and Alvaro Obregón in tow—rose up against the usurper. Although Huerta sent emissaries of peace to the Zapatistas, in light of his conservative credentials and past history in Morelos the war in the south continued and deepened. Huerta soon reinitiated the tactics of summary execution, village burning, and generalized terror with which Madero had experimented for a time. He also implemented a draft. The outcome was the disruption of the pattern of everyday life for more campesinos, many of whom were almost forced into Zapatismo.[32]

The task of leading Zapatismo changed as the movement grew, with Zapata increasingly stepping into roles the government could no longer play. Above all, he became the source of justice and protection for many in the area. In this capacity he was often asked to address the misbehavior of people in his own ranks. Complaints from villagers of forced loans, robbery, murder, rape, and the destruction of property arrived at his camp in a steady stream. Already by the end of 1911 he was well aware of how delicate relations between his forces and the *pacíficos* (noncombatants) of the region might become. He repeatedly instructed his jefes to take from the wealthy so that hunger would not compel the troops to molest the villagers. Those in arms were not to take more tortillas and fodder than the campesinos were willing to give; they were to respect civil authorities that had been chosen democratically; they were to protect civilians. But compliance with such dictates was not easy to enforce in such a decentralized movement, because each Zapatista leader enjoyed broad powers within his own zone of operations. In fact, local conflict was often generated by competition between jefes in neighboring zones who were vying for territory, resources, and power. Zapata continued to issue orders about behavior, sometimes elaborating on past such orders, but often just rehashing them and thus demonstrating how persistent these difficulties were and how great a challenge they might be to his credibility.[33]

One solution Zapata attempted was to charge the educated urbanites who trickled into his camp with organizing and centralizing his movement. Greater centralization would, of course, deprive individual jefes of some of their power, behind which thugs could hide. It would also boost the military effort. As the movement's numbers grew it became increasingly possible to attack larger cities—by 1914 the Zapatistas could seriously threaten Mexico City itself—but to do so, the original guerrilla tactics had to be discarded in favor of the more conventional massing of forces. Zapatismo would never complete the centralization process, partly because of Zapata's loyalty to his rebellion's roots and partly because the urbanites, too, were limited in their ability to shape the movement—as presumptuous outsiders they sometimes merely added a new dimension to an existing dispute.[34] But the growth and evolution of the movement did make Zapata a somewhat more distant leader of troops and provider of justice, and that distance probably enhanced his potential as an object of myth.

Despite Zapata's efforts to limit the misbehavior of his forces and present his movement in a favorable light, recriminations continued to be directed against it from the capital. For Madero, Zapatismo was "amorphous agrarian socialism," a "motiveless and abnormal movement of retrocession," and, of course, just plain "banditry." Huerta's arrival in power did nothing to change these attitudes among national politicians and in the press.[35]

In 1913 the verbal assault on Zapata and his followers began to take book form. In *Veinte meses de anarquía* (Twenty Months of Anarchy), J. Figueroa Domenech described Zapata as a "symbol of banditry and of unbridled demagoguery."[36] Under the pseudonym Héctor Ribot, meanwhile, conservative journalist Alfonso López Ituarte published *El Atila del Sur* (The Attila of the South). Though his tale was novelistic, López

Ituarte sought to legitimize it by providing documentation and claiming to be an eyewitness. A similar assertion of authenticity was made by Antonio Melgarejo, author of *Los crímenes del zapatismo* (The Crimes of Zapatismo), who posed as one of Zapata's earliest collaborators. Melgarejo conceded the justice of Zapata's cause, but argued that the Zapatistas were savages with "uncultivated and poorly organized minds." They were thus beyond Zapata's control. For his part, Zapata was impressionable enough to be incited to greater brutality by one of his first urban advisers, Abraham Martínez. Melgarejo presented the orgies of looting, murder, and rape that resulted in lurid detail and declared that Zapata's "mob" considered such activities "deeds of a Spartan heroism."[37]

Zapatista manifestos and corridos answered this propaganda in kind, denying the validity of first the Madero and then the Huerta regime and accusing federal soldiers of cowardice, cruelty, and barbarism.[38] That was how things stood in July 1914, when Huerta was forced from power by the combined efforts of the Zapatistas, the Constitutionalists, and U.S. president Woodrow Wilson, who had taken an immediate dislike to Huerta and, in April 1914, exploited a diplomatic incident to justify an invasion of the port of Veracruz that hindered the regime's access to arms.

For Zapata the fall of Huerta was a victory only in part, because it remained unclear who would rule Mexico and on behalf of what cause. The Zapatistas could not hope to win the revolution outright; they would have to forge alliances. Here again the urbanites had a crucial role in that it was they who wrote the documents and conducted the diplomacy that presented Zapatismo to public opinion in general, and to the Constitutionalists in particular. But despite diplomatic initiatives undertaken by his urban secretaries, Zapata had not formed an alliance with Carranza, whose troops occupied the capital in August. Like Madero, Carranza was a hacendado from Coahuila, and his primary concerns—as sketched out in the Plan of Guadalupe with which he launched his insurrection—were legality, order, and power. While he would sometimes pay lip service to land reform for political purposes, he was anything but an ardent proponent of Zapata's favorite project.[39] Instead, Zapata turned to Pancho Villa in his search for a piece of a victorious revolution. Villa was a pretty good match for him in class standing, at least, and had become increasingly estranged from his nominal boss Carranza as the struggle against Huerta unfolded. The affiliation of Villa and Zapata, which was consolidated in late 1914, did not, however, end the uncertainty about the revolution's future. By early December, when they rode together into Mexico City, a new war, against Carranza, was already under way.

The behavior of the Zapatistas as they entered the capital changed some minds about them. After reading for years of the barbarous hordes that followed Mexico's Attila, many of the inhabitants of Mexico City expected the worst. But Zapata's insistence on the need for discipline at this crucial revolutionary juncture bore fruit, and the city was soon buzzing about how much better behaved the Zapatistas were than the Carrancistas: rather than simply taking food, they politely begged for it. Publishing houses that had previously churned out anti-Zapata broadsheets opportunistically changed their tunes. Their corridos now praised Zapatista behavior and held up Zapata as a brave and honest hero.[40] Indeed, between mid-1914 and mid-1915 Zapatismo was at full crest, and so was Zapata's national reputation. Poems were written for and about him, and there were so many requests for his photograph that he ran out of prints to distribute. Even the minister from Japan was said to have two such pictures on his desk. In August 1914, when cinematographer José Alencaster filmed Zapata's formal entrance into newly taken Cuernavaca, one of Zapata's compadres, who knew him well enough that he might have thought such a fuss ridiculous, concluded that the event was "of much interest for history."[41]

The Zapatistas began to print their own newspapers in Mexico City as a way of shaping the propaganda there, but aside from participating with Villa in the grand entrance of December 6, Zapata did not personally court the sentiment of the capital. In fact, during the period in which his forces held the city, which lasted, with some interruption, until August 1915, Zapata spent little time there. He preferred instead to tend to affairs in and around Morelos while his educated urbanites represented Zapatismo in the Convention government that he and Villa created. More problematic for image building than Zapata's reluctance to fully engage in it was the fact that some Zapatistas soon forgot his orders about conduct. In the words of one of Zapata's communications, many jefes occupied themselves in the "theaters, cantinas, and brothels" of the city rather than spending time at the front. Some became involved in drunken scandals that included shoot-outs with their fellow Zapatistas or their supposed Villista allies. Nor did the Zapatistas provide strong evidence that they were equipped to govern Mexico. Rather, Zapatista legislators continually clashed with their Villista counterparts, provoking an almost constant series of political crises.[42]

Although Zapata's presence in Mexico City might have improved the situation there, it is no wonder he chose to spend his time at home. Peace prevailed in the Zapatista heartland despite the war against Carranza, and as a successful revolutionary hero, Zapata was virtually worshiped by most of the inhabitants of his region. He constantly received presents—a sombrero, a machete, a "good serape"—and he was often asked, by one village or another, to preside over the anniversary of the birth of the caudillo Morelos or over independence celebrations, or to help celebrate a saint's day or the completion of a new church. In August 1915, the village of Tlaltizapán, Morelos, where he had established his headquarters, threw him a birthday fiesta in the school building, complete with songs, speeches, poems, and skits.[43]

But if the level of acclaim was high, so were expectations, and it was time for Zapata to fulfill his promises. His headquarters were flooded with solicitations of favors, loans, and justice from an exhausted people. Many of these requests came from friends and family, but others were written in terms similar to those Anenecuilcans had used in addressing Porfirian authorities prior to the revolution and thus suggested that, for some, Zapata was the head of a fairly remote government and that payoffs were necessary to hold support. In any event, these entreaties placed powerful demands on Zapata, for they were part of what the fighting had all been about. Addressing small, individual needs, he took babies to the baptismal font and supplied clothing, money, and food—at least in piecemeal fashion—to the aged and the widowed.[44]

The highest expectations, of course, centered on land. Land tenure had been changing hands informally from almost the moment Zapata took up arms, as peasants simply occupied hacienda lands they claimed when they were able. While guerrilla warfare raged, formal land reform would have been difficult and pointless—there was no guarantee that federal troops would not soon return to any given place. But as Zapata gained military control of his region in 1914, it was increasingly possible to apply the dictates of the Plan of Ayala, and he began to outline how land reform should proceed. On January 1, 1915, he demonstrated his seriousness on the issue by having the most powerful and driven of his intellectual crew, Manuel Palafox, sworn in as head of the Convention's new Ministry of Agriculture.[45]

Unfortunately, as campesinos rushed to claim their share of the newly available land, it became obvious that neither oral tradition nor the maps and titles that now came out from their hiding places provided the needed data. Based on these sources, the claims of one community often overlapped those of another. With the common enemy gone, tensions between neighboring villages grew and sometimes burst into open violence.[46] And so, though Zapata put his money where his mouth was and thus earned his lasting reputation as the only one of Mexico's major revolutionary leaders fully committed to land reform, conflict over land festered. Like the misbehavior in the city, this conflict was a manifestation of the centrifugal forces that came with Zapatismo's grassroots origins, forces that would gradually erode Zapata's support by making it impossible for him to live up to the key role of dispenser of justice.

The fundamental problem was that as Zapata attended to matters in and around Morelos, the Constitutionalists were winning the revolution. In late 1914, most observers believed that Villa had the revolution's best army and expected the Convention to make short work of Carranza, who in November set up headquarters in the port of Veracruz as its American occupiers returned home. But Zapata, assigned the task of leading military operations in the south, did not press the advantage, both because Villa failed to provide him with the munitions he had promised and because of the lack of focus within Zapatismo. Given time to recover, Carranza's forces slowly turned the tide. In the spring and early summer of 1915, led by Alvaro Obregón, the Constitutionalists defeated Villa in the great battles of Celaya and León on the plain north of Mexico City. The fate of the Convention government was decided. The Villistas moved north to more familiar ground, and in August the Zapatistas were driven from the capital for good.

The Convention government first fled west to Toluca and then disbanded. With its demise came the end of the intermittent pay Zapatista soldiers had received, pay that had mitigated the strain on local resources in the Zapatista world. Already in 1914 some villages had begun to claim they could no longer feed the growing number of men in arms. Now, as the Constitutionalists nibbled away at Zapatismo's periphery and then invaded Morelos in early 1916, the destruction of renewed warfare left often desperate Zapatistas competing with each other—and with equally desperate pacíficos—for basic necessities. Although the difficulties of war were not new, there was no longer any recourse to the wealth of hacendados and merchants, which had already been appropriated.[47]

Under these circumstances, many of Zapata's jefes apparently abandoned the effort to promote goodwill, demonstrating instead the recognition that coercion and terror could be useful in dealing with campesinos who would no longer voluntarily support the war effort. As a result, many villagers learned to flee to the mountains as quickly from Zapatistas as from Constitutionalists during the last years of the revolution, and it was only natural that some made deals with the Constitutionalist invaders to avoid being punished as adherents of Zapatismo.[48] After mid-1915, there was also a wave of desertion from the Zapatista army as less than fully loyal jefes began to look elsewhere for the winners of the revolution. Whether or not the pacíficos and soldiers who abandoned the movement directly blamed

Zapata for the conditions that prompted them to do so, it seems unlikely that he was—for them and for many others in his area of operations—the immaculate revolutionary icon he would later become. Judging from the attitudes of several prominent Zapatista generals who left the movement, there was substantial criticism of his failure to control his troops and of diplomatic and military decisions that seemed to have produced the current difficulties.[49]

Naturally, Zapata took steps to deal with the growing tensions. In mid-1915 he began to recommend that villages complaining of crimes protect themselves with armed patrols, and in May 1916 he ordered them to do so. He also ordered, in some cases, the public execution of Zapatistas engaging in chronic banditry. As a document that outlined the rights and obligations of villages and troops put it, the goal was to "demonstrate with deeds that the era of abuses has ended."[50]

Zapata also hoped to show "the people" that the Zapatistas were "capable of founding a government" and "establishing the Administration of the Revolution." To that end he reconstituted the Convention in Morelos, though its Villista component had gone north after Mexico City fell. This purely Zapatista Convention developed a program addressing such broadly national concerns as land reform, political and religious liberties, education, and labor rights before the Zapatistas brought it to an end in April 1916.[51] In late 1916 and early 1917, Constitutionalist troops withdrew from Morelos as a result of Zapatista tenacity, disease, and the necessity of chasing rebels elsewhere. Now with more opportunities to implement policies that might firm up his support, Zapata set to work creating state and local governments. He also established the Center for Revolutionary Propaganda and Unification, which, as its name indicates, distributed propaganda and tried to resolve conflicts among jefes and between soldiers and pacíficos. In addition, it directed a set of new juntas—called Associations for the Defense of Revolutionary Principles—that were being chosen in villages the Zapatistas controlled. These associations were to hold Sunday meetings to publicize Zapata's laws and manifestos, oversee public education and elections, and, in general, push the cause at the local level.[52]

With the Constitutionalists in charge in Mexico City, Zapata again became, in both press and public pronouncement, the leader of ignorant bandit hordes. More problematic, however, was Carranza's summoning of a constitutional convention. The Constitution of 1917 that this convention produced was markedly progressive on such issues as the protection of national resources, education, labor rights, and land reform. Though this was not the sort of constitution that Carranza had hoped for, he reluctantly accepted it, and it served his interests in that it tended to undermine the legitimacy of such rebels as Zapata who were identified with causes that it addressed. In the eyes of many, who had no way of knowing that Carranza would not fulfill the provisions of the new constitution, there was nothing left to explain Zapata's ongoing rebellion except that, as a Carrancista corrido put it, he was among those who "only in robbery seek / the way to prosper."[53] The constitution also strengthened Carranza's position by paving the way for presidential elections, which he easily won.

This new assault on his legitimacy was especially troublesome for Zapata because, with his military fortunes ebbing, he increasingly pinned his hopes on attracting new allies. Particularly after early 1917, when Gildardo Magaña became his chief advisor, Zapatista ambassadors scoured Mexico in search of other regional caudillos, semi-retired revolutionary politicos, and disgruntled Constitutionalists who might be willing to join in a unified revolt against Carranza.

As part of this diplomatic initiative, the Zapatistas sought to counter Carrancista propaganda in a series of manifestos directed to a national audience. On January 20, 1917, for instance, a "Manifesto to the Mexican People" began, "the nightmare of Carrancismo, overflowing with horror and with blood, is almost over." This document then charged that Carranza was "an ambitious man without scruples," that his collaborators did not "represent the revolution, nor order, nor progress," and that his soldiers were a "tumultuous avalanche of unbalanced and rapacious men." Those lucky enough to avoid being killed by this mob had been plunged into misery as the Constitutionalists ran the economy into the ground. The good news, though, was that the Mexican people had come to recognize Carranza for what he was, and the Zapatistas now asked them to help turn him out. Once in power themselves, they offered respect for authentic property rights, more stable conditions for business, and the acceptance of everyone "except the enemies of the popular cause." Addressing urban workers in particular, the manifesto submitted that a plot of land would allow them to "exchange the slavery of the factory for the glorious liberty of the fields."[54]

The strategy was to attack Carranza's legitimacy, appear optimistic about winning the revolution, and broaden Zapatismo's potential constituency by arguing that it was a realistic and flexible alternative to the current regime. Subsequent manifestos aspired to largely the same effects. Unfortunately, talk of a Zapatista victory was too far divorced from reality to be convincing. Despite Zapata's attempts to contain it, the strife within the movement continued. The seriousness of that strife was clear in mid-1918, when Zapata repented of his earlier weapons policy and decreed that firearms be licensed by both civil and military authorities to lessen the chances that villagers would use them against Zapatista soldiers.[55] There were even rumors of plots within Zapatismo to assassinate Zapata himself. At the end of 1918 the Carrancistas again invaded the state of Morelos, driving Zapata's remaining forces into their mountain hideouts.

In March 1919, Zapata's increasingly anxious search for allies led him to a young Constitutionalist colonel, Jesús Guajardo, who had supposedly fallen out with Pablo González, the commander of Constitutionalist forces in Morelos. In a letter of March 21, Zapata invited Guajardo to join his movement. Guajardo quickly informed González, and González saw a chance to finish his frustrating work in Morelos, please his boss Carranza, and set himself up for a run at the presidency in 1920, when Carranza's term expired. At González's bidding Guajardo accepted Zapata's offer, "in view of the great difficulties that exist between Pablo González and I."[56]

After some delay, Zapata met Guajardo on April 9 at a train station south of Jonacatepec, Morelos, and they arranged a rendezvous for the next day at the hacienda Chinameca. According to eyewitness Salvador Reyes Avilés, author of the official Zapatista report on Zapata's death, Guajardo's troops were already at the hacienda when Zapata arrived with 150 men on the morning of April 10. While Zapata's forces waited beneath the trees, Zapata and Guajardo made military plans. Rumors that the enemy was approaching soon interrupted them, however, and Zapata took thirty men into the hills to have a look. Finding nothing, they returned to Chinameca shortly after noon. Guajardo was now inside the hacienda building, and he soon sent out two men to invite Zapata to join him. Zapata surely knew it was a gamble, but after talking under the trees a while longer, he ordered ten men to follow and headed toward the hacienda gate. As he approached the gate, wrote Reyes Avilés,

the guard appeared ready to do him the honors. The bugle sounded three times, the call of honor, and when the last note fell silent, as the General arrived at the threshold, in a manner most treacherous, most cowardly, most villainous, at point-blank range, without giving him time even to clutch his pistols, the soldiers who were presenting arms fired their rifles twice, and our general Zapata fell never to rise again.[57]

TWO

THE REGIONAL CULT

As Zapatista veteran Carmen Aldana remembered it in 1974, Zapata had a compadre named Agustín Cortés, a campesino from Tepalcingo, Morelos. Like Zapata, Cortés "wore a large mustache, but he was larger and fatter" than "*mi general.*"[1] According to Aldana, Zapata mistrusted Guajardo, who had been brutal in his treatment of the Morelenses. The revolution was rife with betrayal, and there had already been many attempts on Zapata's life. So Zapata was cautious as he went to meet Guajardo, and Aldana, too, was worried. Zapata even questioned whether the beer Guajardo sent out from Chinameca hacienda that day—to where Zapata and his soldiers waited under the trees—might be poisoned. He refused to drink it, despite the heat. In Aldana's estimation, there was simply no telling what the shameless Carrancistas would stoop to, and that is why Zapata did not enter the hacienda but sent Cortés instead.

Aldana knew that because people had closely examined the body after the shooting. They looked for the finger, and when they saw it was there they knew it was not Zapata. Then they performed for the Carrancista soldiers who were watching. "Now, sons-of-bitches," they bellowed to the other locals, "you are truly orphaned, they have fucked your father, say goodbye to him." Others filed by, checking the corpse for themselves, and everyone said, "good-bye *mi general*," because they knew they would otherwise be beaten. But then "the word spread." Zapata had another compadre, an Arab, whose name Aldana had forgotten. This Arab always traveled with him, and on that day both the Arab and Zapata disappeared. The Arab took him to his land, and a young boy took Zapata's horse once the shooting was over. Later, the horse was given to the president of Mexico. No one had seen Zapata since, and "until today we don't know where he is." Having had no word for so long, Aldana speculated, it seemed unlikely Zapata would return.

While Aldana's memories had decades to develop before they were recorded, many began to wrestle with the events of Chinameca immediately. "Most treacherous, most cowardly, most villainous"—the body was not yet cold, we might surmise, before Reyes Avilés began to fumble for the words that would start loading Zapata's death with meaning. "Thus die the brave," he continued, "the men of dignity, when the enemy, to stand up to them, resorts to treason and crime."[2]

As this new stage in the political struggle over Zapata's image began, the Carrancistas had the advantage of having the body. While the Zapatistas fled Chinameca in disarray, Zapata's corpse was thrown over the back of a horse and Guajardo began a victorious ride north. His entourage passed through Villa de Ayala and Anenecuilco, arriving in Cuautla shortly after nine that evening. Pablo González had witnesses waiting to identify the body before a judge, and as they did their work he telegraphed Carranza with his congratulations. Their "special plans," he reported, had forced Zapata into combat with Guajardo, and Zapata was "killed in the fight." González asserted that his death was an important step in the pacification of the region, and in the hope of maximizing its effect he ordered that the body be "injected" so photographs could be taken the following day. In that way, "those who desired to or might doubt" could see "that it was actual fact that the famous jefe of the southern region had died." González directed that the population of Cuautla be informed of Zapata's demise, and bands from the Constitutionalist garrison marched through the streets, playing reveille. People began to gather on the plaza. In the early hours of April 11, the injection finished, the body was presented to the public at the police station. It remained on display for nearly twenty-four hours, and thousands came to look.[3]

On April 11, the Mexico City newspapers *Excélsior* and *El Demócrata* requested that Zapata's body be displayed in the capital, since "there had been assurances on many occasions that Zapata was dead and later he appeared in other places."[4] Carranza passed on this chance to calm metropolitan fears of the southern Attila, however, arguing that to send his body to Mexico City "would be to do honor to his unhappy memory." Instead, González sent the photographs. The bloodstained clothing Zapata had been wearing would eventually make its way to the city as well. There it was placed for a time in a showcase in front of a newspaper building facing the Alameda Central, a downtown park. Back in Cuautla, the viewing done, just after 5 P.M. on April 12, Zapata's remains were "placed in a pine box, without paint," and carried to the cemetery while a movie camera recorded the scene. González presided over the funeral, accompanied by other Constitutionalist officers, there, presumably, to keep order. The pallbearers were men who had been jailed as Zapatistas, some of whom had helped identify the corpse. There were also hundreds of people from around Cuautla, including three of Zapata's female relatives. Probably sisters and a cousin, they have been variously identified; one is sometimes called his mother, though she was long dead. Zapata's body was placed in a simple grave marked with a wooden cross that gave his name and the day of his death. González ordered the gravediggers to bury the body deep, so "Zapatista fanatics" would not try to move it.[5]

Zapata's death provoked a feeding frenzy in the newspapers. On April 11, the headline of *Excélsior*, a publication closely linked to Carranza, was already asserting that his passing meant the death of Zapatismo.[6] *El Demócrata*, meanwhile, which was generally supportive of Obregón's political ambitions, gave some of Zapata's history, described him as a "roving marauder," and made reference to his "idiosyncratic personal cowardice." On the following day both publications were able to offer the photographs of the corpse to their more skeptical readers. *El Demócrata* arranged them in a montage. In the most striking of the images, excited young soldiers propped up the bloated head of the corpse so the camera might leave no doubt (see Figure 2.1).[7]

In the days that followed, the press displayed a fascination with the details of Zapata's demise—as seen from a Constitutionalist perspective—and stressed Guajardo's bravery and skill. On April 12, *Excélsior's* correspondent reported that Guajardo and his men had been outnumbered at Chinameca and that Zapata, having an "instantaneous presentiment," reached for his weapon first. But Guajardo reacted with "astonishing velocity," and once the shooting began the Zapatistas simply tried to escape. On the next day various papers broke the news that a woman had informed Zapata of the Carrancista plot and that Zapata, in turn, had invited Guajardo to a dinner where he planned to kill him. Now the presentiment was Guajardo's: realizing what was up, he avoided the ominous meal by feigning illness.[8] This story might be true, but it was also a way, from the Carrancista perspective, to try to temper any outrage over how Zapata had died by suggesting that Guajardo was in a situation in which he had to kill or be killed. *El Demócrata* added that the promotion to brigadier general that had been part of Guajardo's reward—along with 50,000 pesos—was "meager recompense for the immense service he has done for the cause of civilization. Today the people of Morelos, Guerrero, Oaxaca, Puebla and Mexico state should raise triumphal arches to him and declare him their benefactor."[9] The story *Excélsior* told on April 14 had Zapata riding into an ambush much like the

FIGURE 2.1

*Showing off the corpse. (Archivo General de la Nación, Mexico City,
Archivo Fotográfico Díaz, Delgado y García.)*

one Reyes Avilés described, with the shooting beginning at a sign prede-
termined by the Constitutionalists—the sounding of the bugle. Guajardo,
who was inside the hacienda drinking with three Zapatista jefes, dispatched
his guests at point-blank range. This version of events was largely corrobo-
rated by Guajardo's official report to González of April 15, which counted
almost three thousand Zapatistas present when the ambush occurred.[10]

Meanwhile, the interconnected issues of Zapata's remains and the remains of Zapatismo continued to prey on the minds of both journalists and
Constitutionalists. "With respect to Zapata's corpse," reported *Excélsior* on
April 12, Zapatista captives of the Carrancistas "said they did not remember
having seen that man before." At first, "no one imagined that the cadaver,
bathed in blood and still warm," was that of Zapata, but then, "with terror
painted on his face," a Zapatista prisoner who had helped bring Zapata and
Guajardo together—a man named Eusebio Jáuregui—made the identification. As Guajardo and company carried Zapata's body north, this account
continued, "men, women, and children emerged from the humble huts of
the hot country" to watch the procession. "All of those that contemplated
the cadaver agreed in asserting that it was that of Emiliano himself . . . and
began to recall the outrages they had suffered at Zapata's orders."[11]

The next day, *Excélsior* claimed that the campesinos who viewed Zapata's
corpse displayed their fear of him by trembling "from head to toe." Then, in
describing the funeral, a different article in the same issue noted that the locals were "dismayed and demoralized" by Zapata's death, adding that "many,
before viewing it [the body], doubted that the man they judged invincible
had died." Interestingly, on April 14, *Excélsior* noted that the Carrancistas in
Cuautla had had similar doubts. Upon hearing that the body was on the way
they took precautions, "given the possibility that Guajardo had fallen into
the hands of Zapata . . . and it was the rebel leader who approached Cuautla
with his troops." The author of this article was quick to point out, though,
that when Guajardo and his soldiers arrived, "all the doubts were dispelled."
For its part, *El Demócrata* argued on April 13 that Zapatismo was basically
through, but then, in a twist of perspective, remarked that Zapata "has taken
in the consciousness of the indigenous population the proportions of a myth."
It was therefore necessary to "finish off the legend" by undertaking land reform in Morelos in accordance with Constitutionalist law. González himself bluntly contended that since the Zapatistas fought not for principles but
out of "blind faith" in Zapata, the movement was now over. He and his soldiers had already noted a "great depression" among the people of Cuautla—
a depression that would soon cause the Zapatistas to surrender.[12]

In short, accounts of Zapata's death produced by the Carrancistas in collaboration with the journalists of Mexico City were evidently colored by the desire to justify the means employed to kill him, by some tendency to exaggerate the exploits of war, by the personal political motives of González, and by plain miscommunication. The inconsistencies on the subject of local reaction to Zapata's assassination were generated in part by hopes that the struggle against Zapatismo was over. Surely also significant, though, was the desire of both the journalists and the Carrancista officials who informed them to do what they could to turn these hopes into reality by convincing Zapata's followers that the fight could not continue.

A third partial explanation for those inconsistencies has to do with the way death affects the living. For most people, death and that which is considered sacred have been intimately related. Death is among the moments of passage in an individual's life that are usually marked by ritual. It is sacred, perhaps, because it is understood as an occasion when the heavens and the earth meet as the deceased moves between them. Some scholars have contended—convincingly, I think—that it is the most important of those moments, even the very source of religious feeling, because of the fear it generates, the mystery that presses for explanation.[13] As we have seen, death has long been central to Mexican culture. Death, wrote Octavio Paz, illuminates the lives of Mexicans. "Tell me how you die," he continued, "and I will tell you who you are."[14] The ways in which Christ and Cuauhtémoc and Hidalgo died were critical to their heroic stature, and the same was already becoming true of prominent revolutionaries, such as Madero, who had preceded Zapata in death. Death, then, can make powerful appeals to memory, and it obviously demands that a life be summarized. Recent difficulties had worn away at belief in Zapata, but now, on learning of his passing, many of those who had tired of the hardships of war must have recalled, in a context of considerable emotion, the promise and the successes of earlier years, the fixity of purpose, the sincerity of the effort to implement land reform. It seems probable that a reevaluation of Zapata was already under way in the first days after his death, and that it complicated even the most honest efforts to read that death's implications.[15]

Demonstrating such a reevaluation is tricky because it is hard to get into the minds of historical actors who did not record their impressions at the moment in question. Still, there are scattered clues about the recasting of memory around Zapata in such sources as Oscar Lewis's oral history account of the life of Pedro Martínez. An inhabitant of Tepoztlán, Morelos, Martínez left the failing movement in 1916 for the relative safety of Guerrero. But when he heard of Zapata's death, he informs us, "it hurt me as much as if my own father had died! I was a zapatista down to the marrow of my bones. I had a lot of faith in Zapata's promise, a lot of faith. I did indeed! I was one of the real zapatistas."[16]

Real Zapatista or not, Martínez had chosen to leave the Zapatistas, and he continued to nurse grievances about the movement when Lewis interviewed him, beginning in 1943. "I didn't have the kind of character suited to the Revolution," he complained. "I was not good at it because I was not base enough."[17] We will never know when Martínez's memories of Zapatismo and of Zapata hardened into the shape they had taken, nor whether it was Zapata's death, the coming of peace in 1920, or the Mexican state's subsequent appropriation of Zapata that motivated his return to the Zapatista fold. His description of Zapata as a father figure may have been mere hypocrisy, given that his identity as a Zapatista soon became crucial to a career in local politics. Or perhaps he remembered Zapata positively as a way of dealing with guilt about having abandoned the cause for which Zapata died. It is also possible that he always admired Zapata, never blaming him personally for the violence and hunger that forced the flight to Guerrero. Aside from his professed emotions when he learned of Zapata's demise, the argument that it was Zapata's death that caused Martínez to reassess him finds support in attitudes about self-serving politicians that had been honed on long experience. For the campesinos of Tepoztlán, it has been written, the only proof of the unlikely possibility that a politician was clean was his martyrdom to a cause.[18] Perhaps only death could cleanse Zapata of the political role he had taken up with so much misgiving.

Similarly provocative inconsistencies can be found in the story told by Luz Jiménez, who witnessed the revolution from the northern fringe of Zapatista territory, in the village of Milpa Alta in the Federal District. Jiménez's specific memories of the Zapatistas concentrated on the murder, rape, and destruction they perpetrated. "When the men of Zapata entered the town," she claimed, "they came to kill."[19] Despite those sordid details, when she told of the arrival of Carrancista troops, Jiménez asserted that the villagers of Milpa Alta would "never forgive him [Zapata] for leaving us in the hands of the enemy."[20] And yet on some level there was forgiveness, for the editor of her account, Fernando Horcasitas notes that Jiménez identified Zapata as one of her three heroes, since he was "the only man who fought for the poor."[21] Jiménez's ability to identify with Zapata and his followers despite displaying few concrete memories of them that were positive suggests that she may have finalized her opinions after Zapata's death. When that might have occurred, as in the case of Pedro Martínez, is something of an open question. Her work as a model during the 1920s for muralist Diego Rivera,

who often painted Zapata, is probably significant, but it is also noteworthy that in speaking of Zapata's death she endowed him with considerable
nobility. "Though he knew he was going to lose," she observed, "his spirit
did not fail him." [22] Together, the somewhat dissonant memories of Pedro
Martínez and Luz Jiménez might support the notion that Zapata's death
inspired a rapid reshaping of regional feelings about him; they certainly
caution us against assuming that local and regional variations of his hero
cult got an uncomplicated or automatic start.

Whatever the degree of devotion to Zapata in the Zapatista homeland
at the time of his death, Zapatismo's remaining leaders believed both that
appealing to memories of him might help revive their moribund movement
and that it was necessary for them to help shape those memories. On April
15, they produced a manifesto that, in its first paragraph alone, referred to
Zapata as the "fiery apostle of *agrarismo*"; the "redeemer of the indigenous
race . . . energetically representative of the Mexican soul, overflowing with
virility and rebellion"; a "glorious predestined one"; and "unyielding, immaculate, unbreakable." Stressing that Zapata's ideals would not die with
him, the authors of this document argued that, far from discouraging the
people of the region in which he operated, his death had "provoked virile
indignation" among them. The manifesto then compared Zapata to other
heroes, like Hidalgo and Morelos, who had been betrayed, and argued that
the cause would soon triumph, because "Zapata died when it was possible
for him to do so, when his meritorious work of disseminating ideas was
over." He could now "live his life of an immortal tranquilly." [23]

It was far from self-evident, however, that Zapatismo could continue
without Zapata, because Zapatista unity remained problematic. As we have
seen, already before Zapata's death internal conflict and increasing defec-
tions had rendered Zapatismo ineffectual as a fighting force. Now these
problems were exacerbated by contention over who would head the struggle. Under these circumstances it is not surprising that Zapatismo's leaders—even as they competed among themselves for Zapata's mantle—found
his memory useful for inciting his former followers to unity and greater effort. Pointing out that Zapata had hated intriguers and traitors, a circular
that probably came from jefe Genovevo de la O argued that "he died a
victim of the most infamous of betrayals and we, out of duty, love of the
cause, and respect for his memory, should die before earning the epithet of
traitors." [24] In the fall a manifesto that reported a vote that made urbanite
Gildardo Magaña the new leader of the rebellion exhorted Zapatistas to
follow "the glorious road that the already immortal Zapata has traced out
for us." [25]

Several important Zapatista jefes—including de la O—missed that vote, however, and Magaña's claim to the leadership of a united movement remained tenuous at best. Then, in November 1919, he abruptly surrendered to the Carrancistas and convinced others to do so as well. De la O, who was among the many Zapatistas who refused to follow Magaña's example, criticized those who surrendered in a December manifesto, noting that some people "have been discouraged by the belief that these bad citizens GENUINELY REPRESENT General Zapata."[26] Far from representing Zapata, de la O continued, their names would be placed with those of the "mass of Judases" from which Mexico had suffered. In January 1920, Magaña rejoined the Zapatistas in the mountains, but the damage was done. De la O rejected his leadership. and that spring de la O and Magaña made separate arrangements to join the rebellion of Alvaro Obregón, who overthrew Carranza in a brief uprising that ended the violent revolutionary decade.[27]

Corridos also helped give Zapata's death significance. Marciano Silva wrote his "History of the Death of the Great General Emiliano Zapata" shortly after Chinameca.[28] After opening with a brief survey of revolutionary history, in which he described Zapata as "a redeemer of the world," Silva entered into the events leading up to his death by taking an elaborate shot at Pablo González:

> Carranza gave Pablo González
> Command of the forces of the south without vacillating,
> So that the ideals of Zapata would die,
> Because he saw he could only save himself from that Sparta [sic],
> By having more cunning than military valor.

Silva stressed Zapata's honorable behavior, as opposed to the deviousness of González and Guajardo, who were barbaric "pirates." One act of barbarism was the killing of fifty-nine soldiers under the command of Victoriano Bárcenas, who left the Zapatistas in 1918 to join the Constitutionalists and had beleaguered them ever since. Zapata had requested that these soldiers be brought to justice as a test, and when he learned of the massacre, he fell "thoroughly into credulity." Silva then detailed the other steps that brought Zapata to Chinameca. He also asserted that (contrary to Constitutionalist claims) Zapata had only 150 men with him, compared to the 600 under Guajardo's command. Ultimately, he sang, Zapata entered the hacienda, "because the brave never fear the cowardly / because their only coat of arms is honor." After killing Zapata, in this account, Guajardo felt himself "an Alexander" and took the body to Cuautla as if it were "a trophy." The response of the Morelenses to the "sad end / of the man who fought for a national good" was tears and anguish, while the "insolent" Carrancistas wandered the streets of Cuautla, ridiculing the people of the town and inviting them to come identify the body of "their father." In another, similar piece on the same subject, Silva closely followed the wording of Reyes Avilés's official report in describing how Zapata was shot. Here he added that Zapata, "like Christ arrived at the end of his journey / to liberate our race from oppression." In general, Zapata the individual, as distinct from the movement, now began to attract more attention from corridistas, some of whom obviously felt the need to honor his memory differently than they had honored his presence.[29]

Despite the exhortations of their leaders, some Zapatistas agreed with the Carrancista insistence that their movement was over with Zapata's passing. "The wings of our hearts fell," recalled one, and many of the young men—or boys—under Zapata's command later noted, as did Pedro Martínez, that it was as though their own fathers had died.[30] One veteran, Constancio Quintero, remembered that he was in the hills when the news that "they just fucked the Jefe" arrived. Quintero's colonel "cried like a child," while other members of the group "took the saddles off their horses and threw them down, such was their despair."[31] It was a heavy blow to those who had stuck with Zapata through every trial and who still hoped that the revolution might fulfill their goals.

Obviously, these observers accepted that the body was Zapata's. "He was dead," asserted another veteran, "no one more dead than him."[32] But this was not the only way that Zapata's sympathizers chose to react to the word from Chinameca. The pains that Pablo González took to inject, photograph, and display Zapata's body, his order that it be deeply buried, and the occasional mention in the papers of the possibility of doubts concerning Zapata's demise all hint that not everyone accepted accounts of his death.

If ways of thinking about Zapata were truly in flux in the immediate aftermath of the ambush at Chinameca, it should come as no surprise that the idea that he had not died in that ambush took shape quickly. Indeed, a corrido entitled "Most Important Revelations of the Family of the Deceased Emiliano Zapata" demonstrates that such rumors were already in the air when it was first published in 1919.[33] This corrido, urban in origin and anti-Zapatista in attitude, indicates that "someone revealed in secret / that the dead man was missing / a mole above the mustache" that Zapata had. Then, in a 1928 publication, Carlos Reyes Avilés, brother of Salvador, wrote of having met an old man in late 1919 who would not accept that

Zapata had died.[34] In 1930, anthropologist Robert Redfield published a more detailed account of this train of thought, based on fieldwork he had done in 1926 and 1927 in Tepoztlán. "It is not known whether Zapata still lives or whether he was really killed as reported," one of Redfield's Zapatista informants told him. "Some say he is in Arabia, and will return when he is needed. For myself, I think he still lives."[35] Redfield also noted that this argument, which he believed to have developed gradually since Zapata's death, was taken up in a corrido of the period. "The singers have circulated," this corrido asserted, "a phenomenal lie, / and everyone says that Zapata already / rests in peace in eternity." But this was not the case. Rather, "since Zapata is so experienced, / alert and intelligent / he had thought beforehand / to send another man in his place."[36]

An oral tradition was in the making in Morelos, and periodic references to stories of Zapata's survival in written sources demonstrate that it persisted over the following decades.[37] Unfortunately, our access to this strand of the myth of Zapata is mediated by writers from the city, many of whom traveled to Morelos looking for peasants they expected to be simple and quaint. These writers often romanticized the stories they heard and may even have prompted some of them; at a minimum, they filtered them through their urban lenses. Thankfully, in the 1970s researchers from the National Institute of Anthropology and History (Instituto Nacional de Antropología e Historia, INAH) undertook a thorough and methodical oral history project that recorded a great deal of speculation about how Zapata eluded Guajardo and what happened to him thereafter.

In this oral tradition, as the 1919 corrido suggests, Pablo González's display of the body was a key event. "I know he had a scar on his cheek," said Redfield's informant, "and the corpse that was brought back from Chinameca had no scar. I saw it myself."[38] In 1938 a newspaper article written for the anniversary of Zapata's death described an exchange in Yautepec, Morelos, between a local doctor and an Indian named Pancho. Pancho asserted that he knew Zapata had not died because he had seen the body; the doctor responded with a rationalist's interpretation: people who examined the corpse claimed that it was missing the wart Zapata had on his left cheek, but the wart had been removed by a bullet.[39] In 1952, another informant explained that villagers who saw the body said it lacked a "mark that looked like a little hand," apparently a birthmark, that Zapata had on his chest.[40] In 1968, a journalist spoke to a group of Zapatista veterans who speculated on the subject. Their doubts about Zapata's demise, the report explained, were due to their understanding that the most renowned Zapatista identifier of the body, Eusebio Jáuregui, had in fact immediately cried out that it

THE POSTHUMOUS CAREER OF EMILIANO ZAPATA

was not Zapata, "basing his claim on specific signs that he knew perfectly." This explained why Jáuregui was executed on the following day.[41]

Later versions focused on other physical features. In an INAH interview of the 1970s, one veteran pointed out that while Zapata was missing a finger, the body presented as his "had its fingers complete."[42] Another old Zapatista noted not only the finger but his belief that Zapata had had a black mole that the corpse was missing, as well as a scar on his calf where a bull had gored him.[43] Others said the body was simply too fat. Some, like Carmen Aldana, claimed that Zapatista sympathizers had told the Carrancistas the body was Zapata's to avoid being beaten or killed.[44]

Accounts of such reactions to the body continue until the present. In 1996, *Excélsior* reported on the ancient Zapatista Emeterio Pantaleón, who stated, "we all laughed when we saw the cadaver. We elbowed each other, because the jefe was smarter than the government." Pantaleón then added material that had by then long been conventional, referring to the finger, the mole, the scar.[45] Though his advanced years made it just plausible that he had really visited the corpse, there was no danger that stories of Zapata's trickery at Chinameca would die with Pantaleón and whatever other last representatives of his generation were still around. Also in 1996, a far younger and more highly educated resident of Morelos explained to me that Zapata might indeed have avoided the trap.

How, then, had he done it? Either because Zapata actually did know of Guajardo's intentions or because the newspapers that developed the story that he had been tipped off stimulated local imaginations, the oral tradition consistently included the notion that he had survived because of premonition or warning. Apparently because the followers of such exalted individuals as Zapata often come to believe their leaders are too clever to be trapped, this is a common element in heroic myths.[46] The result was that Zapata sent another man in his place. Redfield's corrido identified Jesús Delgado as that man, and subsequent informants took the story further. Prospero García Aguirre, one of the INAH's interviewees, explained that a crying woman told Zapata of the trap just before he was to enter the hacienda. She had learned of it from her husband, who was a major under Guajardo. García Aguirre added that one of the most important Zapatista jefes, Francisco Mendoza, had assured García Aguirre's informant that Zapata had not been killed. Mendoza had explained that Delgado, a virtual double, had traveled with Zapata with the intention of dying for him if necessary. Further proof, in García Aguirre's eyes, for the supposition that Delgado had replaced Zapata was that "the unification [with Obregón] came and Jesús Delgado did not appear."[47]

Other accounts identified Zapata's double as Agustín Cortés; or Joaquín Cortés, a compadre from Tepoztlán; or Jesús Capistrán, a member of Zapata's staff and, again, a compadre; or simply a cousin. Zapata's son Nicolás was less interested in the details, revealing only that the person who really died was "some *pendejo* [dumb-ass] from Tepoztlán."[48] Some interviewees even supplied the speeches with which the double persuaded Zapata to make the switch. "I will only be missed by my family," reenacted one, "but you, compadre, would be missed by the whole country."[49] Another had the noble alternate say: "Compadre, I come to die for you; I only entrust you with my woman. Do me the favor of giving me your clothes, your sombrero, your spurs and the horse."[50]

If Zapata lived, where did he go? During the first decades after Chinameca, reports usually explained that he was either in hiding or had gone to Arabia, taken there by a compadre of Arab or other Middle Eastern descent. Wherever he was, he was safe from "the ambushes of his enemies."[51] The interviews of the 1970s offered greater detail. One of the most elaborate histories of Zapata's posthumous travel was that presented by Serafín Plasencia Gutiérrez, who asserted that his sister, a spiritualist, knew that Zapata had not died at Chinameca.[52] From her he discovered that a Hungarian or Arab compadre had taken him to either Hungary or Arabia—he was imprecise about the geography. There Zapata learned "certain languages and was doing well. They loved him like a god." Later, he returned to Morelos and had a girlfriend in Cocoyoc; he dressed like a *ranchero* to call on her.[53] Ultimately, though, he stopped visiting his home state. "The Arabs no longer let him come," Plasencia explained, "because he had many enemies: all of the hacendados, all of the politicians, everyone here in Cuautla was against him." He had died twenty or thirty years prior to the interview, "in his bed, over there in Arabia."

García Aguirre got his information on this issue from a different source. He had an aunt who sewed for a woman of Arab ancestry in Cuautla, and that woman had proclaimed, on returning from an extended trip to the Middle East, that Zapata was in Arabia. The government, she added, took great care of him, and he had "a better house than the president of the Republic." García Aguirre added that he himself had run into an old man who claimed to be Zapata's father-in-law—he probably meant the father of girlfriend Gregoria Zúñiga—and was living in Zapata's house in Quilamula. The old man maintained that he had proof, at home, that Zapata still lived, but García Aguirre was unable to go see that proof immediately, and the man soon died. García Aguirre concluded that Zapata had finally died, about twenty years before this 1975 interview, in Arabia.[54] Emeterio Pantaleón's version was that Zapata lived for a year in a cave close to a volcano. He then went to Tepoztlán, where he had a girlfriend. Still later, with a compadre and his wife, Josefa Espejo, he went to Acapulco, where he boarded a warship bound for Arabia. There he died in 1967.[55]

For some of the INAH informants it was not so easy to reconcile Arabia with local appearances. One noted that he had been told that Zapata had gone to the Valle Nacional, in Oaxaca, and not to Arabia, as many said. He had lived there under the alias Miguel Coria until dying about five years earlier.[56] Yet another version was that of Miguel Cabrera Rojas, who had it on the authority of a friend who had outfitted them that Zapata and his compadre simply went south, "far from Chinameca."[57]

Interestingly, this body of myth does not directly address a key question, which is why Zapata would have chosen to leave. True, the war was going badly, but if he left merely for self-preservation he was hardly setting himself up for hero status. But for those among his erstwhile supporters who had come to wish simply that the violence would stop—and there were many in this category—Zapata was an obstacle to peace. From this perspective his departure was an act of sacrifice that could only improve his reputation. For those for whom this was an unspoken part of the story of Zapata's survival, we might also hypothesize that thinking of Zapata's disappearance as a departure rather than a death was a way of assuaging guilt at having wished it would all end—perhaps even making a deal with the Carrancistas—and then hearing about Chinameca.

Another possible explanation for Zapata's exit was that he left to wait for a more propitious time. Whether he remained in Mexico or became a world traveler, the idea that Zapata might return was imbedded in the speculation. Writing in the late 1920s, United States historian Frank Tannenbaum stated that the "Indians" of southern Mexico, "will to this day tell a stranger that Zapata's spirit wanders over the mountain at night and watches over the Indians and that he will return if they are mistreated."[58] The skeptical doctor interviewed in 1938 maintained that the campesinos believed Zapata "watches that justice is done for the humble and that his work of redemption is continued. On the day oppression returns, he will return to liberate them." In 1949, a journalist reported a slightly more complicated view: "Zapata lives hidden, watching over us; but he has promised to come when they have fulfilled all his ideals, to share with us the fruit of his struggles—or when they try to take our rights away."[59] Decades later an INAH subject confided that Zapata was getting an education, and that he would return when he had received his bachelor's degree.[60] Another reported that around 1927 a peasant had seen Zapata, who asked him, "Hey, buddy, don't you recognize me?" The campesino had known him before

1919, but he was hard to recognize now: "he had shaved his mustache," and he had a mole, but it was red. He was, moreover, balding and dressed in *huaraches* (sandals) and loose, white cotton *calzones*, peasant garb in which Zapata, when he lived, chose not to present himself—at least not for the camera.[61] Finally, for some time a group of Zapatista veterans gathered annually on April 10 in the expectation that Zapata would return on that date to again lead his people in pursuit of justice.[62]

As the years passed, hope for decisive action from Zapata grew harder to maintain. In 1979, the daughter of Francisco Franco—the man Zapata had appointed to protect the documents that supported Anenecuilco's land claims—asserted that Zapata had returned but had been too old to continue the struggle.[63] Others simply received sporadic midnight visits from him, or saw him on his white horse in the mountains, as if he were keeping watch.[64] Indeed, the post-Chinameca history of Zapata's horse is an interesting facet of the myth, so closely was his power associated with that animal. But for many the surviving horse was merely a souvenir of Zapata, a substitute for him, not an expression of future possibilities. Constancio Quintero stated that the horse, though "wounded in the withers, and close to the tail," survived Chinameca, but Zapata did not. Domingo Yedra Islas testified that "they killed Zapata, but his horse escaped; it escaped, but he fell dead." And, as we have seen, Carmen Aldana claimed that a boy took it away and gave it to the president.[65]

What emerged, then, was a complicated messianic drama. The notion that Zapata might reappear to pursue his brand of social justice placed him in the company of Jesus Christ, Shiite Islam's hidden imam, King Arthur, and Quetzalcóatl (see the Introduction), who had allegedly promised to return from the East to recover his central Mexican throne. A comparison with Portugal's "hidden king," Sebastiao, is also instructive. Sebastiao was ostensibly killed in battle in 1578, but there were difficulties in the identification of his body, and many expected that he would come back to bring renewed glory to Portugal.[66] Expectations of Zapata's return alone do not make him exceptional or godlike, given that Mexican folk culture recognizes the annual return of *all* dead on the Day of the Dead. But Zapata was also explicitly associated with various religious figures. In the 1970s, Zapatista veteran Agapito Pariente claimed that Zapata, "like the prophet Moses," had retired to private life. Pariente was perhaps comparing Zapata's disappearance to the time Moses spent among the Midianites before being called back to Egypt to liberate the Hebrews, as a way of emphasizing that Zapata had not abandoned his followers and would himself return.[67] The corridos of Marciano Silva also compared Zapata to Moses, already during

Zapata's lifetime, as a liberator of his people. Shortly after Zapata's death, Silva indicated that, "like Christ, [he] arrived at the end of his quest / to liberate our race from oppression."[68] Another interviewee compared Zapata to her village's patron saint, Santiago, because of his role in protecting the community from Carrancista attacks.[69] Such comparisons do, of course, make Zapata extraordinary, and the complex of messianic ideas about him did much to give him his lasting mythical power.

It is impossible to reconstruct precisely how Zapata's myth developed in the local arena over the decades after his death—how one account led to the next—but individuals evidently took the liberty of piecing together elements of the stories as they saw fit, and the variations are many. In some cases the reworking of the basic narrative seems largely the result of confusion. One veteran, for example, said it was Jesús Delgado who died, and that Delgado, like Zapata, lacked a finger; this account made this particular reference to the body, which traditionally proved that it was *not* Zapata's corpse, into part of the reason Delgado could pass for him.[70]

An apparently more intentional way of recasting the story came from those who did not believe Zapata had survived Chinameca but who appropriated parts of the accounts of those who did. Through decades of retelling, various events leading up to Chinameca have become like Stations of the Cross on the way to Zapata's Calvary: the letters he exchanged with Guajardo; Guajardo's taking of the town of Jonacatepec at Zapata's orders to prove his loyalty; and the subsequent meeting of the two men at Tepalcingo on April 9. One of these oft-evoked acts in Zapata's tragedy was Guajardo's capture—and the eventual massacre—of the forces of Victoriano Bárcenas. Most Zapatista authorities have stated that Guajardo oversaw the slaughter of these troops in the hope of winning Zapata's trust. Some, however, have contended that Zapata presided instead, including Constancio Quintero, who reported that one of the men about to be shot shouted to Zapata, "Don't kill me, general. I'll tell you what they're going to do to you tomorrow," but then the shots rang out. Still, Quintero added, Zapata's jefes warned him not to trust Guajardo. Then, when Zapata stubbornly started his ride toward the hacienda gate, he was intercepted by a *soldadera* who insisted they were going to kill him.[71] Zapata became furious. "Gossipy old women," he supposedly exclaimed, "you go around starting rumors instead of thanking Guajardo." Ignoring all warnings, Zapata continued on to his death.[72] A slight variation specifies that the soldadera was from Guajardo's forces and puts these words in Zapata's mouth: "Thanks very much for your information, but I advise you to go make tortillas or cook some beans and don't bring me gossip."[73] One informant claimed that he himself had offered warnings that were ignored, asserting that despite the apparent proofs of loyalty from Guajardo, "we still told Zapata that this is a betrayal." [74]

INAH interviewee Angel Abúndez traced out another possible interpretation. "Men who are men," he reasoned, "must die to demonstrate manhood. So, for me he is dead, because he demonstrated that he died like Jesus Christ; he died to defend the people, and Jesus Christ did the same, and so he planned his life so the rest could be saved. . . . If he hadn't died, the thing wouldn't have any value." [75] For Abúndez, the events at Chinameca remained transcendental, but the fact of Zapata's death, his martyrdom, was more important than the notion of survival—which was, in any case, a watered-down form of resurrection; no one was suggesting that Zapata had literally risen from the dead. What he had done, from Abúndez's point of view, was imitate Christ by going knowingly to his death as an act of sacrifice. [76] Some believed that this advance toward death was a long one. Pedro Martínez maintained that on the promulgation of the Plan of Ayala in 1911, Zapata had stated that he knew it meant his death. [77] This willingness to die in self-sacrifice echoes not only the Christian story but those of many other heroes, including Mexico's Niños Héroes, who, according to legend, sacrificed themselves in 1847 in hopeless defense of Mexico City's Chapultepec castle against a U.S. invasionary force.

It bears pointing out that Zapata's regional myth has not been limited to musings about his alleged death. There are various accounts of riches he had sealed in caves high in the hills, the kind of tales that might be told of any outlaw. [78] Probably more significant are the stories that demonstrate that he was destined for greatness. In Morelos they say, related a journalist in 1934, that "when Zapata was born, there was a star shower that filled the inhabitants of Anenecuilco with wonder. The old people who knew of Emiliano's birth explained that when such a thing occurs, the new child who comes into the world favored in this way will be prominent in life." [79] Another early sign came at the baptismal font, where a woman claiming to be Zapata's godmother observed that "when a priest from Cuautla gave him the salt, the baby swallowed it without making signs of crying. For that reason the priest announced that he would be ill-tempered." [80] The point, perhaps, was that a measure of irritability is necessary to produce a revolutionary. A third account of predestination, to be discussed in the following chapter, illustrates Zapata's commitment to the land at a young age.

How, then, can we generalize about the peasant myth that rose up around Zapata after his death? First, despite its many variations, it demonstrates substantial continuity in its basic elements. One might also suggest that there is continuity in the type of logic visible, say, in García Aguirre's belief that Jesús Delgado must have died for Zapata because he vanished.[81] Similar thinking appears in two arguments made for Zapata's survival in 1938: if Zapata did die, then why does his son Nicolás not attend the ceremonies held annually on the anniversary of his death; and why had Zapata's sisters "never dressed in mourning?"[82] In a related vein, Zapata's daughter Ana María declared in the 1990s that her father certainly had died, since he would not otherwise have abandoned his family.[83] The logic underlying these statements contains various expectations about interpersonal relationships; it also demonstrates how people in relatively small communities can scrutinize the actions of other community members. It is a logic that exists close to the ground, generated by experience, by lives rooted in the geography that produced the stories being told, so that the speaker can point when telling a story—Zapata slept over there, his horse passed here, Chinameca is just down the road. Supplementing the immediacy of Zapata's presence in this geography are the images of him on the altars in the homes of the region and his evocation during rites of passage—marriages, baptisms, graduations.[84] Still more, Zapatismo remains a living force in Morelos, embodied not just by whatever ancient veterans still stand but by Zapata's descendants, who are rumored to be more numerous than officially recognized. However factual such rumors may be, they are a provocative continuation of the days in which villagers hoped Zapata would take up with a local woman, hopes gradually transferred to at least hypothetical children and grandchildren.[85] Personal connections and local geography, in other words, infuse the myth in Morelos in a way that cannot be duplicated elsewhere; the peasant myth comes from communities not merely imagined but also small enough to be experienced in substantial degree.[86]

The continuity of mythical elements suggests that the oral tradition has been strong and important to locals. That strength may come, in part, merely from the entertainment value of storytelling in a rural and thus not thoroughly "modern" world. But memories of Zapata have been much more than just a way to pass time. In the 1970s, one old Zapatista divulged that people had killed each other fighting over whether Zapata died at Chinameca.[87] In any event, the peasant myth that arose in the aftermath of Zapata's death is crucial for the story this book has to tell because it was there that the positive interpretation of Zapata got its footing. During his lifetime there was no guarantee that Zapata would achieve lasting heroic stature even in his home state; it was the nature and timing of his death that dictated that. As we will see in the next chapter, the way in which the revolutionary fighting ended then provided the conditions in which Zapata's myth could grow and spread from its regional roots.

THREE

FORGING A NATIONAL ZAPATA, 1920–1934

As muralist Diego Rivera sometimes claimed to remember it, he fought alongside Zapata in Morelos in 1911. Zapata, he maintained, received him with open arms because it was Rivera's father who taught him to read before the revolution. This was proof, from Rivera's point of view, that Zapata was not the illiterate the "reactionaries" described in trying to discredit the people's cause. "Much of the time," Rivera elaborated,

> I worked with a former schoolmate named Penioroja. An able mechanic, Penioroja had invented a small, simple bomb, so designed as to blow up only the baggage cars of trains. This saved the locomotives, which were useful to the rebels. It also spared the lives of the passengers, most of them the very people for whom the revolution was being fought.

As luck would have it, Penioroja's invention was exactly the size of Rivera's paintbox. "That is why," Rivera explained, "in this period, my artistic output showed no appreciable increase." Instead of painting, he became a specialist in blowing up trains, while also serving as a link between "our secret organization in the city" and the Zapatistas. Still more, he maintained that he developed a plan to assassinate Porfirio Díaz to end the bloodshed as quickly as possible.[1]

But the government learned of Rivera's activities, the story continued, and made plans to charge him with treason and execute him.[2] He was thus forced, reluctantly, to leave Zapata's side, sneaking away to Havana with the intention of joining the revolution in northern Mexico from there. But in Cuba he heard from friends in Paris, who "desired a report from an eyewitness, so I continued my trip in that direction." He remained in Europe for the next decade, but ostensibly never stopped dreaming about Mexico and its struggle. This, he said, was reflected in his cubist painting of 1915, which he called *Zapatista Landscape*. It depicted "a Mexican peasant hat hanging over a window box behind a rifle," volcanoes in the background. While he later pronounced his cubist experimentation, in general, a waste of time, he believed that this work was "probably the most faithful expression of the Mexican mood that I have ever achieved." Even Picasso supposedly liked it.[3]

Zapata, Rivera asserted, was the "initiator of the independence of the Mexican earth, who wanted only those who worked it with their hands to possess it." But since the "reactionaries" sought to have him remembered as the Attila of the South, licking the bones of the landowners clean, Rivera felt he had the work of the revolution to do.[4] When prominent intellectual José Vasconcelos, who had been appointed Obregón's minister of education, asked him to return to paint the walls of Mexico with images of the revolution, he jumped at the chance. It was to be art for the people, publicly displayed for all to see, not more art for the bourgeoisie to hoard.

Rivera painted Zapata five times in the mid-1920s at the Ministry of Public Education (Secretaría de Educación Pública, SEP). This was not because he wanted to emphasize heroes—Mexican society was his avowed subject—but because he thought Zapata was the rare leader who authentically represented the people. In one panel he painted the process of land distribution as it was being carried out in the 1920s. He put Zapata in the picture among campesinos listening to a politician speak. Here Zapata was dressed as a charro, not wearing calzones like most of the others, and while the others watched the politician he looked straight at the viewer, apparently to demand compliance with the constitution's promise of land.[5]

Putting Zapata into a 1920s scene erased the line between life and death, and emphasized the value of memory.[6] Rivera had heard the campesino stories, so maybe Zapata was not dead, who was to say. At any rate, he erased that line in other panels, too. He painted Zapata as Christ resurrected, looming up from death wrapped in a red robe and made holy by an orange mandorla that surrounded him. This time he was flanked by two seated Indian women holding corn and wheat in their hands, heads lowered in humble worship. Another of the famous muralists of the era, David Alfaro Siqueiros, called this Rivera's "Saint Zapata" and accused him of being a "mystical Zapatista."[7] Rivera answered that, despite his talk of the people's revolution, Siqueiros did not understand the implications of doing art for the masses who made the revolution. It was partly Rivera's desire to address this audience that prompted his use of a corrido to link some of the scenes at the ministry together, though the corrido he employed—actually a composite of three corridos—shows no sign of a campesino hand in its composition.[8]

Never an admirer of Zapata, Vasconcelos charged that Rivera had fallen "into the shamelessness of covering walls with effigies of criminals."[9] Still, Rivera found more work, painting at the National Agricultural School at Chapingo in the mid-1920s as well. Here the theme was naturally the land, so Zapata had to be present. He placed the dead Zapata, in the same red shroud in which he rose at the ministry, beneath the earth, feet-to-feet with Otilio Montaño, co-author of the Plan of Ayala. Flourishing above them was a field of corn, roots drawing strength from the blood of the martyrs. It was yet another resurrection, this time through the natural cycle of death and rebirth, Zapata symbolizing the land and also the fatherland, Mexico. Rivera reworked this theme in a textbook illustration at about the same time. Meanwhile, on the door at Chapingo he did another Zapata, with the inscription, "Those who are good will always be with Zapata."[10]

At the end of the decade he began work on the stairway of the National Palace. There on the huge western wall he painted the entire history of Mexico.[11] For the top of the central arch he started with the idea of an allegorical figure of Mexico as a protective mother, embracing a worker and a peasant. But he decided to change it. Instead, he inserted three martyrs— José Guadalupe Rodríguez, an agrarian leader who had just been assassinated; former Yucatecan governor and *agrarista* Felipe Carrillo Puerto; and Zapata. Together they held a banner that read "Land and Liberty," an excellent three-word summary of Zapata's demands that has been much associated with him, though not a rallying cry he invented or accepted as his own.[12] Behind them were campesinos, but all one could see was the tops of their sombreros, massed together like the halos of a medieval icon.

Again he had two projects going at once. He was also working on a commission from U.S. ambassador Dwight Morrow to paint the history of Morelos in the palace of conqueror Hernán Cortés in Cuernavaca. His goal was to turn the palace, which had been a monument to the Spanish conquest, into a memorial of Indian persistence. In the final section of this history, he painted probably his most admired and reproduced Zapata (see Figure 3.1). This time Zapata was dressed in calzones—white, of course— and leading a white horse with one hand. He was also holding a machete. Behind him were campesinos, ready to work the land they had won. A dead hacienda administrator lay at Zapata's feet. Rivera made Zapata a peasant this time, an Indian, at least from the perspective of urban Mexico, wearing white to reflect his purity and in particular the purity of his relationship with the campesinos and Indians of Mexico.[13] He painted a second Zapata here in tribute to printmaker José Guadalupe Posada, whom he claimed to have met as a child in Mexico City. Imitating one of Posada's prints, he

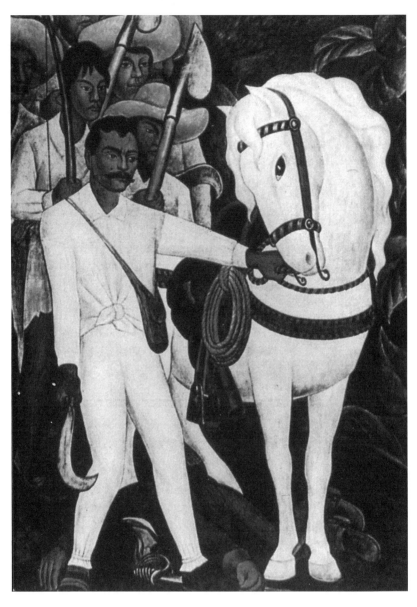

FIGURE 3.1

Diego Rivera, Revolutionary Agrarista Emiliano Zapata, *1929–1930.*
Fresco, Palace of Cortés, Cuernavaca. (© 2008 Banco de México Diego Rivera
& Frida Kahlo Museums Trust. Av. Cinco de Mayo No. 2, Col. Centro,
Del. Cuauhtémoc 06059, México, D.F.)

depicted Zapata holding up a rifle with his right hand and grasping the hilt of a saber at his waist with the other. He was draped in a patriotic sash with Mexico's colors and, of course, his signature cartridge belts—here he was a charro. Posada himself borrowed the pose from a photograph taken after Zapata entered Cuernavaca early in the decade of war (see Figure 1.1).[14]

While Rivera's efforts to instill Zapata with greater iconic presence were fundamental to the creation of the caudillo's image, we cannot entirely trust the stories he told. He was not, in 1911, the warrior, spy, or fugitive he claimed to have been; however sincere his revolutionary sentiment, it did not extend so far as to put him in harm's way.[15] Moreover, the title he gave his 1915 cubist work, *Zapatista Landscape*, seems to have been an afterthought. He also perhaps exaggerated his role in changing attitudes about Zapata in Mexico City, for they had already begun to shift when he returned from Europe. That story begins with the politicians.

For ambitious Pablo González, the assassination of Zapata almost immediately became part of a campaign for the presidency, which Carranza was scheduled to vacate in 1920. Running against fellow general Alvaro Obregón and Carranza's hand-picked successor, ambassador to the United States Ignacio Bonillas, González sought to project himself as a successful military leader and a sincere revolutionary—the "pacifier of the state of Morelos" and that state's true agrarian reformer—though there is little evidence that he was either. In her campaign biography of González, Hermila Galindo, the revolutionary period's foremost suffragette and a woman deeply concerned about sexual violence, melded support of González's ambitions with her own agenda when she got to the subject of the bestial Attila of the South.[16] Galindo conceded that there may have been, at the base of Zapata's soul, "some embryonic sentiment of liberty," but he hardly deserved the credit González's enemies were giving him as they sought to make him appear "legendary and gallant." Galindo also indulged in conventional rhetoric when she charged that those enemies were either reactionaries themselves or at least revolutionaries gullible enough to be fooled by reactionaries; she added her fear that the "reactionary" press would soon be mentioning Zapata in company with founding fathers Hidalgo and Juárez. She also claimed that those who were making "a political weapon of the death of Zapata" did not understand "that the attacks made on General González with this motive wound with rejection the entire revolutionary regime." Thankfully, however, she found that sensible, dispassionate opinion was with González on the issue of the death "of the violator of maidens, the underminer of all rights, the profaner of all virtues, the man-beast who presented a living example of the regression of humanity toward the epoch of troglodytes."[17]

Despite the deeply entrenched metropolitan disdain for Zapata, then, there were people outside of Zapata's home region who expressed reservations about the means used to kill him and may even have considered his cause just, at least in part. In an autobiography written decades later, Luis L. León, who would serve as secretary of agriculture in the administration of Plutarco Elías Calles (1924–1928), claimed that Zapata's death "produced great popular discontent," undermining worker and peasant support for Carranza and González. León added that he told Obregón three days after Zapata died that the assassination of "don Emiliano was shameful for the revolution." Obregón supposedly responded that "this crime reveals a lack of ethics in some members of the government and also of political sense, since peasant votes in the upcoming election will now go to whoever runs against Pablo González."[18] Another Constitutionalist observer, Vicente Estrada Cajigal, who in 1930 became the first governor of Morelos elected under the rules of the 1917 Constitution, remembered that the way Zapata had died was one of the stains on Carranza's record.[19] Though the memories of politicians are notoriously self-serving and there would soon be good political reasons to claim that one had always identified with Zapata, these accounts, added to Galindo's defensiveness, suggest that the manner of Zapata's death did gain him some sympathy in non-Zapatista circles.

Despite Galindo's efforts, González's campaign fizzled, leaving him little opportunity to shape memories of Zapata to his liking. Obregón, the revolution's most successful general, seemed on the way to electoral victory. Carranza, however, was adamant that Bonillas—whom he probably expected to control—should have the presidency. In pursuit of that goal he tried to arrest Obregón. But Carranza's support had been eroding for years. He had been unable to end the violence or solve the economic difficulties the revolution had created, and he had largely ignored the promises of the new constitution. Obregón fled the capital with the help of surviving Zapatistas, while an uprising, the Revolution of Agua Prieta, broke out on his behalf in his home state of Sonora. Much of the revolutionary army soon joined it.[20] The Zapatistas aided Obregón for several reasons. Although Obregón had been a member of Carranza's faction, he and Carranza had been on the outs, more or less, since 1917, when Obregón left Carranza's cabinet. After that time Zapata had had his eye on Obregón as the revolutionary figure who best combined power and some sympathy with Zapatista goals.[21] Furthermore, Obregón was not among those who celebrated Zapata's demise in 1919, if only because González was his political opponent. Thus the Zapatistas joined Obregón's coalition, and on May 9, after a few weeks of fighting, Obregón and Genovevo de la O entered Mexico City together in triumph while Carranza fled toward Veracruz. Later in the month Carranza's career ended much as had Zapata's, when he was killed in the mountains of Puebla by troops loyal to Obregón. Obregón made a Sonoran collaborator, Adolfo de la Huerta, interim president, and began to prepare for fall elections that would sweep him into executive power.

Obregón was a masterful politician. He understood that Mexico had just experienced a largely rural revolution in which people had taken up arms to demand land, and he realized that that demand would have to be addressed before political stability could be reestablished. He also understood that it was Zapata who had voiced that demand best. It only made sense, then, given the presence of the Zapatistas within his coalition, that the memory of Zapata be used to firm up campesino support. To this end, the new regime found scraps of power to throw to Zapatistas who would help lend credibility to its nascent Zapatismo. Gildardo Magaña and Genovevo de la O became division generals in June when the Zapatistas joined the federal army, with de la O taking over as military commander of Morelos. At de la O's bidding, Zapatista physician José G. Parrés was appointed governor of Morelos. Miguel Mendoza L. Schwerdtfeger, another Zapatista of urban background, became general secretary of the National Agrarian Commission, which oversaw the land reform process. Various other Zapatista scribes and advisors, most originally from outside Morelos, became federal congressmen or received positions in the agrarian or education bureaucracies.[22]

Foremost among Obregón's new Zapatista allies was Antonio Díaz Soto y Gama. A lawyer by training and a self-proclaimed anarchist, Díaz Soto y Gama had a considerable career of radical politics behind him. He had participated in the creation of the Mexican Liberal Party (Partido Liberal Mexicano, PLM) that pestered Porfirio Díaz in the decade before the revolution. He had also helped found an important labor organization in the capital, the House of the World Worker (Casa del Obrero Mundial, COM), during Madero's presidency. He joined the Zapatistas in early 1914 and quickly became one of Zapata's most important spokespersons, representing him most famously and controversially at the Convention of Aguascalientes, at which, in late 1914, the various revolutionary factions briefly sought to create a unified government after the fall of Victoriano Huerta. Obregón offered Díaz Soto y Gama the Ministry of Agriculture, but Díaz Soto y Gama apparently felt that a job in the administration would be too constraining. Instead, he established the National Agrarian Party (Partido Nacional Agrarista, PNA), which he represented in the national legislature from 1920 to 1928.[23]

The Agrarian Party was only one among many new parties, and like most of them its strength was limited to certain regions. Under Díaz Soto y Gama's direction it was significant, nevertheless, in that it offered nearly unconditional loyalty to Obregón. It essentially offered Zapata's loyalty as well. Díaz Soto y Gama encouraged his fellow Zapatistas to fall in line behind the established authorities by noting that Zapata "constantly exhorted us to sustain an unbreakable union among all revolutionaries."[24] He also curbed his radicalism in ways that supported Obregón's more moderate approach to land reform, becoming, for instance, an adamant anticommunist. Díaz Soto y Gama now remembered that when Zapata was asked by an enthusiast of communism about that doctrine's applicability in Mexico, he had pounded the table in front of him and cried, "The devil! I want a piece of land for myself, not for the state."[25] In 1923, Obregón presented Díaz Soto y Gama with an oil painting of Zapata; the agrarian leader's fawning reply was that it was the ideal gift, both because it depicted Zapata and because it came from a great revolutionary.[26] Ultimately, Díaz Soto y Gama arrived at the conclusion that Obregón was the "executor of the thought of Emiliano Zapata."[27] He was locked in. In return for his backing, the Agrarian Party became influential, and Díaz Soto y Gama was able to argue that de la Huerta and Obregón heard and attended to Zapatista needs. From his new vantage point he pushed the land reform agenda, fought to get Agrarian Party candidates elected, and petitioned for benefits for Zapatismo's veterans, widows, and orphans.[28]

But the new partnership between Zapatismo and Obregón was not without tensions. One was simply that Obregón hailed from northern Mexico, where revolutionary ideology had a strong developmentalist cast, and he believed too much in the sanctity of private property to undertake the thoroughgoing land reform for which Zapata had fought. Díaz Soto y Gama's praise notwithstanding, Obregón would only be interested in handing out land in regions where it would gain him political clout. Land reform moved quickly in Morelos, but in some parts of the country it did not proceed at all.[29] It was precisely such shortcomings on the land issue that would make Zapata as symbol so valuable to the incipient state.

A second difficulty was that Constitutionalists had fought Zapatistas through much of the revolutionary decade and had ultimately killed Zapata. True, Carranza was out of the way, but many other key figures in that conflict remained, including González and Guajardo, who had avoided supporting Carranza during Obregón's uprising. Luckily for the budding relationship between Zapata and the Obregonistas, in late June 1920 Guajardo rebelled in the northern state of Nuevo León. According to Antonio

I. Villarreal, then de la Huerta's secretary of agriculture, Guajardo "rose up in arms because he was choked with worry. He knew he was accused of a base betrayal that was repugnant to the sentiment of nobility of the nation." Villarreal added that Guajardo's "enemy is not the present government nor any of its men, but his own remorse." This, however, was disingenuous. The present government *was* aligned against Guajardo, as Villarreal revealed when he implied that Guajardo's rebellion had solved the administration's problem over what to do with him. *Excélsior* reflected the prevailing attitude toward him by calling him the "assassin of Zapata," and Pablo González alleged that Guajardo had been mercilessly harassed. In other words, Guajardo's decision to rebel was likely related to the emerging official posture toward the memory of Zapata. If so, then Zapata now had his revenge, for Guajardo was soon caught and executed. González, too, was implicated in the revolt and faced a court martial, but after a few days of theatrics he was allowed to go into exile.[30]

This sacrifice of Guajardo and González was apparently critical for the Zapatistas. One informant from Tepoztlán told Robert Redfield that the Zapatistas themselves had killed Guajardo, and an oral tradition concerning a plot among Zapatista leaders to do just that lingered at least into the 1970s.[31] Pedro Martínez, meanwhile, claimed that de la O had demanded that Obregón execute Guajardo before de la O would support him, "so Obregón had that Guajardo killed and then Obregón became a zapatista." A later interviewee seconded Martínez's understanding on this issue, adding that Carranza's death was part of the bargain.[32] Although many members of Obregón's triumphant faction had fought against Zapata and learned to hate him, the most obvious culprits in his death had now been collectively assigned the role of Judas in his messianic drama and removed from the scene. Several others demonstrated great agility in avoiding blame, the case of General Antonio Ríos Zertuche being perhaps the most astonishing. Though Ríos Zertuche played an indispensable role in luring Zapata into the ambush, it was subsequently he who commanded the firing squad that ended Guajardo's life, clearing the way for him and his fellow Obregonistas to carry out a remarkably quick adoption of Zapata.[33]

One of the main ways official Mexico now embraced Zapata was by commemorating him on the anniversary of his assassination. In 1920 there was surely some sort of local or familial ceremony at his gravesite, but with Obregón's rebellion against Carranza just then brewing it had to be low-key, and it seems to have left no record.[34] In April 1921, however, Obregón was ensconced in the presidency and national politicians were well on the way to forgetting Zapata's "bandit" past. The Zapatista governor of Morelos,

Parrés, declared April 10 a day of mourning in the state and joined the Agrarian Party in organizing a commemorative event. The main speakers, Díaz Soto y Gama and still-Secretary of Agriculture Villarreal, glorified Zapata and asked their audience to be patient as the government's land reform project unfolded. Díaz Soto y Gama asserted that Zapata represented "perennial convulsion" and that he was "in everyone and everything, in the light and in the shadows: Zapata is a symbol of human vindication." *El Demócrata* embarked on an obviously conscious policy of mythmaking, seizing the occasion to depict Zapata as a "modest Indian farmer," a "defender of Democracy," and a "sincere and patriotic Mexican" whose movement had never received support from abroad.[35] In an editorial later that month, the old Porfirian intellectual Francisco Bulnes commented facetiously on the proceedings. Noting that Zapata was already beginning to acquire a "fervent cult," he suggested that if agrarianism accomplished all that was then being promised for it, the towns of Morelos would need to be given Greek names and "from all parts of the world pilgrims will come to the village of Ayala, leaning on magical staffs and loaded with pearls and flowers that the angels will scatter over the classical bronzes of the tomb of the Prophet."[36]

When April came around again, in 1922, an editorial in *Excélsior* put the case against Zapata's official rehabilitation more bluntly. The revolutionary press, this piece argued, had dedicated itself to glorifying Zapata, attributing to him "noble and fertile ideals of popular regeneration." This, the author asserted, demonstrated that Mexicans were losing the ability to tell good from evil. "Zapata had no ideals," the article continued, "nor did he employ generous means to realize them." Far from a hero, he had instead been "the most vulgar of our revolutionaries . . . without principles, without the slightest smattering of education . . . his work was that of an Attila who converted Morelos into a heap of debris and shed torrents of blood." Perhaps even more damning in that political climate, this writer insisted that Zapata was anti-Obregonista, given that he had opposed all government and order.[37]

But neither Bulnes's sarcasm nor the reservations expressed in this editorial could match the forces increasingly arrayed on Zapata's side. In 1922, the administration honored the day by promulgating a new set of regulations for land distribution, while the metropolitan newspapers announced that the commemoration of Zapata's death would exceed the past two "in solemnity." At Obregón's request, the Secretary of War sent a military band to Cuautla, along with a commission that deposited a floral offering at the gravesite. Speakers such as communist teacher, author, and congressional deputy Rafael Ramos Pedrueza and General Francisco Múgica complained of Carranza and called Zapata "the redemption of the rural proletariat."[38] The rather conservative newspaper *El Universal* fumbled noticeably, both with the facts—it indicated that Zapata had been killed at Tepalcingo and buried in Tlaltizapán—and with how to fine-tune its editorial position. With specific reference to both Guajardo and González, this paper took the position that "now that the hatreds have vanished we know that his [Zapata's] enemies glorified him with their treachery"; it also remarked that Zapata had become, in particular, "a symbol for the agraristas." On the other hand, it presented an account of Zapata's death in which it sometimes relied on "facts" that had been imparted by the Constitutionalists. Among these was the potentially absolving claim that there had been more Zapatistas (1,000) than Carrancistas (500) at the ambush, so that a fearful Guajardo was forced to act quickly to protect his troops. *El Universal* did not yet demonstrate much desire to make Zapata a hero, but it was trying to portray him in a new light.[39] For its part, *El Demócrata* maintained that Zapata's fame was already worldwide, as was the condemnation of the crime of Chinameca. It also did a better job than *El Universal* of getting the basic elements of the story of Zapata's demise straight.[40]

In 1923 the authorities of Morelos organized "solemn civic ceremonies" in Cuautla, "which assumed true importance." The Secretary of War was represented by a commission composed of eight generals, but this time Obregón sent an envoy of his own, perhaps a recognition that remembering Zapata was not primarily a military matter. He also helped cover expenses and provided trains to carry celebrants down from Mexico City. The capital's municipal orchestra made the trip too. Governor Parrés greeted the visiting dignitaries at the train station and accompanied them to Zapata's grave. There Cuautla's schoolchildren planted trees; "various villages," including Anenecuilco, were awarded land as part of Obregón's agrarian reform; and inaugurations were performed for the night school "Emiliano Zapata," a new newspaper, and the First Agrarian Congress of Pueblos of the State of Morelos. Representatives of national, state, and local governments, the military, and peasant and worker organizations all placed floral wreaths at the burial site. That evening there was a *velada*—a musical-literary event—which was reportedly well-attended.[41] Not everything, however, was as "solemn" as it might have been. Led by Gildardo Magaña, several Zapatistas had just formed an alternative agrarian organization, the National Agrarian Confederation (Confederación Nacional Agraria, CNA) and public bickering broke out between members of that group and representatives of the Agrarian Party.[42] Still, 1923 saw noteworthy progress in the shaping of commemorative practices, both with regard to who attended and to incorporating rewards for the locals into the proceedings, without which their willingness to cooperate with the federal government on these anniversaries might have been more limited.[43]

More momentous still was the ceremony of 1924, when Plutarco Elías Calles, who would inherit the presidency later that year as Obregón's hand-picked successor, made what was essentially a campaign stop. As the pre-eminent military hero of the revolutionary conflict, Obregón did not need to spend a great deal of his own time worrying about symbolism. Calles, on the other hand, who lacked Obregón's military reputation, was happy to accept the opportunity the ceremony provided. Like previous commemorations and those that would follow year after year, this ritual was organized not by the national government, but by local and state officials and prominent Zapatistas. In particular, Governor of Morelos Alfredo Ortega, Díaz Soto y Gama and his Agrarian Party, and Genovevo de la O—still state military commander—made the arrangements.[44] They surely imagined that the presence of Calles would further honor and legitimize Zapata and advance his agrarian agenda, and in that they were not mistaken.

FIGURE 3.2

Commemorating Zapata's death. (Fondo Gildardo Magaña, Archivo Histórico de la Universidad Nacional Autónoma de México, Instituto de Investigaciones Sobre la Universidad y la Educación, Universidad Nacional Autónoma de México.)

Besides Calles, the guest list included officials from Obregón's cabinet, national congressmen, and representatives of state and local governments from the states of Mexico, Puebla, Hidalgo, Guerrero, Tlaxcala, Oaxaca, Veracruz, Jalisco, Michoacán, Sonora, and San Luis Potosí. Also in attendance were officials of Magaña's National Agrarian Confederation and various other agrarian groups, five thousand peasants from Morelos and the Federal District, and such interested individuals as Diego Rivera, who was presumably there to soak up some of the atmosphere he was trying to capture in his murals.[45] Cuautla prepared well for the occasion, erecting a series of triumphal arches, covered with flowers, banners, and Mexican flags, that straddled the street leading from the train station to the graveyard. Calles arrived at the station at 11:30 in the morning with many of his fellow notables. There he received a tremendous ovation from the crowd that was waiting, and then helped form a parade that filed beneath the arches. It was a march of symbolic occupation, a reclaiming of territory by representatives of a national government that had had great trouble exercising power in Morelos since the revolution broke out in 1911.[46]

At the cemetery a series of speakers took the podium. Federal deputy and Agrarian Party member from Zacatecas Lauro G. Caloca called Zapata a Mexican martyr; and the representative of the Ministry of Agriculture and Development asserted that he was "the greatest reformer in Mexican history" and that his work was already too well rooted in Mexican hearts to be destroyed. Crisóforo Ibañez, an agrarista from Puebla, condemned capitalism and avowed—in an early statement of one of the most-repeated adages attributed to Zapata—that the land "should belong to he who works it." [47] One speaker addressed the crowd in Náhuatl (the language of the Aztecs); another criticized politicians as a group and asked those listening to be thankful they had a clean politician, in Calles, who would implement Zapata's program without corruption. It sounded good, and "vivas" for Zapata and Calles ensued, but the dirty politicians escaped unnamed. They were just rhetorical devices, straw men for Calles to trample, early examples of the empty criticism, the radical posturing, that would become stock practices on April 10. Calles then stood to deliver the most significant phrase of the verbal barrage: "the agrarian program of Zapata is mine." "I only want to tell you," he added, "that the hero rests in peace, that his work is over, and that from today forward present and future generations of campesinos will pass through the breach that he opened in the heart of humanity." Later, people piled floral wreathes around Zapata's gravestone until it was completely covered, and then there was a banquet featuring *platos típicos*, at which, the papers noted, peasants and urban politicians sat down together while the presidential band played. There had been, *Excélsior* summarized, "a true overflowing of enthusiasm, especially among the popular and peasant classes." [48]

Once the elation subsided, however, it became evident that Zapata was not yet everyone's hero. In fact, even before the anniversary, on April 3, an editorial in *Excélsior* demonstrated that the media were still not all willing to let praise of him go unchallenged. Singling out Díaz Soto y Gama as the main architect of Zapata's posthumous reputation, the author of this piece noted that Zapata seemed on the way to "apotheosis, as if he were an immaculate apostle or a demigod." To glorify such an ignorant criminal, the editorial continued, would be "one more lie in our history." [49] Then, after April 10, a chorus of interested parties and commentators demanded that Calles explain what, precisely, he meant when he adopted Zapata's program. An editorial in *El Universal* argued that Calles could not make Zapata's program his own because the Constitution of 1917 recognized private property while Zapata—"who had the confused vision of a primitive and barbarous semi-communism"—did not. On the defensive, Calles soon conceded that he accepted Zapata's agrarianism only in its general outlines, in that both had sympathy for the poor. [50] If it was useful to have his name linked with that of Zapata, Calles had just learned, it was best that the nature of that association remain vague. There were too many conservatives and Constitutionalists around who were unwilling to forget the hard feelings of the past and, with its control of the country still shaky and many of the material challenges of rebuilding still to be met, the state was not yet able to put much energy into advancing Zapata's cult or the revolutionary nationalism of which it would become a part.

Still, news of Zapata the agrarian hero continued to be hammered home in commemoration after commemoration. Additional acts of memory also began to be held in Mexico City. There was a velada in the capital organized by the National Agrarian Confederation as early as 1924, and 1928 saw an event at an experimental Indian boarding school called the House of the Indigenous Student. There María Dolores Pérez, speaking for the Radical Socialist Party of Tabasco, identified the proletariat (not merely the peasantry) as Zapata's constituency, language that reflected labor's growing importance on Mexico's political scene during the 1920s as the government-linked Regional Mexican Labor Confederation (Confederación Regional Obrera Mexicana, CROM) rose to prominence. Also present was Díaz Soto y Gama, who had recently led the charge to amend the constitution—with Obregón in mind—to permit the reelection of a past president after an intervening term. Now Obregón was campaigning to recapture executive power and, though there had been no open break between him and Calles, tensions between their followers were high. Favoring his own strongest supporters, Calles had arranged that the Regional Mexican Labor Confederation, rather than Díaz Soto y Gama's Agrarian Party, help direct the Cuautla festivities.[51] And so Díaz Soto y Gama remained in the capital to pronounce that Zapata was the great defeated one, but that "there is another hero who continues his work, Alvaro Obregón, the victor." Stressing Zapata's religious aspect, he indicated that Zapata knew "that he would go to martyrdom, that he would not see the triumph of his ideals."[52] In the capital this martyrdom was not quite the same as it was when peasants discussed it in Morelos: martyrdom for a specific cause in a specific corner of Mexico. Rather, reinforcing the earlier rhetoric of Lauro Caloca and in combination with the Zapata that Diego Rivera was then developing, Díaz Soto y Gama was helping make Zapata a martyr for the *national* ancestral homeland.[53]

In 1930 a specific metropolitan site for commemorations was established when an agrarian organization marked the house near San Lázaro train station where Zapata had once stayed with a marble plaque.[54] But on April 10, 1931, this was not the only place in the capital where Zapata was remembered. One ceremony was undertaken by university students at a night school named for him. Another occurred at the Alvaro Obregón Civic Center, again tying Zapata to Obregón, who was now a fellow martyr of the revolutionary process, having been assassinated in the summer of 1928 after winning reelection. Each of these gatherings included a contingent of Zapatista veterans, which gave them the stamp of authenticity. There were also ceremonies in the schools, and in particular at the Francisco Madero School, "in order to unveil the plaque that will commemorate the fact that there the workers of Colonia Morelos placed the first bust of Emiliano Zapata."[55]

Zapata's national cult was also built on literary offerings, including the corrido. Immediately after his death, urban writers disseminated a number of corridos that were critical of him. A clerk at the National Palace named Arturo Espinoza wrote two such pieces in 1919: "Most Important Revelations of the Family of the Deceased Emiliano Zapata," and "The Treasure of Emiliano Zapata."[56] In the former, Zapata's mother complains that she predicted his death when he rose up in arms, but that he refused to listen. Full of macho posturing, he instead replied, "I'm a man and I never back down, / nor do I ever retract my promises." He then went off "destroying villages" until "the sword of justice / cut short that life of horrors." The second example concerns the treasure of pearls, silver, and gold that, according to legend, Zapata had hidden in Morelos. The jewels, Espinoza wrote, were "mute witnesses" of terrible scenes that would "forever stain them." In this author's estimation, then, Zapata was both an arrogant and ungrateful son and the murderous bandit that public opinion in Mexico City had long considered him to be. Two other corridos of the period, meanwhile, told spooky tales of Zapata as ghost and *calavera* (skeleton).[57] The "Corrido of the Ghost of Emiliano Zapata" reported that his specter appeared on dark nights:

> One hears the sound of his spurs,
> His horrible curses
> And, teeth grinding,
> Believes that he brings great legions.
> He extends a rigid hand
> and life dilates within him . . .
> Across the southern countryside goes
> The ghost of Zapata.

More subtle was the work of Eduardo Guerrero, who established a printing press in the capital toward the end of the revolutionary decade.[58] Guerrero's "Sad Farewell of Emiliano Zapata" presented Zapata reflecting on aspects of his life, reporting on his death, giving instructions to his followers and, especially, saying nostalgic goodbyes to the local mountains, various Morelian towns, and the Mexican nation. In many respects this corrido was sympathetic to its subject. The string of goodbyes humanized Zapata, and along the way we hear him profess his faith in God and learn that he had hidden money in a cave for his "beloved mother." Those sympathetic touches, though, failed to hide the general message. Apparently written before Carranza lost power, the corrido had Zapata say, "Attila they called me / those who fought me, / but now everything is ended / and died he who they feared." To reinforce the suggestion that "everything" was over, Zapata added a telling piece of advice for his followers:

> It's time to forget the quarrels,
> return to work the land,
> so that more blood doesn't run
> on the plains or in the mountains.
>
> So that my death is fecund
> and brings Peace and happiness
> to the state of MORELOS,
> where my grave is.

The assertion that Zapata's death should mean the end of the fighting in Morelos was, as we have seen, precisely the reading the Carrancistas sought to give it. How that message played in 1919 is uncertain, but the painter Dr. Atl (birth name Gerardo Murillo) claimed in 1921 that this song was popular in Morelos and the state of Mexico, and in the 1950s it was reportedly among the most favored corridos in Zapatista territory.[59]

After 1920 the urban milieu began to generate corridos that echoed the change of heart exhibited at commemorations. "Of the Death of Emiliano Zapata," by the poet Armando List Arzubide, was one such work.[60] List's corrido opened with a traditional invitation: "Listen, *señores*, hear the corrido, / of a sad occurrence; / by ambush was killed in Chinameca / Zapata, the great rebel." The date of Zapata's death, it continued, would remain in the memory of the campesino "like a blemish in history." List then told of Zapata's life, calling him "the bogeyman of tyrants" who "loved the poor / wanted to give them liberty." Sprinkled throughout the work were stanzas that presented rabbits, grasshoppers, and sparrows—among other onlookers from the natural world—as they reacted to Zapata's passing. All of nature mourned Zapata in this corrido, demonstrating the universal implications of his death. Guajardo, on the other hand, was a "felon" for having embraced Zapata (greeting him with an *abrazo*) though he intended to "sacrifice" him, which was done "from behind, at point blank range." One of the last stanzas that evoked nature read, "little riotous arroyo / what did that carnation tell you? / —It says that the *jefe* did not die, / that Zapata will return." "At the edge of a path," the corrido concluded, "there was a white lily, / to the tomb of Zapata / I took it as an offering." Sympathetic to the peasants' struggle, List thus pointed toward the popular origins of Zapata's myth in several ways: by adopting the corrido in the first place, by suggesting that Zapata did not die, and by making the graveside experience personal rather than official.

Another urban imitator of the genre was Baltasar Dromundo. Dromundo aspired, he wrote one Zapatista, "to be considered in the front rank . . . of enthusiasm, of clear revolutionary vision, and of constant militancy in favor of the memory of Emiliano."[61] His "Corrido of the Death of Emiliano Zapata" was first published on April 10, 1934, by the General Office of Civic Action of the Department of the Federal District. It was thus the product of that year's official commemoration.[62] A pioneer in giving women in the revolution what one scholar calls "romantic visibility," Dromundo picked up on the strand of the oral tradition that maintained Zapata had been warned by a woman or women prior to his death, suggesting that the woman in question was "the mistress of his [Zapata's] love."[63]

Zapata woke early and troubled on the day of his death, Dromundo wrote, and the unnamed woman lying beside him responded to his concerns by reminding him that,

> Yesterday I told you that I have
> the black presentiment
> that the Government will kill you.
>
> Go far from these lands
> because later it will be too late,
> and if the Government kills you
> the Indians will die of hunger.

As he often did in the oral tradition, Zapata dismissed these concerns sharply, calling them superstitions and adding that, "Guajardo wears pants / and with him I will win." Later in the corrido Dromundo, like List, gave a nod to notions about Zapata's posthumous career, writing that the Carrancistas buried him deep because they feared he would emerge "to return to the fight." The author's own position on Zapata's survival, however, was merely that Zapata's saying, that the land belongs to those who work it, remained alive in the Indians of Mexico.

Dromundo's corrido was published with a note that declared that it was "deliberately popular," and that both lyrics and music were "of the people." It is not, in fact, a good imitation of a popular corrido, but like the work of List and Rivera it vividly demonstrates the bridging that occurred between metropolitan and campesino meditations on Zapata as the new revolutionary order took shape.

Corridos were not the only literary means by which Zapata's significance was explored in the first post-revolutionary years. Armando List Arzubide's older brother, Germán, published *Emiliano Zapata: Exaltación* (Emiliano Zapata: Exaltation) in 1927, a pamphlet popular enough to run through at least four printings by 1936.[64] Germán List Arzubide had served under Carranza for seven years—for a time as his secretary—which hardly recommended him as a biographer of Zapata. But he was one of the founding members of the 1920s avant-garde literary movement called *estridentismo* (stridentism), and like other members of this movement he became a strong proponent of social reform. That apparently led him to believe that the revolution should do justice to the cause of Zapata, "the great dead one."[65] His short book began with Zapata's death. When he then turned back to the early years of Zapata's life, List presented one of the first written accounts of a much-repeated story with an apocryphal ring. When Zapata was eight or nine, the story went, a neighboring hacienda appropriated some of Anene-cuilco's lands. On being informed that this had just occurred, Zapata's father grew pale and, frustrated and helpless, began to cry. Zapata then promised to recover the lands when he was grown.[66] His life, then, was one of unwavering preparation for and service to this single cause.

List's adult Zapata was a patriarch. In his "visage there was an infinite gentleness" and in his voice, when he spoke to his Indian followers, the "softness of infinite love." He ruled Morelos like a benevolent dictator, respected by all, never contradicted. List envisioned Zapata on his horse: "tall, thin, steady—with the attitude, the conduct of robust certainty that, among ten thousand, would have caused him to be recognized immediately as the awaited one." "He must," the author added, "have passed like an earthquake of sublimity" among his rough troops.[67] In case the messianism was not entirely clear, List directly compared Zapata and Christ. Zapata was not, he wrote, a Christ of defeat, waiting for the next life, but rather one who demanded the reign of God on earth: "Christ the horseman, who gives sermons for the hopeless with his carbine."[68] For List, Zapata's murder was the worst felony in Mexican history and, ironically, he compared Pablo González to Attila the Hun, traditionally Zapata's alter ego.[69] While he and other "spirits that reason circumscribes" could not adopt the popular conviction that Zapata lived on, List did give the hero a legacy. Zapata's final words to his faithful were that while he lived they would have their land, but when he died they would need to defend it, "with their weapons in hand." He knew that "false redeemers" would seek to exploit his work, but he left "his men the path to arrive at victory." List believed Zapata represented the ideal that the youth of Mexico needed, wounded as they were by the revolution and World War I.[70]

Then there was *Cartones Zapatistas* by Carlos Reyes Avilés.[71] The preface of this book, which was produced as part of the 1928 April 10 commemoration, declared that its only objective was to spread word of the ceremony, which was, "deservedly . . . taking on the character of national homage." Support for the publication, however, had come from Congressman Ricardo Topete, who was a "great proponent of revolutionary youth and of Obregonismo, which promoted the government of equality and justice of which Zapata had dreamed for his people."[72] In fact, Topete was head of an alliance of parties supporting Obregón's reelection, a strong sign that Reyes Avilés's book was not, for everyone, only about honoring Zapata.[73]

The work was organized in a series of short chapters—the *cartones* (studies or sketches) of the title—dedicated to several important Zapatistas and such topics as the Plan of Ayala, Marciano Silva and, of course, Zapata's death. Chapter 2 presented Zapata's life, depicting a man with "an iron will, forged on the anvil of all the sorrows and vexations suffered by his race since the time of Cortés." [74] The chapter on Zapata's death was more explicit about his background. Reyes Avilés stressed his subject's humble beginnings, which helped explain his sympathy for the poor. He had, for example, "felt his shoulders bleed from the lash of the foreman" and, having shared in the extreme misery of his fellow campesinos, he "carried within himself the weight of all the injustices suffered by his followers." [75] To account for Zapata's death, Reyes Avilés had to explain how Guajardo could have fooled him. He started with the claim that, due to his background and experiences, Zapata was generally mistrustful, but he then made an argument also made by Germán List Arzubide: Zapata "had the nobility of a gentleman who was a slave to his word" and was "ignorant of the viciousness and the lowliness of the ruffian." [76] Reyes Avilés recorded that Zapata visited his movement's headquarters, hidden on the slopes of the volcano Popocatepetl, shortly before his death. There, on learning of an article written about him in the United States, he had exclaimed "now I can die" because the word was finally out that the Zapatistas were not bandits. He then, in faultless messianic style, "went righteously toward his sacrifice." [77] The author next printed his brother Salvador's report on Zapata's death, with its many details on the courting of Guajardo. With Zapata's assassination, he wrote, "Guajardo, imbecilic instrument of Betrayal, threw the first shovelful of mud on the today already putrid political cadaver of Pablo González." [78]

The final two chapters dealt with Zapata's posthumous career. In the first of them, entitled "Emiliano Zapata was an Obregonista," Reyes Avilés had Zapata himself tell us that, "Obregón is a true revolutionary . . . it is the cause of the people that Obregón serves." The ability to recognize that commitment in Obregón, the author periodically informed his readers, was a "clear example of [Zapata's] prescience." In the last chapter, which covered the commemoration of 1928, Reyes Avilés again reflected on current politics when he recorded that there was unity at that event because "the sectarianism of the pseudo-political parties" had been abolished. Here the reference was to the absence of Díaz Soto y Gama and his party, which, as we have seen, had lost its central role in organizing the Cuautla commemorations. Doling out praise for both Obregón and Calles, Reyes Avilés was navigating the tricky political waters with the National Agrarian Confederation, of which he was a founding member.[79]

A third ostensibly historical contribution to Zapata's memory came from the pen of Octavio Paz Solórzano, father of the renowned poet who shared his first two names. After joining Zapatismo in 1914, Paz Solórzano first served the movement as a propagandist and later as a representative in the United States. When Obregón came to power Paz returned to Mexico and joined the Agrarian Party. In 1929 and 1933 he published, in *El Universal*, a series of 28 articles that covered various episodes of Zapatista history.[80] Strangely, most of these pieces examine the period prior to 1914, when Paz Solórzano had no relationship with Zapatismo. He depended, in other words, on a combination of hearsay and imagination, and there is much here—such as the fanciful dialogue he records—that suggests a sizable dose of the latter.

Paz Solórzano's Zapata was a striking charro, with a "superbly trimmed sombrero of great dimensions, mounted on a spirited steed with a magnificent saddle embroidered in silver." As such, he was "a genuine representative of the true national type." He had "a gaze that was gentle but penetrating and always scrutinizing when it came to interesting issues." He was possessed of great natural intelligence, a love of history, remarkable foresight, audacity, and fearlessness.[81] This Zapata frequently noted that he was comfortable, economically, prior to 1910, and so had not joined the revolution for his own gain. While Reyes Avilés made Zapata poor to stress his solidarity with his people, in other words, Paz sought to emphasize his incorruptibility. He also claimed that Zapata had never been a peon and that his enemies attributed such pre-revolutionary status to him in order "to diminish his dignity."[82] Paz Solórzano often used dialogue to demonstrate Zapata's fairness and wisdom. Faced with the disagreement between Gabriel Tepepa and Pablo Torres Burgos about Tepepa's looting, for instance, Zapata attempted to mediate. "Look, Gabriel," he explained to Tepepa, "if we've taken up arms it's not to execute people or to rob, but for a very just and great cause." Torres Burgos then received the following instruction: "Pablo, it's necessary to be more benevolent with the men that follow us."[83] Finally, Paz Solórzano also acknowledged labor's growing power by having Zapata attest that he was concerned not just with the plight of campesinos, but with workers as well, "because I have seen those unhappy miners of Huautla [Morelos] spend the entire day in the mine and come out exhausted."[84] There was plenty of icon-making language in these essays, but Paz's most important contribution may be that he humanized Zapata with his colorful details, his stilted dialogue, and his discussion of such personal qualities as Zapata's tendency to swear. The result was a less formal icon than those developed by List or Reyes Avilés.

Together these chroniclers of the 1920s and early 1930s laid a foundation for those who would write and speak about Zapata in the future. Described as voceros—spokespeople—of the revolution, the people who produced these works were a varied lot in terms of ideology, talent, and political connections. As a result, there was no general agreement about Zapata. In fact, putting all the perspectives together would yield a patchwork image of him much like Rivera's cubist rendering of a Zapatista.[85]

Most voceros did, however, eventually find state employment. Like Díaz Soto y Gama, Carlos Reyes Avilés and Paz Solórzano obtained congressional posts in the 1920s; they later received other official appointments. In the 1930s, Germán List Arzubide would be selected for two good positions in the Ministry of Public Education. For his part, Dromundo was to serve as personal secretary to the governor of the state of Durango. By the 1950s and 1960s, he became a leading promoter of the ruling party and, ultimately, director of the department of Social Action for the Federal District.[86] They did not all serve at the same time and, since the revolution had no firm ideology, there was no ideological litmus test for government employees. In fact, during the 1920s, as Obregón and Calles struggled for power in a still highly decentralized political world, toeing any official line was difficult because those lines that existed were unclearly marked and subject to erasure. Still, the voceros of Zapata did share upper or middle class status and urban backgrounds with the men who ruled Mexico, and because the state was growing in postrevolutionary years opportunities in public life inevitably captured their attention.[87] Even people who considered themselves Marxists often contributed to the hero-worship of Zapata, contrary to the creed they professed, in which classes are understood to be the movers of history, not individuals.[88] In sum, while the state was far from controlling cultural production, Zapata was a political issue and there were political—and economic—stakes for those who wrote about him. Perhaps this is why, despite the independence and variety of these invocations of Zapata, they did have common elements and—in conjunction with the commemorations and the images of Rivera—they had roughed out by the early 1930s the profile of a Zapata that was acceptable to the new regime.

One of the features of that profile was simply that, as in the peasant cult, Zapata's death and body were central to the process of remembering him. If his death, as I have argued, challenged the campesinos of his home region to recall his life as a whole and in doing so perhaps adjusted attitudes about him, in Mexico City it prompted a hasty about-face. That abrupt change of outlook was due in part to regime change, of course, as Carranza fell and other Constitutionalists not as implicated in that death took over. Political expediency was important as well. But given the hold that death has on the human imagination, we should not discount what Dr. (and Senator) Pedro de Alba wrote in 1924: that the "sacrifice" at Chinameca washed away whatever personal defects Zapata may have had, that with death there came a purification that separated the actual man from the figure he had by 1924 become.[89] Zapata's cult was not only about death. In Anenecuilco his birthday was remembered annually, and the day on which the Plan of Ayala was promulgated, November 28, also drew ritual attention. But the day of his death was the most important of the three, and his death was the most significant event in what was written about him. Moreover, reinforcing the local scrutiny and interpretation of the body described in Chapter 2, Zapata's cadaver was of great value in that the site where it was buried became sacred ground and thus the place where rituals devoted to his memory were first undertaken on anniversaries of his death. The establishment of this sacred ground meant that claims made over his remains—largely those of the new state, which controlled the rituals—surely gained from them a degree of holiness, or at least legitimacy, of their own.

A second tendency was the broadening of causes that Zapata represented. Initially linked to the agrarian reform issue, Zapata quickly became a representative of social reform in general—"the greatest reformer in Mexican history"—in the constructions of many who contributed to his myth. In part this occurred because of changing social and political dynamics, in particular the growing influence of organized labor—the "proletariat"—to which those who used Zapata's image sometimes wanted him to speak. Lower class heroes were scarce, after all, so why not make him pull double duty? Whether intentional or not, this trend also served to make Zapata fuzzier, which might keep him from demanding policies that were too specific. The trouble Calles encountered when he espoused Zapata's program showed how inconvenient a sharply drawn Zapata could be.

Associations between Zapata and Indian ethnicity were also developed on the national stage during this period. Dromundo and Germán List Arzubide were among the many authors who either labeled him an Indian or identified Indians as his core constituency. Far more influential than these written sources, though, was the calzón-clad Zapata Rivera painted at Cuernavaca. Those calzones meant Indian to much of urban Mexico, and this particular image of a sometimes, possibly Indian Zapata would echo down the decades. Rivera's prodigious energy and talent made him perhaps the single most powerful interpreter, and promoter, of the revolution's meaning, and the results of his labors were forceful when he funneled them into images of Zapata. Indians—and by extension an Indian Zapata—were fundamental to the process through which Rivera brought his brand of communism to earth in Mexico, and without his Cuernavaca mural there might be far less that is Indian about the Zapata people imagine today.[90]

Indians were also fundamental to the ways in which various Mexicans sought to redefine their nation after the revolution. The emerging revolutionary ideology with regard to ethnicity—initiated by such voceros as Andrés Molina Enríquez and Manuel Gamio, but adopted and shaped by the state—began with *indigenismo*. Indigenismo was a movement of urban and intellectual types, often anthropologists, who valued the presence and role of the Indian in Mexican life. The basic attitude was perhaps not so different from the position I attributed, in Chapter 1, to Marciano Silva: Indians were a fundamental part of Mexico, but they had been badly mistreated; it had been one of the motives of the warfare, and was now among the revolution's main responsibilities, to address Indian rights and needs. Indigenistas broke from the Porfirian outlook in that they were interested in more than just claiming the Indian past—the hero Cuauhtémoc and the cultural accomplishments of pre-Columbian peoples, for instance—but with the future and the potential of present-day Indians and how they might best fit into the nation.

The indigenistas of the period, both within and outside of the government, generally concluded that the revolution needed to integrate the Indians into the mainstream of Mexican culture, while perhaps letting them keep what were deemed their best or most authentic traditions. In a book entitled *The Cosmic Race* (1925), José Vasconcelos firmly established that, in ethnic terms, the mainstream was mestizo—the result of the cultural and biological mixing of the conquered Indian and the conquering Spaniard. Indigenismo thus nested within a broader body of revolutionary thought that declared that Mexico was a mestizo nation.[91] The coexistence of these two ideas about ethnicity helps explain why Rivera often painted a very different Zapata. When Zapata appeared in his charro outfit, he was no Indian. Rather, he was the Zapata that Paz Solórzano remembered as "a genuine representative of the true national type," and that Rafael Ramos Pedrueza called, during the 1930 commemoration, "the most vigorous representative of Mexican nationality." Here again he was asked to do double duty, because Rivera and others understood that a Mexican hero had to be, at least at times, a mestizo and thus a model of what the assimilated Indian might become.

Yet another facet of the general story was the machismo with which Zapata, as charro, was endowed. Zapata's machismo is plain in the many accounts of his death in which he dismisses—often roughly—the forebodings of women who try to stop him on the way to Chinameca. It is also evident in works that emphasize the brutality of the conflict and in descriptions of him as a charro. Germán List Arzubide writes of Zapata giving sermons with his gun, and his brother Armando's corrido includes the following two stanzas: "smoking tranquilly he [Zapata] walks serenely / among the bullets, / and yells:—Boys, to these men, dead-of-hunger / we must give them their pambazos [common bread, but also blows]"; and "—When I have died—he [Zapata] says to a subordinate— / you will tell all the boys: / with weapon in hand defend your ejido / as men must do." [92]

This was not a case of the postrevolutionary state making Zapata into a macho with the help of a handful of voceros.[93] First of all, as Chapters 1 and 2 show, he had long been viewed as a macho on the local scene. Indeed, the examples of Zapata's machismo cited in the previous paragraph come either from popular sources or from writers seeking to capture the local flavor rather than, for example, state officials speaking at commemorations. Zapata as macho, gun in hand, did not especially suit the interests of Mexico's political elite, which wanted to build peace and prosperity, and enhance governability, after a long civil war. This is part of what Calles was getting at when he proclaimed that Zapata's work was over.

In pursuit of those government goals the Indian Zapata could be useful. In the conceptualization of Molina Enríquez and Gamio, Mexico's mestizo nation had been created by sexual congress between the male Spanish conqueror and the female Indian. This understanding reflected a tendency to associate Europeans with active, "male" attributes and Indians with characteristics that were passive and "female."[94] To the extent that such attitudes were diffused throughout the population, then, an Indian Zapata was a passive, feminized Zapata, stripped of his macho, rebellious past. Machete in hand and corpse at his feet, Rivera's Cuernavaca Zapata was hardly intended to model passivity, but in helping to Indianize and thus perhaps, indirectly, feminize Zapata, in the long run this image may have bolstered the postrevolutionary order.

The larger aim of the new rulers was to make Zapata into one of the nation's many founding fathers: a patriarch rather than a macho, a Zapata who could be inducted into the "revolutionary family" beginning to take shape in official rhetoric and, as a pillar of the state, stand complacently alongside revolutionaries who had been his enemies in life.[95] The prospect of Zapata becoming a founding father was something Hermila Galindo foresaw already in 1919. It was what national officials hoped to accomplish when they honored Zapata as a notable ancestor at his commemorations, and conjectured about the impact he would have on future generations. And it was an appeal, of course, to what was understood to be the traditional Mexican family, which signified order in general and, in particular, underlined the value of traditional gender roles that a decade of warfare had eroded. Some women, after all, had gone so far as to join the fighting, but in the telling of Zapata's tale they were largely props, foils for his strength of character.

Macho and patriarch are not, of course, incompatible. Recall Paz Solórzano's image of Zapata as charro, which is immediately softened by reference to his gentle gaze and natural intelligence. Similarly, Germán List Arzubide leavened Zapata's machismo with "infinite gentleness." But the Zapata that official Mexico wanted remembered was either the "modest Indian" *El Demócrata* described in 1921 or the firm but loving father who could send messages of hierarchy and, in particular, male control over women. The politicos had little use for the sexual prowess, the potential for violence, and the other physical achievements of the drinking, gambling, womanizing, horse-riding Zapata who captured the imaginations of Morelenses. Stories of Zapata's sexual conquests, his military exploits, and his bloody threats persisted as elements of his myth, but they did not persist primarily because they were emphasized in the speeches of politicians who held them dear, but because those attributes were valued in the rural milieu from which Zapata came.

The state would only partially achieve, by the early 1930s, the objective of forging a Zapata who represented order. The fixation on order was ironic coming from a revolutionary government and doubly so when it was Zapata, who had fought nearly every other revolutionary group, who was being honored. It is hardly surprising, though, in light of the moralizing tendencies of some revolutionaries and, more importantly, the political need to send messages of order *restored* after ten years of fighting. And so in 1931 the authorities declared "that the ceremony in memory of Zapata will be characterized by its essentially patriotic purpose, suppressing all of the manifestations of dissipation that have occurred in previous years."[96] While this was perhaps the period's clearest expression of the drive for orderliness at the commemorations, it was also order that was being invoked in 1922 and 1923 by expectations that ceremonies would be more "solemn" than they had been. The fact that veladas, with their ideally seated audiences, were significant components is more evidence of such hopes. The idea was to keep commemorations of Zapata—and other revolutionary rituals— from becoming new occasions for popular revelry like the celebration in September of Hidalgo's *Grito de Dolores*, which started the independence struggle.[97]

The repeated exhortations on behalf of solemnity demonstrate that order was not easy to achieve. In part this was because of the tensions and disagreements among those engaged in remembering Zapata. Reflecting different opinions not only within the media but among politicians, news-paper editorials critical of the unseemly speed at which Zapata was mov-ing toward official apotheosis were hardly solemn. Even Zapata's disciples could not always behave, as evidenced by the quarrel at the velada of 1923. Another part of the story is simply that not everyone shared the official no-tion of what commemoration should entail. Leopoldo Castañeda of Santa Marta Acatitla, in the Federal District, recalled an April 10th spent with Paz Solórzano, who helped villages around Santa Marta get land during the 1920s. Paz Solórzano traveled, on the day in question, from Mexico City to Santa Marta to convince Castañeda and others to accompany him to Cuautla. Due to the spontaneity of their trip they arrived late, after the rit-ual was over. Some of them—including Paz and Castañeda—nevertheless decided to make their way into town, where Paz Solórzano's "friends from there saw us and immediately took us to hear music and corridos that every-one repeated with pleasure and received with shouts of appreciation." The drinking soon commenced—it could not be otherwise with Paz—and an impromptu commemoration of Zapata, quite different from the orderliness sought by the organizers, was underway.[98] Another example would be the way in which village celebration—including the singing of the traditional birthday song and a breakfast of tamales and coffee—has surrounded the official program at Anenecuilco commemorating the birth of Zapata, thus making the event, in general, less formal, less orderly, and less under state control.[99]

A final aspect of the early years of Zapata's cult is that it does seem to have served as the bridge between politicians and peasants that the politi-cians who adopted it hoped it would become. That is not to say that this bridge was a steady one. Politicians had their say about Zapata at the an-nual commemorations, but the national administration did not directly run those commemorations and it made little effort to use Zapata to model some kind of "new man."[100] Rather, officials were frequently on the defensive and merely seeking to hang on to power. They therefore largely contented themselves with incorporating a Zapata already developed in Morelos into the broad myth of the Mexican nation, while simultaneously claiming that Zapata for themselves in hope of enhancing their legitimacy by linking state and nation.[101] Nor did the politicians control the voceros, who are best understood as mediators between the political culture of the state and the various constituencies that their writing touched. Voceros sometimes sent out messages that were convenient from Mexico City's point of view; they collected and published information gathered from Zapata's followers, thus making it available to politicians in need of such material; but any given author might also advocate, for instance, a more thoroughgoing agrarian reform than those who ran national administrations found agreeable.

Furthermore, however much Rivera talked about painting for the people, there was no assurance that the people—and particularly peasants, who were largely illiterate—were listening to the messages aimed in their direction. So how were the messages received? The best evidence comes from the commemorations, which Zapata's local supporters took seriously despite their increasingly official nature. In 1921, for example, *El Demócrata* mentioned the tears of the women of Cuautla and the "fervent exclamations" of the children. It also recorded the following inscriptions on the wreaths brought to the grave by humble Morelenses: "To you, General Zapata, because you were our liberator and our father"; "General Emiliano Zapata: you will always live among us"; "For my General Emiliano Zapata, because all of my children died with him."[102] Decades later an observer recalled that similar emotions had been at work during the 1928 ceremony, noting the "deep devotion with which peasant women contemplated, surrounding it, the final resting place of the Martyr of Chinameca." The same witness compared the fervor of peasants attending the commemoration to that of pilgrims at Mecca, asserting that no other Mexican commemoration could compare in this regard.[103]

This level of emotion demonstrates that commemorations were not *merely* official events, that campesinos found them meaningful too— Zapata's son Mateo remarked that he attended commemorations "because I believe it is my obligation," not because government officials wanted him to.[104] But did peasants listen to the rhetoric of politicians? That is harder to demonstrate, but it was reported that at the 1926 ceremony stories Díaz Soto y Gama told about Zapata—including a version of Zapata's youthful promise to recover village resources—"so stirred the listeners that some of them cried."[105] Moreover, some Morelenses did accept the argument— transmitted so forcefully by Díaz Soto y Gama—that Obregón continued Zapata's agrarian reform.[106] Marciano Silva, a good barometer of regional opinion, wrote corridos praising both Obregón and Calles.[107] More evidence of messages communicated—or at least attitudes shared—comes from the corrido "At the Tomb of the Heroes," which was probably written by a popular singer rather than an urban imitator.[108] This work starts by comparing Zapata with Hidalgo, submitting that if the Spanish should attempt another conquest, "we will always have Señor Don Emiliano on our side, / he will go in defense of our flag." The corridista then mentions the ceremony for which the corrido was written, noting that Zapata received "laurels and wreathes." The final strophe reads:

But finally, noble caudillos, I take my leave,
Señor Eufemio [Zapata's brother] and also Don Emiliano,
God bless you always with his hand
in order to liberate our Mexican people.

Here, then, the practice of commemorating Zapata and the idea that Zapata could someday return are interwoven with a strong dose of the nationalism the postrevolutionary state sought to foment, again suggesting considerable interaction and compatibility of local and official ideas about Zapata's meaning.

Zapata functioned reasonably well, then, as a bridge between Mexico City and Morelos, politician and peasant, precisely because the politicians could not impose their vision of him. In comparison to the efforts made to control revolutionary symbolism, say, in the Soviet Union, the postrevolutionary regime in Mexico did not really even try in the 1920s.[109] Communications moved across the bridge in both directions—if the government was able to convey its message that Zapata's revolution continued, it is equally clear that both commemorations and the written offerings of voceros were influenced by popular practices, predilections, and memories. Not surprisingly, under those circumstances, there were benefits for both sides. Zapata helped justify the policies of national politicians, who used him to construct the edifices of state and nation and to reaffirm alliances with local and state officials. But Zapata's followers were getting something they needed too. Zapatista intellectuals received government jobs, and land reform was well under way in Morelos. Perhaps just as important, symbols like the one Zapata was becoming both justify policies and are justified by them. As Zapata became a founding father of the revolutionary state it was being acknowledged, after a decade of warfare in which most of those who had governed in Mexico City called them bandits, that the Zapatistas had been right all along.

FOUR

MAKING ZAPATA OFFICIAL

Serving as a physician among the Zapatistas during the revolution's epic phase, Dr. José G. Parrés recalled in the 1930s, he was struck by how Zapata always rose to the occasion. Though his enemies accused him of being vice-ridden and much had been written about his use of alcohol, for the Zapata Parrés observed alcohol was never a problem. As a small agriculturalist, Parrés wrote, Zapata engaged in "physical labor greater than the strength of his organism—considering the food he could acquire—would allow him to do. This made it necessary for him, on occasion, to have a few drinks with his friends, without it constituting a vice." But later, when he came into contact with educated people during the revolution, he gained consciousness of his responsibility to take a stand against alcohol's effect on the body and "its impact on every principle of authority." When one of his intellectual advisors developed a drinking problem, Zapata reacted strongly. Drunkenness, he told him, was inexcusable in someone with an education, and the problem was soon corrected.[1]

Zapata was "healthy and strong," indicated Parrés on another occasion, with a "friendly and attentive temperament." He was a "man of character, unbreakable in his decisions, tireless in the struggle, energetic in the fight." In every battle he led the way. He was also "gifted with a spirit of justice," wishing for equality among all men. He lived in such a way that he could "maintain contact with the proletarian class, with the noble goal of always feeling and never forgetting the hardships and miseries of those people for whom he was a redeemer." If he arrived at a *ranchería* (small settlement) where only one bed was available, he would give it to someone who needed it more. He always protected the weak against the strong; indeed, Parrés had once seen him, "full of indignation, punish in public a jefe" who mistreated the campesinos. He never sold out, despite many good offers, never took a cent for himself from all the money that passed through his hands. He even worked his own land during the revolution to feed his soldiers and family.[2]

As we saw in the previous chapter, Parrés became governor of Morelos after Obregón came to power. In that capacity he worked to see that Zapata was properly honored and—though Obregón never attended a commemoration—felt he had the national administration's support in that endeavor. For Zapata's collaborators, he explained to the president, his cult took on the "noble proportions of a communion of ideals." After coming together in his name, as they returned to their homes, "his disciples found themselves renewed in the faith that their Caudillo possessed and gave themselves to their liberating labors with greater zeal, hearts full of a high disinterestedness in personal gain."[3]

According to Parrés, Cárdenas matched Obregón in his sympathy for workers and campesinos, and so, as Cárdenas's undersecretary of agriculture, he continued to feel that he walked in Zapata's footsteps. Like Cárdenas, he testified, Zapata was a "strong believer in the ejido, separating himself completely from individualism," as the Plan of Ayala clearly showed. Zapata had also understood that the campesinos needed the credit and agricultural schools with which the Cárdenas administration had supplied them.[4] During the Cárdenas years, he noted, with a logic that reflected the contortions of official memory, "historians and authorized revolutionaries" were busy assigning the men who gave their lives for the revolution their correct historical places. To that end, he had a document that proved Zapata's great honor. Unfortunately, he could not reveal that document, because it shed negative light on people who continued "to be discussed because no historical judgment on them has yet been reached." To do so would violate Cárdenas's policy to "suppress differences among the prominent factions of the Revolution and advocate for their unification."[5]

During the 1930s, and in particular with the advent of President Lázaro Cárdenas (1934–1940), the central government began to take a larger role in advancing Zapata's cult. Political crisis in the late 1920s seems to have played a crucial part in bringing about this change. The first and greatest manifestation of the crisis was the Cristero Rebellion (1926–1929). During these three years the Catholic Church, which had been the bane of liberal Mexicans since independence, stopped administering the sacraments. Meanwhile, many thousands of peasants, mostly in west and north-central Mexico, took up arms in rejection both of the strong anticlericalism and, ironically, the somewhat active land reform program of the Calles regime. Then, in 1928, Obregón was assassinated shortly after his reelection. His death came at the hands of a deeply religious artist upset by Calles's posture toward the church, but Díaz Soto y Gama immediately charged that Calles and his labor supporters were behind it as they tried to keep Obregón and his loyalists from impinging on the Callista status quo.[6] Such suspicions were fueled, no doubt, by the way Calles did step into the power vacuum. He did not continue in the presidency, which would have been dangerous in that political climate, but rather assumed the extraconstitutional position of *Jefe Máximo*—the "Supreme Chief," behind and above the presidency—which he would play for the next six years as three puppets rotated through the executive office.

Calles took these setbacks to postrevolutionary consolidation seriously. During the *Maximato* (1928–1934), as the ensuing period became known, social reform in general and land reform in particular screeched to a halt, apparently on the premise that they were the reason for the turmoil. On the other hand, important political and cultural initiatives were undertaken. Calles understood Obregón's death as a warning against the personalism that had characterized the revolution. In the fall of 1928, he proclaimed an end to caudillos and set about creating a new revolutionary party he hoped would transcend individual leaders and the multiparty factionalism of the 1920s. The result, in 1929, was the birth of the National Revolutionary Party (Partido Nacional Revolucionario, PNR), a major event in the process of institutionalizing the revolution. This party, which brought together all "revolutionaries" under one umbrella, represented the founding of a single-party system. It also meant an end to the kind of evenly matched competition between Obregón and Calles that had characterized the years preceding 1928, and thus the greater possibility that a single official line would emerge from the postrevolutionary state, within which individuals could fit their visions of Zapata.

Given the revolution's factionalism, regionalism, and varied interests, uniting it within one party was a challenge. It could not be done in a single stroke. Luckily for Calles, some of the organizational and rhetorical groundwork had already been laid—in Obregón's coalition building, and in invocations of revolutionary unity like that made by Carlos Reyes Avilés when he wrote about the 1928 Zapata commemoration. There was also the conceit, mentioned in Chapter 3, that all revolutionaries belonged to a single "revolutionary family." Not surprisingly, these ideas were reiterated as the PNR was founded, but they were also reinforced by new cultural initiatives, particularly in the realm of education.[7] The ultimate aim of educational policy was summarized by Calles in 1934. "It is necessary that we enter," he announced,

> into a new period of the Revolution, one which I would call the period
> of the psychological Revolution or that of spiritual conquest. We must

enter this period and take power over the minds of children and youth, because youth and children do and must belong to the Revolution.[8]

There would be no quantum leap in terms of the state's engagement with culture during the 1930s, both because that relationship was already developing in the 1920s and because, in the 1930s, the state would not become an all-controlling juggernaut.[9] But with close attention to the minds of the revolution's next generation, Calles evidently imagined, the revolutionary family might become a less dysfunctional unit.

The trend toward greater attention to culture—and to education in particular—on the part of the state continued under Cárdenas. Rural school building and funding for education increased dramatically and "socialist education" became the rage, though it was often less about socialist doctrine than simply education with social goals. Cárdenas also pursued greater national unity through the use of radio, perhaps most notably with the 1937 creation of the weekly *National Hour*, during which the government took over the airways, interspersing cultural and educational features with official announcements.[10] The Cárdenas regime also followed the path of Callismo with respect to the construction of the ruling party, broadening the membership in 1938 by dividing it into peasant, labor, military, and "popular" (middle-class and business) sectors. To reflect its changed nature, he renamed it the Party of the Mexican Revolution (Partido de la Revolución Mexicana, PRM).

The crucial difference from the days of the Maximato was that Cárdenas complemented the ruling elite's drive for greater control and cultural presence with broad social reforms. Calles chose Cárdenas for the presidency, and he probably did so, in part, because he thought he could control him. Another likely motive, though, was that Cárdenas was identified with the left, reformist wing of the party, and his selection would help appease the growing number of Mexicans who, goaded by unfulfilled promises and the difficulties of the Depression, were clamoring for social change. One big part of the Cárdenas story is thus the maneuvering with which he broke free from Calles's influence, but the biggest part of that story is that in gaining the independence to enact his own programs he became the great implementer of the constitution's many social provisions. Workers received a higher minimum wage and had their right to strike recognized; peasants got land, 49 million acres of it. But in exchange for that land they had to accept the tutelage of the state: the education it offered, restrictions on what they could plant if they wanted loans, and mass organization in a new national peasant confederation tied to the party. This did not bode well for the liberty that had been half of Zapata's program. Still, in the 1930s, the negative implications were not yet obvious, and the land distribution in particular, more than twice that awarded by all previous revolutionary administrations together, placed Cárdenas in a unique relationship with Zapata's image.

Zapata fits into this picture as one part of the cultural offensive and thus one part of the revolutionary elite's effort to enhance its power. Given the many initiatives of individuals and groups to honor Zapata, the state did not have to create him anew. It merely had to take advantage of some of the opportunities that offered. One group with plenty of ideas was the National Committee for Integral Homage to Emiliano Zapata, led by Zapatista intellectual Jenaro Amezcua. This organization formed in 1931 to ask that Zapata be awarded the official title of *Benemérito* (national hero), that the day of his death be recognized nationally as a day of mourning, that the city of Cuernavaca be renamed for him, and that his name be inscribed in letters of gold on congressional walls. The committee also suggested that a statue of Zapata be erected in Mexico City in one of two prestigious locations: either in a *glorieta* (traffic circle) on the Paseo de la Reforma or near the Alameda park, where Manuel Tolsa's celebrated statue of Spanish King Carlos IV (generally called "El Caballito") stood.[11]

This group was not the only one—and probably not the first—to suggest such honors, and even as it laid out its agenda, the national Chamber of Deputies resolved, in June 1931, to place Zapata's name on its wall alongside that of Venustiano Carranza. History, the act stated, had by then had the opportunity to rule on these revolutionary leaders, pardoning "trifling errors." It was now important to present children and youth with "the distinguished figures, the venerable icons" of the revolution. A speaker added the insight that Carranza and Zapata were now united under the banner of the PNR—a fact surely not lost on Zapata's partisans.[12] The following year the days of Zapata's birth and death were declared, respectively, days of celebration and mourning in the state of Morelos.[13] April 10, especially, was on its way to being explicitly incorporated into the nation's ceremonial life, dedicated, in the words of the ritual calendar published in 1935, to the "greatest and most sincere AGRARISTA and defender of the campesinos produced by the revolutions of Misters Madero and Venustiano Carranza." Though the wording had elements of a backhanded compliment, April 10 now took its place—admittedly a minor one—alongside such patriotic festivals as those of September 16 (independence) and November 20 (Revolution Day). From the 1930s on flags would be set at half-mast for Zapata, and schoolchildren would learn of "the character of this defender of the humble."[14]

Another key development of the early 1930s took place in Cuautla. Discussion of creating a monument to honor Zapata's memory started during the 1920s. In 1927, the newly formed National Peasant League (Liga Nacional Campesina), acting on the proposal of its delegates from Morelos, announced a plan to build a monument to the "martyr of Chinameca" in his home state. The monument was to be financed by contributions from the nation's campesinos, through the purchase of a pin bearing Zapata's portrait and the "Land and Liberty" slogan. The league advocated a pyramid constructed of stones that would be sent from all the nation's ejidos and other peasant communities and organizations, each stone engraved with "a dedication or thought alluding to our agrarian struggle." Atop the pyramid would stand a statue of Zapata, in which he would appear "supported on a mauser in the serene and self-confident bearing of one who is conscious of his strength." At his side there was to be "a giant sickle," also bearing the "Land and Liberty" motto. The league desired to avoid "the vulgarities of bourgeois art," and its leaders believed that this design—"very Mexican and very campesino at the same time"—would accomplish that goal. Diego Rivera did the preliminary sketch of the monument and offered to make the model and oversee work on the project.[15] Though those who made these plans did not mention it, their conviction concerning the suitability of their design probably owed much to the mausoleum Zapata had ordered built in Tlaltizapán to house the bodies of prominent Zapatistas, which had taken the form of a small step-pyramid.[16]

The monument the league envisioned never came to fruition, but the idea of honoring Zapata in this way was in the air, a new departure for a revolution that had not until then concerned itself with statues, preferring to put its resources toward what seemed more practical ends.[17] By late 1931, work on a statue, funded by the state government and revolutionary veterans, was under way. The statue was to be located in one of Cuautla's main squares, the Plaza of the Lord (Plaza del Señor). To make this plaza suitable for Zapata, a committee formed to undertake its "beautification," which included the "establishment of a garden, benches and electric lighting, all of the most refined, modernist taste." Still, not everything would be modern: the renovations were to leave space for the traditional fair of the second Friday of Lent, for which Cuautla was regionally renowned. Thus was a new layer of revolutionary meaning being superimposed on a place with older associations in a way that again paired Zapata and Jesus Christ.

On April 10, 1932, the thirteenth anniversary of his death, Zapata's remains were exhumed and placed beneath the statue—Pablo González could not have buried him deep enough. Cuautla awoke on that day, claimed

Excélsior, as it did on days of "great celebrations." Agraristas arrived from around the state to a city again adorned with triumphal arches, which were decorated with slogans and portraits of Zapata. At dawn, federal forces with their military bands "traversed the principal streets," playing marches, and in general there was "greater solemnity" than on the previous anniversaries, owing to the intention of moving the body. Calles, now the Jefe Máximo, did not attend the commemoration as expected, but other authorities did. Vicente Estrada Cajigal, officially governor of Morelos but at that time serving as head of the Department of the Federal District, presided over the event in representation of both Calles and President Pascual Ortiz Rubio. It was he who had initiated work on the statue. The acting governor of the state, José Urbán Aguirre, was also present, as were governors of other states, congressmen, and, of course, peasants and their representatives. In a front-page article dedicated to the commemoration, the official newspaper of the revolution, *El Nacional*, characterized those in attendance as the leaders of "our social movement."[18]

The ceremony began with a parade of agraristas, federal forces, and government officials in their dark suits. Zapata's remains were taken from where they lay—beneath a marble angel with drooping wings that had been placed over his grave sometime in the early 1920s—and put into a small black box "with some incrustations of gold."[19] The bones fit nicely, according to a Zapatista veteran who witnessed the ceremony. The box was carried the short distance to the plaza by Zapatistas Emigdio Marmolejo and Andrés Pérez, one dressed in the white calzones of the peasantry, the other in his military uniform (see Figure 4.1). As Zapata's body was placed in the cavity beneath the new statue, a bugle sounded honors three times, recalling Chinameca in 1919. A police band then struck up the funeral march, and Estrada Cajigal unveiled the plaque that renamed the square the Plaza of the Revolution of the South.

The dedication of the statue followed. The work of Moisés Quiroz, the statue depicted a serious, sympathetic Zapata on horseback, dressed in his charro best, and beside him a man or boy *El Nacional* identified as a "humble Indian" (see Figure 4.2). Zapata's figure bent slightly to rest its hand on the campesino's shoulder, apparently listening and offering advice or consolation in a paternalistic manner. It was not nearly as macho an image as the one the Liga had envisioned, but the politicians agreed that "the likeness of General Zapata was notable."[20] Speeches followed the unveiling. Though his true feelings about Zapata were at best mixed, Estrada Cajigal gave a "panegyric to the southern hero." Urbán spoke too, assuring the crowd that, "Zapata is with us, converted into ideas, to make us better, and he lives in

FIGURE 4.1

Moving Zapata's remains to the new statue, April 10, 1932. (Fondo Gildardo Magaña, Archivo Histórico de la Universidad Nacional Autónoma de México, Instituto de Investigaciones Sobre la Universidad y la Educación, Universidad Nacional Autónoma de México.)

the heart of the people that extols and exalts him." Finally, flowers were laid at the base of the statue on behalf of various states and officials. Leaving a lamp burning at the site, the prominent visitors and their retainers then retired to "an orchard on the outskirts" of town for lunch.[21]

The rise and momentary triumph of Cardenista reformism can be traced in the discourse of the commemorations that followed. In 1934, Francisco S. Elías, cousin of Calles, wealthy landowner, former governor of Sonora, and now secretary of agriculture and development, was still a mouthpiece for the conservative leadership of the Maximato. Elías drew on a broad array of books and previous commemoration speeches, thus demonstrating how the myth of Zapata was accruing over time. In his story of Zapata's youthful promise to recover village land, he expanded on one aspect of the original account by focusing on the Indianness of Zapata's mother, who had an "enigmatic countenance," a "racial gruffness of expression," and "eyes of obsidian, of an Aztec idol."[22] It was an affirmation of the revolution's desire to reach out to the indigenous population via an Indian Zapata, but the imagery was remarkably racist. It would have fit poorly within

FIGURE 4.2
The 1932 statue. Photograph by the author.

the position that Cárdenas was beginning to articulate, which entailed offering Indians the opportunity to choose from elements of Mexico's national, "modern" culture without demanding that they surrender their
own traditions in exchange.[23] Elías also demonstrated that state officials
were not in lockstep by presenting a strikingly macho Zapata, who, as a
youth, had engaged in fistfights in his hometown to see that justice prevailed. He added that Zapata had had many women, whom he courted
with the help of a troubadour who played the "most exquisite songs of our
folklore."[24]

The ceremony of 1936 stood out for the drama that swirled around it.
Cárdenas was scheduled to appear at the Cuautla ceremony but instead remained in Mexico City to deal with a political crisis: after a two-year struggle with Calles, he had finally managed on this day to send the Jefe Máximo
and his closest collaborators into exile. In the words of *Excélsior*, this converted the velada held in Zapata's memory at Mexico City's Palace of Fine
Arts into one of the "most historically important political-social gatherings
of recent times." As a "multitude of peasants and workers" filled the air
with vivas for Zapata and Cárdenas and cries of "death to Calles," peasant organizer Graciano Sánchez stood to say—echoing, ironically, Calles
in 1924—that Zapata could now rest because Cárdenas's program was saving the revolution. That sentiment was undoubtedly well received, but the
big sensation of the evening was the speech of Emilio Portes Gil, who had
been the first, interim, president of the Maximato in 1928–1930 and was
now president of the PNR. Portes Gil was razzed at first by a "strong group
of communist elements," but he soon won over the crowd. Contradicting
rumors of his ongoing support of Calles, he denied having been Calles's
puppet while in the presidency and pledged his loyalty to Cárdenas. To illustrate that loyalty with reference to Zapata, he announced that the best
possible homage to Zapata was "to proclaim, from this rostrum, the task of
peasant unity," which Zapata had "proclaimed and sealed with his blood"
and Cárdenas was now pursuing. Again, too, there was the nationalism:
Zapata, he declared, "is the most Mexican and most pure symbol of our
social revolution."[25]

During the 1939 commemoration at Cuautla, César Martino, agricultural engineer and congressman, spoke in representation of the recently
formed (1938) product of Cárdenas's drive for campesino unity, the National Peasant Confederation (Confederación Nacional Campesina, CNC).[26]
Martino called Cárdenas the "most loyal continuer" of Zapata's work and
noted that the peasants were "tranquil" because Cárdenas was giving them
what they had fought for:

credit, schools, irrigation, markets for the sale of their goods, the organization of rural life on a higher plane, and material and spiritual tranquility so they can feel themselves free men—all cardinal points of the authentic program of Zapata.

"It appears to us," he added, "that twenty years after being assassinated in Chinameca, Zapata is rising, satisfied, and giving his hand of a peasant and fighter to Cárdenas." The tone was one of self-congratulation. Martino was talking not about work yet to be done but about what had been accomplished. And though no one present could have fully appreciated the magnitude of the accomplishment, Cárdenas's reorganization of the party signified the consolidation of power, for that party, that would last for many decades. A "rising, satisfied" Zapata, hand extended, *had* been a significant part of that story, and the peasantry *would* be relatively tranquil in the ensuing decades. At least for members of the political elite, congratulations were due all around.[27]

The hardest work of state and nation building, however, was not done at these commemorations, nor were they the main way in which the state used Zapata to forward its agenda during the 1930s. Education was more important. Ever since the fighting ended, revolutionary leaders had been interested in the power of education to instill Mexico's masses with nationalistic sentiments and make them more productive citizens. Already in 1921 the federal government was trying to get schools under the jurisdiction of its just created Ministry of Public Education rather than the control of the states, localities, or (worst of all) the church. It was settled at that time that the national government could create schools that it would run anywhere in Mexico, though other, non-federally funded schools would also continue to exist. An interval of impressive rural school building, intended to pull the "backward" countryside into the nation, had followed under the leadership of Vasconcelos. Later, much of the anticlerical onslaught that helped produce the Cristero rebellion was aimed at undermining the church's role in education.

Judging by primary school textbooks, developments in Zapata's cult during the 1920s had no impact on what schoolchildren learned about him during that decade. History texts were not yet a major item on the agenda of the Ministry of Education, and since Vasconcelos considered Zapata a criminal, he made no effort to enhance how he was remembered. Rather than aggressively bringing the revolution to Mexico's children in new textbooks, schools relied on works written during the Porfirian period, sometimes with brief addenda that surveyed the recent conflict.[28] So what did textbooks say about Zapata? A good example is Rafael Aguirre Cinta's widely used work for primary schools, *Lecciones de historia general de México*.[29] Ignoring social issues, Aguirre Cinta contended that Zapata rebelled against the revolutionary regime in 1911 because, given his ignorance, he was unduly influenced by revolutionary politicos angry that Madero had frustrated their designs on power. He added that when Madero ascended to the presidency in November, Zapata "did not fulfill his promise to lay down his arms." Aguirre Cinta did ultimately mention that Zapata was defending the principles of agrarianism, but in that passage he belittled the word "agrarianism" by putting it in quotation marks.[30] The 1926 edition of the work followed the same vein, indicating that Zapata represented no social cause: the land issue was a false one and Zapata was merely an obstructer of order.[31] Individual teachers may have qualified or refuted such lessons in the classroom, but they were on their own in finding the information with which to do so.

During the 1930s, Calles's concern with molding the minds of future generations meant things began to change. Despite much complaining about the superstitions of the masses, the goal was not necessarily to turn Catholic Mexicans into rationalists; rather, it was along the lines of what Calles meant when he talked about a "spiritual conquest." Moisés Sáenz, who had been Calles's undersecretary of education, asserted that the hope was to "keep the movement of the [religious] rite but to change its meaning"—to effect a "transfer of sacrality" from the church to the nation, thus making the nation the sacred object of religious feeling and, presumably, adding to state power in the process.[32] In pursuit of these goals, Secretary of Education Narciso Bassols oversaw a program of action education during the early part of the decade, which dovetailed nicely with the socialist education the party called for in 1933. In both cases, education was tied closely to social reform, and several communists, including Bassols, the List Arzubide brothers, and Rafael Ramos Pedrueza, obtained important positions in the ministry. Teachers became proponents of new hygienic practices, of worker and peasant organization, and of land reform, especially once the Cárdenas regime got under way. In each of these endeavors they were agents of the central government intended to push its programs—and with them its power—into the countryside.[33]

Demanding that all primary schools (federally owned or not) have their textbooks approved by the ministry and observe national holidays and civic commemorations, the new regulations of 1932 were another manifestation of the changing face of education.[34] The desire to occasion a transfer of sacrality was evident with respect to these holidays and commemorations, and it also became clear in the way the revolution's first generation of text-books, now finally being written, utilized Zapata. One example is Alfonso Teja Zabre's *Breve historia de México* (Short History of Mexico, 1935). Aimed at the upper grades of primary school, Teja Zabre's work spent more time on the revolution than had texts of the 1920s, tallying the contributions of diverse revolutionary leaders while downplaying their rivalries. The author credited Zapata with having given Mexico, in the Plan of Ayala, "the prole-tarian basis of the distribution of land," and listed him among the radicals who had pushed the revolution forward. It was the reiteration of a notion that had by now become commonplace: that the agrarian provisions of the constitution, in Article 27, were Zapata's gift to the revolution—this despite the fact that no Zapatista had had a hand in the drafting of that document. The corollary to that proposition, already aired by Díaz Soto y Gama dur-ing the Obregón years, was that Mexico was getting the land reform Zapata wanted. Demonstrating how important visual images of Zapata were to the way he was remembered, Teja Zabre included two: a detail of a Rivera mural at the National Palace that pictured Zapata with Otilio Montaño, Madero, Villa, and various other revolutionaries; and Posada's engraving of Zapata with gun, sword, and cartridge belts.[35] Another text, *Simiente* (Seed), which was directed explicitly at rural schools, indicated that if peas-ants had land they owed it to Zapata, who defended the principle, "land for everyone, land without foremen and without landlords." The present gov-ernment, this book made clear, was also part of Zapata's legacy.[36] José M. Bonilla's *Historia Nacional* (National History, 1939) asserted that Zapata, a representative of the "mestizo race," had given the revolution its revolution-ary, socialist character.[37]

One important new publication reached out to isolated rural teach-ers to educate—or indoctrinate—them: a periodical, put out monthly by the Ministry of Education, called *El Maestro Rural* (The Rural Teacher).[38] During the 1930s, *El Maestro Rural* demonstrated tremendous devotion to the Zapata cult. The December 1933 edition, for instance, printed one of Rivera's images of Zapata from the Ministry of Education in which cor-rido singers, with their memories, conjured up the deceased Zapata. It also conveyed the account of an engineer who claimed to have come in contact with Zapata when the caudillo was a *mozo*—servant—prior to the revolution. This informant indicated that there was nothing striking about Zapata at that time, describing him instead as a typical Mexican. The author of the article in which this story was included expressed approval of that description, which was better than talk of predestination because it meant that other, regular people could rise when needed, "from that obscure rural mass," as heroes, intuitive guides, and liberators. The article also mentioned that Zapata was more closely tied to "mother earth" than other heroes—another hint of his suitability as a symbol of the Mexican nation.[39]

In February 1934, *El Maestro Rural* used Rivera's Cuernavaca depiction of the Indian Zapata leading a white horse (see Figure 3.1) to illustrate a sentimental poem by one Manuel Ramírez Arriaga. Addressed to Zapata, this work managed to praise him through reference to his dislike of paper money: "Zapata: you are as pure / as the silver / of the solid peso / that you minted in Guerrero." In the inevitable reference to his subject's death, Ramírez Arriaga wrote, "you fell / because you never wanted / to compromise with life to protect yourself." Finally, this author averred that since his death, Zapata's heart, "open like your countryside, / in a people's eucharist, / is given in every place / in which a mouth of a redeemed Indian / eats the bread of the ejido plot."[40]

Two months later *El Maestro Rural* again used Rivera's Indian Zapata—this time on its cover, to mark the annual commemoration.[41] Much of this issue was devoted to Zapata. Drawing heavily from the book of Germán List Arzubide—the final chapter of which was reproduced elsewhere in the issue—one article maintained that, "unlearned, Zapata was the owner, like Morelos himself, of a natural talent that illuminated for him the path to the future." Two corridos were also printed in full: that of Armando List Arzubide and Eduardo Guerrero's "Sad Farewell of Emiliano Zapata." Finally, Rivera's SEP image of Zapata with the corrido singers was again reproduced. Photographs of Zapata made the cover of both the November 1934 and the April 1935 issues. On the former of these occasions it was Zapata as charro in recognition of Revolution Day; on the latter, *El Maestro Rural* used a soulful headshot that accentuated the caudillo's dark, sad eyes (see Figure 4.3).[42] The April 1935 issue contained an article on Zapata's death, and photographs were sprinkled throughout. The heavy use of both visual and literary images of Zapata continued throughout the decade in *El Maestro Rural*, with the obvious intention, on the part of the Ministry of Education, of making the schoolteacher the "principal priest" of Zapata's cult. How fully the journal achieved that end is open to question, but it did provide evidence of some success when it printed photographs of murals of Zapata that had been painted on school walls as the Rivera tradition rippled into the countryside.[43] Complementing the textbooks, *El Maestro Rural* played a critical role in making it, as one former student observed, "unlikely a child would leave primary school without knowing about Zapata."[44]

FIGURE 4.3
*Zapata up close. (Archivo General de la Nación, Mexico City,
Archivo Fotográfico Hermanos Mayo.)*

Then there were the books that focused on Zapata alone. One such volume was Baltasar Dromundo's *Emiliano Zapata: Biografía* (1934).[45] Now deeply involved in April 10 commemorations, where he sometimes spoke in representation of the PNR, Dromundo devoted substantial space to Zapata's personal life, discussing both his childhood and his women. Zapata, he contended, was "macho in an elevated sense," noble in his treatment of the women he developed relationships with and always taking the time to romance them. He was also, according to Dromundo, attentive to family duties. When evidence of Zapata's roving eye threatened to undermine the noble macho argument, Dromundo escaped ingeniously, asserting that Zapata took responsibility for the children of any woman he slept with.[46]

Though Dromundo's efforts won him that year's National Prize for Literature, more significant in making Zapata official was Gildardo Magaña's *Emiliano Zapata y el agrarismo en México* (Emiliano Zapata and Agrarianism in Mexico).[47] Magaña began to publish parts of this project, which eventually reached five volumes, in *El Nacional* during the early 1930s; the initial volume appeared in 1934. When Cárdenas arrived in power, Magaña, who, like the new president, hailed from Michoacán, saw his political fortunes rise—along with those of several other Zapatistas.[48] Previously he had received little by way of official appointment, but in 1934 Cárdenas made him governor of Northern Baja California and in 1936 gave him the same job in his home state. In 1939, Magaña even started a long-shot campaign to succeed Cárdenas in the presidency, but he died that year, at forty-nine, of a heart attack. In any event, one of the ways he benefited from his association with Cárdenas was getting government support to publish and circulate his book.

Magaña's objective was to rescue "the martyr of Chinameca" from what he described as the forgetfulness of the authorities and "the indifference of other revolutionary writers."[49] He had emerged from the decade of fighting with many boxes of documents that he identified as the archive of Zapata, and his history was based in good part on them—in fact, it reproduced many of them in full. He also relied on the work of other Zapatista authors, including *Cartones Zapatistas* and a small book on Zapata and education by his own co-author, Carlos Pérez Guerrero, who would complete the final three volumes after Magaña's death.[50] Finally, he drew from the oral communications of a wide circle of informants, often presenting this type of material in dialogue form. One of the best stories conveyed in this way concerned Zapata's first encounter with Madero. In this discussion, which occurred in Madero's Mexico City office, Magaña let Zapata display his wisdom and foresight on such topics as the failure to disband the federal army that would eventually, under Huerta's direction, turn against Madero. As the meeting wore on, Zapata—who was armed—became frustrated with Madero's gradual approach to social change and his demand that Zapata's forces disarm before the land reform they fought for had been accomplished. The following exchange ensued:

> Zapata: Look, Mr. Madero. If I, taking advantage of the fact that I am armed, take your watch and keep it, and after some time passes we meet again when we are both equally well armed, would you have the right to demand that I return it?
> Madero: Of course, general! I'd even have the right to ask that you indemnify me for the time that you used it unjustly.
> Zapata: Well, that is exactly what has happened to us in the state of Morelos, where a few hacendados have taken the lands of the *pueblos* [villages] by force. My soldiers, armed campesinos and entire villages, demand that I tell you, with complete respect, that they want to proceed immediately to the restitution of lands.[51]

However questionable dialogue published many years after the fact may be, Magaña's presentation makes this piece of folk wisdom deeply memorable. With its drama and touch of speechmaking, it has a romantic quality also found in the story of the child Zapata's promise to recover village land. It is a scene ready for the movies, and in fact it would be used, almost verbatim, in Elia Kazan's 1952 Hollywood film *Viva Zapata!*, to be discussed in Chapter 6.

Magaña's narrative approach was to cast his net broadly. He focused on the land issue, as the title indicates, and of course Zapata was a big part of that, but he also developed a general discussion of the revolution. In the first volume he started with the ancient antecedents of the ejido and discussed the caudillo Morelos and revolutionary precursors before getting to Zapata, roughly one hundred pages in. In volume 2, due now to breadth of coverage rather than historical background, Zapata hardly appeared at all. The lack of focus helps explain why, when the work ended after five volumes, he and Pérez Guerrero had only reached 1914. By taking such an inclusive approach, though, Magaña could survey the terrain of the early revolution from the vista of Zapatismo.

Magaña's Zapata was not much different from the Zapata his predecessors had described. He was characterized by "his immense intuition and unbreakable faith," along with "clear vision, inflexible character, and honor." He was energetic, simple, sincere, unruffled by difficult times; he knew each of his soldiers and where they came from. He had no "personal ambitions, nor hunger for command, nor desire for power," and thus could not be bought by those who offered him land and money to betray his cause. He was both "the brain that thought and the arm that acted"—a refutation of charges that his ideological program was merely the work of his advisors. Given such traits, it is hardly surprising that he had the trust and love of the "enormous mass of the disinherited" as he led the most important social movement in Mexican history. Still he had not been properly valued and rewarded. One measure of that was that Pablo González had been allowed to go into exile, where he lived comfortably on what he had stolen during the revolution, while Zapata's daughter, María Elena, had recently died of poverty and disease.

From Magaña's point of view, although Obregón and Calles had enacted Zapata's program, land remained the great revolutionary issue that still required resolution. What undermined "the real, effective, noble, just, elevated, and pure agrarianism of which Zapata dreamed: FREE LAND FOR THE FREE MAN" was the fake agrarianism of corrupt politicians. This was not a problem of factions—Magaña struck the revolutionary family theme perfectly—because there were honorable revolutionaries in every camp. Rather, there were a few Judases, unidentified here, that thwarted the efforts of the well-intentioned majority.[52]

There was some machismo in Magaña's Zapata, but not much. At different points in the narrative he had Zapata threaten to hang Madero and inform us that he left his fear in an old pair of pants. He also mentioned his subject's "ability as a charro."[53] Though Magaña often lost track of Zapata for many pages, there was also some tendency to give him more credit than he probably deserved—he attributed to him, for instance, a great deal of power and presence, across the state of Morelos, during the electoral agitation of 1909 and 1910.[54] On the national scene, Zapata's big tests were dealing with Madero and "the reaction." Magaña went easy on Madero—he was, after all, a member of the revolutionary family. Ultimately, he argued that Madero was a great "apostle" and idealist, but that he failed in his dealings with Zapata because he was not a good leader, his errors due not to bad intentions but to his inability to understand that he needed to govern with the men and ideas of the revolution. This made him vulnerable to the reaction, which was always plotting and which undermined his government.[55] Zapata, meanwhile, forged straight ahead, eyes always on the prize:

He wanted the improvement of the masses in every sense; he wanted the flowering of the virtues of the Indian and the worker in general to be promoted; that to his lips be given bread, light to his mind; that he be allowed to achieve the condition of a human being with the right to all the opportunities to rise; that he simply have justice done for him, without the effeminate fear of displeasing the nation of the North that, in any event, has no reason to be displeased.[56]

This multivolume work was a major milestone in the study of Zapata, but Magaña had yet more in mind. In 1938 he compiled a collectively written volume, entitled *Ofrenda a la memoria de Emiliano Zapata* (Offering to the Memory of Emiliano Zapata), for free distribution at the nineteenth anniversary of Zapata's death. Intended to help exalt Zapata's "personality and his work," the collection started by highlighting the significance of his death by printing Salvador Reyes Avilés's original report on the subject.[57] Magaña's own contribution followed, noting that "the more one studies him [Zapata], the more he is purified; as one gets to know him, he grows, he becomes enormous." [58] Later chapters, from Zapatistas Fortino Ayaquica and Juan Torices Mercado, helped launch Magaña's presidential bid by directing much of their commemorative fervor in his direction.[59] Ramos Pedrueza, too, wrote on behalf of a pet cause. Though no Zapatista, he claimed to have met Zapata during the revolution, which allowed him to testify that the martyred caudillo had had a clear understanding of the Russian Revolution. Bearing witness, as did several other authors, to Zapata's international cachet, he also listed several "great socialist thinkers" from outside Mexico who viewed him as "the most pure of the Mexican revolutionaries." [60]

Although Zapata has never drawn the degree of attention from creative writers accorded to the revolution's other "popular" caudillo, Pancho Villa, some novelists and playwrights did begin to build on the foundation of "fact" established by the first historians and chroniclers.[61] One of the early works of Mauricio Magdaleno, who would become a well-known novelist, screenwriter, and sometime politician, was a play, first staged in Mexico City in 1932, called *Emiliano Zapata: Pieza en tres tiempos* (Emiliano Zapata: Play in Three Acts).[62] This work's initial scene concerned the fate of Zapata's collaborator on the Plan of Ayala, Otilio Montaño, who had been accused of treason for releasing a group of prisoners. Magdaleno's Zapata was "tall and energetic," dressed in a dark charro suit, with an expression that was "distrustful, gentle, sad." He moved his lips while he read to himself, a sign that Magdaleno's interpretation would not always be flattering.[63]

Montaño complained that Zapatismo had become "a party of bandits."[64] Zapata answered by reminding Montaño that he had once told him that they needed intellectuals to manage the troops, who would otherwise run riot. He implied that Montaño had been of little help in this regard. Eventually, Zapata revealed that he knew Montaño had been conferring with the Carrancistas—he was, in other words, on the way to defecting—and Magdaleno made the sin still blacker by indicating that his discussions had been with Pablo González.[65] As they talked, Zapata and Montaño were informed that the Carrancistas were attacking, apparently having been tipped off by Montaño. Zapata fled, but not before ordering that Montaño be shot.[66]

The second and third acts concerned Zapata's own death, yet another reflection of the significance of that event for how he has been remembered. Zapata, now dressed in black, was negotiating with Guajardo. He apparently believed—just as Dromundo's corrido had him claim—that Guajardo would tip the scales of war in his favor.[67] Tired and discouraged by his brother Eufemio's recent death, Zapata expressed his desire to settle down with his girlfriend Remedios, even citing the disgraced Montaño on the destructiveness of war. The discussions with Guajardo were covered in considerable detail, as is almost always the case in stories of Zapata's death—the various events that lead toward Chinameca are like stations of the cross, as I suggested in Chapter 2, and not only for the peasants of Morelos. As this scene ended and the next began, Remedios expressed her misgivings about Guajardo.[68] Zapata, meanwhile, talked dreamily about achieving the Zapatista ideal, which was essentially a male paradise: the working of the land, sugar cooperatives, "the smoke of the huts . . . the women making tortillas . . . the men content."[69] He instructed Remedios to keep her gossip to herself, but she tried to stop him from going into the hacienda, predicting that "there is an ocean of blood in front of you." Zapata threatened to hit her, and then, before leaving, uttered the final words to his people about the defense of the land that Germán List Arzubide had recorded.[70] The audience did not witness the ambush, but two of Guajardo's soldiers subsequently carried the corpse across the stage.

Magdaleno's play was different in its intentions toward Zapata from the idealizations of such writers as the brothers List. The account of Montaño's execution telescoped events that happened at various times and to several people, but it was a fairly realistic reflection of the toughness of the conflict and the compromises that came with it. Montaño's death, foreshadowing that of Zapata, suggests a balance: Zapata as a victimizer as well as a victim. The machismo he directed toward Remedios was probably meant to demonstrate that victimizer role as well. For Magdaleno, Zapata was a tragic figure in the classic sense that his character flaws led to his downfall, though ultimately Magdaleno had him glorified, transfigured in death.[71]

Like many others, Magdaleno was acutely conscious of the process to which he was contributing. Despite the ambiguity of his play, he proclaimed himself, at least by the end of the decade, "an enthusiastic admirer of the human figure of the apostle Emiliano Zapata." In 1935 he wrote:

> one day, perhaps, Mexico will turn its face and no longer encounter Zapata except in the form of a symbol. To such a degree and with such intensity does this figure possess the earthy qualities of myth. But myth— disintegration of the concrete personality, pure and fleeting—is an attainment of human immortality that comes only through the senses of the people, creator of myths.[72]

His concern was primarily that of a writer of fiction, to describe the ties between the human and the heavens, not to make Zapata official. Still, like all else produced on the subject, his play was now potential fodder for the government propaganda mill.

Another revealing work, published in 1932, is the historical novel *Tierra* by Gregorio López y Fuentes. López y Fuentes focused his narrative on rank-and-file Zapatistas rather than on their leader, but the novel ended with an extended gloss on Zapata's demise and reactions to it. On learning of Zapata's death, one character called him his "little father" and fell from his horse to twist in the dust with grief. "He didn't cry," López y Fuentes wrote, "he howled, roared, wailed. It is the symbolic grief of all of the campesinos of Morelos at the notice of the death of the general."[73] In Cuautla, however, the body was exhibited, and in "low voice" the legend began that it was not Zapata's.[74]

The death by betrayal of López y Fuentes's protagonist, Antonio Hernández, echoed that of Zapata, but there was one difference: "everyone is sure that Antonio Hernández is quite dead, but no one knows where he is buried. In contrast, everyone knows where General Zapata is buried, but no one in the area believes he has died. . . . "[75] Rumors of Zapata sightings circulated and the villagers awaited him expectantly, one of them cleaning his gun to be ready when he was called. But the book ends by assuring us that "there is nothing. Only the perfect silence of the fields. . . . "[76] Here the thrust of the story was about the movement, not the individual, but much as I reasoned in discussing the oral histories of Luz Jiménez and

Pedro Martínez in Chapter 2, Zapata's death called him to attention, redirecting that thrust. Death was what brought him to the center of things for López y Fuentes; for corridistas such as Marciano Silva; to some degree, at least, for other Morelenses; and ultimately for Mexico in general.

A final noteworthy literary endeavor is Armando List Arzubide's play, *El asesinato del Gral. Emiliano Zapata* (1938).[77] Like Diego Rivera's murals and like his own corrido of the previous decade, Ministry of Education employee List Arzubide explicitly located this play within the revolution's cultural program—it was simple, "popular" art meant for broadcast over the radio to instill revolutionary virtues in the masses. Interestingly, the first two of the play's three acts focused not on virtue but on vice in the form of the villains González and Guajardo. González referred to Zapata as "an Indian guarachudo" (an Indian in sandals), a standard slur that demonstrated the speaker's wickedness by putting him on the wrong side of the Cárdenas regime's pro-Indian policies. For his part, Guajardo soliloquized about his unbounded ambition. "This is the opportunity I was hoping for," he said, "I leave here a General or the devil take me." In act three, set at Chinameca, various events were compressed and given new significance. Two women arrived to speak to Zapata, but not, as usual, about the impending assassination attempt. Rather, they complained about the depredations of former Zapatista Victoriano Bárcenas. As we have seen, Guajardo's execution of Bárcenas's soldiers was a conventional part of the story, but List Arzubide ignored Bárcenas's status as a lapsed Zapatista as well as Zapata's consequent vendetta against him as a traitor. Here Zapata merely said he had heard complaints about Bárcenas before and asked Guajardo to remove those who misbehaved from his forces. Guajardo then ordered that the men of Bárcenas be shot, and they were massacred off stage. Zapata, normally credited with ordering this massacre and sometimes with carrying it out, was thus not implicated in the bloodshed. Consistent with the regime's desire for a kinder, gentler Zapata, he merely declared, "perhaps the punishment was too harsh, colonel, but for the first time justice is done for the families of the peons injured without mercy by government troops." Soon Guajardo and Zapata went off to look at a horse Guajardo claimed he wanted to give his new commander, and Zapata was ambushed from behind—as in List Arzubide's earlier corrido, this was of course a twist that symbolized the treachery. Anonymous Indians then appeared, yelling that Zapata, "the only defender of the poor," had been killed.

List's extensive treatment of the villains, Magaña's mention of "the reaction," Ramos Pedrueza's analysis of the limits of land reform before Cárdenas, and many other declarations that encircled Zapata were conditioned by the ideologically rich climate of the 1930s. In Mexico as in many parts of the world, the frustrations of the Great Depression and the signs of the coming of World War II produced strong ideological currents. Communists like Ramos Pedrueza and Armando List wanted a Zapata who would help them push the revolutionary agenda ahead, not one who would simply legitimize what had already been done. But as they sought to guide and deepen the revolution's social reformism, they increasingly faced the ire of both traditional conservatives and members of a fascist movement called Sinarquismo that grew rapidly into a serious political force during the period.[78] Other Mexicans simply embraced the strident nationalism of the era—Magaña's somewhat gratuitous gripe about the United States was a play for this constituency. Cardenista reform proved to be a polarizing process during troubled times. Thus, while there was a growing consensus among those who ruled about where Zapata should fit within the revolutionary family, debate about how he should be remembered did continue, both among adherents of the diverse and evolving ruling party and between them and those on the outs with the regime.

Sometimes arguments about Zapata seem trumped up for political or literary effect. It was not the case that, despite the claim made for Magaña's work, the authorities had forgotten Zapata, however peripheral he may sometimes have seemed to their more practical endeavors. At other times issues were so belabored that debates bordered on the ridiculous, as in the case of the extended newspaper exchange in 1933 between Zapatistas (old and new) and their foes over whether or not Zapata had truly been "intransigent." One participant in this debate sought to sully Zapata through association with Pascual Orozco and Orozco's relationship with "reactionaries."[79] Countering arguments included the assertion that Orozco's plan, unlike that of Carranza, at least mentioned land reform and other socioeconomic issues, and a reminder that Zapata had, after all, executed Orozco's traitorous father.[80] Even Manuel Palafox, a former Zapatista intellectual who had left the movement in disgrace, chimed in to question the legitimacy of a document published by one of Zapata's accusers and to note that Orozco had accepted Zapata's plan, not the other way around.[81] Zapata, his many defenders concluded, did not compromise; Zapata, they added, did not back down.

Still, the ideological divisions of the Cárdenas era were often given clear and meaningful expression in discussions of Zapata. Not all textbook authors of the 1930s, for instance, rushed to adopt Zapata as hero. Gregorio Torres Quintero began to publish his *La patria mexicana: Elementos de historia nacional* (The Mexican Fatherland: Elements of National History) during the Porfiriato, and it had run through many editions. Despite abundant opportunities to rewrite to suit prevailing trends, in his 1939 edition he indicates that Zapata (and Villa) *rebelled* against Constitutionalism—certainly not a neutral description of the break in revolutionary ranks that occurred in 1914. He also notes, with ill-disguised scorn, that revolutionaries "have not ceased to praise Zapata" since the death of Carranza.[82] Meanwhile, the efforts of those who did climb aboard the pro-Zapata bandwagon were hardly received with universal praise. Baltasar Dromundo complained bitterly of the criticism his biography had attracted from Catholics, former Maderistas turned counterrevolutionaries, "ambushed liberals, and all of that species, not always classifiable, of saboteurs of the revolution." Still, he valiantly maintained that they would not succeed against either his book or the memory of Zapata, because "in this work of cleansing the figure of Zapata of the opprobrium and lies with which intellectuals and journalists for rent have varnished it, nothing can stop us."[83]

The period's biggest debate over Zapata's merits was provoked by the return from exile, in November 1937, of a man who had been expelled from the revolutionary family many years before: Pablo González. According to one observer, González returned to Mexico much changed—now a "calm, fat old man"—but Zapata's rehabilitation and his own political downfall had long been paired in his mind, and there they had festered. González was angry about land reform and that Zapatistas had found their way into the government, and his San Antonio, Texas, exile had not precluded his involvement in opposition politics and at least one failed rebellion. As proof of his lasting anti-regime commitment, he would soon join the opposition to Cardenismo.[84] But first, on November 10, a sympathetic newspaper article hypothesized that he had not really participated in the plot to kill Zapata.[85] Two days later, González set the record straight in an interview with *La Prensa*. He reminded the newspaper's readers that though Zapata was now categorized as an apostle and martyr, he had been nothing more than an outlaw when he died. González thus had no problem admitting—in fact, he did so with glee, or at least self-righteousness—his active involvement in Zapata's assassination.[86]

A firestorm of criticism ensued. On the following day *La Prensa* sought to balance its coverage by extensive reference to Magaña's book, and by inviting others to contribute to the discussion of Zapata's merits.[87] One response came from Jenaro Amezcua and Carlos Pérez Guerrero of the Union of Agrarista Revolutionaries of the South (La Unión de Revolucionarios Agraristas del Sur, URAS). Led by the chronic organizer Amezcua, this group had formed in 1935 in answer to Cárdenas's plea for peasant unity, likening that appeal to Zapata's old drive to unify military opposition to Carranza.[88] Another failed attempt to unite the Zapatistas, the Union became an intermediary between the state and some of the campesinos of south-central Mexico, whom it eventually helped bring into the National Peasant Confederation. It also worked to get former Zapatista soldiers accepted into the army and to secure pensions for widows and orphans.[89]

Given this close association with the regime, the tack of its response to González was predictable. It was unfortunate, Amezcua and Pérez Guerrero contended, that González was not really answering questions about Zapata's death but rather merely reviving Zapatista indignation and thus "at the point of provoking a division within the revolutionary family." They noted that González seemed proud of having killed Zapata and complained that he "still wanted to throw mud on the unsoiled memory of his victim." They then offered documentary evidence—again, with recourse to Magaña's opus—that Zapata was far more than the irresponsible rebel González described. He was the voice of the campesino masses, and all González had done was make him a martyr. The authors closed by assuring their readers that their dispute with González would not evolve into a broader conflict between Zapatistas and Carrancistas; time had made them realize that revolutionaries had been disunited due only to a lack of understanding, which was being overcome "little by little." Their grievance was with González alone, who was a blemish on the Carrancista record.[90]

Next, the Union created a Revindicating Committee Pro-Emiliano Zapata to deal with González's return. Appointed president of this committee was Senator Agustín G. de Castillo of Sinaloa, apparently chosen because, in the name of the campesinos of his state, he was willing to take an especially strong stand against González: he argued that either González should be punished or Zapata's name should be removed from its place in the Chamber of Deputies. Amezcua became the committee's vice president. The committee then debated how González and his associates should be penalized "for having blackened the pages of our Revolution by eliminating the most idealistic of its Caudillos," and laid plans for a national propaganda blitz in defense of Zapata's good name. It soon communicated its positions on stationery that incorporated both a photograph of Zapata's dead face and a quote from González admitting to having helped kill him. There was also an extended passage, ostensibly from Zapata but written, in truth, by Otilio Montaño in 1913, which stated that Zapata preferred the "death of Spartacus" to living in chains.[91]

González responded to Castillo's accusations and threats by indicating that he did not remember Castillo from the days of revolutionary fighting, which led him to believe "that you were a last minute revolutionary"—a taunt that suggested he had joined the revolution to collect rewards rather than fight. González also contested the secondary charge that he had stolen equipment from the sugar mills of Morelos when he was stationed there, claiming he had never heard it before.[92] He had no hope, however, of responding point by point to all of the protests that arrived at Cárdenas's office from every part of Mexico. An agricultural cooperative in Puente de Ixtla, Morelos, put it this way: "we protest with due energy the arrival of Pablo González in the Republic, because he caused countless and unspeakable excesses and abuses for all of the inhabitants of our beloved state of Morelos, besides being the director of the cowardly assassination of General Emiliano Zapata, standard bearer of Agrarianism."[93] The administration considered prosecution, but the attorney general determined that the statute of limitations on Zapata's death was up. The outcry was sufficient, however, to preclude González from rejoining the army.[94]

In general, the Union of Agrarista Revolutionaries of the South was busy during the latter part of the Cárdenas administration, probably infused with a greater sense of urgency by González's reappearance. In December it returned to an old issue, petitioning the national legislature to grant Zapata the designation of Benemérito, a measure, it argued, that both public opinion and Cárdenas supported. Other unresolved issues it again broached were those concerning a statue in Mexico City and a name change for Cuernavaca.[95] The Union continued its energetic efforts to shape memories of Zapata by beginning to present, at 1938 and 1939 commemorations of the Plan of Ayala and of April 10, the Emiliano Zapata Medal. Among the first winners were Dromundo, Díaz Soto y Gama, Magaña, Rivera, Silva, Salvador Reyes Avilés, and Amezcua himself—a virtual who's who of Zapata's mythifiers.[96]

If controversy over Zapata's memory was a sign of the times, the final great controversy of the period was the presidential election of 1940. There were several candidates within the official party. Though apparently still on Cárdenas's good side, Magaña's campaign implicitly rejected Cardenista land reform by stressing the rights of individual small property holders rather than collectively held and sometimes collectively worked ejidos. This defense of small property seems to have been a smoke screen for the protection of larger property holders, who prospered in Magaña's Michoacán while peasant organizations did not.[97] This did not stop Magaña from exploiting his close association with Zapata. His campaign biography indicated that, though he was not from Morelos, because of his sympathy with the poor he "ran to enlist in the hosts of Zapata."[98] But if Magaña used his prestige as a Zapatista for conservative ends, it was also true that even Cárdenas had come to believe that headlong reform had to end for the time being. He scuttled his reform program in the poor economic climate that followed the 1938 oil expropriation, and his feeling that it was time to consolidate was also evident in his choice of a successor, as he eventually threw his support behind moderate Manuel Avila Camacho instead of his close ally on the left, Francisco Múgica. With that support, Avila Camacho easily captured the ruling party's nomination.

In the general election, though, a serious challenge was brewing. Representing broad frustration with both social reform and nondemocratic procedures, General Juan Andreu Almazán stepped into the fray at the head of a coalition of parties on the right. Almazán had a checkered revolutionary past. A native of Guerrero, he was involved in the agitation against Porfirio Díaz. In April 1911, he encountered Zapata along the Morelos-Puebla border, claimed to be an emissary from Madero, and made Zapata official head of the revolution in Morelos. They then participated in several armed engagements together.[99] In the fall of that year they met and collaborated again, now both on the run from the interim administration of Francisco León de la Barra. But Almazán soon left the Zapatistas, and in 1913 he joined Victoriano Huerta—who made him a general—after the coup against Madero.[100] In these new circumstances Almazán informed the press that Zapata was a bandit. After Huerta fell and the war between the Zapata-Villa coalition and the Carrancistas began, Almazán apologized, and Zapata, needing the artillery and expertise that Almazán possessed, forgave him. Almazán spent the final years of the fighting lurking at the fringes of Zapatismo, more closely affiliated with the conservative movement of Félix Díaz (nephew of Porfirio) than he was with Zapata.[101] Always the opportunist, in 1920 he made a deal with Obregón that again put him on the good side of the revolution. While there he received several nice military appointments and government contracts for road and railroad construction, which made him rich.[102] But as the 1930s ended Almazán again displayed the more conservative instincts he had indulged with Huerta and Félix Díaz, deciding to challenge the revolutionary party's electoral machine from the outside.

During this campaign Almazán frequently evoked Zapata, despite his largely conservative following and despite speaking out against ejidos. His campaign biography avowed that "having followed Zapata is the best reward for a Mexican fighter of the epoch" and that Almazán had been Zapata's "loyal collaborator" because his own humble origins made him love and understand "pariahs." The rough spots in his dealings with Zapata, it continued, were created by Zapatista conspirators jealous of his intimacy with their jefe—intimacy that, it hinted, probably gave him some influence over what appeared in the Plan of Ayala. In the end, the mutual respect with which the two men held each other triumphed over the schemers, and Almazán was still acting on that respect when he helped track down the rebellious Guajardo after Zapata's death.[103] The biography gave the relationship with Zapata a striking amount of space, and Almazán's speeches added still more to this propaganda line. "Sons of heroic Cuautla," he declared before Zapata's statue in late 1939, "inhabitants of the glorious state of Morelos, veterans of General Emiliano Zapata . . . you well know that I knew his secret, I heard his doctrine from his own lips, and at his side in combat."[104] Almazán's use of Zapata was perhaps not quite as preposterous as it may seem. Magaña, too, had come to oppose ejidos, after all, and both Paz Solórzano and Dromundo had drawn on Almazán's memory and inflated his role in the history of the movement in their written accounts.[105] Moreover, Zapata's daughter Ana María, head of an organization called the Union of Morelos Women, supported the Almazán campaign, calling the candidate the heir of her father's ideals.[106] Still, Almazán might have had trouble getting away with it had Díaz Soto y Gama not cranked up the old Agrarian Party for his benefit.[107]

During the 1930s Díaz Soto y Gama, largely out of politics since his attacks on Calles after Obregón's death, had written occasional newspaper articles about Zapata and his movement. The Zapata he fashioned was a vehicle for the expression of his own anticommunism, which grew stronger in the face of such manifestations of Cárdenas's land reform as the collectively worked ejidos of the Laguna region of northern Mexico, which were indeed patterned on the Soviet model. There may also have been an element of personal vendetta involved: Díaz Soto y Gama apparently believed Cárdenas had caused him to lose two of his classes at the National Autonomous University of Mexico (Universidad Nacional Autónoma de México, UNAM).[108]

In any event, a 1938 article revealed that his Zapata was an individualistic ranchero, not a peasant, who—as Magaña also wrote—stood for "free land for the free man." Underlining this emphasis on liberty—he used the word *libre* again and again—he noted that this meant land "without individual tyrannies, but also without tyrannies exercised by the state or collectivity." Díaz Soto y Gama seemed to foresee how the strings the state attached to the land it distributed, as it took over the direction of the agrarian economy from the haciendas that Cárdenas's reforms were decimating, would smother the productivity of much of the Mexican countryside. He then ran straight into the arms of Almazán and his wealthy backers, asserting that in southern Mexico there was no desire to make the ejido the base of a national economy that would feed the millions. That would have to be done by the capitalists, who had a spirit of enterprise still rare in the countryside. Díaz Soto y Gama did not write that Zapata had a place in his heart for agrarian capitalism, but he did not deny it either, and the way he put his article together made it seem as if it were so. The choice to be made in the election of 1940, he argued, was between Mexico and Russia, Zapata and Stalin.[109]

The ruling party countered the effort to make Zapata over in the image of Almazán. One part of the official position was spelled out clearly on April 10, 1936, when, as we saw in the opening of this chapter, José Parrés had precisely the opposite memory of Zapata from the one Díaz Soto y Gama was adopting. Zapata, he believed, had rejected individualism and strongly advocated the ejido.[110] Later, Amezcua evoked Zapata in offering Avila Camacho troops to fight Almazán if political tensions generated a rebellion, and Manuel Palafox refuted Almazán's agrarista credentials.[111] Communist Party member and Cárdenas admirer Miguel A. Velasco, meanwhile, directed attention to the incongruity of the coalition opposing Avila Camacho in colorful terms, charging that the foreign doctrine of fascism had succeeded in uniting Díaz Soto y Gama and Pablo González "in the same dunghill." [112]

When the mudslinging was done, of course, Avila Camacho won the presidency by an unlikely tally. The official party had probably not stolen the election, but it certainly gave its candidate many more votes than he had earned. Complaints about fraud ensued, but in the end the ruling party and its Zapata, though slightly changed by the experience, rolled on.

At the national level, then, in terms of basic meaning, the Zapata of the 1930s was not unlike his 1920s counterpart. He was a symbol of agrarianism and of social struggle in general, a representation of the nation, a founding father with a touch of the macho. Moreover, there was still a mix of private and public motives and contributions behind celebration of Zapata. What changed was that during the 1930s, proponents of a new ruling party with a greater interest in molding culture seemed to have realized that if Zapata was developing into a national symbol, they needed to have a firmer hold on him. In the 1920s the state did little more than pay for some murals into which Zapata happened to be painted and make sure that representatives of the central government appeared at annual commemorations. In the 1930s, though neither Calles nor Cárdenas went out of the way to mention Zapata in their speeches, there were letters in gold, a Cuautla statue, positive textbook depictions, and Magaña's state-subsidized and state-distributed history. Most important, there was the Cardenista land reform. Despite the reservations of Díaz Soto y Gama and Magaña and the strings attached to the land, many understood this process as the fulfillment of Zapata's program. At the April 10, 1940, commemoration, Vicente Lombardo Toledano, Marxist leader of the Confederation of Mexican Workers (Confederación de Trabajadores de México, CTM), which had taken over from the Regional Mexican Labor Confederation as the official labor organization, put that sentiment nicely. "Lázaro Cárdenas," he asserted, "who has enriched with his work the initiative of Zapata, is the best Zapatista in Mexico. Those [Zapatistas] who oppose the development of his work, those who oppose him, are traitors to their jefe."[113] Nor was it only politicians who felt this way, as images of Cárdenas and Zapata began to be placed side by side in peasant homes in southern and central Mexico.[114]

When Graciano Sánchez and César Martino suggested that Zapata could rest, they might have meant a couple of different things. Most directly, of course, they were referring to the accomplishments of Cárdenas's reform project, but a second set of accomplishments had to do with the way the institutionalized revolution emanating from Mexico City continued to take over events at Cuautla and insert them into a postrevolutionary civil culture. In the practice of hero worship and the employment of funerary wreaths, this new civil culture drew from the prerevolutionary past while adding new hero cults and placing value on revolutionary ideas to which those cults had become attached. This entailed the routinization and institutionalization of Zapata's charisma—memories selected, crystallized, linked to the state—making Zapata a sturdier bridge between politicians and peasants.[115] Viewed from 1940, Zapata's use as part of the state's cultural project must have looked like a brilliant success; after all, it had helped accomplish a land reform that was quite different from the one Zapata and his followers had demanded. From the perspective of those running the system, it would surely have been best had the evolution of the southern caudillo's meaning ended there.

In reality, though, there would be no rest for Zapata. The state had developed an effective official Zapata, but it had not coopted him. It had simply joined Morelenses in honoring him, and this meant certain tensions would persist. Politicians might borrow some of their language from the locals, as when Governor of Morelos José Urbán spoke of Zapata living on, but they were not using it to say the same things. The Morelenses who argued that Zapata did not die at Chinameca put him in the context of a popular messianism, while Urbán and company sought to encourage a transfer of sacrality to the religion of nationalism by making Zapata a secular saint. Continuing in this vein, one might add that the state's Zapata, dead and only metaphorically resurrected, represented a peasantry that had been defeated in the revolution and could therefore be consigned to the past while Mexico modernized—as it would do with great zeal after 1940. That would explain the repeated suggestions that Zapata take it easy. Zapata as a man-god who was still in some real sense alive, on the other hand, could be a threat in the present.

Similarly, demands made of the state in Zapata's name by inhabitants of his home region were often both specific and personal, and thus poles apart from the eloquent glosses on the martyr of Chinameca by political orators. In 1933, Inés Aguilar and José Hernández Zúñiga wrote to President Abelardo Rodríguez requesting, as Zapata's widow and son-in-law, the use of two trucks to visit Cuautla on April 10 and 11, "and monetary aid, like other governments have provided." [116] As long as a reformist government continued to hear and answer such local demands, the contradictions between state and popular memories and uses of Zapata—founding father versus macho warrior, land and party as opposed to "Land and Liberty"—would remain latent. That did not mean they were not present. Even within national politics some controversy remained, as evidenced by Zapata's involvement in the 1940 electoral battle. By attaching Zapata to a divisive reform program and making him a pillar of the postrevolutionary state, the Cárdenas regime had placed an additional burden on his memory. Zapata could not yet be taken for granted; the wounds of the past had not yet healed.

FIVE

A MODERN ZAPATA FOR A GOLDEN AGE, 1940–1968

"Emiliano Zapata was a bandit," began Jesús Sotelo Inclán's *Raíz y razón de Zapata* (1943). "He assaulted, burned, assassinated. He filled Mexico with fear." Continuing in this vein, the author added that since Zapata was illiterate, his intellectuals, demagogues all, manipulated him like a puppet, and if there was any ideology behind his movement it was the product of their learning. Nor was he an effective leader of troops; rather, he led his forces in running from combat and never won an important victory. Since he died, "upstart revolutionaries" had attempted to make him into a new Mohammed, but that was just the propaganda of the opportunists who had come to power. Then, on the second page, Sotelo Inclán took the other side. "Emiliano Zapata was an apostle." More, greater than a real man, he was a symbol, champion of the campesinos, hope of the dispossessed. He was a genius of guerrilla warfare who fought because of the injustices of his place and time. Proof of his purity was that he died "so poor he left no inheritance to his family." True, corrupt revolutionaries had found ways to profit from his memory, but their betrayal of the revolution did not detract from Zapata's selfless contributions.[1]

These, Sotelo Inclán maintained, were typical positions of Zapata's detractors and supporters, positions he hoped would die with the old revolutionaries who perpetrated them.[2] Like many others, he had been bewildered by these crosscurrents. To know the truth—which, he imagined, lay somewhere in the middle—"dispassionate historians" were needed who would evaluate the arguments of both sides "with absolute impartiality." Surely it was possible now to find them among the younger generation, with so much time passed since Zapata's death.

Sotelo Inclán himself had been only six years old in 1919—too young, perhaps, to have his own position—but there was some family history. Supposed Zapatistas had killed his great uncle and ruined his grandfather's livelihood in San Lucas, in the Federal District near Xochimilco. When they finally burned down the latter's house, he came to live with Sotelo's family. After that, talk of Zapatista bandits surrounded the budding author, and he grew up in the anti-Zapatista camp. Schoolteachers had tried to change his mind with their official accounts, but that just made him stubborn. As he recalled it, every child in Mexico City knew Zapata was a bandit. Later, at the National University, he had a course with Díaz Soto y Gama, who exalted Zapata, "making him the principal theme of his class." Again it seemed like propaganda, and Sotelo Inclán and one of his friends would argue with the professor when they could, "so that I was a guerrilla fighter, you could say, of the classroom, against Emiliano Zapata." Given his experience, though, Díaz Soto y Gama won the arguments and, ultimately, Sotelo's grudging respect.[3]

But all this left him interested in knowing more. His first inclinations were literary. He wanted to write a play about Zapata, whom he envisioned like a character from Shakespeare, enveloped in "shadows and terrible passions." As he began to explore the theme he discovered that the people who mistreated his grandfather were not Zapatistas; they just used Zapata's name for their own ends. Eventually he went to Morelos to learn more, and witnessed what he called the simplicity and seriousness of the people. He also heard their accounts—and in them their admiration—of how Zapata had avoided the trap at Chinameca. Once, in fact, an old man was ready to kill Sotelo because he believed he had news of Zapata and wanted to know if "they were calling him to the Revolution again." This information, of course, Sotelo was unable to provide.[4]

Though he liked the Morelenses, Sotelo Inclán would not be distracted from his positivistic crusade for the truth, and in particular for the reasons underlying the rebellion. He went to Anenecuilco, which he found to be a place historians had forgotten but one of obvious significance to anyone proceeding methodically, "like a man of science," since it was where Zapata came from. There he was directed to Francisco Franco, an evasive, cautious man whose trust he gradually earned during several trips to the state. Franco was rumored to have some documents, which, Sotelo argued, "no longer belong just to Anenecuilco, but . . . are bound to the History of our Nation." [5] Finally, one day, he brought out, "with great reserve, a tin box, from which he took some old papers. 'Miliano gave them to me before he left,'" he said, "'for them he fought the war against Díaz and against Madero, Huertas [sic], and Carranza.'" Franco now entrusted the documents to Sotelo Inclán.

This was Sotelo's breakthrough. It was fascinating how Franco talked about when Zapata left, not when he died, because he was among those who believed he had survived Chinameca. (Sotelo's own position was that it was true Zapata did not die, because he would be reincarnated in new caudillos when it again became necessary to defend the land.)[6] But more intriguing to Sotelo was that, as Franco explained, these were the documents that proved Anenecuilco's right to the land. "Those papers completely changed the vision I had of Zapata," Sotelo wrote, "and revealed him as an authentic representative of the aspirations of the people." From then on his story, for Sotelo, became one that was "admirable and full of greatness." It was comparable, in fact, to those of national heroes Morelos and Hidalgo, themselves once accused of being criminals. Sotelo Inclán now became a historian, with the goal of leaving a true accounting to future generations. He also became an advocate, during the Avila Camacho administration, for the creation of a museum to house Anenecuilco's documents, but had no success.[7]

The way to understand Zapata, he came to believe, was to explore the history of his village. It is there in the title of his book: the "root and reason of Zapata" was Anenecuilco. Anenecuilco's history went back, he discovered, about seven hundred years, and over much of that time, especially since the Spanish conquest, it had been fighting to hang on to its land. Assigned the task of defending village interests were leaders traditionally known as *calpuleques*. Zapata was a mestizo for Sotelo, not an Indian, but Anenecuilco was an Indian town and calpuleques continued to serve there across the generations, though the name of the position changed over time. Zapata himself was a calpuleque, Sotelo insisted, "not more, not less."[8] The elders scrutinized his behavior and background, and when they chose him it reflected their belief that he was worthy of following the illustrious calpuleques who had come before him.[9] He was not, then, the great enlightened one, the magical intuitive, or the apostle sent by divine providence that revolutionary orators made him out to be. He was just a "simple man," Sotelo argued, "in intimate relationship with the life of his offended and exploited" village. That village was the true hero of the story; Zapata was just one of its best expressions.[10]

Sotelo Inclán made a good case, but Anenecuilco was far from the sole context for Zapata during the early 1940s. Another crucial part of the picture was World War II, which combined with the 1940 elections to set Mexico on a new, more conservative course. One could see the change coming already in the late 1930s, when some Morelenses, perhaps influenced by Sinarquismo and surely motivated by the squabble with the United States and Great Britain over the oil expropriation, began to argue that Zapata was alive and fighting in Europe alongside the forces of Adolf Hitler. This explained "why the Germans were winning so many victories."[11]

After the late 1941 attack on Pearl Harbor, though, the managers of Zapatismo chose to side with the Allies in the conflict—as did the government of Avila Camacho. Now speaking out most forcefully for Zapata was a new group, the Zapatista Front (Frente Zapatista), which was formed on June 23, 1940, by Zapatista veterans and their family members. It was in part an effort to institutionalize the coterie that had formed around Gildardo Magaña now that Magaña was dead, and in part a way to reject Jenaro Amezcua's appropriation of the role of chief Zapatista organizer. Amezcua's Union of Agrarista Revolutionaries of the South continued its own operations on Zapata's behalf, charging the Zapatista Front with destroying Zapatista unity precisely when the fatherland, given the threat of totalitarianism, might need them most. But having never managed to turn his revolutionary service into an official post, Amezcua lacked the clout to compete with his better connected former comrades, and soon faded from view.[12]

The Front picked one former governor of Morelos, Zapatista Elpidio Perdomo, as its first general secretary, and another, Parrés, as its secretary of agriculture. Three of Zapata's sons—Nicolás, Mateo, and Diego—were also part of the group. Serving as titular president was Lázaro Cárdenas himself, whose willingness to lend his name helped the Zapatistas surmount the bickering that had broken out over leadership positions. Cárdenas's role also underscored how profoundly connected the Front was to the ruling party. Its declaration of principles included praise for the Plan of Ayala and for the land reform of Obregón and Cárdenas. It asserted that the government should take care of Zapatista veterans and act on the principle that "the land belongs to the person who works it." It also made recommendations on agricultural credit, cooperatives, and technological aid. On political and religious questions the Front pledged to take no position, cooperating with whatever administration was in power.[13] Five years later it reinforced that pledge of servility by asking Avila Camacho to check the agenda for its first national convention because it did not want to "dissent in the least" from the policies of the present regime.[14]

In conception, the Zapatista Front seemed to be about serving the needs of surviving Zapatistas rather than remembering Zapata, and the document that recorded the practical business of its creation was remarkably free of references to the hero. But that was not true of public pronouncements, and so it is not surprising that, soon after Pearl Harbor, the Front drafted Zapata to help it respond to the Axis offensive. In a communication of December 17, 1941, the Zapatistas demonstrated their patriotism by offering

Avila Camacho whatever men he might need to deal with the arrival of the war on American shores. They added that the current government faithfully supported the principles for which they had fought, and reciprocated by drawing from one of Zapata's old manifestos the appeal that the people be ready to sacrifice themselves, if necessary, for the fatherland.[15]

Zapata also backed the war effort on April 10, 1942, at a velada at Mexico City's Hidalgo Theater. There Senator Vicente Aguirre proclaimed that the National Peasant Confederation was rallying behind the administration during the crisis. After all, he continued, Zapata did fight for the cause of liberty.[16] Two years later, at another metropolitan commemoration, another spokesman for the confederation argued that Zapata was one of the greatest figures "not just in the history of Mexico, nor in the history of America, but in the history of the world." His growing name recognition outside Mexico was a point of pride, especially at a time at which the international order was in flux and Mexico's place among the nations of the world was a major issue. This speaker then indicated that the struggle of peasants during the Mexican Revolution was not unlike the present Allied cause, because World War II was largely being fought by peasants for democracy and land. When it came time to make peace, he suggested, Mexico should urge that Zapata's program "be spread over the entire world"—Zapata, in other words, might serve as the basis of a new world order.[17]

Mexico's role in the fighting of the war was limited to sending a somewhat symbolic air force squadron to the Philippines. Not, then, a war of blood and guts from a Mexican standpoint, it was rather war as a launching pad into what observers then and now have called "modernity." Mexico provided substantial support by sending a wide array of raw materials needed for the manufacture of weapons to U.S. factories. Under the provisions of the Bracero Program that began in 1942, Mexican labor moved north as well—mostly to agricultural jobs—to remedy the labor shortage the war caused in the United States. In addition to these contributions, the uncertainty in Mexico about whether the war might threaten the country more directly—German submarines did, in fact, sink some Mexican oil tankers—helped give invocations of sacrifice and patriotism made in Zapata's name a meaningful context. The war endowed the revolutionary family with greater unity, unity that Avila Camacho used to steer domestic policy in a direction that meant the definitive end of the reformism of the Cárdenas years. Real wages began to go down and land reform slowed dramatically, while official rhetoric sought to make Mexicans forget the class and cultural differences, and interests, that had driven policy during the previous decade.

What, then, were Avila Camacho's goals with regard to domestic policy? Clues can be found in the 1941 commemoration, a momentous episode in the history of Zapata's memory because the president, seizing on his first opportunity to do so, attended the ceremony in Cuautla. By becoming the first sitting president to visit Cuautla on April 10, Avila Camacho established a new precedent: every head of state, for the remainder of the century, would make that pilgrimage at least once during his six-year term. Avila Camacho's speech was broadcast over the radio. In it he asserted that Zapata should be honored by "making the land bloom and produce fruit." It is necessary, he continued, "to honor him in the field, in the good harvest that brings well-being not only to the homes of the workers, but that will strengthen the economy of the country and become a basis of support for its greatness." Avila Camacho conceded that the government had responsibilities to the countryside, but added that it needed the help of the private sector, from small property owners who might help *ejidatarios* (recipients of ejidal land), and from those who could supply credit or undertake irrigation works. "The Mexican countryside," the president indicated, "offers all men of good will a great opportunity to serve their legitimate aspirations of gain and the creation of national wealth at the same time."[18]

The Cárdenas regime, too, had sent peasants and workers strong messages about the need to produce, but only now, in the 1940s, did a Zapata appear that the business community could love. If Cárdenas sought to divide the pie more evenly, Avila Camacho was announcing that he was primarily interested in making it bigger. With its heightened demand for Mexican goods, the war provided opportunities for economic growth, and Avila Camacho did his best to capitalize on them. He capitalized so well, in fact, that he presided over the start of a thirty-year period of unprecedented economic expansion, called the Mexican Miracle or, sometimes, the Golden Age. Initially, this growth was partly based on the greater productivity in the countryside that Avila Camacho appealed for at Cuautla, but the more significant new departure was in industrialization. Limited in its ability to buy manufactured goods from its traditional suppliers because of wartime shortages in the United States and Europe, Mexico now became more ambitious about building an industrial base of its own. Cheap loans, tax exemptions, and high tariffs that protected against foreign competition all helped Mexican industry gain a better foothold. Greater encouragement of foreign investment was another important part of the puzzle.

By the time Avila Camacho made way for the administration of Miguel Alemán (1946–1952) a boom was under way, and Alemán and his successors would deepen it. But the boom would not have equal benefits for all sectors of Mexican society. Those with money to invest had opportunities to increase their wealth, and others rose into a growing middle class that provided services essential to the new economy, but many of the poor continued to struggle for subsistence. The land reform process had largely destroyed the hacienda system, but now the expanding government became the arbiter of campesino destinies. Seeking to feed poorly paid urban workers cheaply and thus subsidize their employers, it limited peasant enterprise through control of prices, credit, marketing, and the processing of agricultural goods. Despite Avila Camacho's exhortations, campesinos constrained by government policies would have little opportunity to produce more, and even if they could, the extra product would be skimmed off on behalf of the nation's "greatness." They had land, but Mexico's peasants would remain the poorest segment of society and hopes for increasing agricultural production for the market—and the resources to support such production—were largely directed toward larger landholdings, especially in the northwest corner of the country.

Given this lack of material support for Zapata's main constituency, the ruling party's rhetorical commitment to him needed to be strong, and it would not hurt if Zapata continued—as he had in the hands of Avila Camacho—to speak out in favor of the brand of progress Mexico was now pursuing. Government officials, in any event, were willing to give it a try. In 1949 at Cuautla, for instance, Roberto Barrios, a founding member and now secretary general of the National Peasant Confederation, addressed some of his comments to President Alemán, who was in attendance. The peasants desired, Barrios reported, "that a project of industrialization be planned and . . . applied to all branches of agricultural production," and that the development of rural activities harmonize with the "process of industrialization in which the Government is involved." Barrios also indicated that those same peasants believed "that only work gives one the right to possess the land." This clever twist on the slogan, "the land belongs to those who work it," moved its focus from the claim on land and placed it squarely on the responsibility to work. The head of the federal government's Agrarian Department, Cástulo Villaseñor, liked it so much that he repeated it, with relish, five years later. Zapata, he revealed, "knew to see in work the primary condition that gives one right to the land. That, ladies and gentlemen, was the great lesson of good citizenship that Emiliano Zapata bequeathed us." [19]

A more extensive look at the Cuautla ceremony of April 10, 1950, demonstrates how such verbal claims were reinforced by ritual. This commemoration occurred in the middle of the Alemán presidency, which, as a result of its public works, deep corruption, nationalistic rhetoric, and promotion of industrial capitalism, is often considered the crowning expression of the Golden Age. We might thus consider it a classic statement of what Zapata meant to those who then ruled Mexico.

It is noteworthy, first of all, that Alemán was again present. Having initially attended the event in 1942 as Avila Camacho's representative, he appears to have decided that the symbolism of Zapata was an indispensable part of the legitimacy he sought to project. Backing him up were cabinet officials, members of the national congress, representatives of state governments, members of the National Peasant Confederation and the Zapatista Front, and generals drawn from each of the main revolutionary groups in hope of illustrating that factional dispute had truly been transcended.[20]

Decorations similar to those of 1924 beautified Cuautla and surrounding villages. Alemán arrived at about eleven in the morning and climbed into a convertible adorned with flowers and several of Cuautla's most attractive young women. Together they rode from the edge of town to the plaza, where a platform and podium were situated in front of Zapata's statue. This commemoration was, as they had all come to be, as full of words as it was of flowers. The president of the Zapatista Front, Adrián Castrejón, who had reputedly been at Chinameca thirty-one years before, praised Zapata as an incorruptible visionary. "We [veterans] feel our chests inundated with emotion when," he intoned, "we come to this site where a monument is raised to his [Zapata's] memory to recall him with affection and reverence." Castrejón assured Alemán of the Front's "unyielding" loyalty and asked him to keep up the good work. Roberto Barrios again said his piece, asserting that "the agrarian problem could be considered finished" and that the government's job now was to organize and improve existing ejidos.

Speaking for the ruling party (after 1946 called the Institutional Revolutionary Party, the PRI) was the federal deputy from Morelos, Norberto López Avelar. López Avelar's presence was an incitement because he had fought under Guajardo during the revolution and was charged by some Morelenses of participating in Zapata's assassination. Zapata's son Nicolás even believed he had delivered the coup de grâce, and another accuser insisted he had been one of the young Carrancista soldiers who had held up the head of Zapata's corpse for the camera. In 1958 López Avelar would prevail over those suspicions to become governor of Morelos. On this day he had merely to deliver his address, which he did, railing against conservatives and communists—Mexican leaders were intensely engaged in the cold war—and recommending that they come to Cuautla for a lesson in the revolution's home-grown ideology.[21]

There were nearly three hours of speeches in all. The event also included the usual floral offerings, and the president and other officials mounted a brief honor guard in front of Zapata's remains. At some point Alemán received Zapata's widow, Josefa Espejo. Eventually, a contingent of motorcyclists started the annual parade. Behind them filed thousands of peasants of the Zapatista Front, who—according to the mouthpiece of the organization, *El Campesino*—marched in perfect order, holding up thousands of pictures of Zapata as a demonstration of "discipline and respect toward their leader." Also marching were a women's contingent, athletes, schoolchildren, and a delegation of revolutionaries who had fought under Pancho Villa.

After the ceremony, Secretary of Government (Gobernación) Adolfo Ruiz Cortines, who would succeed Alemán as president in 1952, spoke to the press. Ruiz Cortines noted that Zapata was one of those who had contributed to the progress of the nation. He reinforced and clarified Barrios's message by announcing that Mexico's land had largely been distributed, but that the government was focusing on irrigation, roads, schools, and productivity planning to help peasants help themselves. Coming down hard on the need for irrigation, he added that if Zapata still lived, water would be his top priority.[22]

The speeches, then, emphasized progress and indicated that peasants would continue to receive material benefits from a revolution in which Zapata fit as both founding father and martyr. The speakers talked as if it were obvious that the revolutionary process was ongoing: much like a shark, a revolution must keep moving or cease to be a revolution, and these officials prodded it to motion, if only in their oratory, while social reforms waned. They also made sure their listeners knew that Alemán represented the continuation of the revolution in general and of Zapata's work in particular. The parade, meanwhile, demonstrated unity and orderliness. Motorcyclists and students, Villistas and Zapatistas were all part of the revolutionary family that gathered together to put on a harmonious show. Order—along with "discipline and respect"—had infused this celebration of revolution, which was a display of power, alliance, and the positions of diverse groups within the community that it brought together. The order displayed was now an *accomplishment* of the revolutionary state, not the aspiration it had been during the 1920s. The motorcycles, of course, symbolized technological progress, and the children stood for progress too—they were the ultimate product of the revolution, and its future. The athletes were representatives of "modern" sports also played in Europe and the United States and proof that the revolution had created a healthy, productive nation.[23]

The participation of a women's contingent was additional evidence of modernity. When women's groups marched in Zapata parades they assumed a collective, public position at odds with traditional notions about women's roles. The presence of Zapatista Colonel Rosa Bobadilla at the head of the women's contingent during the 1949 Cuautla procession surely reminded many observers of how revolutionary circumstances had permitted or forced women to break with some of those customary ideas.[24] But women had their contingents primarily because they, like other sectors of society, had organized and mobilized once the fighting was done. Conditions for such activities were especially good in the 1930s, when there was talk within the Cárdenas administration of giving women equal rights and integrating them into national life. It was in that climate that Ana María Zapata became head of the Union of Morelos Women, which ultimately gained a membership of perhaps eight thousand, while still in her teens. She achieved that position at such a young age largely out of tactical considerations, and the tactics were clear when she evoked her movement's "strong links to the Agrarian Revolution led by my father, Señor Don Emiliano Zapata" in asking the Morelos state legislature to give women the vote. She also used her name to press for government aid for the widows, daughters, and sisters of dead revolutionaries, and voiced her desire for a political career—if only a woman had the right to pursue one (women did not win the right to run for office or to vote at the national level until 1954). If she were a man, she pronounced, she "would carry [my] father's banner far."[25] Interestingly, Jenaro Amezcua, too, incorporated strong advocacy of women's rights into his Zapatismo.[26]

World War II and the subsequent rush to modernity further challenged conventional wisdom about where women belonged. As the Braceros traveled north to the United States, more jobs opened up for women outside the home. Mass media—in the form of comic books, radio, film, and, in the 1950s, television—brought advertisements for lipstick, high heels, and stylish dresses into more and more homes. Comic books and radio, in particular, fashioned the stereotypical *chica moderna* (modern girl) who used those advertised products, spoke her mind, and, until her marriage, made her own money and paid her way. The media also provided information about the unconventional private lives of such models of female modernity as painter Frida Kahlo, actress María Felix, and dancer Nellie Campobello.[27]

Thus, though feminist demands and societal changes encountered strong opposition from more conservative women who chose Catholicism over revolution—and from anticlerical politicians who feared women's votes would support the church—it became politically necessary and conventional to recognize women as part of the revolutionary order.[28] The Zapatista Front therefore included a secretary of "feminine action" from the beginning, and it tried, in its paternalistic way, to do more for women than just seeking pensions for widows of the revolution as Zapatista organizations had always done. In 1950, for instance, the Front gathered members of its Feminine Sector from all over Morelos. One man who spoke at this meeting noted Alemán had recently donated, presumably at the Front's urging, ten sewing machines to female family members of deceased Zapatistas, including Zapata's widow, Espejo. A second male agent of the Front then prodded those attending to get with the government's program, asserting that Mexicans needed to work—in this case, on their sewing machines—to increase productivity. To focus on that goal, he advised, it was best, "for the moment, to abandon politics."[29]

The sewing machines suggest that the role of women in the Mexico Zapata's image helped define was not one of equality. Official appeals to patriarchal values and the revolutionary family, discussed in Chapter 3, were efforts to put women back in their places after the fighting was done—or at least in a place where they could be controlled. Alemán's convertible ride with the young ladies of Cuautla and the paternalism of the Cuautla statue at which that convertible arrived are evidence that that goal had not changed by 1950. Zapata's machismo persisted as well. Though the macho aspects of Zapata's character were still not great favorites of the regime, his vigorous manliness proved impossible for some commentators to ignore. In a 1952 article for a historical journal on Zapata's family, vocero Mario Gill suggested that Zapata's legendary success with women was due not to "don Juanism, but to his plentiful virility." "What *rancherita* [little country woman]," he swooned, "could have resisted the elegant charro, always mounted on magnificent horses, surrounded by an aura of poetry and legend?" Letting his imagination and the generous interpretations of local informants carry him away, Gill then informed his readers that none of Zapata's women were offended by his infidelities and that he was equally considerate of them all. For Zapata, he concluded, "the cult of the woman was an extension of the love of his people, of the love of the land." Another authority informed those who attended the 1955 commemoration in Mexico City that Zapata was "made of the incorruptible metal with which are forged the masculine virtues of the legitimate Mexican."[30] The place of women in Mexican society was gradually changing, and both the change and its halting, constrained nature can be observed in the story of Zapata's posthumous career. The women's contingent was indeed a case of women claiming Zapata, but they seem mostly to have been struck dumb on the subject by its patriarchal and macho nature. Though women had made invaluable contributions to the revolution, as pacíficos and sexual targets they were also among the conflict's major victims. For them, finding uses for memories of Zapata would not come easily.

What the 1950 commemoration at Cuautla demonstrated, in sum, was that Zapata was steadily becoming removed from anything he did or said. In part this was done consciously by politicians like Ruiz Cortines who prefaced policy offerings with claims about what Zapata would want if he were alive and thus sought to mediate between Zapata and changed circumstances by incarnating the continuity of his program. In part, though, this effect can simply be attributed to the passage of time. Writing on the occasion of the 1949 commemoration, Teodoro Hernández looked back nostalgically, not to memories of Zapata, which he did not have, but to the commemoration of 1928, where he heard the village bands play, watched the veterans, and witnessed the "deep devotion" of peasant women mentioned in Chapter 3.[31] The celebration of 1950 was, then, at least as much a commemoration of postrevolutionary civic culture and the institutionalization that it reflected—of past Zapata rituals, which had become history—as it was of Zapata's death and life. Reflecting this ongoing routinization of Zapata were new honors: in 1954 Congress declared April 10 a national day of mourning, and in 1959 Zapata's portrait was placed next to that of Cuauhtémoc in the art gallery of the National Palace.[32]

The messages generated at commemorative ceremonies were reinforced and broadcast by textbooks. A 1954 publication of the Ministry of Public Education on the Mexican Revolution came down especially hard, in Zapata's name, on the nationalism that underpinned the new unity of the post-Cárdenas era. A "typical national figure," Zapata had struggled to save the peasants from having to "leave national territory to cultivate other fields in foreign lands." If this was true he had clearly failed, for the Bracero Program continued until 1964.[33]

J. Jesús Cárabes Pedroza's, *Mi libro de tercer año: Historia y civismo* (My Third Year Book: History and Civics, 1966), was part of a program, started in 1959, in which the Ministry of Public Education took further charge of what primary school students read by producing its own textbooks. These it distributed, at no cost, to public and private schools all over Mexico. Cárabes streamlined the revolution in such a way that one revolutionary never confused issues by fighting another. Madero first rose against Díaz, and was then deposed and killed by the treacherous and reactionary Huerta. Carranza took over the leadership of the revolution and produced the constitution. Cárabes then discussed the rights the constitution provided to workers, which was followed by the appearance of Zapata, who embodied the peasants and their revolutionary gains. The section on Zapata began by declaring, "No doubt you have heard the name of Emiliano Zapata. Some street or school in your town is surely named after him." This, in 1966, was a safe bet. Zapata, it continued, fought "tirelessly" to return lands stolen by haciendas to the peasants, but the author did not indicate when he fought or against whom. Zapata was thus extracted from the revolutionary warfare because there was no way to include him in it without undermining the revolutionary family's stability in third-grade minds. Cárabes added that the government had done justice to peasant demands, "giving campesinos land and the means to cultivate it" and undertaking irrigation works to bring water to that land. The theme of progress was reinforced when one turned to the next section, which was entitled "The Progress of Mexico" and crowned with a picture of the man then occupying the presidency, Gustavo Díaz Ordaz (1964–1970).[34]

For the sixth-grade audience some of the rivalries of revolutionary siblings were exposed, and the case for Zapata's connection to progress was made more directly. Eduardo Blanquel's *Mi libro de sexto año: Historia y civismo* (1966) affirmed that Madero stood for political change, but that others—among them Zapata, Villa, Obregón, and even Carranza—wanted social revolution. Once Huerta was removed from the scene "there were differences and even battles among the principle revolutionary leaders," who did not agree about how best to achieve social change. They were, nevertheless, "all heroes," because together they made Mexico more just and improved conditions for development.[35]

Again, though, old themes did not disappear as new ones emerged. A compendium of materials meant to help teachers prepare for commemorations, for instance, included a poem that reminded them of Zapata's Indian aspect. "The silenced Indian, the sleeping Indian," this poem asserted, "woke to the cry of 'Revolution,'" and Zapata was the "man of the race of the exploited / of the pariah race" who liberated them.[36] In a 1954 compilation for primary school students, a poem by José Muñoz Cota pursued similar ends. "The Indians, the Indian children," the author wrote, "those who grow up aching / to devote their lives to the field, / see him [Zapata] pass with love."[37]

Various Zapatistas also made written contributions—in ways generally amenable to the regime—to the image of Zapata during this era. One accomplishment was the completion of Gildardo Magaña's multivolume work, which the Zapatista Front entrusted to Carlos Pérez Guerrero, who had collaborated with Magaña from the beginning. With support from the Ministry of Public Education, where he was employed, Pérez Guerrero published volume 3 in 1946—Parrés made sure Avila Camacho received the first copy that rolled off the press.[38] Six years later all five volumes were published together at the Alemán administration's expense, the final two seeing print for the first time. The Zapatista Front oversaw the work's free distribution to revolutionary groups and government officials around the country and, since there were not enough copies for everyone requesting it, made plans to publish it serially in *El Campesino*.[39]

Pérez Guerrero largely adopted the narrative strategies Magaña had developed, though he lacked even Magaña's limited organizational skills. He cast his net broadly; he put noble words in Zapata's mouth; and he made an immense effort to unite the revolutionary family. Apparently in response to critics, he reiterated the argument, developed in volume 2, that Madero's behavior toward Zapata was not the product of bad faith. He even found something positive about Carranza and Pablo González, allowing that Carranza had "great virtues" and that even González's victories against Huerta were victories of the revolution. Still, it was Carranza's fault, not Zapata's, that revolutionary unity was not achieved in 1914.[40] Zapata, after all, had no "ambitions of command and power" and had always wanted such unity. Zapata was, of course, still the leading spokesman for land reform, and his influence on Villa was critical in this respect since Villa was not precise in his thinking on the issue.[41] Finally, and right in step with mid-century priorities, Pérez Guerrero's Zapata was a nationalist. When he learned of the U.S. invasion of Veracruz, Zapata had said, "I felt like my blood was boiling."[42]

Another source of Zapata lore was the work of Serafín M. Robles, one of Zapata's former secretaries and a dedicated member of the Zapatista Front, who cranked out numerous articles for *El Campesino*. His contribution, as he described it to Alemán when he sent him a sample, was to write on Zapata's efforts "in defense of the peasants, relating anecdotes and traits of the Southern Caudillo."[43] Among his topics were Zapata's prerevolutionary life, his magnificence as a charro, his incorruptibility, and his rejection of communism.[44] He also recognized the appeal of accounts of Zapata's death, which he published both in April 1950 and in April 1953. In the 1950 piece Robles captured some of the flavor of popular messianism in reliving for his readers "the most horrendous assassination of our days"—expressing revulsion over Zapata's death continued to be a tactic used by his promoters to seize the moral high ground. Zapata, Robles noted, was the "humble son of Anenecuilco," as was Jesus Christ of Galilee, and like Jesus he did not flee death, though he might have done so given the "great cunning and distrust he demonstrated in eight years of armed struggle, in which his enemies could never capture him, alive or dead." And so, though he had a presentiment of danger on that day at Chinameca, he chose to die and fructify the fields of Morelos, and the entire nation, with his blood, thus realizing his destiny.[45] The 1953 account repeated much of what Robles had written three years earlier, though some of Zapata's quotations underwent changes. Most striking here was Robles's take on Zapata's final thoughts. "I'm not sorry about dying," Zapata said, "because I have already fulfilled my duty. I'm sorry for the villages and my soldiers. I pay with my life for having incited them to rebellion, but they, how will they be treated after my death by the governments that are established?"[46] It was a crucial shift of perspective from List Arzubide's account in which Zapata's ultimate advice to his followers was that they stand up for themselves; it was also perfectly in accord with the Zapatista Front's tendency to pin its hopes on official largesse.

Yet another noteworthy contribution was a book by Díaz Soto y Gama, who in the 1950s was making a comeback. At least by mid-decade, Díaz Soto y Gama had returned to the Zapatista fold by joining the Zapatista Front.[47] He was also featured in the SEP publication, *The Mexican Revolution*, as a "great friend of Zapata," and someone whose life "came to interpenetrate to such a degree with that of Zapata, that he is one of the few who can really say he knew Zapata's life thoroughly." To interest its young readers, this book recorded Díaz Soto y Gama's take on the story of the child Zapata pledging to retrieve stolen lands. In this telling, he subtly switched the focus to the Zapata family's use of the lands rather than their collective, village ownership, though he cited the same informants as had Germán List Arzubide and thus almost certainly got his information from the same book by Julio Cuadros Caldas. Milking the theme of individual initiative, he noted that at age fifteen, Zapata rented a small parcel from a nearby hacienda, on which he worked with "an indescribable perseverance" to grow melons for the market.[48] The general message was, of course, likely to please the current regime, which may explain why Díaz Soto y Gama was forgiven for his indiscretions with Almazán. As a measure of that forgiveness, in 1958 the Senate presented him with the Belisario Domínguez Medal of Honor. Since Domínguez was the senator from Chiapas who paid with his life for speaking out against Huerta's 1913 coup, the medal was surely meant to recognize its recipient's relentless willingness to speak his mind, and he must have felt vindicated. At the ceremony at which it was presented, members of the audience yelled "Viva Zapata" as Díaz Soto y Gama walked to the stage, and one journalist remarked that "he was not ashamed of having been and continuing to be a Zapatista."[49]

Díaz Soto y Gama's book, *La revolución del sur y Emiliano Zapata, su caudillo* (The Revolution of the South and Emiliano Zapata, Its Caudillo, 1960), was largely a compilation of newspaper articles he had written over the previous three decades. Readers might have expected great things given the author's unparalleled acclaim as Zapata's confidant, but the book offered little new information based on personal contact with the hero. In fact, it relied, sometimes strangely, on written sources. Magaña was the main authority on Zapata's relations with the Madero and Huerta regimes; agronomist Marte Gómez supplied the information on the land reform of 1915; and Salvador Reyes Avilés did the same for Zapata's death.[50] Díaz Soto y Gama even relied extensively on Paz Solórzano. At one point he presented as an eyewitness account—though without naming his source—Paz's version of events that Paz could not have been in Morelos to see.[51] Part of the explanation may be that Díaz Soto y Gama turned eighty the year the book was published; at one point he confides that a story by Serafín Robles, to whom he also resorted often, was more reliable than his own memory.[52] Still, we get the author's by now expected take on a number of issues: Zapata was an individualistic ranchero, not a communist; he was a Christian; and he made decisions without the counsel of his secretaries, who merely gave them form.[53] Little here is surprising except the discussion, franker than most, of the violence in which Zapatista forces engaged. This the author finds unsurprising since they were participating, after all, in a social revolution.[54] Instead of new insights, then, the book was a compendium of stories previously told by Díaz Soto y Gama and others; it was the word on Zapata, accumulated over decades, as related by his urban advisors.

Still, it did provoke some reactions. Politicians and journalists seized on one quotation in particular that Díaz Soto y Gama attributed to Zapata: "they pursue me for my only crime," he had Zapata say as Constitutionalists drove him from Tlaltizapán in 1916, "which is to want those who are hungry to be able to eat." Díaz Soto y Gama had published this line at least by 1938, but the book revived it, and it was repeated publicly several times in the coming years.[55] Chronicler Alfonso Taracena, meanwhile, called Díaz Soto y Gama's work a whitewash and argued with him over its negative depiction of Madero and whether Zapata dallied over Huerta's offers of alliance before deciding to fight him.[56]

Finally, essayists seeking to explore *lo mexicano*—what it meant to be Mexican—in the wake of the revolution began to incorporate Zapata, demonstrating that his rapid journey to the center of national identity was complete. By far the most influential of these works was poet Octavio Paz's *The Labyrinth of Solitude,* first published in 1950. Influenced by his father,

Octavio Paz Solórzano, and by Díaz Soto y Gama, who became his professor and friend, Paz identified Zapata as the revolution's truest expression.[57] Zapata appealed to Mexicans, he suggested, because he had "the plastic beauty and poetry of our popular images," and because Mexicans valued fortitude in the face of long odds more than they did victory. In addition, Paz indicated that death was critical to Mexican self-identity—"tell me how you die," he wrote, "and I will tell you who you are"—and that Zapata had died correctly, "as he had lived: embracing the earth. His image, like the earth, is made up of patience and fecundity, silence and hope, death and resurrection." For Paz, Zapata's achievement was nothing less than making a modern Mexico, a redefinition of Mexico, possible by taking Mexicans back to their Indian roots, where they could begin to find themselves. In leading them to those fundamentals, Zapata could help restore a sense of collective identity, thus breaking down the solitude Paz found at the heart of Mexican life.[58] The argument for community suited the state, as did the notion of Zapata as a modern Indian—or at least an Indian key to modernity—who might therefore somehow help modernize Indians as a group.

Zapata was not only of interest to those who relied on words to express their admiration. His mounting status in urban culture was evident in 1953, when choreographer Guillermo Arriaga introduced him to the world of dance—first in a performance in Bucharest, Romania, and then at Mexico City's Palace of Fine Arts. Arriaga himself took the part of Zapata, while the female lead represented the land. In the "mythological cycle" that this dance revealed, writes one authority, Zapata was born of the land, and "the chained land armed Zapata's chest with the cross of cartridge belts." An "energetic, virile, impetuous, emotional dance" ensued, in which "the entire body of the ballerina" expressed the anguished clamor for Land and Liberty.[59]

Members of a Mexico City printmaking group called the Taller de Gráfica Popular (Popular Graphics Workshop) also made generous use of Zapata's image. Placing themselves within a printmaking tradition that went back at least to José Guadalupe Posada, they sought to produce work, much like the muralists', that was public and popular and would convey their leftist political and social concerns. They naturally turned to Zapata as a central motif. Mariana Yampolsky, better known as a photographer, did an engraving that presented him in his youth, gaining his revolutionary resolve. Looking warily out from a hiding place, he watched as a foreman whipped peasants while they dug and other campesinos trudged past, carrying immense burdens. A hacienda building and a collection of boxlike homes for the peasants stood in the background. Other images followed Rivera's mural at Chapingo in making Zapata embody the earth. One of the Taller's founders, Angel Bracho, made him a mountain overlooking protesters in one print, and Jesús Alvarez Amaya showed him actually holding the earth at the end of a furrowed field. Salvador Romero illustrated a plot of corn that transformed itself into Zapata's dead—or sleeping—body. Another convention was to depict him on horseback, often among his troops: Erasto Cortés Juárez represented him, in engaging folk-art style, posing calmly on his horse at the center of his cultural universe, a hut, corn, the earth, and three spades arranged around him (see Figure 5.1). He also appeared as a warrior. Arturo García Bustos, a student of both Rivera and his wife, Frida Kahlo, portrayed him holding up a gun in one hand and equipped, again, with those crisscrossing bandoliers that were by then well-established elements of his iconography. Looking and pointing straight at the viewer, García Bustos's Zapata asked the question—which was printed beside him— "You, what have you done to defend the conquests for which we gave our lives?" Taller members rendered similar resolute gazes in a number of busts, Zapata's head usually beneath a large sombrero suggestive of a halo. In doing so, they helped make him into the conscience of the revolution he was becoming. Finally, there were the inevitable depictions of Zapata's death. Gabriel Fernández Ledesma, for instance, designed a death scene in which the grim reaper came to collect Zapata's body from a sheet on the ground where it lay, a mound of corn before it, mourners and cornstalks behind. In the background his troops apparently prepared to continue the struggle. Zapata was essential to these artists who thought of themselves as revolutionaries, so they turned to him frequently. But despite their convictions, they really delivered only a still more sanctified Zapata, not one who stood in clear opposition to the growing conservatism of the miracle years.[60]

In this time of conscious modernization, new media became increasingly important in fostering Zapata's image. Growing numbers of people had access to the radio and could therefore tune in, for example, on April 9, 1950, when the government's station, XEDP, dedicated its *National Hour*— broadcast by all radio stations in the country—to Zapata's memory."[61] Since the 1940s were the golden age of Mexican cinema, it is hardly surprising that there was also talk of making a film of Zapata's life. A Quirico Michelena y Llaguna wrote Avila Camacho in 1943 to pitch the idea of bringing Zapata to the screen, promising to reconcile his work "as much as possible with the historical truth." He already had the support of the Zapatista Front and, he claimed, Mexico City's Spanish colony, of which he was perhaps a member, but he clearly felt the need for presidential backing—probably of the monetary variety—as well.[62]

FIGURE 5.1
Zapata on Horseback. *Print by Erasto Cortés Juárez,*
18.5 × 13 inches. Courtesy of Jaime Erasto Cortés.

Maybe because that backing did not materialize, Michelena's movie was
not made, but in 1950 the Front had another cinematic project in mind,
entitled *Emiliano Zapata and the Mexican Revolution.* The screenplay was
written by Porfirio Palacios, a congressional deputy from Morelos and the
Front's secretary general, whose father had died with Zapata at Chinameca. Thinking big, the Front intended to do both Spanish and English

versions and seek broad distribution in the United States. The director, the Zapatistas imagined, would be the illustrious Emilio "El Indio" Fernández, and the Spanish version would star three of Mexico's most famous actors, Pedro Armendáriz, María Félix, and Dolores del Rio. Vivien Leigh or Jennifer Jones, they thought, would suffice for the English rendition, but they had not yet identified the ideal gringo Zapata. Consideration of Leigh perhaps reflected dreams that this movie would have an appeal comparable to the American blockbuster *Gone with the Wind* (1939), in which she had starred. The Zapatistas hoped for government support to get the movie made; proceeds were slated for charitable works in Morelos.[63] The Alemán administration did explore the possibilities, but the report was not promising. No company in Mexico wanted to touch such a project due to the "riskiness of the theme, since the Zapatistas want them to make the film an elegy to Zapata and his work." There were doubts, too, about the Front's ability to get U.S. distributors to meet its expectations. Finally, two already copyrighted screenplays on Zapata presented obstacles—one of them was by Mauricio Magdaleno and presumably similar to his 1932 play.[64] For these reasons, this initiative went no farther than the first.

Though the Zapatista Front was sometimes annoying, the regime could nearly always count on its backing, and occasionally it acted directly as an agent of social control. One good example concerns the electoral challenge posed by General Miguel Henríquez Guzmán against PRI candidate Ruiz Cortines in 1952. Already on April 10, 1951, at Cuautla, Palacios looked ahead to the election in calling for campesino unity and discipline under the tutelage of the National Peasant Confederation and the Front. In answer to the Henríquez campaign's occasional evocations of Zapata, he also made sure his listeners knew which side Zapata was on: they should all follow Zapata's example, he advised, which was "the best guide," and thus avoid the division some sought to sow in the coming elections. The PRI, he added, in case there were doubts, "represents the postulates of the Revolution."[65] The following May *El Campesino* avowed, with regard to some vaguely described unrest in Oaxaca, "that the authentic person of the field who fought for the ideals of Zapata does not participate in uprisings and knows enough to be on the side of the constituted authorities." Agitators, in fact, were "bad Mexicans" and thus in danger of falling out of the national community.[66] One such agitator, as it turned out, was the perennially frustrated Amezcua, who was arrested in Puebla for activities on behalf of the opposition. His former comrades did not stand up for him. Rather, *El Campesino* served notice that Amezcua had never been a member of the

Front, "because those who belong in the files of the Zapatista Front are conscious of their responsibilities and duties as soldiers of the Revolution." [67]

There were, in its defense, a few occasions on which the Zapatista Front, or at least some of its members, did adopt independent positions. Though the Front never stopped praising Alemán's ostensible agrarianism in general terms, it did not support his reform—which was among his first initiatives—of Article 27 of the Constitution. To do so would have been difficult, since Alemán's changes protected larger holdings on lands producing valuable goods for the market and gave landowners a new legal tool to defend their properties against expropriation.[68] Another rare example was a rather more dramatic one: the involvement of one of the Front's leaders, José María Suárez Téllez, in Guerreran state politics during the early 1960s. After a long career that included stints in the Communist Party and as a PRI functionary, in 1960 Suárez Téllez brought the Zapatista Front of Guerrero into a coalition of popular groups opposing the corruption and brutality of Guerrero's governor. Backed by these grassroots organizations, which included some Zapatista veterans, in 1962 he campaigned to become governor himself against the PRI candidate. He was instead awarded an extended stay in jail. Out of this initiative emerged the Liga Agraria del Sur Emiliano Zapata (Emiliano Zapata Agrarian League of the South), in conjunction with talk of class warfare against the bourgeoisie that revealed the influence of the Cuban Revolution of 1959.[69] Suárez Téllez thus served as a link between the conservative Zapatista Front and a new, more radical Zapatista organization and, ultimately, to a man named Genaro Vázquez Rojas. As we will see in Chapter 7, Vázquez Rojas would continue to shake up Guerreran, and national, politics for some time.

Still, to find much criticism of the way in which the state used Zapata we need to look elsewhere than the Zapatista Front. Some observers continued to reject the cult of Zapata altogether. Rubén Salido Orcillo, who taught history, simply seemed offended by what he deemed to be exaggeration when he complained in 1960 that one day soon someone would insist that "the only hero worthy of being remembered is Zapata, and that the study of our nation's history should be divided into two parts: before Emiliano and after Emiliano." It was the same sarcastic tone adopted by Francisco Bulnes when he criticized the emerging cult back in 1921. In another article, Salido Orcillo reported that one of his brightest students had recently done research on Zapata and learned that he was a "distinguished intellectual, one of the great minds of the Revolution . . . an assiduous reader of Voltaire, trained in the school of Jean Jacques Rousseau, and familiar with the ideas of Montesquieu." When Salido expressed concerns about whether the child had sources on which to base those conclusions, the answer was immediately forthcoming: the information came from a talk recently given in Stockholm by Mexico's ambassador to Sweden.[70]

Most who spoke out publicly against Zapata, though, were motivated not by historical standards but by their personal histories. Despite all the talk of revolutionary unity, aging Constitutionalists were no better than aging Zapatistas at forgetting the factional lines that had divided them during the revolutionary conflict. The memories would persist as long as these veterans lived, and forgiveness was sometimes hard to come by. Alvaro D. Bórquez Alméndrez, a Constitutionalist who had fought the Zapatistas under the command of Pablo González, was aghast at the tendency to compare Zapata to independence hero Morelos and wondered whether everyone had simply forgotten that the Zapatistas blew up trains and tortured and assassinated their enemies. Others sought to defend Guajardo, insisting on the original Constitutionalist position that it was he who was outnumbered at Chinameca, not Zapata, and that the engagement was not, therefore, a criminal ambush.[71]

But memories were slowly dying with the vessels that carried them, a case in point being Pablo González, who passed from the scene on March 4, 1950. In the wake of his death, Alemán helped González rankle the Zapatistas one last time by ordering that he receive the honors traditionally accorded a general of division, including having his body covered by the flag; González's wife, moreover, was awarded a pension of a thousand pesos a month. Porfirio Palacios responded with a rambling letter to the Mexico City dailies and a speech in the Chamber of Deputies. From the Front's point of view this was another slap at Zapata, and Palacios asked how it was possible, on a day on which he had been absent, that not a single congressional representative spoke out against the pension. It was, he said, larger than any pension ever provided to a descendant of Hidalgo and more than ten times as much as was received by a widow of one of Zapata's jefes.[72]

While González could never have hoped to cast off his anti-Zapatista past even if he had wanted to, others allowed themselves to be swayed by the prevailing political culture despite what they might have remembered. Some were perhaps worn down by the dull beat of pro-Zapata arguments, others may simply have been able to let bygones be bygones, and many surely recognized that political advancement might depend on signing up with the friends of Zapata. Carrancista José Mancisidor repented that when young, he had fought for individual men instead of ideals and thus wound up in Morelos waging war against the Zapatistas. He recalled, though, that after observing the struggle, he was troubled by the excessive Carrancista brutality, and ultimately concluded that, "in the humble peasants who were fighting daily for the land with the desperation with which I saw them fight was found the real, permanent, and profound meaning of the Mexican Revolution."[73] By contrast, when Antonio I. Villarreal spoke for revolutionary veterans at a commemoration in 1941, he glossed over his own conversion experience. Making the case, based on historical documentation, that both Carranza and Villa had been "in full accord" with the Plan of Ayala, he seemed to forget how miserably he had failed to communicate Carranza's supposed appreciation of that document at a crucial moment in 1914 when, with a chance to avoid a new round of warfare on the line, he visited Zapata as Carranza's emissary. Presumably he hoped others would forget as well.[74] However the conversion really occurred for Mancisidor and Villarreal, we can rule out moral considerations as a motive for the pro-Zapata expressions of Senator Ruffo Figueroa of Guerrero. When campaigning for his place in the Senate, Figueroa, nephew of two prominent Guerreran revolutionaries who had clashed with Zapata when he was alive, found it useful to praise Zapata and his followers. Once the position was his, however, he returned to the family tradition, indicating that "Zapata was a remarkably bloodthirsty individual."[75]

Opposition parties also tried to adapt Zapata to their purposes. Under the increasingly conservative conditions of the era, Mexican communists sought to hold on to the Zapata they had developed more or less in accord with the Cárdenas regime. A velada held at Mexico City's Hidalgo Theater in April 1942 honored not just Zapata but also an international cast of communist leaders: Brazilian Carlos Prestes, Earl Browder of the United States, and Mexico's own José Díaz, a labor organizer from Jalisco.[76] Rafael Ramos Pedrueza stood at this celebration to describe a dinner he allegedly had with Zapata in 1911 in a cafe in front of Mexico City's old Principal Theater. Zapata, as he described him, was a charro, and "the most Mexican of the revolutionaries and the most revolutionary of the Mexicans"— communists, too, felt the pull of nationalism during the war. As Zapata spoke respectfully about land reform, continued Ramos Pedrueza, he suddenly "became multiple." It was not Zapata but rather all Mexican heroes that sat with Ramos, "all of the dispossessed mestizos, our rural mass torn up by the Porfirian regime." Zapata was a "brother" in arms of the caudillo Morelos, but the authorities had called him an Attila and a bandit, the sort of labels, Ramos Pedrueza noted, now directed at the communists. Cárdenas, he added to huge applause, had been "faithful and obedient to the will of Emiliano Zapata."[77] Some years later Miguel Mendoza López

Schwerdtfeger, one of Zapata's intellectual brood, ran for president on the Communist Party ticket, noting that his status as a Zapatista proved he had always been with the people.[78]

Parties from the other end of the spectrum—even those that generally rejected the revolutionary tradition—sometimes sought to use Zapata as well. In 1951, Carlos Pérez Guerrero founded a group he called the Confederation of Precursors and Veterans of the Liberating Army of the South (Confederación de Precursores y Veteranos del Ejército Liberator del Sur). The Zapatista Front responded by charging him with trying to divide them and indicated that some members of the new group belonged to the conservative Partido de Acción Nacional (National Action Party, PAN) the Almazán campaign had helped generate. In that context, the Front accused, they were exploiting "the memory of the righteous and upright man that was our jefe."[79]

The harshest and most direct critique of the official Zapata came from Morelos. Though by the 1940s the political force of Zapatismo was on the decline in the state as Zapatista veterans disappeared from the scene, some oppositional sentiment did live on.[80] Undoubtedly, there were some Morelenses who continued to receive government messages about Zapata precisely as officials wanted them received: in a way that would give them warm feelings of inclusion in a national community and a modernizing experience that Zapata embodied. Thousands of people were, after all, involved in such events as the April 10 parades through Cuautla's historic streets, and many were surely swept up in the patriotism. But if officials seemed intent on overwhelming the locals with words and flowers until remembering Zapata became an exercise in mindless patriotism—or at least a numbing routine—their strategy was not entirely successful. There was grumbling in Morelos that demonstrates that not everyone was numb and that for many the patriotism wore off soon after the parade was over.

The dissatisfaction was partly related to the shortcomings of the land reform process, and this was true most famously in Anenecuilco. Sotelo Inclán complained at some length in his book about the plight of this village, and at the 1946 commemoration a Zapatista Front speaker made remarks that amounted to a petition from Anenecuilco to Avila Camacho to resolve its land problem. Competition for land in the area was so intense that in the following year Cuautla police murdered the most outspoken proponent of Anenecuilco's claims, Zapata's confidant Francisco Franco.[81] In 1949 Alemán addressed the issue, again on the April 10 stage that Zapata provided, promising to compensate Anenecuilco for land that confusion in the 1930s had put in the hands of neighboring Villa de Ayala. But that compensation was not forthcoming, and the head of Anenecuilco's ejido, Joaquín Quintero, and his supporters got in touch with Alemán in 1952. Reminding the president of his promise, this group complained that Cárdenas had caused the problem, which was inappropriate given that their village was "the cradle of the Agrarian Revolution." "We're irritated by waiting and waiting," the document continued and, after threatening to settle things themselves with Villa de Ayala, asked that Alemán not send troops to stop them.[82] Despite the benefits of Zapata's example, this was not a problem that was easily solved: later in the same year another faction in the village—called the cradle, this time, "of the caudillo Emiliano Zapata"—complained of the abuses committed by Quintero's group, which, according to the second group, was working against the interests of the ejidatarios.[83] These disputes over land around Anenecuilco were ongoing, and people involved in them often used Zapata to reinforce their claims while implicitly questioning whether an inattentive government had earned the right to do the same.

Members of Zapata's family raised more personal concerns with national leaders in Zapata's name. Daughter Ana María asked Alemán at both the 1949 and 1950 commemorations to increase her government pension. As with Anenecuilco's demands, Alemán apparently sounded generous on April 10, but in 1952 Ana María was still waiting for her money.[84] Asserting that she and her mother had been completely forgotten despite her father's defense of "Land and Liberty," she added in 1952 that she would like a plot of land and a car she could rent out to make money.[85] It appears that she was mollified with political position instead. In 1953 she was appointed the substitute secretary of the Feminine Action section of the National Peasant Confederation, and—women having finally won political rights—in 1958 she became the first female congressional deputy from Morelos. Though he had himself managed to bargain his way into some power, her half-brother Nicolás accused her of having agreed to support their father's reputed assassin, López Avelar, for governor in return for the latter post.[86]

Many other Zapata relatives complained of being shortchanged and impoverished. Sons Mateo and Diego received some educational aid, and in 1942 Governor Elpidio Perdomo asked the federal government to send them to the National Agricultural School at Chapingo, where Diego Rivera had painted their father's image, to be trained as agronomists. Again promises were made, but at least for Mateo they were not fulfilled. Left with few resources, he ran as a candidate of the PAN for state deputy from Cuautla in 1950, using his name "demagogically," in the estimation of one observer, "to attack the Revolution." In the next election Mateo was convinced to run as a PRI candidate so the ruling party could demonstrate its ownership of Zapata, but the PRI did not see the arrangement through to victory for Mateo. Perennially discontented, Mateo came to believe that, "some day we'll resume the fight, and when that moment arrives I will demonstrate that I am, besides being a Zapata, a Zapatista."[87] At about the same time, a grand-niece of Zapata's expressed a similar sentiment. "If Emiliano were alive," she avowed, "he would rise up in arms again."[88] In 1952 Mario Gill added his slightly ominous perception that the myth Zapata had not died had previously been waning, but that lately, given conditions in the countryside, it had started to find new devotees.[89]

A look at the state newspapers is also instructive. If the attention paid by national politicians toward Zapata, Zapatistas, and Morelos had initially been flattering, much of that wore off as the Golden Age wore on. A 1950 editorial in the Cuernavaca paper *El Informador* looked toward April 10 with something less than enthusiasm, noting that "the pseudo-Zapatistas, sycophantic beings who have accumulated large fortunes in the shadow of the caudillo of the south," would, as always, be present, and that these politicians were responsible for the lasting exploitation of the peasantry.[90] In another Cuernavaca paper at the end of that decade, the postcommemoration headline read: "Again They Assassinate E. Zapata." Beneath that charge was a cartoon image of Zapata held upside down, a giant hand holding a knife in a stabbing position above the body. Around the hand and knife, in tiny letters, were the words "bankers," "false revolutionaries," and "demagoguery." An article on page 2 explained that even as they uttered their "elegant phrases" about Zapata, corrupt functionaries were busily plundering peasant land in Morelos. "This is how," it asserted, "Zapata is assassinated every time a false revolutionary breathes." Mourning their lost lands, another article claimed, the campesinos "prayed quietly on the 10th," finally convinced that Zapata had died, since that was the only way to explain what was happening.[91] Then there was the editorialist for *El Eco del Sur* in 1966, who asserted that ten paces from the house in which Zapata was born, people lived in the same conditions that had surrounded him at birth. "Who are these people," he continued, "that live amid trash, crap, parasites, misery, promiscuity, hunger, and mud? They are those who descend in a direct line from Emiliano Zapata." They were also, this author believed, almost angry enough to start another revolution.[92]

Taking a different approach was a *Presente* editorial of 1962, which charged that though Zapata was remembered everywhere, "no ceremony has had an authentic Zapatista character." The Zapatista survivors who showed up at commemorations were few, and they "looked like intruders, because of the way they dragged misery, age and sadness behind them." Also critical of the superlatives hurled at Zapata by politicians, the author of this piece remarked that many of the "revolutionaries of this epoch arrived [at Cuautla] in brand-new Cadillacs, Buicks, Chevrolets, and Mercedes Benzes." Then the real attack began, and there was no hesitancy about identifying culprits. "Roberto Guzmán Araujo," the article went on,

> lost control of his oratorical frenzy while heaping praise on his dear friend, the agrarian representative, who is a sworn enemy of the campesinos, and it appeared that the equestrian statue of the caudillo moved. If he [Zapata] still lived, he would be accused of social dissolution.[93]

Another way in which journalists criticized commemorations was to complain about the mistreatment of the children and campesinos drafted to participate in them. In 1966, the Cuautla paper *Polígrafo* indicated that there were to be two changes in ceremonial practice. Recently the parade had come first, with the result that members of the official retinue, installed at a platform in front of the statue, were forced to turn their backs on that monument to watch the contingents file past. Then the students and ejidatarios who had marched in the parade—and who could not politely escape—had to remain standing "beneath the sun for as long as the demagogic speeches of the politicians lasted... until disbanding at the end of the program." The new arrangements would put the speeches first, which meant only those interested in the blather of men who knew nothing about the revolution had to be present. The officials would then switch to a second table, in front of the church, to observe the parade.[94] Despite the talk of changes, *Polígrafo* offered a similar set of complaints the following year. As always, children and peasants had risen early only to be kept waiting in the sun because the program began later than planned. When the politicians at last arrived, they were accorded space in the shade from which to speak. "An insipid march," the article added, "followed the demagogic act in which there were only three orators, but each of them tried to break the record for length of speech." Later there was a big spread—at taxpayer expense—for the governor and his friends, which produced "many drunks... due to sorrow over the death of Zapata."[95] The acute anger behind such comments was not, of course, directed at Zapata, but there was little evidence in the local press of efforts to resist his appropriation by official Mexico by offering an alternative interpretation of what he stood for. Instead, it sounded as if Zapata were an ordeal imposed on Morelenses during these occasions.

One person who did offer such an alternative was Rubén Jaramillo, the most prominent agrarian leader in Morelos since Zapata. Jaramillo was an ex-Zapatista who had left the movement in 1918, before the fighting was over. He did so motivated by the same disillusionment others were experiencing at the time, but later he seems to have given an account of the speech he supposedly delivered on disbanding his troops—a speech that demonstrated that he still held Zapata in high esteem, and blameless for the misbehavior of his followers.[96] In the late 1930s, he became active in promoting peasant interests to the administrators of the state-owned sugar mill at Zacatepec, which was opened at Cárdenas's instigation in 1938 and named, of course, after Zapata. Because of his organizational efforts, Jaramillo was stripped of his claim to ejidal lands in 1940. In 1942 he led a strike over control of the mill and the problem of credit. In 1943 he took up arms for the first time, under his Plan of Cerro Prieto, which was based in part on the Plan of Ayala, though also motivated by military conscription instituted during the war. He accepted amnesty the following year. In 1946 he ran for governor of Morelos as a candidate of the Agrarian Labor Party of Morelos, and also opposed Alemán's candidacy for president. Six years later he ran for the same office while supporting the opposition presidential campaign of General Henríquez Guzmán. He was subsequently driven again into rebellion, which lasted until 1958, when he accepted amnesty from the government of President Adolfo López Mateos (1958–1964). In 1961 he led a land invasion and spoke out publicly against the choice of López Avelar as governor of Morelos. His case was resolved, in 1962, just like that of Francisco Franco, when he was killed, along with family members, by government thugs.[97]

Given his background and activities, it is not surprising that some Morelenses associated Jaramillo with Zapata, and that some Zapatistas joined his struggle. An unidentified informant explained that when Jaramillo was fighting, the government could not catch him because "the people protected him and he was very intelligent, like Zapata. When someone sent Zapata some kind of invitation he did not go, but sent someone else instead."[98] Another comparison had to do with Zapata's incorruptibility. According to a second witness, López Avelar offered Jaramillo a sizable sum of money, a house, and a car in exchange for giving up his fight. Jaramillo responded that he came from a poor background and then added, "my father was a revolutionary with Don Emiliano, and I was a little young, but I was also in the Revolution with my father." Jaramillo then concluded that he might be willing to accept the money if it came from López Avelar's pocket, but since it belonged to the people it should go to those who were more needy.

The mention of Zapata was not incidental—the teller of the tale, and perhaps Jaramillo before him, brought Zapata in, however obliquely, to help establish an ethic.[99] And if there was a hint of the temptations of Christ in that account, a third informant brought Zapata, Jaramillo, and the devil together explicitly. Zapata, this story went, like Hidalgo, Juárez, Christ, and Jaramillo, was a man "of progress" who had been killed, in the end, by the "Prince of the World"—the devil, who in this instance manifested himself as the PRI. Revolutionary politicians claimed they were doing what Zapata "ordered and dictated," s/he continued, but "if Zapata returned again to live in these times, as often as he was resuscitated he would be killed, because the regime of the PRI is very distinct from the regime of Zapata. That is what I discussed with Jaramillo." Jaramillo himself put it this way: if we supported the government, "we would make ourselves accomplices of those who are betraying Zapata in the land of Zapata and in the name of Zapata." A corridista once described Jaramillo as "a second Zapata" and these examples demonstrate why. Perceptions such as these helped give him the legitimacy necessary to direct local frustrations against an unresponsive state, and Zapata and Jaramillo have continued to be paired in death.[100]

These forceful expressions, by some Morelenses, of frustration over the lack of fulfillment of Zapata's goals seemed sometimes to generate an official echo, albeit a weak one, especially during the presidency of López Mateos. The contention that there was still revolutionary work to do—and thus that the revolutionary party was indispensable—became during the miracle years a standard element of official Zapata events, where it came up occasionally in rotation with more frequent assertions that the peasants had already received what Zapata fought for. But during the López Mateos administration this sentiment was occasionally delivered as if it were not just a throwaway line. In some respects, López Mateos was a breath of fresh air after eighteen stifling years in which the revolution's social goals were—in practice, if not rhetoric—virtually forgotten. Younger by twenty years than predecessor Ruiz Cortines, he was still in his late forties when he took the job and by all accounts a dynamic figure. Perhaps motivated by the rising social divisions that rapid economic growth had occasioned, he defined himself on the left within the party, and to some degree his populist style and his policies backed that up. Dissidents were often treated brutally during his administration—Jaramillo is a prime example—but rewards for those who cooperated were significant. López Mateos presided over a renewal of agrarian reform, distributing some thirty million acres of land, more than any previous president but Cárdenas. Other policies included enhanced medical care and pensions; greater expenditures on education, especially in rural areas; and the construction of low cost housing for Mexico City's teeming masses, now around six million strong.[101]

During a 1958 campaign stop in Cuautla, López Mateos delivered a speech in which he indulged in extensive hero worship of Morelos, Hidalgo, Guerrero, and Zapata. In speaking of Zapata he was frank about the constructed nature of national heroes—though not about the role of the state in that process. Zapata, he asserted, was an excellent example of how people purify the images of the men they venerate: "with regard to him one can say that the sentence, 'the Republic remembers the virtues of its great men and forgets their defects,' has become reality." What remains for us, he continued, is "the sober image of the incorruptible fighter: what remains is the pure ideal of a country, Mexico, that has always known the land is the redoubt of freedom." In response to a concern raised by Ana María Zapata, he added, "the banner your father raised is not preserved in a display case; it is in the hands of the Revolution, in the hands of the party that represents the Revolution in Mexico."[102] Despite this reference to the by then unfounded linkage between the ruling party and revolutionary action, López Mateos was taking a different approach than other leaders of the period. In a world in which officials who spoke of Zapata generally sought to mystify rather than clarify, his allusion to Zapata's purification was surprising enough that some listeners might have taken away hope from the "display case" remark. The leaders of the Zapatista Front, however, probably heard nothing after the suggestion that Zapata might have had a defect.

In 1960 López Mateos made his requisite visit to a Cuautla commemoration. Again his performance exhibited some frustration over past accomplishments and suggested a willingness to take action usually missing in such events during the miracle period. The most significant part of the trip was the energy with which the president worked. After attending the Cuautla ceremony, where he gave ejidatarios 896 certificates for urban plots, he traveled through a number of villages—Oaxtepec, Totolapan, Tlalnepantla, Tlayacapan, Itzmatitlán, Casasano, Oacalco, and Yautepec—inaugurating such public works as electric service, systems providing potable water, and small irrigation projects as he went. When he arrived at his last stop, Cuernavaca, around seven in the evening, he found, at least according to the newspapers, an excited crowd of 40,000 people waiting. The state congress designated him a "favorite son" of Morelos, and López Mateos countered with another reference to the need to take action in Zapata's name. When there is no one in the country, he declared, that "suffers ignorance, unsanitary conditions, misery, or injustice, we will have realized the ideals of Emiliano Zapata and, in addition, those of Morelos, those of Hidalgo, and those of Juárez."[103]

Then there was the speech, in the capital on April 10, 1962, of a young lawyer and sometime functionary named Miguel Covián Pérez. Covián Pérez began by noting that the peasants continued to be the "most miserable" of Mexico's classes. Receiving enthusiastic applause from the campesinos of the Federal District for that assertion, but only "timid" responses from the politicians present, he went on to allege that "Zapata does not rest, because his people have been betrayed." True, he said, the reactionaries had been beaten in the countryside, but they had been defeated by those who bought and sold the revolution. Covián Pérez was true to tradition in that he neglected to provide names of corrupt officials, but that might be forgiven in such an emphatic damning of the system. Similar rhetoric had graced the stage of Zapata anniversaries before, but Covián may have stepped just beyond the bounds of acceptable demagoguery, and it was perhaps no coincidence that in the following year Federal District officials decided there would be no speeches at the Mexico City commemoration. Possibly taking strength from the more open climate, however, the Zapatista Front recruited Covián to speak for it at Cuautla.[104]

All this may have been nothing more, though, than another part of the broader populist drama—the shifting signals, the appeals to nationalistic emotions, the obscuring of real intentions—with which the ruling party sought to keep people looking the wrong way while it put money in the hands of capitalists it hoped would deepen Mexican development. In fact, López Mateos's entire presidency might be chalked up to the need to give advocates of social reform some passing, confusing hope. That certainly seemed to be the case when the next PRI president—chosen by López Mateos himself, just as all of the ruling party's presidential "nominees" were picked by their predecessors—was the conservative Gustavo Díaz Ordaz (1964–1970). Díaz Ordaz distributed a lot of land, but he was no agrarian reformer. Rather, he handed out land of low quality for political effect and provided campesinos with little financial support. His presidency brought about, at best, a return to routine protestations regarding Zapata and, at worst, a demonstration of how insipid that language could be.[105] Two examples of the latter should suffice. In 1966 an obsequious article in *Excélsior* declared that "only time separated Zapata from" the buck-toothed, buttoned-down lawyer, guardian of the revolutionary status quo, in the executive office.[106] Two years later, Senator Andrés Serra Rojas averred on behalf of the Zapatista Front that "today Emiliano Zapata is indisputable; only a stupid person could dispute Emiliano Zapata." Serra Rojas then delivered what he apparently hoped was the indisputable corollary to Zapata's indisputability: that Díaz Ordaz was a sincere agrarista.[107] It was just not so, and after twenty-eight years of the Mexican Miracle there can have been few observers who did not know it.

But even if López Mateos was just a calculated populist blip on the screen of Mexican history, his ability to fool people, and thus raise hopes, may have been meaningful. Among those who supported him was Díaz Soto y Gama, the perpetual critic, who had not encountered a chief executive he could embrace since Obregón. At the Cuautla commemoration of 1961 he exhorted Zapatista veterans to unite in a single Zapatista Front so they could fight for progress behind López Mateos, "standard-bearer of the Agrarian Reform." But if he raised expectations, this standard-bearer did not, or could not, improve conditions in rural Mexico in any meaningful way, so ultimately those expectations were dashed. López Mateos not only handed power to Díaz Ordaz, he also quickly vanished from the political scene, suffering a serious stroke soon after leaving office, which undermined his health until his death in 1970. For his part, Díaz Soto y Gama, the loudest Zapatista, died in 1967, to be eulogized while a banner bearing Zapata's image hung behind his coffin.[108] Those who found hope in the López Mateos years would have to look elsewhere now.

The real test of the power and importance of the official myth of Zapata—and by extension, of the revolution's cultural project in general—is how well it worked when no longer reinforced by the material rewards offered, in particular, by the Cárdenas regime. The predictable visit of each president to at least one Cuautla commemoration demonstrated that the revolution's rulers believed that Zapata as founding father could help limit the damage to their rural support as they enacted policies that favored the city over the countryside. They were right. To be valuable to the regime, the official Zapata did not have to convince everyone at all times. It had merely to mystify enough to keep people divided at any moment about what the relationship between the state, the nation, and Zapata was and how or whether memories of Zapata could be used to challenge government policies. It did not have to win over anyone completely; it had only to foster a kind of cognitive dissonance in individual minds through the association of Zapata, for instance, with progress or the war effort. People could grouse, but they were apparently unable to imagine a different Zapata than the one first worshipped in Morelos and then appropriated by the state. Unable to do that, they could not harness the righteousness of *the* emerging symbol of the revolution's conscience to their purposes. And with the Mexican national community now fundamentally defined as a revolutionary one, that was a serious shortcoming, which made rallying effective resistance difficult. True, drawing legitimacy from his past association with the caudillo, Rubén Jaramillo took up arms in Zapata's name, and Henríquez Guzmán wielded Zapata's memory in an opposition campaign for the presidency that Jaramillo supported. Moreover, in the early 1960s in Guerrero, the Emiliano Zapata Agrarian League of the South was born. These were interconnected reflections of an ongoing, regional Zapatismo that would play a crucial role in helping to turn Zapata against the state, but not until after 1968.

Judging from the evidence presented above, the official Zapata enjoyed his greatest success—within the period under discussion—during the 1940s, perhaps because of the novelty of the era's developmentalist policies and the confluence of war, nationalism, and economic growth. The regime's use of Zapata did not, however, render its policies and behaviors invisible. By the 1950s more observers perceived a disconnect between the lessons of Zapata and Golden Age realities. Criticism came from several directions. Sometimes it was partly disguised as ridicule, as when *Excélsior* exposed the pretense and ambition of official Mexico in its coverage of the 1953 Cuautla commemoration. When President Ruiz Cortines and about fifty functionaries ascended the platform, the paper reported, various officials "attempted at all costs to find seats close to his [Ruiz Cortines's], with the result that the platform was on the point of collapsing. Some of the boards fell with a great crash and a disorderly flight ensued, the President thus being delivered from such bothersome subjects." [109] The following year an *Excélsior* cartoon pictured an orator conjecturing in front of a crowd of politicians and military officers about what Zapata would have done if he "had had the 'H' bomb." In other cases—most strikingly in the newspapers of Morelos—the tone was more serious and the complaints were not veiled, despite the usual assumption that the government, through various forms of coercion, exercised substantial control over the media. [110] At any rate, evidence that many Mexicans were unwilling to cede Zapata to the ruling party was ample, even if they did not yet know what, precisely, they might do with him themselves.

SIX

PUTTING ZAPATA ON THE MAP,
1920–1968

Agustín N. Ortega remembered the 1940 commemoration of Zapata's death well.[1] He was in Cuernavaca on the ninth of April when some friends invited him to go with them to the commemoration at Cuautla. He answered that he would prefer to spend the day in Tlaltizapán. That was all it took to get them started, complaining about the politicians that appeared every year at Cuautla. In Cuautla, he joined in, "one feels dizzy upon seeing so many revolutionary dandies, presenting histories in their speeches that are hardly understandable, but still shouting that they are Zapatistas down to the bone." Some of these politicos even managed to squeeze out tears as they talked about how the revolution triumphed, but all they were doing was politicking, looking for ways that they could triumph. The government had forgotten about the peasants who lived in Zapata's old domain.

The next morning Ortega got up early and started for Tlaltizapán, against the tide of campesinos moving toward Cuautla. He reached his destination around eleven in the morning, and instead of a bunch of suits and milling crowds he found an intimate, comfortable scene, just the survivors of Zapata's personal escort scattered around the central square in small groups. They looked sad, he recorded, not with fake tears but with real feeling, because they were remembering what had happened at Chinameca. There was a lot of conjecture about what *had* really happened. Was it true, some asked, as so many people claimed, that the jefe had not died, that one of his compadres, "his double," had stepped in in his place? Was it true "that Zapata had left the country with his Arab friend" and that you could probably still find him in Arabia? Others, whom Ortega found more "radical" in their thinking, argued "Zapata would never have left the revolution in order to escape with his life," because he was a true revolutionary. But those who believed he had survived came back with what they felt was proof: that people swear "they saw him as he was leaving the country; others affirm they saw him when he returned."

Ortega did not recall taking a position himself, but the seriousness of these men, and the importance they attributed to their conversations, confirmed his belief that Tlaltizapán, where sincere homage was done on April 10 year after year, was the place to be. Zapata loved it there, and Tlaltizapán had given him hospitality and love in return. "Because of that, on the date of the anniversary of his death, everyone exclaims: 'Zapata lives… in the heart of the Morelenses and of Tlaltizapán in particular.'"

Ortega understood that where Zapata was remembered was a critical element of his cult. In fact, though we have seen him used for many purposes, his basic meaning can be described in a fairly straightforward way. Looking back from the 1960s, we might say he represented land reform broadening toward social justice in general, and also gradually became an expression of the Mexican nation and thus of Mexican identity. But the precise definitions of those referents—land reform, social justice, revolution, nation, and identity—varied. Their definitions changed over time, of course, but they also varied depending on place: social justice might mean an increased minimum wage in Mexico City rather than land reform. The nuances of Zapata's meaning often depended on where he was remembered because that determined who was claiming him—which community, for the moment, he helped form—and for what cause.

As noted in the Introduction, Octavio Paz wrote that "Zapata dies at every popular fair," which is one way of saying that the claims on him were many.[2] This was especially true in Morelos. While residents of most Morelian communities presumably felt they were important parts of Zapata's story, some claims were stronger than others. There were, in particular, two localities other than Cuautla whose inhabitants thought they should possess Zapata's remains. One of them was Chinameca. Even as Zapata's bones were placed under the statue in Cuautla in 1932, Chinamecans could take comfort in the promise that this monument, built by the state of Morelos, would be "without prejudice to the one of a national nature that was being considered for the hacienda of Chinameca, the place where he [Zapata] was sacrificed."[3] Given the importance of death to Zapata's cult, it is not surprising many felt that Chinameca had a right to such a national Zapata memorial. But more than merely seeking a monument to Zapata, those who stood up for Chinameca often argued that Zapata's body should rest there as well. In October 1931, for instance, the state legislature of Guerrero asked that national, state, and local governments together purchase what remained of the hacienda of Chinameca, locate a statue of Zapata there, and move his body to that monument. This request apparently never received much of an answer. Five years later, the Ministry of the Interior did respond by indicating that Zapata had already garnered enough honors and that he was remembered "in all the nation's communities" on April 10. It did not, however, address the idea of moving his remains so as to make Chinameca a special focus of pilgrimage on that day.[4]

The Chinamecans did not give up. In 1939 the practice began of honoring Zapata there a day late, on April 11, so as not to be overshadowed by the Cuautla ceremony. In the spring of 1940, officials and citizens of Chinameca wrote to Cárdenas to remind him that it was in Chinameca that Zapata had died and to reiterate the request for a statue to commemorate that event. In a recent visit to their village, they claimed, Cárdenas had promised them such a monument, which "would perpetuate his [Zapata's] enormous sacrifice and remind us with veneration of the agrarian cause for which he happily offered his life." In expressing the hope that Cárdenas would comply with this promise before leaving the presidency at the end of the year, the letter resorted to flattery, indicating that he was the only agrarista president Mexico had ever had. On this occasion Chinamecans did not request Zapata's remains. Perhaps they decided it was best to take one thing at a time.[5] Though the Cárdenas regime indicated a monument was being planned, in 1941 the Chinamecans were at it again, with a manifesto that charged, "not even a stone has been raised in this village to recognize the place where the body of the southern hero fell." By the following year things were looking up. Chinameca was then in a position to invite Avila Camacho to the unveiling, at an April 11 commemoration, of a bronze bust of Zapata, displayed on a pedestal three meters high, that had been given to them by the government of Morelos. It was to be erected "precisely in the place where [Zapata] fell dead."[6]

Chinameca's drive for recognition also enjoyed some success during the administration of López Mateos. In 1959, the anniversary of Zapata's death was the occasion for the inauguration of a road from Chinameca to Anenecuilco.[7] In 1964, López Mateos unveiled various plaques, along with a new monument that portrayed Zapata, in high relief, flanked by two peasants—one a warrior and one a woman in civilian dress—who stand slightly behind him. Again, it was placed exactly where Zapata fell.[8]

In 1965, the ultimate goal finally seemed within reach when Governor Emilio Riva Palacio and the state legislature agreed that in the future, April

10 would be observed at Chinameca, where Zapata, "victim of a betrayal, was assassinated, and that his remains should be moved to Chinameca from the place in which they were located." The people of Morelos, the act read, "have manifested their desire that the epic deeds realized in the Morelian campaign be commemorated precisely where they took place, so that our children and youth do homage to our heroes in a way that is historically true." Strangely, the act also indicated that in the future, August 9, the day of Zapata's birth, would be celebrated at Chinameca too, though birth celebrations had always before been the province of Anenecuilco. The government of Morelos had decided, in other words, to place all of the commemorative focus on the place Zapata had died.[9]

Naturally, many in Cuautla were unhappy with this decision. An editorial in the Cuautla newspaper *El Eco del Sur* asked what reason there could possibly be, after Zapata's remains had reposed so long in Cuautla, for "casting them aside in the rough, inhospitable ground of Chinameca." Why should he be taken from the place "where he was known so well and is still venerated and respected?"[10] Arguments such as these ultimately won the day—or at least they have until the present.

The second community challenging Cuautla for possession of Zapata's bones was Ortega's beloved Tlaltizapán. Tlaltizapán's claim was based largely on Zapata's establishment of his headquarters there, in 1914, and his consequent decision to honor the village with the pyramid meant to hold the bodies of his movement's illustrious dead. This claim was strong enough that the Constitutionalists may have briefly discussed burying him there in 1919.[11] Two decades later, in 1939, a "Committee for the Transfer of the Remains of the Caudillo of the Revolution of the South" was circulating a petition, supported by the state legislature, to move the body to Tlaltizapán. The argument, at least as it was put at that time to Cárdenas, was simply that Zapata should rest in Tlaltizapán because the mausoleum he built there demonstrated that such was his desire. In the plaza at Cuautla, the committee contended, the remains were "isolated from those of the group of dead Generals that belonged to his [Zapata's] staff." Prominent Zapatistas who still lived, the letter implied, also hoped to see Zapata at Tlaltizapán; indeed, the committee was headed by Zapata's nephew, Gil Muñoz Zapata, a Tlaltizapán resident who had fought in the revolution. The committee conceded that the lack of a highway leading to Tlaltizapán could be an obstacle, but noted that Governor Elpidio Perdomo was working to get one built. Maybe that was part of the reason other towns in southern Morelos—Tetecala, Tlaquiltenango, Amacuzac, and Jonacatepec—supported the initiative. The committee's communication to Cárdenas ended with the hope that the president's affinity for Zapata would prompt him to intervene in the issue, and Cárdenas apparently did take some steps on behalf of the initiative before he left office.[12]

So far, though, Tlaltizapán has had to settle for building an infrastructure for Zapata's cult without possessing the body. Like Chinameca, Tlaltizapán was trying to regularize its commemorations by at least the 1940s. Those events could, and did, incorporate the mausoleum, and in 1944 two commemorative plaques were added to that structure.[13] Also in 1944, the federal government purchased the old house and mill complex Zapata had used as headquarters, and in July Cárdenas, now secretary of defense, came to unveil a plaque identifying that building. The Zapatista Front then began to push to have the headquarters made into a library, museum, and medical dispensary. The process was slow: by 1955 the local chapter of the Front had started work on the building—paid for by the Zacatepec sugar mill—but the museum was not inaugurated until 1969.[14]

The competition in Morelos for Zapata's remains seems to have been driven by one part practicality and one part pride. Part of the motivation was that there would be public works projects connected to the body, as Tlaltizapán recognized in angling for a highway to facilitate the pilgrimage to Zapata's shrine. State and national politicians made promises to Morelenses on April 10, and the community where Zapata was buried was bound to get its share and more. There were obviously commercial benefits, too: a highway would increase trade year-round, but with or without one, April 10 would be a good day for local merchants. On the pride side of the equation, having the remains would put a community, its inhabitants, and their revolutionary experiences on Mexico's historical map.

The last Morelian community with a special claim to Zapata was Anenecuilco. As the only location where Zapata's birth, rather than his death, was the focus of public memory, Anenecuilco never made a play for his body, which in any case was close by as long as it stayed in Cuautla. As we have seen, though, Anenecuilco did ask for land in Zapata's name, and there were other rewards as well. In 1937 a new school building was erected there—and named after Zapata—as a "palpable and unique demonstration of gratitude for the renowned apostle." At the dedication one child remarked that Zapata had helped lift the villages of the area out of "darkness and ignorance."[15] Shortly thereafter, Jesús Sotelo Inclán raised the idea of creating a Zapatista museum in the house where Zapata was born, "which today one finds totally abandoned and in danger of crumbling into ruins." The museum, he suggested, could deal with Anenecuilco's archeology, ethnology, and history and contain an archive for photographs and the village documents on which he based his book. It could also display objects

Zapata had owned, which were scattered and, Sotelo feared, in danger of being lost. Anenecuilcans, he asserted, were willing to volunteer their labor to save what had been Zapata's home from oblivion and give their documents "the place of honor they merit before the Nation and History." A less ambitious museum, incorporating what were then described as the "ruins" of the house, was a reality by 1960.[16]

Because it was the largest city and the capital of the state, Cuernavaca's commemorations often included visiting dignitaries, and it made sense that there be a monument there. In 1934, students of a local veterinary school—clearly inspired by the strong governmental efforts of the 1930s to undermine devotion to the church on behalf of devotion to the nation—asked that the statue of the Virgin of Guadalupe at the city's northern entrance be replaced by one of Zapata.[17] That initiative came to nothing, but a large statue of Zapata was inaugurated in northern Cuernavaca, on boulevard Emiliano Zapata, in 1954.[18]

Other localities in Morelos settled for less grand and perhaps less regular rituals, organized by schoolteachers and town council members, ejidal organizations, the National Peasant Confederation, and the Zapatista Front. A man named José Saldivar found himself unable to attend the ceremony in Tlaltizapán in 1937 and so remembered Zapata at his home in Colonia Dr. José G. Parrés, "beside the school, with a wake and a funeral wreath, making present our memories in Honor of the Pure Zapatista compañeros and old fighters" who accompanied "the Agrarian Martyr Señor Don Emiliano Zapata." Because the sponsors of the commemoration lacked the money to publish an announcement, only those who lived nearby attended.[19] In 1955 in Xochitepec, municipal authorities were responsible for the event, which included a parade featuring "beautiful señoritas mounted on fine horses, tractors, and campesinos carrying modern farm implements, which were the attainment, precisely, of the ideals of Zapatismo." The parade passed through Xochitepec's principal streets before ending in the park "Emiliano Zapata."[20] Passing through those principal streets, of course, made that parade resonate not only with the regional Zapatista movement and the national cult but with local history as well. A similar effect came from the practices of the teachers of Tepoztlán, who on April 10 always reminded their classes that five of Zapata's generals had been Tepoztecans. Though the places where Zapata spent time were the most important spots for his cult in the Morelian landscape, many communities sought to emulate Cuernavaca, Cuautla, Chinameca, and Tlaltizapán by affixing reverence for Zapata in their geographies. Temixco got a bust of Zapata, for instance, in 1954, and soon thereafter Zacatepec sought permission from

López Mateos to erect a full-length statue in the fountain at the sugar mill's entrance. The statue was to carry a document with the inscription "Plan of Ayala" and an indication of the presidency during which it was created.[21]

In short, Zapata had enjoyed an intimate relationship with the landscape of Morelos during his lifetime, and Morelenses now sought to attach him, through ritual and visual reminders, to that landscape and thus make the relationship permanent and to some degree sacred. It was not so different from the way Catholicism had been inscribed onto the map, through churches and chapels, rituals and place names, four centuries earlier. Schoolteachers and other government employees took the place of priests in this process, but the same holiday meals of mole were sometimes served. On the northern fringes of the state, at Hueyapan—and, we might assume, in other locations—a particular neighborhood was responsible for Zapata celebrations because its main plaza was named for him, just as specific neighborhoods had long been responsible for honoring their patron saints on their feast days.[22]

Statue building came back into vogue during Mexico's miracle years, another sign of the more conservative climate. As mentioned in the Introduction, Porfirio Díaz believed it important to enhance his regime's legitimacy by using public images of famous men—most notably along the fashionable Paseo de la Reforma—to assert a connection to the Mexican past.[23] From 1910 to 1940, however, the fighting and the struggle after the war to pull the country back together in more concrete ways took priority, and Cuautla's statue of Zapata was one of the few erected in the period. After 1940, with greater resources and, as we have seen, a greater need to claim some connection for their industrializing regime with the revolutionary past, those who ruled returned to this method of displaying history.

When they did so, the Zapatista Front was there to lobby for the placement of a monument to its hero in Mexico City. Talk of a new monument resurfaced during the Front's first national convention in 1945, and the Zapatistas were thinking big. Parrés, then the organization's secretary general, informed Avila Camacho of hopes that the monument not be "inert with respect to social services, but that rooms for a school, library, and a museum should be built." The idea was to ask the nation's ejidos to foot the bill, each paying 200 pesos.[24] Fundraising progress was slow, though, so the Front formed a "Committee Pro-Monument to the Caudillo of National Agrarianism: Emiliano Zapata." The creation of this committee was announced in the inaugural issue of *El Campesino* (1949), which was graced, on page 1, with a photograph of Alemán and the profession that the Front was loyal to him and willing to support any measure that put the "fatherland" first. In return for that sort of allegiance, Alemán signed the constitutive act of the committee and agreed to serve as its honorary president, while the Front's president, Adrián Castrejón, headed the committee in practice. The plan was to convene a competition for the job of constructing the monument and, harking back to the Amezcua-led initiative of 1931, to seek a site along the Paseo de la Reforma. The Front was already writing to peasant communities for their monetary support, so that "every stone, every bit of bronze that forms it [the monument], will signify the work, the effort, and the gratitude of the men of the field, for whom he [Zapata] fought until death."[25]

Two years later the accomplished sculptor Ignacio Asúnsolo and his son Enrique, an architecture student, were engaged for the task. The former offered a plaster model in the paternalistic mode: Zapata as charro, on foot and facing the viewer, a protective arm around the shoulders of a smaller campesino holding a sickle. *El Campesino* reported, approvingly, that the work "symbolized the fatherly affection Emiliano Zapata felt for the campesino." Enrique, meanwhile, developed plans for a building that would house a library and a museum; it would be decorated with a frieze that incorporated Zapata's cartridge belts as part of the design. The architectural plans also included the plaza where the statue would stand and a gateway in which Zapata would appear on horseback.[26] The proposed location was now on the brand-new campus for the National University that Alemán was having built in the southern part of the capital.

By late 1951 this plan had been discarded. In its place was the idea of an equestrian statue—on which Ignacio Asúnsolo was already at work—to be located at Huitzilac, Morelos, a village high in the sierra of Ajusco on the highway between Mexico City and Cuernavaca.[27] At least publicly, the Zapatista Front expressed contentment with the new arrangements, but an organization called the Intellectual Workers' Block rejected, probably at Asúnsolo's request, what it considered an out-of-the-way site. "This capital," the block observed, "deserves a magnificent and very Mexican monument to symbolize our agrarian reform."[28] Perhaps hearing other complaints as well, the young Ruiz Cortines administration returned to the idea of a location for Zapata in the capital while *El Campesino* continued to solicit contributions from peasants, a frustrating endeavor.[29] Huitzilac made do with a statue of Morelos, and in 1953 it was announced at the Mexico City commemoration that the equestrian statue would be erected at a rather nondescript spot south of the city center. There it was to face the Ajusco— the mountain range to the south from which Zapatistas had often looked down on the capital.[30]

Five years later, hearing that the statue was in storage in Mexico City, the village of Anenecuilco made a play for it, indicating it would "be more welcome there since family members of our great Man were still living" in the area.[31] Behind the scenes, the Zapatista Front continued to lobby for a location on the Paseo de la Reforma—ideally at the traffic circle it formed with the streets Sevilla and Mississippi.[32] But neither Anenecuilcans nor the Front would have their wishes fulfilled. Mauricio Magdaleno, now director of the Federal District's Social Action division, pushed the project through to completion at Huipulco, yet another location in southern Mexico City. On November 26, 1958, Ruiz Cortines celebrated the anniversary of the Plan of Ayala by unveiling the statue there, on the city's fringe, south and east of Alemán's new campus. Baltasar Dromundo spoke, as did federal Deputy Moisés Ochoa Campos, a professor and official of the Ruiz Cortines administration in multiple capacities. Ochoa Campos noted that Zapata "gave his life to achieve the symbiosis of the agrarian gospel in a new Mexico." In a comment that is provocative, given the firm fixing of Zapata in Mexico City that the event represented, he added that Zapata was a symbol that was incarnated in Anenecuilco, but that this could have happened in "another corner of the fatherland." Zapata, he continued, "protested the nature of our deepest social problems in order to make the historical integration of Mexico effective and complete." It was just one more contribution to the nationalistic discourse about Zapata meant to reinforce the federal government's credibility, but it was more outrageous than most. By implying Zapata belonged to the nation instead of to the people of a more specific locality, Ochoa Campos baldly decontextualized him, thus reinforcing the symbolism of placing his statue in the capital.[33]

Though frustrated by the location of the monument, members of the Zapatista Front thrilled at language that put their hero at the center of the national stage. They presumably also liked the imposing statue, which a writer for *Excélsior* called Mexico's best equestrian sculpture since Tolsa's turn-of-the-nineteenth-century *El Caballito*.[34] Finally, they might have found solace in the likelihood that a southern location would be more convenient for the campesinos of the Federal District—who nearly all lived south of the city—as they trekked to the commemorations that would be held beneath it. Solace or not, the Front, as usual, was willing to cooperate.

But a statue was not necessarily enough for everyone in Mexico City, where there were some doubts about whether Zapata should remain a Morelense for all eternity. The alternative to keeping him in his home state revolved around a structure called the Monument to the Revolution. This monument was completed in Mexico City in 1938 on the iron frame that was all that existed, when the revolution broke out, of a Porfirian building intended to house the federal legislature. A single monument devoted to the abstract notion of the revolution would, its creators apparently hoped, help break down persistent regional, factional, and ideological differences and contribute to making the revolution understood as a coherent, national movement. From this nationalizing and state-building perspective it made sense to move Zapata's body to the building. There it would join the bones of Zapata's heroic colleagues: between 1942 and 1976, Madero, Villa, Carranza, Calles, and Cárdenas were placed in the four massive piers of the edifice, which together support its huge dome.[35] Carranza's body was the first to be moved to the new monument, in 1942, and despite the fact that Carranza and Zapata had been mortal enemies and that Carranza had colluded in Zapata's assassination, discussion began within days over whether Zapata should rest there as well.[36] In 1946, Avila Camacho's office responded to a request for a new Cuautla statue in a high-handed fashion, indicating that a new statue was moot, since "the federal government is promoting the project of moving to the Monument of the Revolution erected in this capital the remains of those who have offered distinguished services to the Fatherland."[37] The names of Zapata and Carranza had, in the service of national unity, already been inscribed in gold together in congressional chambers. Pairing them in everlasting sleep probably seemed like the next logical step. Still, the federal initiative did not go anywhere at this time, though it did occasionally crop up later in the period.[38]

At the same time, Zapata was making inroads in other areas of the country. His memory doubtless spread in part with the people who descended on Cuautla from all corners of Mexico each April 10 and returned home to tell of their experiences, and in some cases peasant organizations seized on him without needing the prodding of the state, but the most effective vehicle for his travels was surely the national government. While commemorating Zapata in Mexico City was a way of *symbolically* nationalizing him, the revolutionary elite understood that his memory could only serve as a source of national unity if the citizens of those regions of the country he had never visited while alive also had something to remember. Using the land reform process with its ejidal organizations, the organizational efforts of the Zapatista Front and the National Peasant Confederation, and the revolution's cultural project—the educational system, the arts, the mass media—Mexico's rulers therefore pushed Zapata on the provinces. That this spreading of the myth was a conscious process can be seen at least as early as 1934, when the Ministry of Education, through *El Maestro Rural*, recommended that schools hold commemorations on April 10. Subsequently, Cardenista activists sometimes entered churches to replace religious icons with images of revolutionary heroes, Zapata's among them.[39] And when the PNR published volume 2 of Magaña's book in 1937, Cárdenas himself wrote Mexico's governors encouraging them to acquire enough copies for distribution "in schools, libraries, ejidos, union halls, and civic centers... because with it you will contribute to the defense and better understanding of the Social Program of the Revolution."[40] The Zapatista Front complemented such efforts by providing its local branches with instructions on how they should undertake commemorations. Directions for 1953 included the injunction to "choose the most propitious hour" so the general citizenry could attend, as well as schoolchildren and their teachers. The Front also hoped to tie Mexico's provinces into the cult's center by encouraging communities to send representatives to Cuautla, too.[41]

One result of these efforts was the establishment of the final locale of Zapata's cult that has received substantial attention over time from national authorities: Cuatro Caminos, near the collective ejidos of Lombardía and Nueva Italia that Cárdenas established in the south of his home state of Michoacán.[42] The focus of commemorations there was an equestrian statue of Zapata that dated to the Cárdenas administration, when the campesinos of the region paid for it at the president's urging. Frequently the location of ceremonies covered in the national press, on April 10, 1964, Cuatro Caminos even hosted López Mateos, who stopped at the statue for the usual rituals and then traveled through the area, handing out land titles and certificates and inaugurating two cotton gins and an ejidal gas station. Zapata's son Nicolás was also there to give the site the stamp of authenticity.[43]

The way Zapata arrived in the rural, impoverished, and largely Indian state of Oaxaca in southern Mexico is a good—though not typical—example of how he traveled and how he was received. Oaxaca was not far from Morelos, and though Zapata may never have entered the state himself, during the decade of revolutionary warfare small guerrillas operating in its mountainous fringes sometimes identified themselves as Zapatistas—some really had links to Zapata's headquarters and some did not. In either case, the activities of those forces were often perceived as banditry. In part this was because they did appropriate resources from villagers and landowners with whom they came in contact. It was also due in part simply to the fact that they often came from outside the state, and because there were, in Oaxaca, fairly strong movements led by local elites who called themselves revolutionaries but rejected the kind of social change the Zapatistas proposed.[44] Under such circumstances it is not surprising that in 1923, the city council of Oaxaca heatedly debated an invitation from the governor of Morelos—Parrés—to commemorate Zapata's death. Various members of the council argued that Zapata was merely a bandit and an assassin, and in the end no commemoration was held.[45]

Ten years later, Oaxaqueño Enrique Othón Díaz published a poem to Zapata in which he stressed his subject's special powers, describing him as a "receiving antenna / of the aching waves / of the oppressed." Othón Díaz's metaphors did not, of course, represent his entire state. In fact, the author of the epilogue to the book in which the poem appeared criticized Othón for not recognizing that Mexico had gone only halfway, stopping "at Zapata when Lenin waits a bit farther along."[46] Furthermore, in 1934 the Oaxacan Peasants Confederation apparently let the date of Zapata's death slip by without notice. But in that year, of course, Cárdenas became president, and Zapata would now quickly overcome whatever serious Oaxacan resistance remained.[47]

One reason he could do so is that he was closely associated with the Cardenista land reform in the state, during which the number of ejidatarios doubled and peasants were hooked into the National Peasant Confederation.[48] In Santa María del Tule, a town in the central valley, Mario González remembered almost six decades later that Cárdenas "was with Emiliano Zapata. He and Zapata were for the poor people. Zapata was the one who had the idea about taking the land away from the hacendados. Zapata suffered for us. He gave his blood so that the campesinos would have some land to work."[49] When asked directly whose idea it was to organize the local ejido, González responded, "It was Emiliano Zapata." González also asserted that after winning the war, Zapata told his followers it was time to get to work.[50] Cárdenas had visited El Tule and thus established a somewhat personal connection with observers like González, but González also inserted Zapata into local history, making it sound as if he were a contemporary of Cárdenas and an actor on the local scene, working specifically for village interests. While González was old enough to remember the 1930s, residents of El Tule young enough to be his great-grandchildren repeated similar stories, demonstrating that there was a tradition about this hero that passed from one generation to the next.[51] Also noteworthy is the reference to Zapata giving his blood, which suggests that the messianism of Morelos may have found an echo in Oaxaca. Finally, it bears pointing out that González was probably combining impressions of Zapata he received at different times during his long life. The claim that Zapata had won the revolution and told the peasants to work may well date from the post-Cárdenas era, when spokesmen for the national government did, as we have seen, use a victorious Zapata to say precisely that.

Other aged informants from El Tule also had memories of Zapata that tied him to Cárdenas, the poor, and local communities. Carlos Gómez, who was born around 1914, confided that Zapata and Cárdenas were "very closely linked, because, when Cárdenas became president of the Republic of Mexico, he followed the ideas of General Zapata and kept on expropriating land from what they call latifundias." People in El Tule, he added, "think that everything Zapata did is good, because he said that the land belongs to whomever works it." He also commented that it was important that Zapata gave his life for his cause. Elvira Bautista Méndez volunteered that "he gave us our land," which was why "the teachers make a holiday honoring Emiliano Zapata here in town." [52]

In nearby Unión Zapata, Pedro García Sánchez was proud his village bore Zapata's name. "This place is named for Zapata," he indicated, "because we took the land away from the hacendados and we redistributed it here. It is our pride in this legacy here that allows his name to continue." García Sánchez said he learned about Zapata in school; he also mentioned that there was a photograph of him at the local ejidal office. "Several people have come and tried to take that photo," he remarked. "This is an original photo of Zapata. We don't want anyone to take it away.... It belongs here." [53] The village that became Unión Zapata was named Loma Larga when people living in the area and working on surrounding haciendas formed it, in the early 1930s, to meet the population requirements for petitioning the government for an ejido. In 1935 its residents voted to change the name to Unión Zapata, proof that positive attitudes toward Zapata in the area indeed go back to the 1930s, as the interviewees believed. [54] In Unión Zapata, in fact, Zapata figures as part of a modern-day creation myth for a community that physically came together in his name.

Carlos Gómez testified that he first learned about Zapata from April 10 commemorations in El Tule, which were attended by forty to fifty people. He also remembered going to the 1937 velada held at the city of Oaxaca's fancy Macedonio Alcalá Theater, which dated from the Porfirian era. The velada was organized by the Division of Social and Cultural Action of the state's Agrarian Department and the Oaxacan branch of the Mexican Peasant Confederation—the officially supported predecessor of the National Peasant Confederation. The keynote speaker was the gifted orator Dr. Alberto Vargas, head of the Coordinated Sanitary Services of the state, whose address was titled "Hygienic Action in the Rural Milieu." Unfortunately, Gómez probably had trouble hearing, because Vargas was at times drowned out by the noise made by the schoolchildren present. The newspaper *Oaxaca Nuevo* expressed the hope that the teachers would control their charges better the following year. Just as at Cuautla, the ceremony included the placing of floral offerings by officials from local, state, and national arenas—here before an altar specially arranged for the event.[55]

In the following year the Ministry of Public Education "circulated instructions to every school to organize and carry out, on the tenth of this month, solemn commemorative ceremonies of the death of General Emiliano Zapata." The ceremonies, the instructions indicated, should clarify Zapata's "life and meritorious work" for the students.[56] Taking the hint, the inhabitants of San Juan Chapultepec, Oaxaca, held a festival with two objectives: to commemorate the day of Zapata's death and to inaugurate improvements to the primary school, which included general repairs and the building of a new restroom and an open-air theater. Presiding over the act was Professor Rodolfo Mendivi, inspector of the school zone, in representation of the director of education in the state. The program was diverse. The girls of the grade school sang "Las Inditas" (The Little Indian Girls), and there were recitations of "El Agrarista" and "Sangre Campesina" (Campesino Blood). A traditional Mixe Indian dance was performed, presumably by students; students from the rural school of Azompa added a musical number of their own; at some point Mendivi said a few words; and the festivities ended with the national anthem.[57] It was not, perhaps, the "solemn" occasion the education administration requested; in fact, it would appear that Zapata was all but lost in the commotion. It was instead an event more in accord with the sentiments of an editorial of the same day in the newspaper *Oaxaca Nuevo*, which took the position that Zapata's death was a cause for joy, not mourning, "because it provided the opportunity for his arrival at the throne of the immortals."[58] In any event, in San Juan Chapultepec the anniversary of Zapata's death had now been entered into the ritual calendar. In the meantime, memories of Zapata were also being created elsewhere in the state. There was another commemoration at the capital city's Macedonio Alcalá Theater that year, and even the residents of the jail in nearby Etla organized an event in memory of the "martyr of Agrarismo" that incorporated speeches and recitations by the inmates themselves, as well as an opportunity for anyone present to speak.[59]

The Zapatista Front established itself in the state immediately after its founding in 1940, and began to promote the cult.[60] The periodicals of the city of Oaxaca could also soon be counted on to discuss Zapata in April, beyond simply reporting on commemorations. In 1940, *Oaxaca Nuevo* offered a broad mix of positive attitudes toward him. It commented that Zapata was the "apostle of agrarianism" and that "rebellion in him is temperamental; untamable like a noble colt, he didn't permit anyone to impose order on him or exercise attitudes of dominance." It also alluded to the popular myth of his home state in claiming, "one still sees his horse, like lightning, in the fields of Morelos." Finally, it added that Zapata was "already consecrated by the entire Mexican people as the greatest and most sincere defender of the campesinos."[61] There were sometimes fairly straightforward history lessons as well, many of which discussed manifestations of Zapatismo during the decade of warfare in Oaxaca.[62]

In 1945 the state's League of Agrarian Communities and Peasant Unions (a branch of the National Peasant Confederation) asked the Oaxaca city council to name one of the city's parks after Zapata, "so that from now on the acts done in his memory will be carried out in the indicated park."[63] Ten years later, in the village of Yodohino in the state's northwestern corner, the local Zapatista Front and municipal authorities presided over an April 10 ceremony. The flag was set at half-mast, and at ten in the morning there was a procession. At eleven a program full of "declamations" began; in the afternoon, there were sporting events.[64] "Dawn was saluted with music and fireworks" on the same day at another village in this municipality. Later, a parade of ejidatarios, students, teachers, authorities, and the general populace threaded its way through village streets to an "altar of the Fatherland," where students, mostly, presented their thoughts on Zapata.[65] In 1957, Deputy Ramón Ruiz Vasconcelos of Oaxaca spoke at Cuautla as a representative of the National Peasant Confederation, while in the city of Oaxaca 1500 peasants gathered, along with union members and students, at the Macedonio Alcalá Theater. The village bands of Tlacochahuaya and Macuilxóchitl played, and the governor and other dignitaries exhorted the crowd to work and be unified.[66] At a 1965 ceremony at San Baltazar Chichicápam in the center of the state, the ejidal president of San Nicolás Yaxé called for "peace and concord" among the villages of Chichicápam, Yaxé, and Guilá that took part in the event.[67] In 1966, social worker Guadalupe Pérez Baños held a ceremony, largely for women, at the city of Oaxaca's Center of Social Security for Family Welfare.[68]

On April 10, 1962, in the city of Oaxaca, campesino contingents marched from the old location of the League of Agrarian Communities and Peasant Unions to the league's new office, which had been built and equipped by Governor Alfonso Pérez Gasca. Among the streets through which the procession moved were those named for Morelos and Hidalgo; it also passed the center of power in the state, the Plaza of the Constitution, to salute the governor. The inauguration of the new building followed. There was then a "regional dinner," at which peasants of Oaxaca's seven regions presented a "Guelaguetza"—a Oaxacan fiesta with pre-Columbian roots—

featuring dances and "typical clothing from each region." Speeches on this day vaguely linked the state's great hero, Benito Juárez, with Zapata, and the peasants were predictably informed of the importance of hard work. There was the requisite praise for López Mateos and an energetic address by Francisco Hernández y Hernández, leader of the National Peasant Confederation. The land, he asserted,

> continues to belong to he who works it with his own hands, and if it is necessary to return to battle to assure this, let's welcome the battle! Zapata continues to be, in spirit, ready to cross the fields of the Country and finish off the last haciendas.

The headline of *Oaxaca Gráfico* on the following day was, "The Land Is the Fatherland, Defend It." [69] That defense could apparently have started very close to home, for López Mateos had reportedly "snubbed" the ostensibly generous Pérez Gasca recently for his practice of market speculation with corn raised by his state's campesinos.

Toward the end of the period at least one Oaxacan publication voiced the kind of criticism heard in Morelos and warned that the battles mentioned by Hernández y Hernández could indeed come to pass. A 1964 article in the magazine *Oaxaca en México* complained of the demagogues who used "the name of Zapata, immaculate warrior," to enhance their power. "They should be very careful," it cautioned, "because the people of the fields are already awakening, and it is immoral to use the anniversary of the death of the great agrarista that Zapata was to fool, demagogically, our simple people in Oaxaca." Ultimately, however, it was another case of indicting nameless individuals rather than the system, as the article ended with thanks for Díaz Ordaz, who truly believed in the redemption of the peasantry. [70]

In Oaxaca, then, commemoration of Zapata became common during the 1930s, and took many different forms in the decades that followed. As in Cuautla, there was an emphasis on inclusion that extended from peasants to workers, students, women, and, at least in some cases, to anyone who wanted to participate. In Oaxaca, however, that inclusion was not as purely symbolic as it was in Cuautla, where many people were seen but few heard. With fewer officials prowling the Oaxacan rituals, teachers, students, peasants, and even prisoners shared their views. There was broad geographical inclusiveness in Oaxaca as well. Ceremonies were held in the capital, the central valleys, more isolated mountain areas, and the Isthmus of Tehuantepec, which suggests that the hopes of the Cárdenas regime and the Zapatista Front that these rituals take place in every community with a school or an ejido were in some measure met.[71]

Commemorations of Zapata also brought people together, whether it was the apparently feuding villages of Chichicápam, Yaxé, and Guilá or the representatives of Oaxaca's seven regions who gathered in the capital in 1962. As they did so they both appropriated Zapata for Oaxaca and demonstrated that Oaxaca fit into the national community. Zapata was appropriated when Pedro García Sánchez insisted his photograph belonged in Unión Zapata, when parades in his honor traced paths through local geographies, and when ceremonies held in his name included exhibitions of Oaxacan culture. Since the culture on display was largely Indian, his Indianness was accentuated by his presence in the state. On the other hand, discussion of Zapata, land, and fatherland and the use of the national anthem were insistences that Zapata was a national hero as well as a Oaxacan hero in the making, and that Oaxaca demonstrated its place in the national order by accepting him. In general, too, the ritual trappings—wreathes, speeches, honor guards—recalled those used in Cuautla, revealing a well-established national culture with regard to how such things should be done. The advocacy of work and unity, of course, echoed themes at Cuautla perfectly. In sum, the messages could cut either way: Oaxacans would be able in the future to use Zapata for their own, separate ends or allow him to draw them into the embrace of state and nation.

Though all regions of Mexico were encouraged to adopt Zapata's cult, not all would accept it with the same depth of feeling displayed in Oaxaca. Oaxaca's relative openness to Zapata can be attributed to the Cardenista land reform there, the state's rural and Indian character, and its proximity to Zapata's home territory. The neighboring state of Guerrero shared some of these characteristics but was logically even more promising for the cult in that Zapata had led troops there. During the 1950s, at least, various Guerreran villages went so far as to simulate Zapata's body and its trappings on April 10. In Apango, in the center of the state, an honor guard performed in 1951 before "a simulated body of General Zapata."[72] A year later, the "humble peasants" of neighboring Zotoltitlán, "constructed a catafalque where the casket of the southern jefe was simulated" during a fourteen-hour "vigil for the caudillo." According to *El Campesino*, it was an "imposing" act during which, "among copious flowers and the mourning veils, large candles constantly burned."[73] Ejidatarios of Mixquiahuala de Juárez, Hidalgo, meanwhile, got together in 1957 to request that Asúnsolo's equestrian monument be sent to them, since they too had learned it was gathering dust in storage when it could be serving as inspiration to their children. They also professed to have received their ejido on the orders of Zapata himself, via a homegrown Zapatista.[74] Elsewhere, claims were often made in Zapata's name, whatever the feelings behind them, as when citizens of Texcalyacac in the state of Mexico evoked Zapata in a letter asking Avila Camacho for help in rebuilding their Municipal Palace, school, and irrigation system, all destroyed during the revolution.[75] In general it appears Zapata was accepted with enthusiasm in the center and south of Mexico, where conditions bore some similarities to those of Oaxaca.

In the less agrarian, less Indian, and more distant north, on the other hand, rituals associated with Zapata were generally more formal, manifestations of an official cult with limited popular resonance.[76] Here, memories of other revolutionaries, particularly those of Pancho Villa in the states of Chihuahua and Durango, could also be obstacles. Still, conditions for Zapata were not entirely distinct from those in Oaxaca. In the mid-1930s, cultural missionaries from Tabasco went to southern Sonora in support of the Cardenista land reform; they spoke, beneath a mesquite tree, of how Cárdenas was acting on Zapata's initiatives.[77] Providing evidence that such messages were sometimes taken to heart, in 1943 the Feminine League of the ejido of Tepehuaje at Ciudad Jiménez, Nuevo León, asked Avila Camacho for a bust of Zapata, and in the 1960s an independent peasants' organization with northern leadership employed Zapata's image as a rallying point.[78]

Indeed, despite his failure to uniformly conquer the country, a great many Mexicans gathered in observance of Zapata each April 10, which surely produced some of the sense of simultaneous action and sentiment that might help people imagine a nation. In 1950, on the same day Alemán went to Cuautla as described in Chapter 5, the municipal presidents of Ciudad Obregón, Navajoa, and Bacum in Sonora's Yaqui Valley came together to remember Zapata too. Houses were decorated with national flags and the event included two baseball games, a twenty-one-gun salute, a barbecue, and a literary-musical production where a likeness of Zapata was located in a place of honor and the third-grade girls sang a corrido. Pictures of Zapata were passed out to those attending.

At San Pablo Oxtotepec, in the southern Federal District, two Zapatista veterans used the ritual that year to charge that the secretary of defense had still not recognized their military rank. "They demand documents and photographs from us," complained one, "as if the scars that reveal the bullets that perforated our bodies in the struggle were not enough." Adrián Castrejón stopped here to speak on his way to Cuautla, noting that not all villages had yet received land and that the Zapatista Front would not rest until they did. Many people were trying to stop land reform, he added, but they would not succeed because Zapata's "liberating message" was in the conscience of the campesinos.

Also in 1950, at Cacahuananche, Guerrero, the principal act was carried out in the federal school, and floral offerings were made at an "improvised altar to Zapata." At Atlixco, in western Puebla, an "imposing" parade wound through the "principal streets." Zapatista veterans, military and civilian authorities, teachers, students, and peasants from various towns—with their respective bands—marched in the procession. After the parade, Zapata was honored in front of his monument in the small plaza named for him, and there were "endless" floral offerings. Meanwhile, people from the villages of El Atravezaño and Las Lomas in Jalisco and La Palma and Zicuicho in Michoacán gathered at Los Reyes, Michoacán. There

> the bells of the parish church made their sonorous voices of bronze heard through the detonations produced by the fireworks and by the musical notes that escaped from the band as it executed the Agrarista Hymn and the beautiful revolutionary songs, La Adelita and La Valentina.

In Mixquiahuala, Hidalgo, the program included an open podium.[79] It all added up, perhaps, to the nation the new revolutionary elite had hoped to forge out of the revolutionary chaos, but as the veterans at Oxtotepec who took advantage of the opportunities for freer speech at provincial commemorations showed, it was not a nation in which everyone gathered in mindless worship of the caudillo.

As Mexico's participation in World War II demonstrated, Mexican nationalism was not just about forging internal unity but also about occupying a respected place among the nations of the world. To obtain such a position it was necessary to have certain bragging rights within the community of nations, and one of those rights was based in the figure of Zapata, who could be promoted as the world's greatest, or first, or purest agrarian revolutionary (if not very convincingly as the enlightenment philosopher the ambassador to Sweden portrayed). As an *El Campesino* editorial put it in 1970, Zapata was becoming enormous, and in doing so he gave "Mexico an enviable place in the history of humanity."[80] As a result of his ever-increasing size, he sometimes inspired admiration in other parts of the world not unlike that which he enjoyed at home. Chilean Nobel laureate Pablo Neruda wrote a corrido about Zapata, presenting him as a force of nature. "Zapata then [at sunrise] was land and dawn," he wrote, "all along the horizon appeared / the multitude of his armed seed."[81] While such manifestations of international Zapatismo may be interesting, the most fertile foreign ground for Zapata's armed seed was the neighboring United States, a country dramatically different from Mexico but one to which Mexico was inextricably bound, in a love-hate relationship, by history and a common border.

Emissaries from the United States had little to do with Zapata while he was alive, largely because the distance of his headquarters from both the border and the coasts made him less accessible and, they believed, less critical to American interests. After his death, however, many American writers of leftist, progressive, or liberal persuasion were drawn to him by the stories they heard. Among the first to write about him was historian Frank Tannenbaum, in two books, *The Mexican Agrarian Revolution* (1929) and *Peace by Revolution* (1933).[82] Tannenbaum generally followed lines already mapped out by Mexican pronouncements. He described Zapata as an Indian for whom Indians were the main constituency, and as uneducated—the author indicates that Díaz Soto y Gama taught him to read at night by the light of campfires. Zapata, Tannenbaum asserted, had devised the only clear program of the revolutionary decade, and his persistence made the revolution what it was: "a profound spiritual and social change in the total attitude and relationship of the different classes in that country."[83] Deeply admired by his followers for his willingness to fight for his cause until death, he "was obeyed affectionately and implicitly like an old Aztec King."[84] He was also one of the few revolutionaries who stayed true to his ideals, and the most powerful influence shaping the revolution's agrarian program. When Zapata was killed, Tannenbaum maintained, fear spread through the territory in which he had operated, but with the arrival of Obregón in power, "Zapata had won, and so had the Revolution." Finally, he noted the popular myth, indicating that in Morelos they have made a "sacred shrine" of his grave and that "Zapata's spirit wanders over the mountain at night and watches over the Indians and that he will return if they are mistreated."[85] For those Americans who read them, Tannenbaum's books tended to make Zapata the revolution's key player.

Journalist Carleton Beals was also among those introducing Americans to Zapata, in a book entitled *Mexican Maze* (1931). Beals interviewed Díaz Soto y Gama, attended a Cuautla commemoration, and considered Zapata a legitimate agrarian reformer with significant influence on the constitution. In words more colorful than those employed by Tannenbaum, he described him as the "black mustached whirlwind of the agrarian revolution in south Mexico." In writing that his subject possessed the "omnipotence of an oriental sultan," he emphasized, as had Tannenbaum, both Zapata's power in his bailiwick and how foreign and Indian he appeared when viewed from the United States. Also like Tannenbaum, he remarked on the developing myth: "When the sky grows dark and it thunders, people run to the doors of their thatched cabins to see Zapata galloping across the heavens. His figure is outlined in the clouds; his voice echoes in the winds." [86]

A decade later, English writer Edgcumb Pinchon, who had earlier fashioned a book on Villa that became a Hollywood movie, published *Zapata the Unconquerable* (1941). Written in part to debunk an unfavorable book about Zapata—H. H. Dunn's far-fetched *The Crimson Jester* (1933)—the goal of this work was nothing less than "to rescue from the back of a mule where it once hung, bodiless and bloody the head of one of the greatest human beings of modern times." The author claimed to have done his own research in Morelos, and though his account took many of the novelist's liberties, it reads as if that claim was probably true. Pinchon also drew heavily on Magaña.[87] Zapata, he argued, was a perfect reflection of those who followed him. He played up Zapata's skills as a horseman, crediting him with the ability to perform *"el paseo de la muerte"*—the ride of death—in local rodeos, which entailed jumping from the back of one galloping horse to another.[88] He also developed a fictional romantic subplot by introducing a Romanian reporter named Helène Pontipirani, whom Zapata first met when she was a young girl.[89] They continued to get together, off and on, throughout the revolutionary decade, Pontipirani saving Zapata's life and providing him with information, including the fact that Guajardo was planning to trap him. In one scene, after a kiss lit by lightning, Pontipirani asked to be allowed to stay at Zapata's side. "Don't torture me," he responded, "I can't take you into my world. Here is nothing but starvation, filth, blood, wounds, death." If she remained, he continued, he would have to choose between her and his work, "and Morelos would be lost." [90] At about the same time the Zapatista Front was beginning to consider how to bring Zapata to the screen, this British romantic clearly had him ready for Hollywood.

Pinchon was not alone, in the international community, in wanting to get Zapata on film. But the Alemán administration report (introduced in Chapter 5) that evaluated the likelihood that the Zapatista Front could produce a movie about Zapata, noted that both foreign and domestic companies ran into a brick wall when they explored their options. That wall was the Front itself, which tended to demand a cut of the proceeds and "alleged that it had rights to intervene in the filming, in order to prevent Zapata's life from being discredited or adulterated." This report concluded that Zapata's biography was only of interest to Mexicans. To make a movie appealing to an international audience, liberties would have to be taken, "which would surely not please the Zapatistas." A case in point was the speech of the Front's representative at a Mexico City commemoration in 1944. This speaker denounced the Ministry of Public Education for authorizing the filming of a movie in which Zapata was depicted in "an untruthful way." A Señor Allen, he added, who was "a *pocho* of indefinable nationality," had initially brought this project to the Front.[91] In answer to its concerns about how Zapata would be depicted, Allen had conceded that "the merit of the figure of the Caudillo was unimportant," he just wanted to make money. The greatest outrage in the proposed film was that a female tourist from the United States hooked up with Zapata, and from there a "cinematographic idyll" unfolded in which the tourist "guides Zapata until he falls into the hands of an American Reporter." The Front was willing, this spokesperson asserted, to use violence if necessary to keep the film from becoming a reality, and such threats apparently worked, because Allen's film did not get made.[92] Long odds, then, for Pinchon's love story. Allegories that touched on Zapata's experience, such as *El Compadre Mendoza* (1934), had appeared on film, but anything more explicit was likely to provoke a firestorm of criticism.[93]

Pinchon had already approached the movie company Metro-Goldwyn-Mayer (MGM) as early as 1938 to sell film rights to his projected book.[94] Little came of that initiative for several years, but during World War II the U.S. Office for Coordination of Commercial and Cultural Relations between American Republics—a newly created propaganda organ—asked the Motion Pictures Producers Association to look into using Zapata for a war message. Several studios expressed an interest. Perhaps based in part on Señor Allen's exploratory trip south, the eventual answer, though, was that he would be hard to employ in such a manner. After the war, screenwriter Lester Cole began to develop a script based on Pinchon's book for MGM, with Alemán's strong support. Judging from Cole's later comments, it would have been a work of hero worship.[95] But Cole soon became a casualty of a red scare. As the cold war began, the infamous House Un-American Activities Commission (HUAC) started its anticommunist deliberations, and Cole wound up one of the jailed and blacklisted Hollywood Ten. Strangely, it was under these touchy circumstances that director Elia Kazan—who had already been "named" before the HUAC as a former member of the Communist Party—and novelist John Steinbeck entered the story by convincing Twentieth Century Fox to buy the rights to *Zapata*. MGM was more than willing to sell. The instructions of the studio manager, in fact, were reportedly to "get rid of this fuckin' script, this bastard Zapata's a goddam commie revolutionary!"[96]

It seems that Kazan and Steinbeck took the risk of making their film, *Viva Zapata!*, simply because they found in Zapata an irresistible subject. Both avowed that they had long been interested in him, Steinbeck claiming he had interviewed countless old Zapatistas, starting as early as the 1930s, and knew "as much about him [Zapata] from all angles as anyone living." Though he perhaps exaggerated, he *had* spent time with veterans in Morelos and had heard firsthand accounts of Zapata's survival.[97]

When the two men took their vision to Mexico, it was not well received. Because Kazan wanted to shoot the film "precisely where its events had taken place," they traveled south to prepare the way, meeting in Cuernavaca with Gabriel Figueroa, a prominent cinematographer, head of Mexico's film technicians union and a friend of Steinbeck's from a previous visit. Figueroa greeted them enthusiastically but, according to Kazan, when Steinbeck brought up Zapata, his expression changed. Kazan later remembered Figueroa saying Zapata was "next to a saint" and "the hero of every forward-looking patriot here." He also recalled that the cinematographer lamented that Mexicans had not done a movie about Zapata long before. Figueroa's perceptions of the encounter, and the problem, were different: "from the beginning I saw that Kazan... knew nothing about Zapata and Zapatismo and that Steinbeck, despite his unquestionable good faith, had, well . . . very gringo ideas about the whole thing. This I confirmed upon reading the script." Figueroa declined the invitation to join the project. When the script was subsequently evaluated by a censorship board, one censor echoed Figueroa's position: that he knew the history of Zapata and Steinbeck did not. Officials at the Department of Defense, strangely, also had a look—a Zapatista veteran there suggested that Steinbeck come to him for some ideas that would improve the story.[98]

Given the climate of opinion in the United States, Steinbeck and Kazan could not help but have communism on their minds. Both were vulnerable to the sort of treatment endured by Cole in that they had had communist connections in the 1930s. But by the late 1940s both were busily shedding their communist pasts—a convenient move politically, of course, but also a rejection of the brutal authoritarianism of Joseph Stalin. Under these circumstances it is perhaps not surprising that they tended to "smell" the "party line," as Steinbeck once put it, when obstacles arose in Mexico; they quickly concluded, for example, that Figueroa had presented the script to anonymous communists for a reading. In any event, they found themselves criticized for elements of their story they believed to be true: that Zapata had Spanish blood and was proud of it, that he was vain, and above all that he had walked away from national power. Steinbeck assured Kazan that bribes would resolve their difficulties, but they did not. Producer Darryl Zanuck was supposedly informed the movie would be "condemned in Mexico and cause a great wave of anger," and they were unable to secure government permission to film in Mexico. Zanuck instructed them to shoot on the south Texas border instead.[99] Also discarded were hopes of casting a Mexican in the role of Zapata. Steinbeck lobbied for Pedro Armendáriz, the actor the Zapatista Front also had in mind at about the same time (see Chapter 5), in whom he found the "the same face, the same fierceness, the same vitality" as Zapata. Zanuck, however, wanted someone he considered a bigger star. In Marlon Brando, fresh off a triumph in *A Streetcar Named Desire*, he got one.[100]

Steinbeck recognized early in the project that getting reliable information on such a legendary figure would be difficult, but he dispensed with that problem by deciding the local myth was the truth he wanted to communicate: "I am trying to take an Indian's eye view of him," he wrote, "for there are more of them, and to them he could do no wrong."[101] An unwieldy mix of hero worship, talk of predestination, and racial typecasting, his original treatment pleased neither Kazan nor Zanuck, who subsequently helped him boil it down to its essentials. They also painstakingly cut material, largely at the nervous Zanuck's orders, that might make people believe they were "subtly working for" the communists. Zanuck lobbied for pro-democracy messages instead. The studio also engaged in extended negotiations with Mexican censors to get permission to screen it in Mexico. Interestingly, the censors did not care about the negative depiction of Madero, at least according to one account, but were concerned only that Zapata's reputation be protected.[102] What was left included several scenes taken straight from Pinchon, but Pinchon's love story was redirected, focusing on an apparently monogamous Zapata's courtship of, and relationship with, Josefa Espejo. Zapata's drunken and womanizing brother Eufemio, played by Anthony Quinn, was the foil who underscored Zapata's gentlemanly behavior.

Ironically, Steinbeck initially felt that the humanization of Zapata that attention to his marriage would generate was crucial because, committed to the "Indian's view," he found Zapata an unsatisfactory character. "There was no internal struggle in the man," he wrote, "no uncertainty, no barrier of fear to overcome."[103] With the help of his producer and director, though, he soon abandoned this constraining perspective. Discarding discussion of predestination, they now gave Zapata the moral quandary on which the movie would turn: would he take up the cause of his oppressed people in violent revolution, or did he prefer the status of respectable citizen, which was at times just beyond his grasp?[104] Eventually, appeals from his friends and from Madero, his own anger at the injustice that surrounded him, the rejection of his marriage proposal (for the moment) by Espejo's family, and his arrest by local authorities all conspired to drive him into rebellion, but his ambivalence about power and standing, some of which Steinbeck did hint at in his first draft, continued to be a theme throughout the movie.[105]

To draw that out—and to protect themselves from anticommunist crusaders—Kazan, Steinbeck, and Zanuck developed a villain, Fernando, who had not appeared in Steinbeck's original version. A committed communist ideologue, Fernando arrived before the fighting started with a message from Madero and thereafter lurked menacingly at Zapata's elbow. When Zapata's old friend, Pablo, was caught conferring with the enemy because in his estimation their rebellion had gone awry, it was Fernando who prodded Zapata to execute him; when there was power to seize, Fernando insisted that Zapata seize it. In the end, though, Zapata walked away from national power, after becoming acting president, when he discovered it made him just like Porfirio Díaz. Fernando then joined the enemy and began to plot his death.[106] In this account, it was a prescient Espejo who warned Zapata not to go to Chinameca, but he pushed her away. As the ambush played out, Fernando screamed at the Carrancistas to shoot the white horse as well, but it made its escape. Zapata's body was dumped unceremoniously in a plaza, where the village women cleaned it and the men began to speculate that it was not really his. The movie ended with the horse running free in the mountains, which was Zanuck's touch—Kazan speculated that "he'd stolen it, no doubt, from an old Warner western."[107]

Fernando, then, embodied the uncompromising Stalinist menace in a way that should have made it clear, by comparison, to even the least discerning critic, that for the makers of the film Zapata was no communist. He was not even much of a land reformer, given that the movie shied away from depicting the broad redistribution of land he oversaw in Morelos. Still, Kazan would later say he knew the movie would be criticized for being "communistic," but that he refused to be told what to do.[108] It is true, at least, that the changes he made did not get him off the hook with the House Un-American Activities Committee. He was called to testify about the time filming on the movie ended and, in a decision that would forever cloud his reputation, provided the committee with names of Hollywood radicals. He also alluded publicly to two Mexican communists—one apparently being Figueroa—who had sought to influence the film.[109]

Who then *was* Zapata as *Viva Zapata!* portrayed him? Most important for our story, he was a man who had sacrificed himself on three levels: by walking away from any hope of small-town respectability, by surrendering national power, and by finally giving his life to the cause.[110] He was a steadfast and incorruptible hero, but one—much like Jesus Christ, who suffered when crucified because he was human—who did not attain that heroic stature easily. Early in the movie he rejected the leadership role his friends sought to thrust on him by asserting, "I don't want to be the conscience of the world. I don't want to be the conscience of anybody."[111] But in the end, this is precisely what he became, or at least Kazan and company were holding him up to their world as a model, a rare case of a man who was conscientious to the end in painful and confusing circumstances. After all the twists and turns, this was not, ironically, so far from the way the Mexican regime had come to depict him.

Though Steinbeck, Brando, and Quinn were nominated for Academy Awards and Quinn received one, this manifestation of Zapata was greeted roughly.[112] *Viva Zapata!* did poorly in the United States, where Zanuck—probably from lasting political concerns—did little advertising for it and soon withdrew it from circulation. In Mexico City it folded after only one week.[113] On both sides of the border critics lambasted it for numerous sins. In the United States, Hollis Alpert, writing for the *Saturday Review of Literature*, found that efforts to make Brando resemble Rivera's depictions of Zapata had turned out well: the Indiana native was "quite Mexican looking." On the other hand, he complained, "Steinbeck has written it [the script] so that the meaning of events remains beautifully obscure and also free from the criticism of those quick and eager to smell scarlet rats."[114] He concluded that too many liberties had been taken with historical events. In a subsequent issue of the same review, Carleton Beals jumped to Zapata's defense. Promoting himself as an authority who had ridden with the Zapatistas, he declared that Alpert had been too generous in his critique of the "slicked-up interpretation of the great agrarian leader and his times." Voicing the outrage of aging 1930s-style leftists over the renunciation of power that lay at the center of the film, he asserted that Zapata had "committed no such gross betrayal of his followers." Zapata's life could not, he continued, be told as a propaganda piece either for or against communism, "or by making his stark, primitive career into a cream-puff of Gandhi hocus-pocus."[115]

In Mexico the Alemán administration secured a critique from a reviewer who found that the film strayed badly from the historical record, its worst aspect being that it left the impression that Mexico had not responded to Zapata's demand for land. "As a work of art it is uneven," he added, but it was simply another contribution to Zapata's legend, nothing that wounded the dignity of the Mexican nation.[116] Not surprisingly, the Zapatista Front was less complacent. Castrejón and Palacios reported three egregious errors: *Viva Zapata!* presented Zapata as illiterate; showed him "personally executing his enemies"; and made him president, in which office he momentarily rebuffed peasants who arrived from Morelos demanding land. For those reasons they asked first the secretary of government and then President Ruiz Cortines to forbid the film's showing until the errors were rectified. Whether this request had any connection to the movie's short run in Mexico is uncertain, but the negative reception it received there must have gratified the Zapatistas.[117]

In his first script, Steinbeck predicted that Zapata would eventually emerge as "the great and pure man of Mexico and [would] take a parallel position to the Virgin of Guadalupe, as the human patron of the freedom of Mexico."[118] This was no feat of the imagination—Zapata was already well on his way to such standing when Steinbeck wrote—but it is interesting that, in a roundabout way, *Viva Zapata!* helped him take some of the final steps. Much has been written about the challenges, in terms of identity, faced by Mexicans incorporated into the United States following the Mexican-American War (1846–1848), and subsequently by those who migrated across the border. One of those migrants, if only for a few years in the late 1920s and early 1930s, was the muralist José Clemente Orozco, who went north in search of larger commissions. His story is suggestive for ours.

Unlike Diego Rivera, Orozco had never been a fan of the revolution: he depicted its subject matter with ambivalence, and his murals ignored its heroes. He had apparently never painted Zapata. During his stay north of the border, however, he portrayed Zapata twice. The first of those Zapatas appears in a 1930 easel painting that now hangs in the Art Institute of Chicago (see Figure 6.1). This dark, ambiguous work of bold, heavy brush strokes presents Zapata as seen from inside a hut, framed by the light of the doorway. The building's four occupants are all anonymous—in fact, we can see the face of only one—and the nature of their reaction to the new arrival is uncertain. Two of the shadowy figures, one apparently male and the other female, kneel on the floor at the bottom of the painting, embracing each other and each with an arm outstretched. They are tangled together in heightened emotion, for sure, but whether they are begging for their lives, in some sort of agony that Zapata might alleviate, or exalting their hero is anyone's guess. Whatever is happening, the revolutionary context is grim. The painting is full of the imagery of death and violence with which Orozco generally presented revolutionary topics: bandoliers, a dagger, Zapata's blood red scarf, and a blade held by one of the peasants standing in

FIGURE 6.1
José Clemente Orozco, Zapata, 1930. Oil on canvas, 178.4 × 122.6 cm.
(Gift of the Joseph Winterbotham Collection, 1941.35, The Art Institute of Chicago.
© 2007 Artist Rights Society, New York/SOMAAP, Mexico City.)

front of Zapata that rises, within the composition, to touch his left eye. This probably foretells his death—Orozco's friend Alma Reed stated that Zapata's sombrero was meant to evoke a martyr's halo.

Three years later, at Dartmouth College, Orozco placed Zapata in a mural entitled *Hispano-America*, one of a series of panels that examine the "history of America."[119] Zapata can be identified by his mustache, sombrero, and cartridge belts—as we have seen, some of the key iconography—but in other respects the figure does not especially resemble photographs of him, and at least one critic has perceived some of Orozco's own facial features there instead. This Zapata stands in the center of a chaotic, upended landscape, where he is surrounded by greedy politicians, businessmen, and soldiers, some of whom throw themselves on a river of gold coins at the bottom of the panel. He is on the point of being stabbed in the back by an American general. Here Zapata evidently represents the forces of idealism, hope, and progress, which are repeatedly undermined by the corrupt and the selfish in this mural series.

So why the sudden interest in Zapata? Having left behind not only his cultural milieu but also his family, Orozco was sometimes unhappy during his stay north of the border.[120] His observations about the United States, at least as expressed in the Dartmouth murals, were far from flattering, and it is no coincidence that it is an American general who prepares to murder Zapata. Under the difficult circumstances of his voluntary exile, then, we might speculate that Orozco was in greater need of symbols of Mexico such as the one Zapata was becoming than he was under normal conditions at home.[121] Notwithstanding his ambivalence about such patriotic images, they were inevitable facets of his own identity, especially when he moved across an international border to a place where he would be understood and identified as a Mexican rather than, say, as a *tapatío*—a native of Jalisco—as other Mexicans might have described him. In the United States, of course, there was much questioning, undervaluing, and dismissing of that Mexican identity. If Orozco did blend some of his own features into the Dartmouth Zapata, we might therefore assume, it was an acknowledgment of these dynamics of identity. Interestingly, at about the same time Diego Rivera had an exhibition at New York's Museum of Modern Art, for which he redid his calzón-clad Indian Zapata from Cuernavaca in portable form.[122] Rivera and Zapata were by then an old story, but it is significant nevertheless that to this the most prestigious exhibit ever in the United States of a Mexican artist's work—an opportunity to show the gringos what he, the Mexican Revolution, and Mexico were all about—Rivera thought it crucial to uproot Zapata and bring him along.

If Orozco was uncomfortable in New York, imagine the distress of migrants who encountered xenophobia, racism, and segregation in the United States as common laborers. The need for positive images of who they were, collectively, as simply Mexicans—the way they, like Orozco, were now often perceived—was surely strong, and in their mental baggage, at least after the Cárdenas administration had finished its work of diffusion, they carried with them memories of Zapata.[123] Those memories and their associations with Mexicanness were then perpetuated and reinforced in the communities they formed in the United States. In 1932, San Antonio's Spanish-language newspaper included an article that noted the anniversary of Zapata's death in terms by now familiar to us. Zapata fell for Guajardo's ploy, it suggested, because he was a man of his word and expected others, like Guajardo, to share his sense of honor. As his movement crumbled he refused advice to give up the fight, but he did seem to foresee his death. After Chinameca, of course, he passed into immortality.[124] Later in the decade, *El Continental*, the Spanish-language paper of El Paso, recognized Zapata's anniversary with an article entitled, "From Bandit to Hero." This piece reported that there was room for Zapata alongside the region's Villa cult, and that peasants and workers, teachers and students, would commemorate him just across the border in Ciudad Juárez, Chihuahua.[125]

In 1952, Mexican-American needs, memories, and evolving traditions met, in *Viva Zapata!*, a righteous man, and thus a rare positive expression about Mexico in the mass media of the United States.[126] Advertisements in Spanish-language newspapers emphasized Brando's machismo and, in general, "Action! Romance! Emotion!" but surely the movie worked, on another level, to kindle pride.[127] People from around Zapata County, Texas—named for another, local Zapata—still recall Brando and Jean Peters strolling through the town of Roma, which the studio remodeled for the film, as a great event.[128] Fifty years after the fact, newspaper columnist Linda Chávez wrote that this was the first movie she remembered seeing, at the age of five in Albuquerque's Kimo Theatre. "I remember crying out loud in the auditorium Quinn's line as he rode across the screen after Zapata was killed: 'No, no, he's not dead. He's in the mountains with his people.' The movie still brings tears to my eyes."[129] She did not have it quite right—Quinn's Eufemio died before Brando's Emiliano—but *Viva Zapata!* had left a deep impression. In the late 1990s, the leader of a Hispanic organization illustrated a point about the nature of leadership by saying,

> I'm reminded of the story of Emiliano Zapata. When he was about to go and meet with the *federales* [federal troops], it was evident that there

was a good chance he would not return. Some of the members of the community pleaded with him not to go. Zapata turned and said to the crowd, "A strong people do not need strong leaders."[130]

Though far too young to have witnessed such an event, the man who told this story could probably envision Zapata speaking those words because they came straight from Brando's mouth. The power of movies is considerable, and Brando's Zapata probably infiltrated many memories in a similar fashion. He even captured the imagination of New Yorker Edward Rivera—of Puerto Rican ancestry—who saw the movie three or four times, and presumably that of his father, too, who enriched family culture with frequent recitations of the "Discourse on the Anniversary of the Death of Emiliano Zapata, 10 April" he found in an anthology of oratory.[131]

With the 1960s came new uses for the transnational Zapata by the United Farm Workers Union under the leadership of César Chávez.[132] Chávez rarely mentioned Zapata in his speeches, but on Mexican Independence Day in 1965, posters of the caudillo were abundant at the parish hall in Delano, California, when grape pickers gathered to vote for a strike that would last five years.[133] On the wall of the union's office, meanwhile, Zapata appeared—near an image of pacifist Mahatma Gandhi—against a blood-red background, gun and saber at the ready, under the slogan *"Viva la Revolución."*[134] His name was also painted on a fence at the workers' camp in Delano, along with those of Villa, Juárez, and Chávez.[135] In 1966, when union members marched to Sacramento, the state capital, to draw attention to their strike, they performed dramatic readings of their Plan of Delano, which was deliberately written after the manner of the Plan of Ayala.[136] In 1968, muralist Antonio Bernal painted an armed Zapata as one figure in a line of heroes on the wall of the United Farm Workers' *Teatro Campesino* (Campesino Theater) building in Del Rey, California. Marking the start of the Chicano muralist movement, this painting helped establish Zapata as a key element of Chicano iconography.[137]

Elsewhere, 1967 saw the publication of the epic poem, *I Am Joaquín*, by Rodolfo "Corky" Gonzales. An ex-boxer from Denver, Gonzales led an organization called the Crusade for Justice that emphasized Chicano nationalism and demanded civil rights for urban Chicanos. A sweeping tour of history in pursuit of Chicano identity, *I Am Joaquín* claimed Mexican history, culture, and values for Chicanos, something previous Mexican-American groups, which tended to prioritize assimilation, had been reticent about doing. The protean narrator of the poem was not only Joaquín—a reference, apparently, to Joaquín Murrieta, the legendary leader of resistance to Anglo incursion in California—but also Cuauhtémoc, Cortés, Hidalgo, Juárez, Madero, and, of course, Zapata, among others. He was, in other words, the product of Mexican history on both sides of the border and the synthesis of often conflicting forces, as the inclusion of both Aztec resistance leader Cuauhtémoc and Spanish conqueror Cortés demonstrates. Zapata got no more attention than the other heroes Gonzales mentioned, but his contribution to the imagery was not negligible. "I am Emiliano Zapata," the narrator announced, "'this land, / this earth / is / OURS.' / The villages / the mountains / the streams / belong to Zapatistas."[138] On one level, this was merely a way of indicating what Zapata's program was to readers unfamiliar with the history Gonzales found so crucial. But it was also a demand, made on top of Zapata's claims, for the return of the mythical Chicano homeland, Aztlán, identified with the American Southwest, which had been taken from Mexico in 1848. Infused with Zapata's spirit, the narrator insisted that the land in which Chicanos worked belonged to them.[139]

Based on initiatives such as these, by 1967 and 1968 a broader Chicano movement was in full bloom. A central part of the story was the activities of high school and college students, especially in California and Texas, who staged walkouts and other activities in pursuit of community control of schools, Chicano studies programs, and less restrictive university admissions policies. In support of those causes, Zapata posters appeared on students' bedroom walls and broad Zapata mustaches sprouted from their upper lips. Chicano activists later reported that Zapata's image became so ubiquitous at this time in Los Angeles that the police issued an "all-points bulletin" on him.[140] That anecdote presumably started as a joke, but some in positions of power in the United States did recognize the threat Zapata posed. Delano grape grower Bruno Dispoto warned that "Mister Cesar Chavez is talking about taking over this state—I don't like that. Too much 'Viva Zapata' and down with the Caucasians, la raza, and all that."[141] While the precise dynamics of Zapata's movements are murky, it is interesting that Viva Zapata! enjoyed a comeback, during the 1960s, among "minority" students on college campuses and members of the civil rights, student, and anti-Vietnam War organizations that comprised the New Left. Less wedded to models of class conflict than traditional Marxists and strongly influenced by existentialism, these viewers apparently responded to the moral challenges faced by Brando's Zapata, and his ultimate rectitude, in a way Carleton Beals could not.[142]

Shortly after his death, then, Emiliano Zapata hit the road. In using ejido, education, and commemoration to spread the word around the country, officials of the central government hoped Zapata would help both to link localities to them and put a positive face on their revolutionary endeavors in those localities. Local communities competed for statues of Zapata or, if they could make a case, for his bones, as a way of connecting with the state's revolutionary project, a way of gaining recognition and the resources that might come with it. But those who met Zapata as he traveled were not merely self-serving; often, they also came to like him. Looking for better lives but not ready to leave their traditions behind, some migrants even carried him along as they crossed the northern border.

Zapata's cult encountered a variety of conditions. In many ways provincial rituals evoked the Cuautla ceremony, reflecting a collective understanding of what such an event should entail. But though ritual elements revealed the existence of a national civic culture, provincial rituals were not carbon copies of the Cuautla production. Barbecue and baseball demonstrate that all was not formality and order, and in general there was room for freer expression in the villages of Mexico, where an open podium was even a possibility. The active participation of students and inmates in Oaxaca, as well as the incorporation of regional cultural elements, hinted that different localities might generate different Zapatas.

If Zapata was an element in the process of imagining a national community, then, he was also present where local communities were being reimagined in the aftermath of the revolution. In those localities he interacted with landscapes already granted sacred qualities because of the religious, ethnic, historical, and civic meanings they bore—the mountains that gave the inhabitants their character, the fertile lands that had long fed them, the streets where the ancestors had defended themselves, the cemetery where they were buried. When the citizens of Atlixco, Puebla, paraded memories of Zapata through their "principal streets," he occupied, for a moment, the center of local patriotic feeling. His statue in the plaza that bore his name did not keep him at that center, but it did affix him more permanently to the local world.

Zapata did not, of course, completely unite people in places where his myth took root. As on the national scene, not everyone agreed that he deserved to be honored at all. One individual allegedly misbehaved at the 1953 commemoration at Coyuca de Benítez, Guerrero. "He expressed himself," indicated an observer, "with irreverence toward General Zapata" to the point of nearly provoking "a regrettable conflict."[143] In Morelos, meanwhile, local politics often pitted a Zapatista party against others who chose not to utilize Zapata's name.[144] There was also competition for holiness within the cult: in 1955, the president of the Tlalchapa, Guerrero, branch of the Zapatista Front complained of an ejidal official who arrived late at the commemoration with an "insignificant" floral offering. As Zapata's image spread and grew in power, a process of conversion was taking place, but not everyone was thrilled by the new creed.

On rare occasions the opportunity for freer expression that existed at provincial rituals produced direct criticism of the national government. The grumbling we have seen around the edges of the Cuautla event took center-stage at San Pablo Oxtotepec, when Zapatista veterans protested the Defense Ministry's failure to recognize their contributions to the revolution. Symbolically occupied by the federal government, the Cuautla commemoration had become merely a venue for national politicians to make their presence—and priorities—known, but comparable official domination could not happen everywhere. While local and state officials were certain to be present at any given provincial commemoration, it would have taken a highly efficient and coherent state to ensure that they would all regulate the exchange of views about Zapata's meaning in the same way. The complaints at Oxtotepec did not amount to much in the way of rebellion in Zapata's name, but they did suggest what the future might bring. As we saw in Chapter 5, suggestion of that future was clearer down in Guerrero, where well-developed memories of Zapata and the efforts of Zapatista Front leader José María Suárez Téllez helped produce an oppositional Zapatismo that would grow stronger into the 1970s. Officials in the capital had delivered Zapata to the provinces with the goal of uniting Mexicans around him, but in Mexico's sundry corners they were going to encounter some difficulties. Local communities are more easily imagined than national ones: one can know, more or less, the people and the geography of a small town in a way that is impossible at the national level. In such domains, memories of Zapata would be closer to everyday, lived experiences and needs. And that, as we will see, can be profoundly decentralizing.

Zapata also traveled to the United States. There, of course, Mexican authorities could no longer hope to control him—they could stop Kazan from shooting in Morelos, but they could not prevent him from making his film. In the United States, Zapata entered into a relationship with a different state and a different set of economic and social forces. He thus found himself in a new sphere of identity formation, a target of racism and other facets of American culture along with his fellow immigrants. In that different context his meaning changed. In *Viva Zapata!* he was raised up as the kind of hero that made staunch anticommunists in the U.S. government queasy, and during the 1960s, as a Chicano, he challenged social practices, economic power, and political exclusion alike. Because those in political and economic power north of the border had no interest in him as a source of legitimacy—and thus emitted no competing messages—becoming a rebel again, a radical, was relatively simple. As the summer of 1968 began Zapata still enjoyed that status only in various pockets of Mexico and the United States, but this was a situation in which those at the top of the Mexican pyramid might have been able to see trouble approaching.[145]

SEVEN

RESURRECTING THE REBEL

Emiliano Zapata at Work and Play, 1968–1988

In her 1991 short story, "Eyes of Zapata," Chicana writer Sandra Cisneros adopted the perspective of Inés Alfaro (often called Inés Aguilar, see Chapter 4). The mother of Zapata's first two children, Alfaro was little more than a footnote in most accounts of Zapata's life. In Cisneros's hands, however, she got the chance to tell her story while Zapata slept, and in that telling gave us a unique, intimate vision of the caudillo. Touring Zapata's reclining body with tenderness, Alfaro told of "the skin of the eyelids as soft as the skin of the penis, the collarbone with its fluted wings, the purple knot of the nipple, the dark, blue-black color of your sex, the thin legs and long feet."[1] She called him "*pobrecito*"—poor little boy—and noted he had "hands too pretty for a man." His eyes, on the other hand, were "terrible as obsidian," full of the future and "the days gone by," but also, "beneath the fierceness something ancient and tender as rain." Their children, she added, had those eyes too, and would have to live with the legacy.[2]

Alfaro was pleased that when Zapata returned to her from the war—and from his other women—he could sleep as she watched over him, but the other women were a big issue. She expressed her jealousy, in particular, of Josefa Espejo, ostensibly Zapata's "real wife," though Alfaro slept with him first, balancing "that thin boy's body of yours on mine, as if you were made of balsa, as if you were boat and I river." These, she indicated, were their happy days, before *his* revolution began.[3] She tried to resist him, she claimed, because she could see his vanity from the start. She talked of the quality of his clothes and horse, and of the inability of "stupid country girls" to resist the charms of "the magnificent Zapata in his elegant *charro* costume, riding a splendid horse. Your wide sombrero a halo around your face. You're not a man for them; you're a legend, a myth, a god."[4] Only now when he slept—the pose, the outfit, that magical, revolutionary skin shed at the side of the bed—was he sometimes the boy she had known. "Are you my general?" she asked, "or only that boy I met at the country fair in San Lázaro?"[5]

But when Zapata awoke, he always again became the great caudillo, dressing to leave, dismissing her "women's concerns," nothing to say and unable even to joke or sing. The last time you left, she told his sleeping form, "you gave a sigh that would fit into a spoon. What did you mean by that?"[6] Looking back from the end of the revolution, after a decade of killing, Alfaro knew exactly what Zapata was going to. She recalled watching their son Nicolás play with bullet shells, hiding "in caves with the spiders and scorpions," bodies being burned. "The fat ran off them in streams," she elaborated, "and they jumped and wiggled as if they were trying to sit up."[7] Nicolás, she revealed, now traveled with his father so he could learn to be a man.

Despite Zapata's brusqueness, Alfaro confidently asserted that he would always come back, at least until he was killed. They can no longer kill the revolutionary, she declared, but she predicted they would soon kill the boy. And so she was a widow every time he left, "we are all widows, the men as well as the women, even the children. All *clinging to the tail of the horse of our jefe Zapata*."[8] She challenged the Zapata who rode off to war to stay and fight at her side, because "the wars begin here, in our hearts and in our beds." She asked whether he wanted men to treat their daughter as he treated her.[9] Or as a group of men had treated her mother, who had visions and desires, and was caught in a field "with a man who is not my father." After murdering her for doing what Zapata did without a thought, they staked her down, "the star of her sex open to the sky... braids undone, a man's sombrero tipped on her head, a cigar in her mouth, as if to say, this is what we do to women who try to act like men."[10] The cigar and the sombrero could have been a reference to Zapata himself, though this occurred before the revolution, before he became the caudillo. This, in any event, was why Alfaro rejected Zapata's revolution, with its macho trappings.

Alfaro conceded she had belonged to Zapata ever since he claimed her at the fair. He gave her a first "crooked kiss, all wrong, on the side of the mouth. *You belong to me now*, you said, and I did."[11] But she asserted her strength, too, her ability to meet his eyes and possess him when he slept, twist him "like a spiral of hair around a finger."[12] Indeed, we gradually discover, she shared her mother's visions. Offering a dried hummingbird to the Virgin or saying "a prayer in *mexicano* to the old gods," she had the power to fly at night above their "little avocado tree, above the house and the corral" and look down on future memories, long after she and Zapata were gone.[13]

Zapata apparently left Alfaro completely in 1910, years before the time, near his death, in which Cisneros set her narrative.[14] By using her story to rescue Alfaro from obscurity and permit her to voice her view of Zapata, Cisneros reflected a dramatic broadening of options in terms of how Zapata might be remembered. The most fundamental change was that by 1991 he had been resurrected as a rebel, and in most respects that meant the new directions he had taken were charged with great seriousness. But though Cisneros was deadly serious herself in her examination of the violence within traditional gender roles and sexual relations, she was not interested in Zapata as rebel. In fact, even as she explored, and contributed to, the greater flexibility of Zapata's image, she undercut his revolutionary stature by exposing his failure to consider gender inequities.

Her work does represent, however, the discovery, after 1968, that Zapata's image could be more than just a vehicle for earnest political commentary, but that it might convey a certain playfulness too—that this icon Mexican officials and others had rendered unable to joke or sing might even be open to parody and ridicule. Within Mexico's gay community, for example, it was rumored that the macho Zapata had been a homosexual. The claim was undoubtedly, for some, simply a way of ridiculing the machismo by suggesting it was a cover. There was, though, one piece of tenuous evidence: Zapata's periodic employment by the reputedly gay hacienda owner Ignacio de la Torre y Mier, son-in-law of Porfirio Díaz.[15] Whether those who circulated this story believed it or just found it amusing, by presenting Zapata in a pose so strikingly new they were certainly toying with his image.

In the case of Cisneros, the playfulness may already be apparent: together she and Alfaro stripped the icon down; displayed him on his bed in the pose of the classic reclining female nude of Western art; subverted his manliness with pet names and references to his boyhood; rendered him, in sum, silent, passive, vulnerable and thus the embodiment of several of the characteristics traditionally assigned to Mexican women.[16] Turning the tables completely, in fact, Cisneros demonstrated her power by going one step farther than Alfaro could: after having a good look and giving Zapata a verbal, public fondling, she cast him aside much as he did Alfaro. He was not, for her, a useful symbol of the Mexican facet of her identity.[17] The new Zapata was serious business, yes, but there was fun along the way.

How do we get from César Chávez to Sandra Cisneros in Zapata's story? The reemergence of the rebel in Mexico comes first. Zapata had never completely ceased to be a rebel. Despite the general trends, even government officials sometimes recalled him as an "eternal rebel" and conceded that he had indeed fought against other revolutionary factions.[18] He was also mobilized at times against the government, as when, in 1951, members of the union at the textile factory "El Angel" requested permission to hold an April 10 rally on the *Zócalo*, Mexico City's main square and the symbolic center of national power. That permission was not granted, but the workers met anyway, along with members of a "hunger caravan" of Coahuilan miners, an independent peasants' organization, and some students from Mexico City's National Polytechnic Institute. Speakers attacked the regime, and some of those present attempted to take down the flag flying in front of the Supreme Court. According to *Excélsior*, when the police arrived the workers attacked them as well, resulting in the arrest of those the authorities identified as "communist agitators." But though Zapata meant resistance on that day in 1951, and he did so for Rubén Jaramillo as well, these were isolated incidents. Many grumbled about the PRI and its appropriation of Zapata during the Golden Age, but few were ready and able to do anything about it.[19]

Then, in 1968, the rebel Zapata resurfaced in a Mexico City in the throes of rapid change. Since 1940 the modernizing efforts had borne fruit. Mexico had enjoyed one of the world's fastest-growing economies, with an average growth rate of more than six percent and industrial productivity rising still faster. Economic growth brought a population boom, especially in urban areas and most particularly in Mexico City, where much of the new industrial base was located. Home to about two million people in 1940, the capital had roughly nine million residents in 1968, making it one of the world's largest cities. Though far from perfect, the educational programs of the postrevolutionary regime generated the higher rates of basic literacy necessary for this urbanizing world. Mass media supported education, or at least helped disseminate information and ideas associated with growing cities. Lured and prodded by media images and seeking new opportunities, some Mexicans were able to acquire the skills necessary for social mobility and helped swell the ranks of the urban middle class. While these were precisely the sort of changes Mexican leaders sought, change is inevitably dangerous to those flourishing under the status quo, so officials took steps to channel it in ways they hoped would limit the threat. Through an assortment of direct and indirect means—and a combination of carrots and sticks—they sought to moderate media messages and keep them supportive of government power and programs. Social transformation and a sense of broadening horizons thus strained against conventional assumptions within signs that were many and mixed.[20]

The growth of an urban, middle-class Mexico was mirrored by the expansion of such educational institutions as the National University, which now had nearly a hundred thousand students. Reflecting international trends, discontent on university campuses had increased during the administration of Díaz Ordaz, and in July 1968 an apparently innocuous brawl between rival high schools in downtown Mexico City triggered new dissatisfaction when riot police, the *granaderos*, broke it up with what many thought was excessive zeal. University students immediately took notice, other clashes between students and police followed, and by August students at the National University and the National Polytechnic Institute had organized large demonstrations and begun to reach out to other groups—urban workers in particular. The students' main demands were that the chief of police be fired, the granaderos disbanded, political prisoners released, and the World War II–era article of the Penal Code that outlawed "social dissolution"—thus facilitating the jailing of those political prisoners—be repealed.

Zapata entered the fray as the students developed their strategies. During the first days of the movement they had turned to China's Mao Zedong and to Che Guevara—one of the architects of the recent and deeply influential Cuban Revolution—to symbolize heroic resistance. For them, according to one leader, Paco Ignacio Taibo II, "the past was international territory." Mexican heroes such as Zapata "were characters of somebody else's history, with which boring bureaucrats working as professors had tried to uneducate us; they were, at most, the names of streets." [21] Political science student Claudia Cortés González put it somewhat differently. She had never thought of Zapata as a potential symbol because he "has become part of the bourgeois ideology; the PRI has appropriated him." In fact, attitudes toward official heroes were in such a state that López Mateos era legislation made it illegal to defame them. [22] As products of the urban world the students were simply at the opposite pole, in social terms, from the peasants who were still Zapata's major constituency. Ritual and school had brought Zapata to the city long ago, and political rhetoric had repeatedly associated him with social justice in general, with modernization, and with the nation, but he had still not captured the imaginations of the children of the miracle.

These negative attitudes toward the fathers of the patria, however, gave the government's experienced propagandists plenty of fodder, and the students found themselves accused of being the dupes of international communist agitators. The implication was that they were bad Mexicans acting against their country's national interests, and they could not hope to forge alliances with many nonstudent organizations if that was how they were perceived. The movement's leaders responded by deciding they would carry, during their protests, "placards with the portraits of Hidalgo, More-los, Zapata, to shut them up. They're our heroes." One participant seems to have adopted the name "el Zapata," and when the students occupied buildings at the National University it was Zapata—along with Guevara and some others—who was the subject of the murals they painted.[23] Some students drew the line when asked to march with a placard bearing Carran-za's likeness, but Zapata was not as hard a sell, and feelings about Mexico's heroes, in general, soon softened. Famed critic Carlos Monsiváis observed that the "propagandistic tactic became emotional reality: from the belief in the Generation Gap between parents and children we pass to the dis-pute for the meaning of patriotic history."[24] In making this nod to expedi-ency, these students were helping guarantee that Zapata would capture the imaginations of student and other urban organizations to follow. He was completing the acculturation process to become a modern, urban Mexican. Emiliano Zapata was becoming cool.

On August 27 about half a million people, including workers and some peasants, came together to protest on the Zócalo, carrying portraits of Hi-dalgo, Morelos, Juárez, Zapata, Villa, imprisoned railroad union leader Demitrio Vallejo and, still the international favorite, Guevara.[25] It was the largest antigovernment demonstration in Mexican history, and when the police and army moved in to impose their version of control on it at least one student died. Despite this sobering outcome, the administration con-tinued to take a hard line. Much of the explanation for that position lies in the fact that Mexico was preparing to host the Olympic Games that October, making it the first "developing" nation to receive that honor. It was a wonderful opportunity for the leaders of the by now highly insti-tutionalized revolution to demonstrate that revolution's success—partic-ularly in growing the economy since 1940—and thus gain international prestige, attract investment, and lay the foundation for future trade. Díaz Ordaz would do his best to ensure that a bunch of hippies did not ruin the show. The students, for their part, were critical of the massive expenditures undertaken for the games in a country where profound social problems persisted.

In mid-September the movement received a sharp blow when ten thou-sand soldiers invaded the campus of the National University, jailing hun-dreds and destroying the murals that had honored Zapata in an unortho-dox context. That the intimidation was beginning to work was evident in the relatively small crowd—perhaps six thousand—that showed up for a rally at Tlatelolco's Plaza of Three Cultures, in the northern part of the cap-ital, on October 2. There the government dealt the knock-out blow, at least for the time being. As dusk descended, army and police units encircled the plaza, and when helicopters hovering overhead began to drop flares, a massacre ensued. Several hundred people were apparently killed, two thousand wounded, and perhaps as many again jailed. Heavily policed, the Olympics went off without a hitch.

Those students who, alive and not in prison, hoped to continue the struggle now took their Zapata underground. Meanwhile, other young people expressed their frustrations through less direct avenues of protest, such as "La Onda Chicana" (The Chicano Wave), a rock-and-roll movement that also sought to pry Zapata from the regime's grasp. The most commercially successful band of this period was Guadalajara's La Revolución de Emiliano Zapata, the very name of which indicated that the rebel Zapata had survived Tlatelolco. This band had little to say about Zapata—other than putting his image on its album covers—but its members bragged that they had provoked fear of *desmadre* (disorder) in the authorities by conquering Mexico City just as Zapata had done when he captured the capital in 1914. La Revolución de Emiliano Zapata also toured California, where the appeal of a band named for Zapata was high. Another group, Los Locos del Ritmo, had a 1971 hit called "Viva Zapata." Sung in English to dodge censorship, like many of the songs of La Revolución de Emiliano Zapata, this tune asserted that Zapata continued on the road and urged listeners to follow.[26] Where the road might lead, though, was an open question: while an advertisement for clothing in a counterculture magazine borrowed Zapata's likeness to proclaim, "here is what the great guerrilla leader says: *¡moda y libertad!* (fashion and liberty)," folk singer Amparo Ochoa traveled back toward the mythical Zapata's roots with a rendition of Armando List Arzubide's old corrido.[27]

Zapata thus returned as a rebel—or at least an anti-establishment figure—to the center of national power. In many respects this was a watershed in the trajectory of his myth, but it was also part of a broader story. It is quite possible, after all, that this outcome was influenced by his slightly earlier status as a figure of resistance among farm workers, and then students, in the United States. The use in Mexican counterculture of the word "Chicano" and the tour of La Revolución de Emiliano Zapata in California demonstrate, at any rate, that these were not separate worlds. If there was such a link, then it was another example of what one scholar has described in this period as "Mexican youth observing American youth observing Mexico."[28] Another possible source of inspiration existed in Zapata's old stomping grounds in Mexico's near south, where Rubén Jaramillo had carried personal memories of fighting at Zapata's orders into the early

1960s, and where memories of Zapata fueled opposition to oppression in Guerrero.

Whether these three strands of Zapata's myth—one regional, one national, and one international—influenced each other or not, the return of the rebel Zapata was produced by their conjunction during the 1960s. The next step was the emergence, in each of the three settings, of guerrillas fighting in Zapata's name—desmadre of a different sort than that offered by La Revolución de Emiliano Zapata. On the first anniversary of the massacre at Tlatelolco, bombs exploded in the Mexican capital. Two months later a group called the Urban Zapatista Front (Frente Urbano Zapatista, FUZ) assaulted a Mexico City supermarket. In October 1970 this new Zapatista Front robbed a branch of the national bank and in September 1971, in its biggest exploit, kidnapped the director of Airports and Auxiliary Services, Julio Hirschfeld Almada.[29] In the wake of the kidnapping the original Zapatista Front served notice that, despite the confusion of some of its members, it had nothing to do with the iniquitous people that had usurped Zapata's name to "commit their criminal acts."[30]

The FUZ, meanwhile, which ultimately ransomed Hirschfield, released a photograph of him in front of a large poster of Zapata at his most poignant—the headshot that had been used by *El Maestro Rural* in the 1930s (see Figure 4.3). On being captured in early 1972, the organization's leader, Francisco Uranga López, demonstrated that he had learned the lesson of the student movement well. "We aren't taking anything from abroad," he avowed, "we are admirers of Emiliano Zapata and he is our inspiration. Zapata did not finish his revolution because they killed him; we are continuing his work." That work, he added, was against imperialism and the oppressor class, and on behalf of peasants, workers, and progressive intellectuals. Another member, social worker María Elena Hortensia Dávalos de Montero, was pregnant and planned to name her child Emiliano if it was a boy and—reflecting international events on the minds of leftists at the time—Vietminh if it was a girl.[31]

Though the FUZ was beaten, Zapata remained in revolt. Many of the most striking examples of that revolt came from guerrillas operating in the countryside in the hope of imitating the success of Guevara and Fidel Castro in building a revolutionary movement based on support from segments of the rural populace. This is where former schoolteacher Genaro Vázquez Rojas, collaborator with José María Suárez Téllez in opposition politics in Guerrero in the early 1960s, returns to our story. Frustrated with nonviolent methods, members of his movement, the Guerreran Civic Association (Asociación Cívica Guerrerense), gradually armed themselves and retreated into the mountainous terrain of Guerrero, where Zapata too had spent time. By 1968 there was open conflict.[32]

Vázquez Rojas wrote that the assassinations of Zapata and Villa were "fresh in the memory," along with many other murders, including that of Jaramillo, perpetrated by the government over the decades since the revolutionary fighting ended.[33] When Vázquez Rojas himself was shot dead in his car by police and soldiers in 1972, his wife was more explicit about his identification with, and desire to seek legitimacy in, Zapata. She told her children that their father "admired Emiliano Zapata and went to the mountains to fight like him." Like Zapata, too, she revealed, he had once told her, "I will fight until I die" and, again, "these are not ideas copied from abroad." Whether it was acceptable for Vázquez Rojas to claim to follow Zapata, of course, depended on the observer. One reporter commented disparagingly that he had "placed himself above the law, considering himself a new Emiliano Zapata." For his part, the governor of Guerrero gave the group credit for no platform at all, simply charging that its members were criminals who stole and kidnapped to get money for their own use. A Cuernavaca journalist retorted that the authorities of Zapata's time also called him a "leader of outlaws" and a "cattle thief."[34]

A second prominent Guerreran rebel, Lucio Cabañas, headed the Peasant Justice Brigade of the Party of the Poor (Brigada Campesina de Ajusticiamiento del Partido de los Pobres) and was grandson of a Zapatista. Cabañas commented that the death of Vázquez Rojas was sad for the poor, but for the rich and for government officials it was a motive for happiness, "just as the Carrancistas rejoiced at the death of Emiliano Zapata."[35] In fact, linking its opponents to Zapata's assassination was a central rhetorical device of Cabañas's organization. In response to government charges that guerrilla members were criminals, a Peasant Brigade manifesto asserted that this judgment was up to the people, not "to an enriched politician, a bone-licker who made his fortune on the name of a Zapata that they [sic] themselves killed." The massacre at Tlatelolco and other such atrocities, the document continued, did not represent "the justice of which Zapata dreamed."[36] In June 1972, after the Brigade kidnapped Guerreran senator Rubén Figueroa, another message made the point yet again: it is true that we set a trap for Figueroa, it read, but the "bourgeois Carrancista gentlemen" to whom the communication was directed should remember that "they set a worse one for Emiliano Zapata, at Chinameca."[37]

It was no longer a case of the revolution pitted against the reaction. Decades of unhappiness over corrupt "revolutionaries" were finally reaching full expression with Cabañas and his collaborators, who were appropriating the part of the revolution they admired and insisting on the rifts in the revolutionary family that the PRI had tried so hard to bridge. As part of the strategy of turning Zapata against the state, Cabañas made sure to observe the proper rituals. One man recalled him marching into a village one April 10 with more than 150 men behind him; he then launched into a long speech on Zapata and related topics. "The campesino," he said,

> had no doubts about following Zapata; he saw in him his only hope of liberating himself from the situation he was in. Zapata, when he began, did it much like we are doing it, with a few of the most decided taking up arms, those who are not scared by the thunderclap of these (and he [Cabañas] raised his M-2), those that don't tremble when people tell them "here come the soldiers." [38]

Ultimately, the Brigade offered the concept of a nation built around Zapata and separate from the regime, as when it notified the police and soldiers arrayed against it that "to defend the bad government of the rich is to betray the Fatherland of Cuauhtémoc, Morelos and Zapata." [39]

Given the time that passed between the lives of the two men, Cabañas's program was naturally not precisely that of Zapata. As expressed in a letter of 1974, the goal was to "fulfill and exceed the ideals of the Zapatista Revolution, bring the proletarians of Mexico to power," and install a socialist regime. Various documents also demonstrated a strong rejection of U.S. imperialism.[40] Nevertheless, Cabañas's desire to take Zapata back from the state was relentless, and it helped him capture the imagination of many observers. One author seemed especially taken by what he perceived to be Cabañas's incorruptibility, asserting that like Zapata and Vázquez Rojas, he was not tempted by the money that passed through his hands or the offers that were made to him.[41] Another commentator remarked, shortly after Cabañas's death in a late 1974 ambush, that there were rumors in rural Guerrero that Cabañas, like Zapata, had survived his supposed demise.[42]

While the most famous guerrillas of the period were those of Guerrero, there were many more. Operating on the Oaxacan coast and in the mountains of Sonora and Chihuahua was the Emiliano Zapata Revolutionary Brigade (Brigada Revolucionaria Emiliano Zapata, BREZ).[43] And across the border, in San Francisco, a group called the Emiliano Zapata Unit set off several bombs and reportedly plotted the assassination of then-governor Ronald Reagan.[44] By the mid-1970s, though, guerrilla activity was dying out, and in Mexico in particular, the regime had largely defeated the rebels in the field, thus winning this contest over Zapata's memory by force of arms.

However daunting they seemed at the time, in retrospect the guerrillas were not necessarily the biggest threat to the PRI's control over either Zapata or the nation. Other more gradual and subtle developments would also have a great impact. One such development was the publication of a powerful new history of Zapatismo, John Womack's *Zapata and the Mexican Revolution*, which appeared both in English and Spanish in the late 1960s. Adopting a narrative approach, Womack's work was characterized by exhaustive research and—driven by the peasant war that raged in Vietnam as he wrote—a passionate writing style that combined a populist, leftist perspective with down-to-earth colloquialisms and an occasional romantic flourish.

Womack's book was, of course, about Zapata's battle for land and liberty, but it was also about his righteousness: his incorruptibility and simple tastes, his loyalty, his ability to represent his people, his rejection of politics, his intransigence, the regional utopia he created when given the opportunity. "A man obsessed with staying true," wrote Womack, "he could not betray a promise for the life of him," and thus, not unlike Kazan's much maligned hero (Womack liked the movie), he chose at a critical juncture to shun many of the responsibilities of power.[45] Indeed, the author was so intent on denying that there was anything duplicitous about Zapata that he suggested that the professions of admiration for Guajardo in the letters he signed as they arranged their meeting were legitimate—this despite accusations that Guajardo had perpetrated a massacre in Tlaltizapán some years earlier.[46] Ultimately, he credited Zapata and his followers with a pyrrhic victory in that they forced the new regime to undertake agrarian reform, but Womack was no more fooled by the revolutionary family than was Cabañas.[47] His revolution was one in which a single stalwart leader and his followers were ranged against a host of politicking pretenders—Madero, Huerta, Carranza—some who called themselves revolutionaries and some who did not. It was also a revolution that subsequent politicians had led seriously astray.

Too much had been written and said about Zapata by that time for any of these story lines to be entirely new, but Womack's status in American academia—the book landed him tenure at Harvard—the depth of his research, and his engaging writing style gave the arguments he developed a force they had never had before. *Zapata and the Mexican Revolution* was broadly distributed, becoming one of the biggest sellers ever in the United States on a Latin American theme and, in Mexico, eventually being included in a 1980s series of historical classics put out by the Ministry of Public Education, which printed 30,000 copies.[48] According to the usually hard to please Zapatista Front, it was "an objective book" by an "impartial historian," and thus validation by a total outsider of the Front's insistence that Zapata was the revolution's only genuine revolutionary.[49]

Not everyone loved Womack's book. Alfonso Taracena, author of a volume on Zapata in the 1930s, published another, less favorable one in 1970 in which he declared that Zapata had ties to conservative supporters of Huerta and apparently reasoned from there that Womack, as Zapata's defender, was of "Huertista extraction." [50] Still, the high quality and lasting influence of Womack's work, his close relationships with Mexican academics, and his association with President Carlos Salinas de Gortari (1988–1994), who was his student at Harvard in the 1970s, together gave him a certain stature in late twentieth-century Mexican history. In the words of one Mexican scholar, Womack "is acquiring the same mythic quality as his hero. The historic image we have today of Zapata, thanks to Womack, owes much to the populism and Marxism of the United States." [51]

Though much less accomplished, another cultural product of the period, Felipe Cazals's 1970 movie *Emiliano Zapata*, was significant in being the most expensive film ever made until that time in Mexico. It was also the first feature film shot in Mexico that focused, with no indirection, on Zapata's life. That fact in itself is testimony to the difficulties of bringing an icon loaded with so much meaning before a mass audience, and those responsible for the attempt quickly discovered why no one had done it before. It was the first movie for Cazals, who went on to a distinguished career in the business; Zapata was played by Antonio Aguilar, a star of the singing cowboy genre, who dieted for the role.[52]

One of the goals of this work was to be historically faithful, and Cazals did manage to introduce the main characters and events, even in the second half of the story, where *Viva Zapata!* meandered and which most historians ignored. Still, transitions from scene to scene were usually unclear—as if Cazals assumed everyone knew the history—and some details were inevitably misrepresented. Zapata, for instance, married and then bedded a far too white Josefa Espejo, but thankfully the larger truth, the machismo of his character, was captured by the fact that he wore his cartridge belts during the sexual encounter.[53] Aguilar himself did not much resemble Zapata. His mustache, if anything, was too big and his gruff, sonorous voice did not seem to fit, perhaps because it was that of a man who was slightly older than Zapata would ever be. In general, he came off as a comfortably middle-class Zapata—more paternal than macho—who experienced none of the quandaries that weighed on Brando's version. In fact, the only time one senses any internal life was when, working on the Plan of Ayala, he struggled to the conclusion that, "we are not bandits, we are men with God and with law." Cazals pursued authenticity with a great many showy and destructive battle scenes, full of spurting blood, burning buildings, and dead and dying horses, but he displayed little understanding of what guerrilla warfare was like. Whether because Aguilar and Cazals had artistic differences—which they did—or just because the pressure of doing Zapata was intolerable, the seriousness of the endeavor weighed it down. There was not an instant of intentional humor in the film.

In the end, Zapata rode completely alone across a broad plain and into the hacienda with a bedraggled and desperate look on his face that said he knew exactly what was going to happen and was anxious to get it over. The critics agreed it was high time. One remarked that Zapata occasionally "seems to us rather constrained within an inflexible mold, the same observation, we recall, that we made at the time about Zapata-Brando." The problem was, this critic added, that everyone was already familiar with the iconic image of Zapata and, anyway, a wooden Zapata was no basis for a good movie.[54] Another reviewer wrote that the film was "neither a faithful vision nor a betrayal, neither traditional nor modern, neither epic nor ordinary, neither moving nor cold, neither indifferent nor passionate." [55] Cazals was more to the point. It was, he said, *"una mierda negra"*—a black crap—and the worst sin of his film career.[56]

Beyond questions about whether it was a movie anyone would care to see were the political issues. Apparently the only person who liked it was Díaz Ordaz, who gave Aguilar's performance a thumbs-up, a suggestion that it was a sufficiently iconic portrayal for the regime, which did maintain veto power through the censor's office in the Ministry of Government.[57] The Zapatista Front, on the other hand, found scenes that denigrated Zapata. The single example provided in an *El Campesino* article on the subject was that, just as in *Viva Zapata!*, Aguilar's Zapata was personally involved in an execution, in this case leading Otilio Montaño to the wall where he was shot. This, the Front argued, was "inexact": Zapata was absent when Montaño was tried and killed. Reflecting the sad state of filmmaking in Mexico—the golden age of the 1940s was now a distant memory—the movie had been selected for the International Film Festival at Cannes, but the Zapatista Front, certain it "would leave an image of Emiliano Zapata completely distinct" from the truth, persuaded the relevant officials to ground it.[58]

The pain did not pass quickly for the makers of *Emiliano Zapata*. Several years later, apparently imagining that his long-dead brother still had a reputation to protect, General José Juan Guajardo sued Cazals, Aguilar, and company for defamation of character. The newspapers of the time, the plaintiff pointed out, had called his brother a hero, and that was far more important than the opinions of historians, "men who know nothing." It had been a case of a soldier shooting a bandit, and it had not occurred in an ambush, as depicted in the movie, but during a skirmish that broke out when his brother tried to arrest Zapata. Fixated not on Cazals but on Aguilar, who had produced the movie, the aged Guajardo adopted a befittingly macho posture. "If the law does not punish him," he announced at a hearing, "I myself will execute Antonio Aguilar... I have the guts to do that and much more." He added that he already possessed the weapon and ammunition. Aguilar responded that the deceased Guajardo was a traitor and then, preposterously, that "history is not adulterated in the cinema... and it must not be adulterated." For his part, the scriptwriter suggested that the suit be redirected toward the Ministry of Public Education and the universities, since the movie followed history as it was taught and recorded. The suit was dismissed, and another Guajardo did not, apparently, kill another Zapata.[59] In fact, the Guajardos just suffered more humiliation. Porfirio Palacios went on late-night television to present the Zapatista Front's point of view. Managing to sound sensible about the film's content—it was, he said, ninety percent true and ten percent false, as happens in movies—he certified that Guajardo was responsible for Zapata's death and had already been judged by history. "History is history," he reasoned, "however severe it may be."[60] The *Los Angeles Times*, meanwhile, carried Zapatista veteran Jesús Chávez's version of Guajardo's death. "Guajardo cried all night," Chávez confided,

> And, just before the execution, he was so frightened, that he made signs asking for some rum. He also asked for marijuana to build up his courage, but neither the rum nor the marijuana could keep him standing in front of the firing squad. They had to blindfold him and tie him up in order to shoot him.[61]

Astoundingly, Aguilar found a new director and reprised the part of Zapata in a 1988 movie called *Zapata en Chinameca*. As if to guarantee that this effort would also flop, he reused scenes that had been cut from Cazals's "costly production."[62]

Yet another telling event was painter Alberto Gironella's 1972 exhibit at the Palace of Fine Arts entitled *The Burial of Zapata and Other Burials*. This was, in the words of one reviewer, not a traditional art show but rather an "atmosphere," in which the exhibition itself was the work of art. That exhibition included not only a series of paintings and collages but also an array of household objects, photographs of Victoriano Huerta and of Zapatistas sitting at the counter at Sanborn's Restaurant in downtown Mexico City, and sacks of sugar from recent harvests. Using these diverse tools, Gironella meditated on what Zapata had been, what he had become, and what he should be.[63]

Fundamental to the exhibition was a canvas called *The Burial of Zapata and Other Burials*, which evoked the artistic heritage of Spain in that it was patterned after El Greco's masterpiece, *The Burial of Count Orgaz* (1586). The subject of El Greco's painting was the 1323 funeral of a man, Orgaz, of such piety that Saints Stephen and Augustine reputedly descended to earth to preside over his burial. In the lower half of the huge canvas, the two saints lift the count's body while an assembly of priests and the immaculate, mustachioed elite of Orgaz's world look on. Above them the clouds open as an angel carries Orgaz's soul to heaven, where other angels, a heavenly throng, the Virgin Mary, Saint John the Baptist, and Jesus Christ himself await.

Gironella's echoing of this composition begins with a surreal earthly retinue of largely skeletal Zapatistas—or maybe they are all Zapatas (see Figure 7.1). Some of the skulls of these mourners are disfigured by what appear to be bullet holes, but all maintain their mustaches; all, too, have their sombreros, as indispensable to their images as lace collars were to the Spanish gentlemen El Greco depicted. Also appearing at the bottom of Gironella's canvas is a rendition of the photograph (see Figure I.1) of Pancho Villa in the president's chair with Zapata beside him. Significantly, Zapata's body is missing from this painting, the lower central space where El Greco put the saints and the corpse instead being occupied by an indistinct orange mass. This, perhaps, reflects both Gironella's uncertainty about miracles and the doubts of Zapata's followers about the identity of the corpse. Such uncertainties are clearly expressed in the upper portion of the work. In the middle ground the place of the angel and the rising soul is occupied by a volcano topped by a mustachioed skull. The volcano appears to be active: yellow smoke exits the top of the skull and drifts to the right, where it forms a cloud. Visually, the volcano leads us up, or back, to a white horse, on the gallop, at center top. The horse is suspended in heavens that consist of little more than swirling fields of color inhabited by a handful of skulls and faces so spectral they may be nothing more than the viewer's imagination.

Zapata also appeared in other works at the exhibit, most notably collages in which photographs of him are peppered with flattened bottle caps

FIGURE 7.1

Alberto Gironella, The Burial of Zapata and Other Burials, *1972. Oil on canvas, 400 × 300 cm. (Collection of the Museo de Arte Moderno de la Casa de la Cultura de Gómez Palacio, Durango. Courtesy of Emiliano Gironella. Reproduction authorized by the Instituto Nacional de Bellas Artes y Literatura, 2008.)*

FIGURE 7.2
Alberto Gironella, Zapata with Cattle Brand, *1972. Collage on wood, 100 × 80 cm.
(Collection Gironella Parra. Courtesy of Emiliano Gironella.)*

evidently meant to symbolize the bullets of Chinameca. In one such piece Gironella stood a photo of Zapata on a pedestal composed of these bottle caps (see Figure 7.2). Yet another composition employs part of one of the photographs taken at the orders of Pablo González, shortly after Zapata's death, in which Constitutionalist soldiers hold up the cadaver's head. In this work Zapata and several soldiers are enveloped in tin stamped with flower designs, converting him and his killers together into a facsimile of a religious icon. Other pieces in the exhibit brought bulls and bullfighters, Pablo Picasso, and Raquel Welch into the mix, as well as further exploring—and conflating—the burials of Zapata and the Count of Orgaz.

Gironella claimed he began this work because "one day I saw a photo of Zapata's cadaver surrounded by campesinos looking toward heaven, and that image was identical to" El Greco's painting. "I painted Zapata as he had been left," he continued, "as a screen or a sieve. Because there are politicians who benefit from the idea that Zapata is alive.... [A] dead Zapata, riddled, like a sieve, with bullet holes, 'doesn't sell,' it's no good for inaugurating statues in plazas." Gironella also took pride in another effect of his work. The complex arrangement of art and everyday items gave it a baroque character that tied it to the world that produced El Greco's painting, and that brought to mind the chapels of Mexican churches and home altars, perhaps especially altars created for the Day of the Dead. The result was a show that had "a liturgical aspect. People who attended the exhibition spoke in low voices, as if they were in a church."[64]

Not surprisingly, those attendees drew diverse conclusions about what Gironella meant to say. It seems to have been clear to everyone that this was a repudiation of the official practices that had set Zapata's flattened image on that pedestal made of bullets.[65] The inclusion of Picasso and Welch, both still living and in the eye of the media in 1972, suggested a broader critique of how some individuals were fetishized by modern society—a critique that equated the public simplifying and consumption of personages ranging from Welch to Zapata with death. But Gironella did not intend to be "offensive to the memory of Zapata," as one fellow artist charged.[66] Indeed, he named his son, born the year of the exhibition, Emiliano, and had been a fan of Zapata's since at least 1957, when he painted, like Diego Rivera before him, an idealized Zapata inspired by photographs of him with saber and sash taken early in the revolution. What Gironella hoped to do, then, was to identify a purer and better Zapata than the one the officials put on parade, to tell "a more true and less solemn history," in the words of one observer.[67] This he accomplished in the *Burial of Zapata*, which was obviously meant to raise questions about Zapata's myth, but not to destroy it. The exhibit was not, therefore, as cultural critic Carlos Monsiváis complained, about Zapata's burial at all, but rather about "his new death." For Zapata, of course, death meant new beginnings; Gironella sought to rectify memories of Zapata, to cast off the rigid founding father and recover the hero's plasticity, not call an end to the mythification and offer Zapata's ghost a final place to rest.[68]

As guerrillas stoked Zapata's indignation, Womack made him better understood, Cazals and Aguilar warded off their detractors, and Gironella probed the recesses of the myth, April 10 proceedings continued. The fiftieth anniversary of Zapata's supposed death arrived in 1969, and the Díaz Ordaz administration, looking to erase the vision of a government that called itself revolutionary gunning down students in the streets, tried to make it special. Díaz Ordaz asked the Ministry of Public Education to circulate instructions for schools having ceremonies, and plans made mostly at the local level called for the unveiling of Zapata statues and busts at a multitude of sites—too many, claimed *El Campesino*, to list—including the National Peasant Confederation headquarters in the city of Oaxaca.[69] Díaz Ordaz sent Ford 5000 tractors to the ejidatarios of Etla and other Oaxacan communities, and the National Peasant Confederation distributed posters and biographies of Zapata to schoolchildren who attended ceremonies in that state. Said to be organizing twenty thousand acts nationwide, the Confederation also arranged for its leaders in each state to bring earth to Chinameca, where it was deposited "in a cement box with a glass lid" beneath a quote from the Plan of Ayala about the expropriation of land. In Chihuahua the same thing was done on a lesser scale as soil from all of that border state's ejidos was combined at a monument to Zapata in the capital city.[70]

After Tlatelolco, and particularly with the arrival of Luis Echeverría Alvarez in the presidency in 1970, there was a change of tone. The new president faced extraordinary challenges in the bombings and kidnappings of the period and was hamstrung in his efforts to deal with them by suspicions that he, in his previous capacity as secretary of government, had personally ordered the Tlatelolco massacre. In hopes of appeasing those who were disillusioned by the policies and actions of Díaz Ordaz, he imitated López Mateos by infusing the tired revolution with another dose of populism. He allowed for greater democratization and freedom of the press and encouraged, at least publicly, the formation of independent unions. He also sought to demonstrate renewed energy in the countryside. Conceding that haciendas still existed and that the procedure for resolving land claims had been blocked for years, he promulgated a new land reform law in 1972 and gave agrarian reform greater bureaucratic weight by turning the Department of Agrarian Affairs into the Ministry of Agrarian Reform. Both the head of the new ministry and the leader of the National Peasant Confederation took to calling themselves Zapatistas.[71]

Another departure could be heard in a 1973 speech of Luciano Barraza Allande, who, as director general of guanos and fertilizers, had perhaps the ideal title for an orator representing the institutionalized revolution. "Emiliano Zapata is the hero," he proclaimed, "is the primordial representative of the Third World." With this conception he sought common ground with the international leftist discourse of the period, a relatively painless way of appearing revolutionary that was also evident in Mexico's official support of the Cuban Revolution. It made Zapata the representative not of a particular class within the country but of Mexico as a whole and a group of other nations—disadvantaged and exploited but also proud and united—as they confronted the world's economic powers.[72]

The populist opening signaled opportunity to journalists who wanted to dig deeper than usual in their coverage of April 10 activities. This was especially evident in *Excélsior*, which already in 1970, just before Echeverría took power, printed an article that developed a counterpoint between official proclamations at a Chinameca commemoration and the complaints of Zapatista veterans who attended.[73] While government speakers enumerated the benefits peasants had received from land reform, reporter Jaime Reyes Estrada interviewed a representative of about four hundred Zapatista veterans who wanted to complain about living in misery and ask for houses and pensions. Like the Morelos and Oaxaca newspapers, *Excélsior* was now bringing the grumbling that had long existed behind the scenes of these official acts into the public record.

Another good example occurred as Echeverría barnstormed through Morelos on April 10, 1975, providing the usual handouts, being named a "favorite son" of the village of Chamilpa, and taking credit for turning poor peasants into vigorous agriculturalists. One of Echeverría's themes that day was the persistence of *caciques*, local bosses who often frustrated equitable land distribution in pursuit of their own interests and those of powerful patrons. *Excélsior* correspondent Alejandro Iñigo asked several of the governors who were present about the problem, and all were happy to tell him how they were stamping it out or had already done so. Then the leader of the National Peasant Confederation in Morelos, Roque González, alleged that there were "developers who had become caciques" in his rapidly urbanizing state—such an accusation naturally being useful to him because it suggested he was standing up for the campesinos. Iñigo, however, called his bluff, asking for names. "Why," González responded, "the whole state already knows who they are?" He then attempted to change the subject, but Iñigo persevered. "Names," he said, "we insist," and he eventually extracted three of them from the reluctant witness, along with the observation that "there are many politicians from previous administrations hiding behind *prestanombres.*"[74]

In the hands of these journalists, the day of Zapata's death was becoming a public discussion, rather than a monologue, about government policies, the meaning of the agrarian hero, and what one had to do with the other. Much more important for fomenting that discussion, however, were the activities of campesinos. Though some peasants were surely upset by the violent end of the student movement, they had reasons of their own to act more forcefully. Due to rapid population growth since 1940, landlessness persisted as a problem in the countryside despite the agrarian reform. A newer development was that decades of governmental neglect of the ejido sector and mounting environmental problems sometimes related to that neglect resulted, by the late 1960s, in a decline of agricultural productivity that increased the poverty of those lucky enough to have land.[75] Eventually, the government conceded that Mexico, the birthplace of corn, no longer produced enough basic grains to cover its needs, which was both a socioeconomic misfortune and a serious blow to national pride. Exhortations to produce in Zapata's name, under these circumstances, acquired a new urgency. In 1969 the head of the National Peasant Confederation felt the need to assure the crowd at the Cuautla commemoration that the country could still feed itself.[76] At the same event in 1974, Secretary of Government Mario Moya Palencia noted that there was a world crisis in agricultural productivity and that under those circumstances, "production is synonymous with revolution." In pursuit of greater productivity, though, he made only the usual kind of promise, that the government would supply campesinos with more credit.[77]

For obvious reasons, many campesinos did not trust such promises. Beginning in 1972, with a march of hundreds of peasants from Tlaxcala and Puebla on Mexico City, peasant movements—some independent of the state, some not—began to engage in ritual protest on the day of Zapata's death.[78] This was perhaps the most fundamental step in the return of Zapata to rebel ranks. Many of those protests included land invasions, such as the one around Zimatlan, Oaxaca, supported by students, that took place on April 10, 1973. The orderliness with which the day had been infused over the decades now began to erode. Like Gironella and Cisneros, the campesinos were rejecting the Zapata who demanded only hushed respect from his followers. April 10 became instead, as the older patriotic holidays had often been, a day off from the usual rules, but in this case the revelry took the form of overt protest.

Behind the marches and invasions were organizational endeavors, often undertaken with the help of government bureaucrats or officials of the National Peasant Confederation who were encouraged by Echeverría's populism. Ejidos all over the country joined in Unions of Ejidos—including the Emiliano Zapata Union of Ejidos in Morelos—in order to better press their demands.[79] In 1975 the local branch of the National Peasant Confederation at Tulancingo de Bravo, Hidalgo demonstrated the growing anger and defiance in an advertisement in *Excélsior*. The only thing new in agrarian policy, this statement read, is the creation of the Ministry of Agrarian Reform, "but its specialty continues to be demagoguery, deceit, farce, traffic in land, corrupt intermediaries, incapacity, the use of paper organizations, disorganization, chaos." All of that, it continued, undermined the president's drive for increased production, as did the head of the National Peasant Confederation, despite the happy tales he was telling Echeverría about the distribution of credit. "Our homage to the Apostle of Agrarianism," the notice concluded, "is a public denunciation before the Chief of the Nation of what is occurring in the countryside."[80]

Although the National Peasant Confederation took pains to support some manifestations of the rising tide of protest, the new mobilizations threatened its control of rural Mexico, and in general, Echeverría's populism failed as a political solution. In fact, rather than solving problems, his administration yielded new ones. Low agricultural productivity was only one manifestation of an increasingly shaky economy. Inflation, uncompetitive industry, and a peso devaluation served notice that the Golden Age was over. Echeverría seemed to acknowledge the failure of his approach when he turned his back on the freedom of the press he had advocated and removed the editor of *Excélsior*, in 1976, to quiet that paper's criticism of his policies. With his successor, José López Portillo (1976–1982), the PRI swung back toward the right. The new secretary of agrarian reform proclaimed that land invasions would no longer be permitted, it became harder for peasant organizers to find sympathetic officials, and direct repression of campesinos and journalists increased.[81]

Still, protest in Zapata's name continued. One example of such activity occurred at Huipulco, the home of Zapata's Mexico City statue. Surprisingly, given Huipulco's essentially urban location, a small group of ejidatarios who claimed land in the area made their presence known on April 10, 1977. After attending the official commemoration at the monument, they approached a senator with an announcement. For fifty-five years they had possessed documents, they said, making them ejidatarios on twenty-two hectares of land between the Acoxpa and Xochimilco highways, but had been perpetually blocked from working that tract by the authorities and the rich who had other, more urban, uses for it. They intended to invade and cultivate it now.[82] That same day Zapatista veterans again made their unhappiness heard in Morelos. Complaining about their pensions, they added charges against the Zapatista Front, from which they were estranged. It had, they felt, been far too long under the control of Palacios, "who calls himself a Zapatista colonel without having been in the Revolution, but he has enriched himself." [83] To celebrate the 1978 anniversary, more than a thousand campesinos from Veracruz invaded the offices of Agrarian Reform in Mexico City to force an investigation of the ministry's representative in their state.[84]

On a larger scale, in the summer of 1979 Mateo Zapata convoked a National Campesino Congress in Cuautla. Representatives from many peasant organizations attended, some of them—such as Mateo's own National Plan of Ayala Movement (Movimiento Nacional Plan de Ayala)—at least loosely affiliated with the government, and others independent, like the campesinos from Michoacán who were on the point of forming the Emiliano Zapata Union of Communal Landholders (Union de Comuneros Emiliano Zapata, UCEZ). Given the substantial presence of groups allied with the regime, López Portillo himself attended the meeting's final day, along with his secretary of agrarian reform, Antonio Toledo Corro. The final act of the congress took place at Cuautla's Robles Cinema, where Toledo Corro was to speak. The theater was packed, and guards stood watch at the entrance to keep out those without invitations, among them apparently a disproportionate number of people who were wearing calzones. (On a previous day, guards had prohibited Zapatista veterans from entering the museum built around Zapata's house in Anenecuilco.)

Toledo Corro announced that 84,620 hectares of land would immediately be divided. Anxious to know the details, a "dark-skinned" young man in denim then yelled the question that may have been on everyone's mind: "where?" Others in the audience echoed the query, indicated that Toledo Corro should throw his own hacienda into the pot, or just generally booed and heckled. Shaken, Toledo Corro apparently had no clue about the land's location. As the noise level rose, he managed to say that López Portillo intended to bring the agrarian reform to its conclusion; then the president got to his feet and declared the meeting at an end. The guards kept the president and his entourage safe, as they exited, from the looming crowd of campesinos who, with no idea of what had happened inside, hoped for the opportunity to express their needs.[85]

Unhappy with the semiofficial nature of the Cuautla meeting, independent organizations quickly called a second national gathering, which was held at Milpa Alta, in the Federal District, in October.[86] This assembly produced the most powerful independent peasant organization of the period, the National Plan of Ayala Coordinating Committee (Coordinadora Nacional Plan de Ayala, CNPA). It also announced its opposition to plans to move Zapata's body to Mexico City's Monument to the Revolution.[87]

The idea of nationalizing Zapata's remains had come up again in 1971, at the Cuautla commemoration. In a suspicious departure from the traditionally well-scripted and politician-dominated affair, a campesino, Facundo Salazar Solís, rose to take the podium, supposedly "outside the program." His proposal that Zapata be moved was "received with thunderous applause by the thousands attending." The secretary general of the National Peasant Confederation then stood to offer his organization's support of the initiative, and the Zapatista Front immediately backed it too. Several of Zapata's children were present as the request was made and, despite their frequent spats with the regime, sons Mateo and Nicolás soon joined the growing chorus. Moving his body to the capital would, proponents of the idea claimed, reflect and emphasize Zapata's national and international significance.[88] It was obviously an orchestrated performance, and it was not random chance that it happened when it did. Rather, it was an effort on the part of the regime, in the face of rising dissent, to tighten its hold on its now disputed founding father.

Four days later *El Nacional* weighed in on the issue. Telegrams, it indicated, had been pouring into the headquarters of the National Peasant Confederation from all over the nation to support the suggestion "of the campesinos of Morelos" that Zapata be moved to the capital. Oaxaca's branch of the confederation, for instance, called on Echeverría to heed the appeal to honor Zapata in this way, noting that it was a wonderful coincidence that Zapata might be moved just as new agrarian legislation, with its great benefits for campesino families, was being prepared. Another organization, *El Nacional* reported, took the position that Zapata was worthy of the honor as the "true caudillo" of the agrarian movement, which was the essence of the revolution.[89] Elsewhere in the national media there was indignant repudiation of the notion that honoring Zapata by moving him to Mexico City was intended as a substitute for action on agrarian reform.[90]

El Campesino argued that "it is not just" that Zapata's remains were not at the monument. Noting that the Front had raised this idea two years earlier to no avail, one editorial contended that Zapata had, after all, given the revolution its "basic ideology." Echeverría's agrarian reform law was merely the fulfillment of Zapata's plan, and Zapata's ideas had been translated into all major languages and honored in other nations. The editorial conceded that some people felt Zapata should remain in his home state, but it insisted that since he was an international figure, he should go to "the place that has been chosen as the most sublime site for present and future generations to do homage to the most distinguished men of the Revolution." Zapata's failure to take his place at the monument was now especially problematic since the body of Cárdenas, "the standard-bearer of the agrarian cause for which Emiliano Zapata gave his life," had just been placed there.[91]

Nor was it only national opinion that favored the move. On April 18 the Cuautla newspaper *Polígrafo* printed an article that traced the postmortem history of the body. It referred to Zapata's death as an act of betrayal and recalled that "the cadaver still smelled of powder and blood, and already of decomposition" when they carried it to the cemetery two days later. The author of this piece took the position that with the move to the Monument of the Revolution, "the national campesino will have taken a transcendental step in favor of his agrarian hero; but surely Cuautla will lose one of its characteristic and typical festivities of the last forty years."[92] Five days later another piece in the same paper argued that Zapata, like those already present at the monument, had made Mexico better. He had given the revolution social content, and there had been many improvements for the peasantry. While some campesinos were still impoverished, in those cases Zapata represented the ongoing challenge. For all those reasons he belonged in Mexico City.[93]

A year later Baltasar Dromundo, still a Zapatista at heart and representing the Zapatista Front, reiterated the request that Zapata be moved, but for some reason no action was forthcoming.[94] One partial explanation may have been the inconsistency of Mateo Zapata. Whether he complicated things early in the decade is uncertain, but at the Cuautla ceremony of 1978 he refused to sit with the functionaries on the platform and aired his usual complaints about the state of the Morelian countryside. Grumpy again on the following anniversary, he asserted that "my father doesn't need commemorations. He has already had plenty of speeches. Pure demagoguery. Pure empty promises and the campesinos continue as screwed as before."[95] And then, as the idea of moving Zapata finally hit the fast track, on August 8, 1979, the centenary of Zapata's birth, Mateo stated that he would oppose it until there were no political prisoners in Morelos; until the regime complied, in general, with his father's ideals; and until land tenure became more secure—much of the distributed land was still held on a provisional basis, and ultimate title to all ejido land lay not with peasant villages but with the state.[96]

Then something happened, in the next two weeks, to change Mateo's mind, one possibility being that the regime, allegedly maneuvering to coopt the emerging National Plan of Ayala Coordinating Committee, had told Mateo he could run it. In any event, on August 25 it was announced that he and his half-brother Nicolás—who may also have been an obstacle—had agreed to permit the transfer of their father's remains in light of the agrarian policy of López Portillo, which, they declared, had made Mexico's campesinos the "objects of justice."[97] Zapata's move to the capital was scheduled for the following November 20, Revolution Day, which commemorated Madero's call to arms against Díaz in 1910. It was the ideal date for the transfer from the national government's perspective because, like the Monument to the Revolution, it represented and venerated the revolution as a coherent movement, not as a factional competition. The reburial would complete the symbolic incorporation of Zapata into a national revolution that was PRI property.

That was how things stood when the representatives at Milpa Alta took their stand. Their primary argument was that it was unacceptable for Zapata to be placed next to Carranza, and they pledged to take action to prevent it. "All of Cuautla will watch and keep guard that this accord is respected," claimed one representative, "the general always wanted to be in the land where he was born, buried at the side of his generals."[98] A flurry of commentary followed. Morelos Governor Armando León Bejarano weighed in immediately, asserting that moving Zapata "is not an official request, but an old desire of the children of the hero" that no Zapatista organization could possibly oppose. Agreeing to the relocation, then, was a litmus test of true Zapatismo, and León Bejarano was not above suggesting that some people were appropriating Zapatista identities with scarce justification. He added that the government, though neutral, was willing to grant Mateo's condition that Zapata not be placed with Carranza but rather in the crypt with Cárdenas. As far as León Bejarano was concerned, it was now up to Mateo, since Ana María and a son named Diego were firmly aboard and Nicolás had just died.[99]

An editorial in *Excélsior* supported those who sought to keep Zapata in Morelos. Author Javier Blanco Sánchez wrote that if it was true, as he had heard, that the citizens of Cuautla were dead set against the transfer of Zapata, "it would be the first gesture ever of provincial rebellion in defense of the right to possess a historical treasure." This, he believed, would be a positive step, because letting the locals keep the remains of national heroes would foment patriotism. He also pointed out that León Bejarano's statement that moving Zapata to Mexico City was an old dream of his children was nonsense. Rather, he said, they had initially opposed the measure. In the same issue of *Excélsior*, a cartoon depicted a group of campesinos tilting the Monument to the Revolution into the air while one of them explained, "we prefer to take the monument to the remains of Emiliano." [100]

In the end Zapata stayed put because the independent peasants' organizations expressed their preferences strongly, while government officials had obviously decided they could only profit from relocating him if they could do so while pretending not to care. One part of the opposition's case was made in a message from the Milpa Alta congress to Mateo. While they respected his decision to authorize his father's transfer, a spokesman explained, the remains "are the patrimony not of his family, but of the entire people." [101] To counter those, like León Bejarano, who disagreed with that proposition, opponents of the move later made Nicolás heard from the grave. His last words, they reported, had been, "if the government carries off the remains of my father, it is going to take back from the peasants the lands that were given them because of the blood that he shed." [102] Finally, as promised, campesinos did guard Zapata's Cuautla monument, just a few blocks from Mateo's office, as November 20 approached. It remained only for Mateo to change his mind once again. He explained that he had agreed to moving his father "on the condition that the federal government implement the Plan of Ayala." He had since decided that that condition had not been met. [103]

Having won this battle, the campesinos pressed on with confrontational April 10 activities despite López Portillo's tough bearing. Indeed, in 1981 several organizations linked to the National Plan of Ayala Coordinating Committee used April 10 to draw attention to the government's behavior, charging that assassinations, torture, arrests, and evictions of peasants from their land had increased markedly around the nation.

The regime, for its part, was beginning to talk seriously on Zapata's anniversaries about ending the distribution of land and encouraging instead the proletarianization of the countryside that was, in any event, under way. In 1978 at Cuautla, an official from the Ministry of Agrarian Reform argued that a better way to improve the conditions of peasants than letting them work smaller and poorer plots in a country without more good land to distribute was to make them into skilled agricultural workers—instead of landowners—and accord them the rights and protections that workers enjoyed. Serving notice that the media were not entirely cowed, a critical *Excélsior* editorial charged that this was a plan from people who had turned Zapatista premises into slogans of "political mercantilism," embracing Zapata's goal—well-being in the countryside—while entirely rejecting his means. [104]

López Portillo did get a chance to make someone happy in April 1979, by commissioning a new statue for Chinameca. A life-sized bronze based on "photographic information about the saddle and harness Zapata used the day of his death," the statue depicted the martyr of Chinameca, horse rearing up beneath him, under the gate of the hacienda on the spot where he had allegedly died. It was both a representation of Zapata as the shots rang out and, in its power and permanence, another expression of his resurrection. López Portillo did not attend the unveiling, but Governor León Bejarano was there to link Zapata's altruism with the president's efforts "to revitalize the values that will make our nation great: responsibility, honesty, efficiency, participation, and national pride."[105] With this statue in the center of a remodeled plaza, Chinameca would no longer chafe in the shadow of Cuautla; from now on, April 10 celebrations there would rival those held in the presence of Zapata's remains.

But if many Chinamecans felt gratified, not everyone was happy. Diego Zapata, a son of Zapata's who had received an education, lived in Mexico City as an engineer, and grown a "mustache longer and broader than that of his father" while maintaining few ties to the countryside, was in attendance. His message was that of the regime—that "there is no longer land to distribute"—and his reward the disdain of the Zapatista veterans in the crowd.[106] Even Porfirio Palacios had the spunk to complain that yet another wealthy, well-connected politician with shallow roots in the state was being imposed as a congressman; he also declared that Zapata's ideals had not even been "minimally" fulfilled.[107] The newspaper *Polígrafo* commented with the headline, "Pure Demagoguery at the Ceremony of Emiliano Zapata."[108] But López Portillo plodded on with the ritual schedule, visiting Morelos in August—despite the earlier derision at the National Campesino Congress—to celebrate Zapata's hundredth birthday. On that occasion he unveiled a huge bronze in Cuernavaca, handed out land, and inaugurated a stamp that memorialized the event. His own secretary of government rewarded the president with a commemorative medal bearing Zapata's likeness.[109]

Self-congratulation, López Portillo might have thought, was entirely in order, for Mexico seemed on the brink of a remarkable occurrence. As León Bejarano put it in April, "our country is acquiring in the present circumstances and at the world level, an advantageous position, which should assure our greater development."[110] In brief, Mexico's leaders believed the nation was poised for entry into the "first world" on the basis of abundant oil reserves recently discovered in southeastern Mexico. Mexico had become the world's fourth largest oil producer at a time when the prices paid for that oil were high and rising. The new statues of Zapata were but a drop in the bucket compared to what officials now imagined they could do for the people they governed.

Unfortunately, López Portillo badly mishandled the opportunity. The main mistake was that, in a rush to increase spending on public works, social welfare programs, and subsidies for consumers, the administration borrowed heavily from abroad. Both Mexican officials and foreign bankers assumed oil prices would remain high and thus enable Mexico to pay off the loans. The largest loan, incidentally, went to fund the Mexican Food System (Sistema Alimentario Mexicano, SAM), the first serious attempt in decades to increase food production and keep the agricultural sector from continuing to be a drag on the economy.[111] So it was that prolonged inattention to Zapata's rural constituency helped produce some profoundly negative consequences, because a glut on the world oil market developed in the early 1980s and the price of oil plummeted. The debt became unmanageable and the economy headed into a tailspin—characterized by capital flight, high inflation and unemployment, and the dizzying devaluation of the peso—that turned the 1980s into a lost decade for many. Making matters worse, despite the pious moralism often expressed in Zapata's name, untold millions of the dollars that passed through government coffers during the period found their way into the pockets of López Portillo, his close friends, and other officials. When that information came out it only increased the cynicism of a society already suspicious of its government. The general sense of crisis and flux that began in 1982 has continued, essentially, until the present day.

Episodes of protest on April 10 now reached new heights, thwarting regime desires to bring down the final curtain on land distribution.[112] In 1984, a protest called by the National Plan of Ayala Coordinating Committee and other organizations saw an estimated hundred thousand people march from and through eighteen states, from Sinaloa to Chiapas, before arriving in Mexico City, where they snarled traffic hopelessly as they bore down on the Zócalo.[113] The following year the crowd in the capital was perhaps only half as large, but it was equally successful in shutting down traffic and businesses. Demanding a new, democratic agrarian reform law, the distribution of the lands of disguised haciendas, credit and technical support, more effective commercialization of agricultural products, and an end to the stifling bureaucratization and corruption of the state, they visited the Ministry of Agrarian Reform as well as the Zócalo. Simultaneously, marchers in the city of Oaxaca attempted to take over its agrarian reform building, but were held at bay by police. They demanded that lands around Tuxtepec owned by the family of an ex-governor be divided, and complained, too, about the ponderous wheels of the land reform bureaucracy.[114] Several years later, on another April 10, ten thousand campesinos, tired of waiting, simply took the Tuxtepec lands for themselves.[115]

On the 1987 anniversary, an official of the National Peasant Confederation in Oaxaca tried to gain credibility by delivering a virulent critique of agrarian policies. According to an article in the paper *Noticias*, it was a "gesture of honesty very unusual among the campesino leaders of the CNC."[116] The next year a new group with a focus on Indian identity, the National Coordinating Committee of Indian Peoples (Coordinadora Nacional de Pueblos Indios—CNPI), helped other protestors take over Mexico City's central district yet again. Some of the independent organizations that gathered that day signed an agreement to use "radical and even violent means" to take lands they felt belonged to them, while at the Monument to the Revolution the crowd assembled by the National Peasant Confederation for an official commemoration was notably unenthusiastic.[117]

To address the crisis, the new president, Miguel de la Madrid (1982–1988), set in motion a series of sweeping changes on which subsequent administrations would elaborate. With a graduate degree from Harvard, he was the first of a series of three Ivy League "technocrats" to inhabit the presidency. Like Echeverría and López Portillo before them, these were men with bureaucratic backgrounds who gained power in recognition of their administrative abilities rather than by proving themselves in political office. To pay on the mounting debt, de la Madrid cut government spending in an austerity program that meant still more pain for the average Mexican. He reduced government subsidies for consumers, resulting in price increases for basic goods. He laid off employees of the federal government, cut the wages of those who remained, and sold unprofitable government companies. In an attempt to curtail inflation, he imposed wage controls. Despite these harsh measures, de la Madrid enjoyed some popularity for prosecuting some of the most disgracefully corrupt members of the previous administration. It also seemed for a time as though his economic policies were bringing the economy around. Then came the earthquake of 1985, which wrought massive destruction in Mexico City. The earthquake not only drove the economy back into the doldrums, it also added to the discredit of the government, which seemed ineffective in terms both of rescue and relief.

De la Madrid's program was not the program of a revolutionary government, or at least it was not revolutionary by the standards Mexican practice and discourse had established since 1910. Most fundamentally, the state that had only expanded, since the revolution, at least ostensibly to tend to societal needs, was now retrenching, backing off from many of the social and economic responsibilities it had assumed. Some historians have suggested it was also now beginning to shed the symbolism of the revolution, but there is little evidence of that with regard to Zapata.[118] In fact, at Cuautla in 1984 Francisco Labastida Ochoa, secretary of energy, mines and government industries, gave a spirited defense of the state's right to Zapata. Employing key words from the title of Sotelo Inclán's book, Labastida called Zapata the "root of our Nation" and asserted that this root "has already become trunk and fruit, reason and light." The revolutionary government, he went on, had not just acted on Zapata's ideals in the past but continued to do so. The revolution did not stop, but instead "changes with reality, adapts, adjusts," and now the best way to achieve the goal of improved living standards for the peasantry was to take an integrated approach to rural development. That meant, again, getting beyond the fixation on land distribution. Labastida then spoke of the need to increase the security of land ownership, as Mateo Zapata demanded, by properly documenting the distribution that had already occurred. This would allow farmers to settle down, make improvements on their land in the confidence that it would remain theirs, and produce. "To say Zapata," he concluded, "is to say equality and sovereignty, liberty and development, independence and revolution. Zapata is a fundamental axis of our country: the point at which the history of the fight for justice and the promise of a better future come together."[119]

Despite its poverty, the de la Madrid administration imitated its predecessors by trying to buy a closer relationship with Zapata, as in 1986, when the president inaugurated public works valued at three and a half billion pesos—the peso was now a mere shadow of its former self—on an April 10 swing through Zapata's home state.[120] In the late 1980s, Zapata's remains were placed beneath a new monument at Cuautla (see Figure 7.3). This towering statue depicted Zapata standing alone, propping up a gun with one hand and in the other holding the Plan of Ayala. He looked much like a latter-day Moses, with the Plan of Ayala supplanting the Ten Commandments. He was no longer primarily someone's father, as he had been in the 1932 statue, but rather a society's prophet: still patriarchal, but more dominating, intimidating, godlike.

But a speech, a statue, and some infrastructural improvements were not going to turn the tide. In most respects official Mexico was on the defensive when it came to Zapata, and one could hear the defensiveness on April 10. When campesino protestors arrived at his headquarters in 1985, Secretary of Agrarian Reform Luis Martínez Villicaña was unwilling to meet them. The

march was not undertaken by authentic peasants, he maintained, but had political motives at base, since many of its leaders were congressional candidates from opposition parties. He also characterized the National Plan of Ayala Coordinating Committee and other sponsoring groups as "minority organizations." In that and subsequent years, functionaries speaking in Morelos and Oaxaca complained of those who were using economic problems to condemn the government, charged protestors with demagoguery and acting outside the law, and observed that defaming agrarian reform was negative thinking.[121] This was where things stood as the de la Madrid administration struggled to a close.

GOING HOME TO CHIAPAS

At the age of eighty-one, in 1996, Ana María Zapata looked back on an interesting life. I "have been very restless" in my career, she said, having had many government positions, including the office of federal congresswoman during the López Mateos years.[1] She enjoyed politics and had "been a *priista* since the PNR," which was only logical, since she belonged to "a revolutionary family." From her birth in 1915 the Zapatistas had hidden her from federal troops, so she was in the revolution too. Reflecting back happily on a moment of paternal concern, she reported that she had once become ill when she was with her father in the mountains at Quilamula. Her father had to leave, so he entrusted her to the care of Dr. Gustavo Baz, suggesting it would be best for Baz if her health improved by the time he returned.[2] Whatever Baz did it worked, and Baz—probably the one who told her the story—later reported how relieved he was to "have saved himself."

Her father, she argued, was a heroic idealist. He had become "an international figure, because there is no other person like him." He did not want anything for himself. The most charming part of his history, for her, was that when he was a boy "that infamy that the Spanish, those wretches, were committing" happened in Zapata's "own home." They took "the land we had, that provided food for us," and her "grandfather was crying." It was then that her father promised, "When I grow up, I will make sure, with complete respect for the law, that the lands are returned to their legitimate owners." "That's the true story," she added, "and a very nice thing." Over the years she had, she felt, tried to follow in his footsteps, working for the "well-being of the campesinos of the republic." From the time she was a girl, she had always wanted "the people to be well, to live well."

During the 1930s, though still young, she formed a women's organization because "many people died in the revolution, from sons to fathers to brothers." At that time there was real leadership from General Cárdenas, who was "helping the people who had been in the revolution." So they invited him to a meeting they were having in Morelos about a land problem. Almost half the people present were women. He asked her, "Why are there so many women here?" "Because their men fought at the side of my father," she told him. "They died for a just cause, they went with their weapons in their hands." She had asked herself, "how is it possible" that no one was helping these women that made such sacrifices for the revolution? And she resolved to do what she could.

She believed "it was a clean revolution." When her mother was still alive, some journalists interviewed her for a story about how the politicians had not provided sufficient pensions even for the family of Zapata. Her mother said Zapata had been "a magnificent husband," but then, according to Ana María, she got confused. She told them Zapata executed thieves, so Ana María had to interrupt. "No," she asserted, "my father did not order anyone shot." Later the reporter asked where Zapata got his weapons, and again she had to set the record straight, before her mother answered. My father "never compromised himself with anyone to obtain arms," she maintained.[3] He never backed down or sold out, that was how it was.

What were people thinking, she wondered, when they said Zapata did not die at Chinameca, "that he left and did not keep his promises"? How was that possible? After all, he had ten children. If he had been hiding out, "he would have sent a note, right?" But they waited and nothing came, so they knew he was dead. She went to all the commemorations, except when she was in the hospital, and "I am going to tell you something frankly… ambitious politicians took hold of [Zapata's] banner." Or maybe we should call them "mafiosos." A man from the Defense Department, whose name she had forgotten, came one year to a commemoration at Anenecuilco, and he was one of those who had killed her father. And then there was that lowlife, Salinas, who came down and gathered all the veterans and just told them lies. Later he invited her to the presidential residence at Los Pinos to sign his reforms to Article 27 into law, ending land distribution. When Silerio Esparza, governor of Durango, walked up first, people were muttering that he should not sign, but he did sign, she recalled, everyone did. She thought the reforms were bad, and noted that people still lived in "flooded houses, little children without shoes, barefoot, they do not even have anything to eat." What happened to her father's revolution? She was never asked to speak at commemorations, and they did not want campesinos to speak either.

Echeverría, she believed, was the president who had done most to fulfill Zapata's program. He was "like a father with his children," who came to

Morelos and gave people what they needed. And López Mateos once told her, "Señora Zapata, the banner of your father will not be preserved in a display case." Lauro Ortega was a good governor, she continued, despite the new statue he placed over her father's remains, which they called the colossus and which no one liked. The old statue went to a park, which "was a really nice thing for the campesinos." The park was in a neighborhood named for Zapata, where the streets bore the names of revolutionaries and of the towns of Morelos. Around her, on the walls of her restaurant, were pictures of her family and especially her father. Out in the courtyard was the angel that had been the first monument on his grave.

When Miguel de la Madrid chose Carlos Salinas de Gortari as the PRI candidate for president in the 1988 elections he turned the competition for Zapata up a notch. The small, bald economist with the high voice did not look like the resolute leader many felt was needed in those difficult times. But in many respects Salinas turned in a remarkable performance, presaged by his campaign stop on April 10, 1988, at Tlaltizapán. Some elements of his speech that day were conventional. As had Labastida, he invoked Sotelo Inclán when he indicated the need "to go deeply into the root and reason of Zapata, and, committed to his ideals, give renewed force to his aims of justice and equality for all Mexican campesinos." He played to local chauvinism, like the average political hack, when he praised Tlaltizapán as Zapata's true home. But he also developed a short history lesson that demonstrated extensive knowledge about Zapata and the revolution's agrarian history. To finish that lesson, he paraphrased—without attribution—the opening sentence of Womack's book, asserting that the history of Zapatismo was "the history of a people that made the Revolution because they did not want to change." He interpreted that to mean not that these people were backward-looking, rejecting all change, but that "the only change that campesinos do not want is having to abandon their communal way of life." Based on that embellished reading, he argued that one could draw two lessons from Zapatismo: that paternalism was bad policy because peasants will oppose changes thrust on them without their participation, and that the changes they want are those that will reinforce community identities. Like his recent predecessors he chose to focus his rhetoric on Zapata's goals, not the means he had outlined to achieve them, but he did promise, on this occasion, to preserve the material base of communities by keeping ejidal land off the market.[4] Continuing to speak for the campesinos, he assured his audience of the "nationalism of the peasants, their love of the land and their passion for Mexico." Then came the big finale:

I have always imagined a future of liberty and greater justice for the campesinos of Mexico and for all of the nation. Imagining this future, one of my sons carries the name of Emiliano: imagining this future I remember the political testament and the words of Emiliano Zapata: "We will—said Zapata—continue fighting without faltering for the conquest of the land." "We will—said Zapata—continue to raise, with firm hand and resolute heart, the beautiful banner of campesino dignity and liberty." "We will—decreed Zapata—fight to the end." Such is our duty if we want to merit the title of free men and conscientious citizens.[5]

Expressing his agreement with these sentiments, Salinas served notice that he meant to govern with Zapata.

It was only a speech, but it was more powerful than most because Salinas communicated—with reference to his son and his own hopes, with evidence of his knowledge—the rare sense, from a politician, that for him Zapata was personal. To a degree that was true. He had been a student of rural Mexico since his undergraduate days at the National University and had studied with Womack at Harvard. The final result of his formal education was a doctoral dissertation on political participation in the countryside, for which he lived for seven months in three rural communities. Nor was this his first official trip to Morelos. He had kicked off his campaign, the past November, by visiting Zapata's house in Anenecuilco—beginning where Zapata had begun.[6]

Unfortunately for Salinas, the elections of 1988 would be another major blow to the credibility of the PRI regime. During the 1980s opposition parties—and especially the PAN—had increasingly turned electoral reforms, the broad dissatisfaction with the PRI that had, in part, forced those reforms, and the prolonged economic downturn to their advantage. In some areas—particularly in the north—the ruling party had come to face electoral challenges it could barely contain.[7] And with the competition heating up, presidential candidates other than Salinas were making their positions on Zapata known on April 10, 1988. Socialist Party candidate Heberto Castillo found a Zapata statue in Culiacán, Sinaloa, from which he could call for a new democratic and popular agrarian policy.[8] And at Xochimilco in the Federal District, where Zapata and Villa had first met in 1914, Lázaro Cárdenas's son Cuauhtémoc outlined his plans to rescue agrarian reform.

Cuauhtémoc Cárdenas had recently broken from the PRI to launch an opposition campaign for the presidency. Possessed of the ideal name for a left-of-center politician in Mexico—recall that Cuauhtémoc was the Aztec emperor who had fought the Spanish conquistadors—Cárdenas had national heroes besides Zapata he could draw on. But because of the linkage between Zapata and Lázaro Cárdenas in the popular imagination, and because Cuauhtémoc campaigned hard for the support of Zapata's campesino constituency, he was naturally an associate of Zapata in the minds of many. "It seems like the time of General Zapata and General Lásaro [sic] Cárdenas was only yesterday," read a letter Cárdenas received during his campaign, "and now we are with you Engineer Cuauhtémoc Cárdenas."[9] Whom Zapata helped most is anyone's guess, especially since the votes were never really counted. When the early returns from Mexico City put Cárdenas ahead of Salinas, the computer system tallying the vote mysteriously shut down. Several days later the official "results" gave Salinas a narrow majority at 50.7 percent, with Cárdenas some twenty percentage points behind.

Salinas then got to work in an attempt to earn the legitimacy the elections had not accorded him and promote the change he spoke of during his campaign. On the following anniversary of Zapata's death he presided over the usual handouts and talk of modernization in Morelos, but also spoke of the need for a new agrarian reform, because that of the 1930s "has already exhausted its benefits." Change was inevitable, he added—returning to his campaign theme—and Zapata had wanted change so rural traditions and communities could survive. One stop in that year's swing through Morelos was Tlaltizapán, which had recently received funds for urban renewal that would "maintain with pride the place where Zapata chose to construct the mausoleum in which, in the classical manner, his remains could rest."[10]

On April 10, 1990, Salinas was again in Morelos, where his secretary of agrarian reform, Víctor Cervera Pacheco, professed that Zapata's convictions and his vision of the future gave agraristas the principles they needed "to fight for democratic change."[11] Salinas was in Boston on April 10, 1991—remembering, maybe, with Womack—but later that year he visited Anenecuilco to celebrate Zapata's birthday by returning the documents that supported the village's land and water claims, for which Zapata had joined the revolution. These were the papers on which Sotelo Inclán had based his work and which, despite his desire to place them in a museum in Anenecuilco, had remained in his hands for forty-four years. Sadly, he had just died in an automobile accident, but Salinas now fulfilled his wish by inaugurating a museum called "The Struggle for the Land" beside the one that covered Zapata's childhood home. A large mural on the new structure's front wall depicted a muscle-bound, superman Zapata bursting up from beneath the earth with the chain he had broken in his hands. This was where the documents would be exhibited. Salinas took the opportunity to point out that while Zapata had fought for land, he had also fought for the right of villagers to make their own decisions. He reiterated, too, that it was necessary to seek justice and dignity through different methods than the agrarian reform of the past. Lending the occasion scholarly cachet was the presence of Arturo Warman, author of an important leftist anthropological account of land, labor, and Zapatismo in eastern Morelos. Warman now served as Salinas's agrarian attorney general.[12]

With the rhetorical groundwork in place, Salinas then took the leap, breaking his promise to keep ejidal land off the market. Negotiations for his most treasured project, the North American Free Trade Agreement (NAFTA), were under way with the United States and Canada, and at least one of Salinas's negotiating partners, U.S. president George H. W. Bush, knew something about Zapata: he had once been part owner of Zapata Petroleum Corporation, so named because *Viva Zapata!* was playing in Midland, Texas, when he helped form the company.[13] But while Bush's knowledge of Zapata may have facilitated dinner conversation about history or movies, it could not have moderated his general free trade position, since his Zapata had obviously been a proponent of corporate capitalism for decades. If he was consulted, the Zapata who hung in the air between Bush and Salinas would therefore have agreed with them that if NAFTA was to work, Mexican agriculture had to become more competitive and greater opportunities for private capital had to exist in the countryside. This Salinas made clear when, in November 1991, he stood before a large painting of Zapata at Los Pinos to announce the end of land distribution and propose reforms to Article 27 of the Constitution that would encourage private ownership of ejidal lands.[14] His new agrarian model would give ejidatarios individual title to their land in ejidos where two-thirds of the members voted for that change. Once in possession of a title, an ejidatario was free to sell her or his land, thus opening the door to the capitalization of the countryside, the erosion of village communities, and the creation of larger landholdings.

A month later Salinas rounded up 268 representatives of agrarian organizations to ratify a "Campesino Manifesto" supporting the new approach. Among them was Mateo Zapata, who was photographed signing the manifesto, while Salinas and Cervera Pacheco looked on, with an image of his father in the background (likely the same one Salinas spoke in front of to announce the reforms). On the same day the Independent Central of Agricultural Workers and Peasants (Central Independiente de Obreros Agrícolas y Campesinos, CIOAC) and others protested in Anenecuilco by signing their own manifesto, the Plan de Anenecuilco.[15]

The use of Zapata to bolster these policies did not necessarily misrepresent him more than others had done in the past, but Salinas's measures did inspire more controversy than most because of two ironies surrounding the construction of Zapata's myth. The first was that since the 1920s, the regime had used Zapata to sanctify—with questionable accuracy—the agrarian reform it carried out based on Article 27. Over time, the association of Zapata with that article had taken deep root, making an assault on it much like an attack on the hero himself.[16] The second irony was that one thing that clearly separated Zapata's program from the agrarian distribution as it was carried out was that Zapata had hoped for liberty in the form of a decentralized state that allowed for local decision making. The ambitious leaders of the new regime, however, had consistently used land reform to enhance the power of the central government in the countryside. They distributed land, but downplayed liberty as they attached both political and economic strings to that land. The Salinas regime now hoped to emphasize the liberty side of the "Land and Liberty" equation, but that was an uphill battle after decades of official rhetoric that emphasized Zapata's association with land. These obstacles did not mean that all campesinos would automatically reject Salinas's reforms. Glad to be offered more flexible use of their land and not hypnotized by past PRI rhetoric, some were surely happy to vote the way Salinas hoped they would. Others could be pressured and manipulated to do so. But the legacy of the old discourse and practice in Zapata's name did mean that the outcry over Salinas's plans would not soon die down.

In 1992 Salinas returned to Morelos to promise that the titling of lands would progress quickly, that he would clear up the backlog of agrarian cases, and that he would increase the budget for the countryside in each remaining year of his administration. He asserted that Mexico was "changing with the idea of Zapata" and that he would not allow Zapata's heritage to "become an object of discourse and fade away." Ana María and Diego Zapata stood by to affirm that "yes, Zapata would have supported the reforms!"[17] Meanwhile, a new ten-peso bill was released, with an image of Zapata and two hands holding corn on the front, and on the back his old, 1932 Cuautla statue with a factory—probably a sugar mill—standing behind it. It was another honor for the hero and, for the state, another means of claiming him, but it also seemed to bear inadvertent witness to the way his mythification had helped Mexico industrialize on the backs of the campesinos.

Another critical part of the package arrived in August 1992, when Salinas and Education Secretary Ernesto Zedillo—who would succeed Salinas in the presidency—presented the new history textbooks for primary schools they had commissioned from historians Héctor Aguilar Camín and Enrique Florescano. The stated goal was to get beyond the heroes and villains of previous texts to develop a more objective history, but objectivity is often in the eye of the beholder, and Aguilar Camín, in particular, was a friend of Salinas, who had handpicked him for the job. In the new text for fourth graders, Zapata was a one-time supporter of Madero's who rebelled against him for unexplained reasons and thus risked being perceived as a rootless source of disorder and bloodshed. Although the book eventually did identify him as a peasant leader, his agrarian goals were not disclosed. The volume for the sixth graders included more detail on the revolutionary period, but it still did not clarify the relationship between Madero and Zapata or tell who killed Zapata and why. Again Zapata's motives remained rather obscure. Despite his many messages to the contrary, Salinas obviously knew that Zapata stood in the way of his program. Unwilling to take him on directly, he was pursuing a mixed strategy: while playing him for all he was worth, he hoped to use education to shuffle the old man—gradually, gracefully, quietly—off center-stage of Mexican political life. Those hopes were dashed by another uproar, and the government quickly backed down. Salinas and Zedillo aborted the 1992 effort and produced more Zapata-friendly texts the following year.[18]

Meanwhile, the opposition continued its work. In 1990 Cuauhtémoc Cárdenas took over the main site of commemoration, Cuatro Caminos, in his home state of Michoacán, where automobile workers, students, and "groups of Chicanos coming from California" forced the state government to hold its event in Morelia to "avoid confrontations."[19] In 1991, Cárdenas's Cardenista Peasant Central (Central Campesina Cardenista, CCC) was a major organizer of the fifty thousand protesters expected in Mexico City.[20] In 1992, *Excélsior* reported on two marches of "Zapatistas" in Mexico City, which stopped traffic as they now did every year. Among the groups participating were the Emiliano Zapata Eastern Mexico Democratic Front (Frente Democrática Oriental de México Emiliano Zapata, FDOMEZ), the Emiliano Zapata Peasant Organization (Organización Campesina Emiliano Zapata, OCEZ), and the Emiliano Zapata Worker-Peasant Union (Unión de Obreros y Campesinos Emiliano Zapata, UOCEZ). Both marches ultimately arrived at the Zócalo, where participants chanted against "anti-agrarian and privatizing" policies. They also complained about ecological destruction, human rights violations, NAFTA, and—during a stop at the U.S. embassy— the American economic blockade of Cuba. "It was as if," wrote the author of the *Excélsior* piece, "the spirit of Zapata returned yesterday to traverse the city streets."[21]

The *Excélsior* article also indicated, however, that though these manifestations were sizable, they were not as large as they had been on other anniversaries. This did not represent a trend and may have meant nothing, but it is somewhat surprising that, in 1992, with the reforms of Article 27 now in place, the crowd was not larger. One possible explanation is that Salinas was enjoying some success. His policies were challenging fundamental assumptions and generating a great deal of anger, but the economy was also rebounding nicely from the debacle of the 1980s, and Salinas was even expressing the hope, like López Portillo before him, that Mexico was on the verge of joining the "developed" world. Having dispelled perceptions he would be a weak leader, he was taking the offensive, and many Mexicans were willing to concede that he might be on the right track. Then came 1994.

As the first day of NAFTA, January 1, 1994, was to have been a day of celebration for members of the Salinas administration. Instead, in the southern state of Chiapas, a group of Mayan Indians who called themselves the Zapatista Army of National Liberation (Ejército Nacional de Liberación Nacional, EZLN) served notice that Salinas's final year in the presidency would be a difficult one by taking over the city of San Cristóbal de las Casas and several smaller communities by force of arms. A federal counteroffensive quickly drove the rebels back into the Lacandón jungle from which they had come, and a cease-fire was soon arranged, but not before the rebels got their message out. An EZLN declaration of January 2 seamlessly combined the new guerrilla force with Zapata's earlier struggle. Porfirio Díaz, it read, had failed to live up to the laws of the Reform period, with the result that "the people rebelled, creating their own leaders. Villa and Zapata appeared, poor men like us to whom the most basic education has been denied so we could be used as cannon fodder and the riches of our fatherland could be sacked without them caring that we are dying of hunger and curable diseases."[22] The new Zapatistas demanded "work, land, housing, food, health care, education, independence, freedom, democracy, justice and peace"; NAFTA, they said, was a "death sentence" for the Indians.[23]

Much of Mexico was stunned by this the first noteworthy armed insurgency since the 1970s, but it, and its use of Zapata, had been building for some time. Like inhabitants of other parts of the country, Chiapans learned about Zapata through the education system, the land reform process, commemorations, and mass media. In 1962, there was a commemoration at Tuzantán in front of a makeshift altar that held a picture of Zapata and was surrounded by floral offerings. It was noted that Zapata sacrificed his "life and welfare for the campesino," and students delivered poems with such titles as, "Song to Zapata," "To Emiliano Zapata," "Oh... Great Zapata," "The Voice of Zapata," and "Goodbye to Zapata." Then there were basketball games between visitors and locals, the winners receiving prizes from the "beautiful young ladies of the place."[24]

Roughly twenty years later an official commemoration in the capital, Tuxtla Gutiérrez, included the distribution of ejidal rights. A speaker noted that this land reform should quiet "the restlessness that had been prevalent in the countryside for some years," making it possible to concentrate on alimentary self-sufficiency. That same year, peasant groups used the anniversary to protest the increase in repression under López Portillo.[25] In 1985, Governor Absalón Castellanos Domínguez deposited a wreath at Zapata's statue in Tuxtla Gutiérrez and distributed various certificates to campesinos. On the same day members of peasant groups besieged the governor's offices—which were well guarded by the police—while striking bus and taxi drivers partially paralyzed city streets. Still Castellanos Domínguez assured a reporter that "in Chiapas there is no problem." He also expressed his pride that every settlement in the state contained "a work of art as never before in history." "Because a people without monuments," he continued, "is a people without history." Aside from the presence of a governor who refused to participate in the problem-solving rhetoric of the period, none of these events seem markedly different from what was happening in other parts of the country.[26]

But Chiapas was different. Like its neighbor Oaxaca one of the poorest and most Indian states in Mexico, it was also one of the states least touched by revolutionary programs and thus, it seems likely, relatively unaffected by the PRI's propaganda. Zapata did arrive in Chiapas along the same official routes he took to Oaxaca and elsewhere, but not with the same force.[27] He also, however, came to the state along a nonofficial path. As part of the guerrilla current that followed Tlatelolco, outsiders connected to the student movement briefly tried to start an uprising in Chiapas in the late 1960s. Having little success, some of the would-be rebels moved to the northern city of Monterrey before returning to Chiapas in 1972 to begin training as the Emiliano Zapata Guerrilla Nucleus. After considerable difficulties and with the infusion of some additional non-Chiapans, this group reemerged in 1980 as the Zapatista Army of National Liberation, named after Zapata because he "is the hero who best symbolizes the traditions of revolutionary struggle of the Mexican people." Two years later the group helped found—in, ironically, the town of Venustiano Carranza—the Emiliano Zapata Peasant Organization, which became a major participant in ritual protest in the state. Then, in 1983, some guerrilla members entered the jungle canyons of eastern Chiapas to explore the possibility of further developing their army there. Among the leaders of those that moved into the canyons was the man who would become known as Subcomandante Marcos. Many years after these educated outsiders began to work with and try to earn the trust of the inhabitants of the area, according to one account, Marcos took command of the EZLN in 1993 in order to lead it, finally, into rebellion.[28]

As guerrillas with urban backgrounds and Maoist ideas encountered Mayan peasants, who were often illiterate, a broad process of cultural exchange took place, part of which concerned Zapata. Precisely how those exchanges occurred is uncertain, but there is information on what they produced as war in Zapata's name approached. On April 10, 1992, four thousand members of the newly formed Emiliano Zapata Independent National Peasant Alliance (Alianza Nacional Campesina Independiente Emiliano Zapata, ANCIEZ) converged on the offices of the municipal president of Ocosingo while the officeholder fled the scene. Outside the building, according to one account, "the indigenous campesinos of Ocosingo, Oxchuc, Huixtán, Chilón, Yajalón, Sabanilla, Salto de Agua, Palenque, Altamirano, Margaritas, San Cristóbal, San Andrés y Cancuc dance in front of a giant image of Zapata that one of them painted, recite poems, sing and have their say." The participants chanted, *"Zapata vive, la lucha sigue"*—Zapata lives, the fight continues—and one read a letter to Salinas that accused him of ending the agrarian achievements of the first Zapatistas, as well as selling out the country through NAFTA and, in general, "returning Mexico to the times of Porfirismo."[29] The ANCIEZ would fold into the EZLN and disappear when the celebratory ritual protest described here turned to fighting in 1994.

Once the EZLN made itself known to the rest of Mexico, Marcos and his collaborators proved much more adept at manipulating Zapata than did Salinas. Indeed, the EZLN had hardly scratched the surface of Salinas's Zapatismo before something very different appeared beneath it: as noted in the Introduction, only a few days into the crisis Salinas offered amnesty to the rebels in front of an image of Carranza, a clear sign that he chose law, order, and the status quo. Marcos recognized a threat when he saw one, and countered that he would have trouble negotiating with the government now because he could not stop thinking about "Chinameca and the image of Venustiano Carranza" that backed up the president.[30]

But if the EZLN identified with Zapata's faction, it also used Zapata to associate itself with the nation. Taking a hint from the nationalistic turn of the student movement in 1968, it indicated that it had learned its military tactics not from Central American insurgents or other foreign sources but from Hidalgo, Morelos, Guerrero, Villa, Zapata, and various Indian rebels.[31] In a letter to the National Coordinating Committee of Indian Peoples it made Zapata one of the central symbols of the nation when it expressed the hope that "the Mexican eagle [which is represented on the flag] and the Zapata of its [Mexico's] coat of arms" would live forever.[32] The EZLN was not even willing to leave Womack to Salinas. One document mentioned a man named Angel, "a Tzeltal whose pride is having completely read the book of Womack on Zapata. ('It took three years. I suffered, but I finished it,' he says when someone dares to doubt his prowess)."[33]

It was not long before Marcos unveiled a Mayan Zapata who would promote a new way of thinking about the nation. The notion of Zapata as Indian, as we have seen, is an old one, but recent developments had given it greater strength. Most significant here was that part of the general trend toward campesino restiveness and organization visible since the 1970s was the formation of specifically Indian groups—such as the abovementioned National Coordinating Committee of Indian Peoples—and a simultaneous revaluing of Indian identity. Since one thread of his myth made him an Indian, Zapata could participate in such processes. And so it was that when, in 1979, journalists and local historians from around the country met in Morelos to consider how Zapata was regarded in the provinces, the chronicler of the village of Coacalco in Mexico State, Tlakaelel Francisco Jiménez Sánchez, compared Zapata to Cuauhtémoc and called him a *tlatoani*.[34] At nearly the same time, historian Miguel León-Portilla made a scholarly effort to resuscitate Zapata's Indianness in the face of Womack's insistence that he had been a mestizo. Drawing on León-Portilla's argument, Zapata was soon speaking Nahuatl in a comic book history of Mexico.[35]

Much of Zapata's posthumous charisma in Chiapas, then, had to do with the Indian that he could be. Putting that and his connection to the nation together allowed the EZLN to take a new tack in the struggle against the PRI. The key construction was the association of Zapata with the figure of Votán. Through the shape-shifting in which indigenous gods engaged, Votán had acquired several interesting and, as it turned out, useful attributes. In Tzeltal myth he was understood as the guardian of the people, who had given them land and sacrificed himself for "true manhood." He was also tied to the Maya concept of Kukulcan, who was in turn paired with the god of central Mexican origin, Quetzalcóatl (see the Introduction). Votán seems to have been linked particularly to forms of Quetzalcóatl that could transform themselves into Xolotl, the lord of the dead. One of Xolotl's missions had been to go to the realm of the dead—Mictlan, traditionally associated with Chiapas—to gather the remains of the deceased and mold them into humanity; another was to bring corn and fire to the Maya. In short, linking Zapata to Votán would place him, through the intercession of Kukulcan-Quetzalcóatl and Xolotl, at or near the center of Mayan ideas about creation. Nor was this quite all: Votán had played such a critical role in inciting Maya revolts against Spanish rule that in 1690 a bishop destroyed every trace of his existence he could find.[36]

The genesis of the figure of Votán-Zapata is obscure, but Marcos supplied a fascinating explanation in a letter of late 1994. The letter told of a meeting between Marcos and "old Antonio" ten years earlier. Perhaps in the context of recruiting, Marcos began to tell Antonio who he and his fellow outsiders were, including an account of Zapata's trajectory from Anenecuilco to Chinameca. Antonio rejected Marcos's account and offered to tell him Zapata's true history. A long story about the gods Ik'al and Votán followed, in which they learned how to move down a path together by asking questions, which they found were for walking, not staying put. They came to a fork in the path and chose the longer route because they could see the end of the shorter one, but the only way to know where the longer one led was to take it. To walk for a long time, they decided to play on their separate strengths, which were, essentially, day and night. Then Antonio said,

> this Zapata appeared over there in the mountains. They say he wasn't born. He just appeared. They say that he is Ik'al and Votán that went over there to rest on their long walk and that, in order not to frighten the good people, made themselves one . . . and they named themselves Zapata.

After some consideration of the black-and-white duality of Zapata that came from this background, Antonio concluded that he was the "path for true men and women." He then pulled out a small photograph of Zapata that he carried with him as one might carry the image of a saint and gave it to Marcos, saying, "I've asked this photo many questions. That's how I came to be here."[37]

Votán-Zapata made his first appearance in the historical record, appropriately, on April 10, 1994:

> From the first hour of this long night in which we die, say our farthest grandfathers, there was someone who collected our pain and our oblivion. There was a man who, his word walking from afar, arrived at our mountain and spoke with the tongue of true men and women.... There was and there is, brothers and sisters, a person who, being and not being

seed of these soils arrived at the mountain, dying, to live again, brothers and sisters, the heart of this passage itself lived dying.... Votán-Zapata guardian and heart of the people.... Votán-Zapata, timid fire that in our death lived 501 years. Votán-Zapata, name that changes, man without a face, tender light that protects us. Votán-Zapata came coming. He was death always with us. When he died hope died. Coming, Votán-Zapata came. Name without a name, Votán-Zapata saw in Miguel, walked in José María, was Vicente, named himself in Benito, flew in a little bird, rode in Emiliano, yelled in Francisco, dressed as Pedro.... Receive our truth in a dancing heart. Zapata lives, also and forever, in these lands.[38]

Here was Zapata the creator, who linked death and life and had a deep mythical resonance in Chiapas that provided meaning for those "true men and women" who lived and died in this realm of the dead in pain and oblivion. But the references to Miguel (Hidalgo), José María (Morelos), Benito (Juárez), Francisco (Villa), and Zapata himself were not, of course, specifically Chiapan. The line of heroes, the cosmology, stretched away from Chiapas to the nation and back again. A second document of the same day addressed the issue of national politics directly. "The usurper Salinas de Gortari," it charged, "who calls himself 'president of the Mexican Republic,' lies to the people of Mexico when he says the reforms to Article 27 of the Constitution are in the spirit of Zapata. The supreme government lies! Zapata will not die by arrogant decree." This document went on to note the joy of the EZLN that some of the same texts being read that day in Chiapas would also be delivered to fifty thousand people at Mexico City's Zócalo, that Zapata would arrive again at that site, as he had in 1914. "We," it continued, "small and forgotten, raise the image of Zapata in the other heart of the fatherland: that of the mountains of southeastern Mexico." Together the rhetoric and the simultaneity of the events broadcast Zapata across the Mexican landscape while making strong claims for Chiapas as a vital part of the nation.[39]

A year later the new concept of nation the EZLN was building around Votán-Zapata gained clearer expression. "All of us," a missive for the 1995 commemoration read, "are one in Votán-Zapata and he is one in all of us." This nation was not, however, entirely inclusive. Rather, it was based on a rereading of Mexican history generated by conflict, much like those undertaken by previous rebels—leaders of independence and revolution alike—as they struggled to define Mexico. In this rereading Zapata was at the center of a new creation myth for the nation that privileged the marginalized—the Indian and, broadening from there, those who lived in "misery." It was a flashback to the sense of community displayed by Marciano Silva, for whom, I argued in Chapter 1, an Indian seems to have been anyone long oppressed and deprived of basic rights. Excluded from this community were the powerful who, the EZLN asserted, wanted to "defeat and kill Votán-Zapata for good" and had tried to do so both in 1521 and 1919.[40] Among these powerful, a letter addressed to Zapata later suggested, were those, both within Mexico and outside it, that had created NAFTA. The neoliberals in power, this piece complained, "run this country, yours and ours, *mi General*, as if it were a run-down hacienda, a big estate that has to be sold with all of its *peonada* [workers attached to the land], that is, the Mexicans, *mi General*, included."[41]

But the efforts of politicians to kill—or control—Zapata had failed badly. He had instead taken a winding road back to provincial, rural Mexico, where he was again making national demands, much as he did when he first intruded on Mexican consciousness in 1911. The causes he espoused had broadened considerably. Perhaps most remarkably, in the hands of the EZLN he became of greater use to women. As we have seen, women had served as central props in Zapata's story, and they had grieved at his grave. For decades they had paraded and sewed and politicked in his shadow, while schoolgirls sang and danced and recited. But Zapata still always moved with greater ease across class lines than across those of gender.

Then, starting in the 1960s, intermittent suggestions that that might change began to appear, as various women put Zapata to work. As noted in Chapter 7, María Dávalos de Montero of the Urban Zapatista Front planned to name a child for him. At about the same time, in her semifictional biography of Jesusa Palancares, novelist/journalist Elena Poniatowska underlined her subject's admiration for Zapata by making up scenes that put the two together. Interestingly, she also defended him against charges of sexual violence—or at least thoughtless macho complicity in it—that had been leveled by Hermila Galindo and would be raised again by Sandra Cisneros.[42] Daughters and granddaughters of Zapatistas, meanwhile, embraced their ancestors' program by becoming involved in land and other social issues, including Zapata's own granddaughter, Margarita Zapata, a social activist in the capital.[43] In 1984, across the border in Arizona, Fina Román, president of the Morenci Miners Women's Auxiliary, urged that a strike against the Phelps Dodge copper company continue by asking strikers to take to heart a slogan she, like many others, attributed to Zapata: It is better to die on your feet than live on your knees.[44] Chicanas on university campuses wore Zapata T-shirts to assert the Mexican facet of their identities. And then there was Cisneros's assessment.[45]

Despite such precedents, Zapata was still not a symbol for which the Zapatista women of Chiapas often explicitly opted when they spoke of their struggle. Speaking in Tzotzil, one of the predominant languages of the area, Comandante Susan did note, on April 10, 1996, that because of the presence of government forces women had not been able to work "the land that belongs to the poor, that belongs to Zapata, for which he fought and has not died . . . because the government wants to seize us . . . to turn us into prostitutes." Major Ana María joyfully commented that when she went to a village and asked the children who Zapata was, "all of them knew perfectly well."[46] And in 1994, women in Guadalupe Tepeyac opened a restaurant "Che Guevara-Emiliano Zapata" to cater to the influx of journalists and other visitors.[47] But the bigger story was that a commitment to women's rights was a central facet of EZLN ideology. Through the EZLN Zapata became linked to a new "Revolutionary Women's Law" and the associate of many women who occupied highly visible leadership roles.[48] And during the tense standoff in the Chiapan jungle, he even developed into a strong opponent of violence against women (though that does not mean, unfortunately, that such violence ended). Among the first Zapatistas there were female fighters, messengers, and spies, as well as some legislation—written by Zapata's urban secretaries—intended to promote women's liberation, but no previous Zapatistas had ever placed so much emphasis on issues particular to women.[49]

By demanding rights and recognition, women in the EZLN were thus changing what it meant to be a Zapatista, and echoes were heard elsewhere in Mexico. In 2004 an organization called the Army of Zapatista Women in Defense of Water (Ejército de Mujeres Zapatistas en Defensa del Agua) appeared in the state of Mexico. These women, of Mazahua Indian ethnicity, wanted access to water and land, compensation for recent flooding caused by an emergency discharge from a nearby dam, and a development plan for their region. According to eighteen-year-old Iris Crisóstomo, they organized because government officials "didn't pay attention to our men . . . and because we are the ones who go out to wash and carry the water." "We're fighting like Emiliano Zapata," she added, "for our lands, but above all for our dignity." To make their point they armed themselves with rusty shotguns and machetes and besieged a water purification plant, thus demonstrating the threat they could pose to Mexico City's water supply. They also suggested that they "were even disposed to shoot men that attempted, under government auspices, to fool them."[50]

The EZLN, then, gave Zapata's career several ironic twists. Soon after Zapata's death, politicians had adapted some of the religious facets of the popular strand of his myth to their own purposes to argue, essentially, that he was a secular saint who was continually resurrected in them and their programs. Unlike Zapata's Morelos resurrection, of course, this one was purely symbolic. The problem, though, is that such a transfer of sacrality, even if successful, does not entail rooting out the underlying "superstition" that many revolutionary leaders perceived among the masses. The state subsequently took the cult and, presumably, the discourse of symbolic resurrection, to Chiapas. And in that setting the EZLN recovered, for the opposition, the religious feelings that still enveloped Zapata. It did so, moreover, as part of emphasizing Zapata's Indianness, a racial designation many Mexicans had historically associated with passive femininity. But if the government carried an Indian Zapata to Chiapas in hope of incorporating a passive population more fully into the nation, the EZLN answered with an Indian Zapata who took up arms to challenge governmental authority. And it disputed the association between passivity and femininity along the way.

The EZLN was creative in its use of Zapata to forge community and legitimacy, but the mere availability of the symbol was a key part of the story. What other image could have served the insurgents' purposes so well? From their perspective Zapata was the perpetual loser of Mexican history, defeated by the conquerors in 1521, by pro-Spanish forces during the independence struggle, and by the Constitutionalists in 1919. But in defeat he only became a better emblem for indigenous populations that had suffered centuries of discrimination and oppression, and in death he only morphed and multiplied into other heroes and eventually into a national community of heroes. And the EZLN's concept of a national community of heroes disabled the pro-government argument that has cropped up in various forms throughout this book: that heroes made change and, by implication, that regular people could not.

In this context, Zapata's status as the conscience of the revolution, his well-established moral character, was crucial. He was ready to model the "true man and womanhood" that made the Chiapans heroes, that legitimized them, that placed them within a newly conceptualized national community, and that sharply distinguished them from the official handlers of Zapata's myth. "General Zapata was and is," read one proclamation, "the symbol of those who fight for what they believe despite the consequences. The symbol of those who don't sell out. The symbol of those who resist. The symbol of those that don't surrender or lower their banners."[51] One final thought: while land was a huge issue in Chiapas, it was in addressing the other side of that simplified Zapatista formula, "Land and Liberty," that EZLN goals were most provocative. They demanded the liberty long buried in the quagmire of postrevolutionary bureaucracy, but conceptualized differently now, with a specific insistence on ethnic autonomy—ethnic autonomy that Zapata, again, could represent.

Not everyone, of course, was enchanted by EZLN constructions. Despite Salinas's passing use of Carranza, the PRI was not ready to surrender Zapata, and it got support from Mateo and Ana María Zapata, who reacted with suspicion to the Chiapan use of the family name. Mateo indicated that he and his associates represented the continuation of his father's work, and that violence belonged to another era. Ana María noted that "they took the name just to create an impact with the indigenous people."[52] A Oaxacan observer adopted a similar line, suggesting the EZLN "should act within present-day realities and not draw sustenance from the name of one of our heroes of long ago."[53] Up north, the *Wall Street Journal* editorialized that Zapata never sought to "take the capital or to introduce socialism" as, it said, the new Zapatistas did, and that socialism "runs contrary to Zapata's respect for democratic principles."[54]

Elsewhere the reaction was more positive. Immediately capturing the imaginations of many urban Mexicans—as well as an international community of sympathizers—the EZLN became a cause célèbre and Marcos a media darling. Some of these enthusiasts saw most clearly in the new Zapata their own democratic longings. According to one young man, Zapata meant "liberty, liberty, that's cool, isn't it, it's something that has no price... it never tires." But when a high PRI potentate visited the National University in the summer of 1994, the students who greeted him did not explain the attraction, but rather simply yelled that "UNAM isn't *priista*, UNAM is zapatista!"[55] Zapata was now more admired by university students than any other figure in Mexican history, and downtown graffiti informed passersby that, "these days, to be young and Mexican is to be Zapatista." Meanwhile, in August 1994 Alberto Gironella traveled to Chiapas for a Zapatista convention and to hand over to the EZLN—in the form of a painting "dappled with bullets and bottle tops"—his version of a betrayed and rebellious Zapata. The painting occupied a place of honor during one of the convention's sessions, but it disappeared that night when a rainstorm interrupted the proceedings.[56]

Not surprisingly, many of the first Zapatistas also had sympathy for the Chiapans despite the views of Zapata's progeny. Upon his death in 1998, Estanislao Tapia, a reputed witness of the promulgation of the Plan of Ayala, left a message for the neo-Zapatistas: "Tell them they are not alone, that Zapatistas from all over the world are with them."[57] Another veteran commented that the EZLN was a movement of "men of the same race as us.... Those men are completely right. Like Zapata. For that reason, today, sitting in this wheelchair, I still respond to Zapata's name, because whoever defends the poor that cannot defend themselves is a hero."[58] Clearly, there was pent-up demand for the glimmer of hope the uprising offered. For many in Magdalena Ocotlán, Oaxaca, not far from the state capital, the appearance of the EZLN must have felt like the answer to a prayer. There, every year on April 10 since 1957, the ejidatarios had come together to "'take roll' and to voice an 'I'm present, general!' in front of the photograph of the caudillo of the South" that graced a wall at the ejidal offices. Proceedings also included the placement of two bouquets of flowers beside the photo and, "with respect, an old drum and a bugle—final testimony of the group of campesinos that participated in the battle for land and liberty—[were] placed in the center of the table of honor." At this event in 1993, the president of the ejido noted "we know Zapata defended us and that we live thanks to him." Someone else added the belief that he would one day return, because they had come to need him again.[59]

The rebellion in Chiapas was not the only problem the PRI confronted in 1994. That spring, Salinas's choice for a successor, Luis Donaldo Colosio, was assassinated at a campaign rally in the border city of Tijuana by, according to one interpretation, a lone disturbed gunman. Ernesto Zedillo stepped in to take Colosio's place despite unhappiness within the party about what he represented—more technocratic rule—and his lack of personal magnetism. But Zedillo won just over fifty percent of the vote in an election that was quite clean by PRI standards, and that amounted to a cautious vote of confidence in Salinas's free market reforms, which had pulled the economy out of the doldrums of the 1980s. Then, in the fall, came another assassination, this time of the PRI's secretary general, José Francisco Ruiz Massieu, Salinas's former brother-in-law. This fueled rumors that opposing factions of the PRI—one supportive of Salinas's reforms and the other against them—were engaged in discussions over the future of the party they took *very* seriously. Then came the final blow. Salinas was adamant that an electoral triumph be part of his legacy and, fearful of showing weakness, he postponed a much needed devaluation of the peso until after the elections. By then it was too late. In December, owing in large part to the imbalances caused by this politically motivated monetary policy, the peso entered free fall, and the economy followed. To add insult to injury, investigators soon discovered that business transactions in one sector of the economy—the trade in illegal drugs that had blossomed during the Salinas years—had apparently been conducted under the president's nose by his brother Raúl, whose Swiss bank accounts were bulging. Carlos Salinas scurried into exile and Raúl soon went to prison, convicted of Ruiz Massieu's murder.[60]

The 1995 commemoration captured the new situation. Given the spiraling crisis, Zedillo hoped to use the occasion for symbolic damage control and so made the trip to Chinameca himself. Because the stakes in the contest for Zapata had never been higher, in fact, Zedillo, like Salinas, would appear in Morelos often on April 10. In 1995, he was joined there by many other prominent politicians, including Arturo Warman, now secretary of agrarian reform. Zapata's three surviving children were also present. After receiving what a Cuernavaca newspaper called an "effusive" reception from the campesinos, Zedillo spoke in front of the 1979 equestrian statue. He stressed that Zapata's ideals were liberty, justice, and law, and that those ideals formed the basis for the alliance between the state and the peasants. Calling for national unity, he promised "permanent dialogue" with the peasants. He also promised that such policies as the Program for the Certification of Ejido Land Rights and the Titling of Urban House Plots (Programa de Certificación de Derechos Ejidales y Titulación de Solares Urbanos, PROCEDE), with which he and Salinas sought to guarantee individual property rights within ejidos, would help make the countryside productive. The governor of Morelos, Jorge Carrillo Olea, spoke as well, insisting that Zapata's legacy had to do with "the march of the great Mexican people" toward dignity and civil rights, and not with violence, destruction, and the defense of group interests, as some people were interpreting it. Zedillo then boarded a helicopter bound for Guerrero, where he inaugurated a number of public works.[61]

Abandoning "Land and Liberty" for a reference to the slogan "Liberty, Justice, and Law" that Zapata had chosen for the Plan of Ayala was an interesting recourse to an actual text, but it was a pathetic gesture if Zedillo hoped it would put a dent in the link between Zapata and land. In 1995, the myth was much more dynamic in other hands. That was true, as we have seen, in Chiapas, but it was also true in Oaxaca. There, Governor Diódoro Carrasco Altamirano traveled to the town of Loma Bonita in the northeastern part of the state. In the Benito Juárez auditorium he addressed 3000 people, including state functionaries, municipal authorities, and members of peasant organizations. He highlighted his participation in the agrarian transformation being undertaken by Salinas and Zedillo and spoke of the need to resolve land conflicts between communities. He also promised public works in the area.[62]

Carrasco Altamirano added that he accepted the right of people to "demonstrate respectfully" on the day of Zapata's death. Surely he was thinking of what was then taking place in the city of Oaxaca, where fifteen thousand peasants with ties to various organizations were marching to make known their unhappiness with government policies. Approximately six thousand members of the National Peasant Confederation arrived at Oaxaca's monument to Zapata on Eduardo González Boulevard around 10:45 A.M., where they undertook a floral offering and an honor guard. At least two of them removed their hats and crossed themselves before Zapata's image. Also present were several members of a nonofficial peasant group who loudly criticized the National Peasant Confederation's ritual. One of them yelled, "That's an offense, not an offering." [63]

After the National Peasant Confederation left, opposition groups began to arrive en masse. One participant wore a ski mask in imitation of the Chiapas Zapatistas and hung from the Zapata statue waving the national flag, while hundreds of others—not just peasants but teachers as well—chanted against government policies. These protestors removed the flowers of the National Peasant Confederation, undertook a ritual of their own that included more floral offerings, and then replaced the CNC's offerings, but in a different arrangement. On the same day peasants besieged the residence of the state government, shouting "Zapata vive, vive, la lucha sigue, sigue" and scrawling graffiti that recommended specific sexual activities to members of the ruling party.[64]

Although security measures were taken, it was probably no coincidence that Carrasco Altamirano left for Loma Bonita rather than presiding over a commemoration in the state capital as was customary. But he had to plan his escape route carefully, because the city of Oaxaca was not the only place in the state where the day of Zapata's death was, in 1995, a moment of protest. Down on the Isthmus of Tehuantepec, at Juchitán, members of the Worker-Peasant Coalition of the Isthmus (Coalición Obrera Campesina Estudiantil del Istmo, COCEI), militants of the left-of-center Party of the Democratic Revolution (Partido de la Revolución Democrática, PRD) that had formed in the wake of Cuauhtémoc Cárdenas's 1988 campaign, oil workers, teachers, merchants, and others expressed their discontent by blocking roads and occupying government offices and banks. Demonstrations also took place in nearby Tehuantepec, where peasant women were the most visible participants. In the district of Juxtlahuaca in the impoverished mountains of the Mixteca, meanwhile, there was a march of five hundred members of the Bi-National Indigenous Front of Oaxaca (Frente Indígena Oaxaqueña Binacional, FIOB), which was composed of migrant workers of diverse Indian ethnicity who demanded that the governor respond to a petition they had given him the previous year. Yet another march occurred in Huautla de Jiménez, where teachers, peasants, and other citizens of surrounding villages denounced taxes, inflation, and general scarcity.[65] Elsewhere in Oaxaca, and across Mexico, similar events were taking place.

In the years that followed, the PRI's loss of Zapata became ever more apparent. Protests on April 10 criticized the changes to Article 27, the privatization of the electric industry, new taxes, and the U.S. Border Patrol. They demanded political reform, debt relief, more access to credit, liberty for jailed campesinos, and serious negotiation from the government. They carried out land invasions and sought greater unity among their organizations. During the 1980s, April 10 marchers had sometimes carried images of crucified peasants—perhaps representing Zapata, perhaps not—as visual commentary on government policies. In the 1990s, the identification of the crucified figure as Zapata became explicit. In 1997, for instance, *Excélsior* called such a representation "a 'Zapata' crucified by NAFTA." The proximity of Easter can only have lent this particular symbol greater force.[66]

On April 10, 1996, about eight hundred citizens of Tepoztlán, Morelos, members of a movement that opposed the new golf course being planned for that town, gathered for a pilgrimage along "Zapata's Route"—Cuautla, Anenecuilco, Chinameca, Tlaltizapán. Many of them had altars to Zapata in their homes. As they neared their final stop, Tlaltizapán, where they hoped to give Zedillo—who also toured Zapata's route that day—a letter describing their plight, they encountered a roadblock manned by three hundred riot police. "In their zeal to save the president from an outbreak of visual contamination," wrote Carlos Monsiváis, the police acted forcefully, and one of the leaders of the group, Marcos Olmedo, was shot and killed. The first official word was that no one had died and that, indeed, the police had not been armed, but one of the protestors had a video camera, which put the lie to that account. While the authorities recast their stories a new martyr was born.[67]

In signing the San Andrés Accords with the EZLN in February 1996, the Zedillo administration might have undercut some of the protest, but instead of implementing those accords, the president took a hard line on Chiapas, expressing the fear that to grant Indians special rights or protections would undermine national cohesion. This obviously did nothing to discourage other would-be guerrillas, because new rebels continued to appear, frequently on days associated with Zapata. In celebration of Zapata's birthday in 1996, the Popular Revolutionary Army (Ejército Popular Revolucionario, EPR) made its presence known in Guerrero, demanding a new government, a new constitution, and new economic policies. While this group was not as adept at—or interested in—manipulating symbols as the

EZLN, a comunicado of April 10, 1998, indicated that Zapata was a "guide and source of inspiration." [68] Exactly two years later, on a street corner at Xochimilco in the Federal District, the Revolutionary Armed Forces of the People (Fuerzas Armadas Revolucionarias del Pueblo) made an appearance. With covered faces and AK-47s, this group's spokespeople indicated that Zapata, too, had been called a bandit. Addressing Zapata directly, they noted that globalization had made Mexicans "among the worst paid" people in the world. They complained of the decline of national industry, of forced sterilization of "our women," and that "many Mexicans work like burros on the lands of the gringos." Worst of all, perhaps, they charged that the makers of the new system "sought to erase the memory of our culture and even want us to think like gringos." [69]

In the midst of all this, Arturo Warman could only insist that he and other functionaries were Zapatistas too. At Chinameca in 1998 he declared that Zapata "belongs to all of us" and asked that "no one arrogate his name to themselves as exclusive property." He added that the land reform, now finished, had been much broader than what Zapata had demanded; he reiterated that Zapata "belongs to the nation." And to bolster Zedillo's rejection of any special recognition of Indian rights, the distinguished anthropologist of Zapatismo emitted a new interpretation of Zapata's meaning: that he stood for justice "without exemptions or privileges." [70]

In the summer of 2000, after seventy-one years of rule by the official revolutionary party, the PRI lost a presidential election. It did not lose only because it had lost Zapata, but the conjunction of the two defeats was no coincidence. The PRI lost the presidency because the legitimacy of its system had been eroding for decades in the eyes of most Mexicans; because the failures of that system had caused suffering and provoked frustration; because successive PRI administrations had gradually opened up the electoral process in the hope of letting off steam; and because in 2000, angry voters were allowed to have their say. Memories of Zapata were never far from the center of this story. Zapata was a significant aspect of the legitimacy the PRI squandered, and he had developed into a central trope for those who demanded change. As legitimacy disintegrated and anger swelled, he could no longer support the PRI ticket in any way.

Taking over the presidency was Vicente Fox of the PAN, a former Coca-Cola executive with a cowboy attitude from the north-central state of Guanajuato. Fox in particular, and the PAN in general, had risen to power in part because of their practicality. They had abandoned some of the Catholic emphasis with which the party had begun and, though still conservative, had even claimed at times that it was they who could fulfill many of the aspirations of the revolution. They had not, however, embraced the cults of revolutionary heroes. One party president, in fact, had promised that if the PAN came to power, "we would get rid of the revolutionary myths of Zapata or of Calles, of Cárdenas or of Alemán." [71] Pragmatic Panistas are unlikely to have given this promise much thought when it was uttered in 1972, but it was pretty loose talk. A PAN government would also need legitimacy, and it would not have the power to overhaul Mexico's political culture. And so, while Fox was able to avoid April 10 commemorations personally, he soon found that he could not entirely ignore the martyr of Chinameca. What ensued instead was something of a free-for-all as various parties and other political and social groups competed on the new playing field to see who could get traction from Zapata's memory.

This was readily apparent on April 10, 2001. On that day Tlaltizapán concluded its first annual "Zapata Vive!" festival, which included, in addition to commemoration and parade, a theatrical performance, a children's art show, and the screening of a new documentary on surviving Zapatistas, *Los últimos zapatistas, héroes olvidados* (The Last Zapatistas: Forgotten Heroes).[72] During the commemoration, Mayor Matías Quiroz Medina called for the transfer of the "mortal remains of the caudillo of the south, to bury them in the mausoleum that Zapata ordered constructed in 1914 for himself and his generals." Tlaltizapán was not, Quiroz Medina added, just another town. Along with the mausoleum, it possessed "the blood of the caudillo fixed in the clothing he wore when he died," as well as the best-maintained museum of Zapatismo in the state.[73] Moreover, he contended, the people of Tlaltizapán "venerate and respect the history that permits us today to have free governments, clear thoughts, and a country with dignity." For all these reasons, he believed, Zapata's place was in his mausoleum "at the feet of father Jesus." A second local official provided context for Quiroz Medina's last comment by indicating that Zapata was a man of great faith who often attended the church in the atrium of which his mausoleum had been built. This speaker also pointed out that other important leaders of the movement—Emigdio Marmolejo, Jesús Capistrán, Pioquinto Galís—had been buried there, and that Zapata should be permitted to "rest with his compañeros, who are waiting for him."

In Cuautla, meanwhile, there were several ceremonies in Zapata's honor. The city government turned out early to deposit a floral wreath at the feet of his statue. Moments later the governor of Morelos, Sergio Estrada Cajigal of the PAN, arrived with other representatives of the state government.[74] They, too, left a floral offering. Shortly thereafter a scuffle broke out between representatives of the governments of Cuautla and Ciudad Ayala (previously

Villa de Ayala). Both entities wanted to control the ceremony soon to be enacted by leaders of the state PRI. Pilgrims from Tepoztlán arrived during the spat and performed their own brief ceremony, which echoed with that defiant mantra, "Zapata vive, vive, la lucha sigue, sigue." Eventually, the folks from Ciudad Ayala won the field. They got their sound equipment and speakers' table set up just before National Peasant Confederation and PRI officials arrived to make their speeches. Despite a conspicuously small audience, one orator professed that in coming elections the PRI would be "the option Zapata wanted."[75]

Then there was the official, national tribute at Chinameca. Here Estrada Cajigal, having made his way south from Cuautla, noted that the revolution was finally bearing fruit because Mexicans were "no longer fighting with weapons, but rather with the vote." Also during this ceremony, Secretary of Agrarian Reform María Teresa Herrera Tello, representing Fox, insisted the president knew Zapata stood for a commitment to social justice, "which will be taken up again by the federal government." Fox was not, she added, "trying to cancel the history of Mexico." Looking on were members of a group of retirees from Zacatepec, whose banners indicated they were hungry because they had not received their pensions in four months.[76]

In 1994, then, Zapata turned up in Chiapas, where, at the head of a newly conceptualized Mexican nation, he relived some of his rebellious youth. Officials of the ruling party were learning the hard way, if they did not already know, how valuable a symbol he was. This was not the first violence in Zapata's name during the post-1968 period, and ritual protest continued to challenge the sense of order and sacredness the postrevolutionary state, and many ordinary citizens, had tried to instill in the April 10 ceremonies. Ironically, those who were building an oppositional Zapata repeatedly took advantage of the religious aura of the day: the commemorations were to some extent protected arenas of expression, Zapata's symbolic weight requiring that the authorities be cautious about cracking down on protest.[77] Facing occasional violence and rising outspokenness, politicians could no longer claim Mexico had achieved Zapata's utopia—people could, after all, consider their own living conditions. Nor could they do much with the tired line that the revolution still moved forward, its sights set on Zapata's goals, because it had simply taken too long. During the Salinas administration more serious discussion of policies and problems emerged on April 10, displacing some of the empty rhetoric. But few celebrants of Zapata wanted to hear what Salinas and company had to say, or accept the policies he offered.

Though tensions were high, for a moment the tattered web of political culture seemed to hold. After all, the PRI did win the 1994 election. And if the mass demonstration in Oaxaca in 1995 represented the symbolic capture of the city, the word "symbolic" is critical: it was not an uprising but, in essence, an insistence that politicians negotiate more seriously and find a way to bring the disillusioned back into some national consensus about Zapata, the revolution, the direction of Mexican life. The drive to negotiate was apparent even in Chiapas on April 10, 1995, as the state and the EZLN agreed to return to the bargaining table.[78] But though government discourse about Zapata had become more serious, the PRI was also, in 1994 and 1995, proving itself seriously corrupt, seriously inept, and perhaps seriously murderous as well. None of this helped the party in the struggles over Zapata's memory, and it lost the battle for Zapata, as well as many other battles in the war for legitimacy. As the century closed it lost the presidency, too, and the competition for Zapata entered a new, more multipolar, stage.

But the history of Zapata during this epoch was not only about that contest. It was also about the explosion of Zapatismo as Zapata continued to travel to places he had never been before—and at an accelerated rate. In addition to his trip across racial divisions and geographical regions to Chiapas, Zapata moved with increasing power across the urban-rural divide, gender lines, and the border with the United States.

The willingness to play with Zapata's image that developed, mostly among urbanites, after 1968, helped produce Subcomandante Marcos, of course, but it also helped create an audience with which the Chiapas construction of Zapata would resonate and which was ready, in general, for a more lively interpretation of Zapata than the state offered. That demand was met in part by the feature film *Zapata: El sueño del héroe* (Zapata: The Dream of the Hero) by the accomplished director Alfonso Arau (*Like Water for Chocolate*, 1993).[79] Alejandro Fernández—like Antonio Aguilar before him, a popular singer—was cast as Zapata in his first movie role.

By the time it reached the screen in 2004, this film already had a long and complex history. The project started in the United States as the brainchild of director Gregorio Nava (best known for *El Norte*, 1983), who claimed he had wanted to do a film about Zapata since he was a boy. He considered making it a musical at one point and put novelist E. L. Doctorow and musician Paul Simon to work on that vision, but he eventually generated a magical realist script instead. Nava sold the idea to Walt Disney Studios, but Disney liked neither Nava nor the screenplay and so turned to Arau. Subsequently, Disney backed out entirely, and Arau decided to produce the film himself, in Mexico. In the meantime, trying to start over, Nava approached Hollywood star Antonio Banderas about the lead role, but he soon faced protests from Chicano groups about the Spaniard Banderas's light skin.[80]

Arau, too, courted controversy, in this case by demonstrating little concern for historical accuracy. He did shoot the film in Morelos and claimed to have conferred with the locals—including some of Zapata's descendants—but his attitude toward historical veracity was different from that of Cazals. "I am a storyteller," he pointed out, "not a historian." He also noted that "the so-called official history of Zapata comes from a government that was in power for 70 years, so why should anyone believe that version?" He sought instead to "portray a spiritual, human Zapata with weaknesses and flaws not unlike those of Jesus Christ."[81] Part of his motivation for that approach, he avowed, was that he had a dream "in which Zapata appeared and asked him to tell the revolutionary's true story, and not the false 'cardboard' story that has become dogma in history books." Zapata also ostensibly told him to do it in Spanish and in Mexico. This would naturally differentiate the film from *Viva Zapata!*, which Arau characterized as typically gringo, though he was not above imitating Kazan in places, as when he had his cast reenact the photograph of Zapata with Villa in the president's chair.[82] While Arau embraced the mystical Zapata, Fernández joked about his role, another sign of how times had changed. When reminded by a reporter that Zapata's motto was "Tierra y Libertad" and asked about his own, he replied, "*Vieja* y Libertad!"—vieja in this context meaning his "old lady," or woman. His ideal life, he explained, was "a ranch, of course, a good vieja and a good mule, and that the mule not be too vieja [old] and the vieja not be too mulish." In case that was not enough machismo to qualify him to play Zapata, he postured that he was "brave, very brave, like a Mexican charro."[83]

Like Cazals in 1970, Arau set a new standard for spending on a Mexican movie. There was also a large advertising campaign and the biggest opening day ever in Mexico, on 650 screens. But the film was almost universally panned. Some attacked it for being too Hollywood or being a bore, but much of the critique came from those who wanted it to be good history. From his Harvard lookout, Womack disputed Arau's Mexicanness, remarking that "people who live in Los Angeles, like Arau, have fantasy views of what Mexico is all about."[84] Mateo Zapata was ready to sue even before the movie's release, after hearing broadly circulating rumors that Arau planned to give Zapata a male lover. What the critics missed was that Arau captured, at least in part, the direction Zapata's myth had taken. Based on his research "with the shamans of Morelos," he depicted Zapata as the reincarnation of Quetzalcóatl and Cuauhtémoc, predestined to be a warrior and the guide of his people.[85] The director gave his hero a moral dilemma similar to the one he faced in *Viva Zapata!*: as a mestizo, he could go either of two ways—an Indian wife and a light-skinned, high-society mistress illustrated the tension. Ultimately, Zapata accepted his destiny and chose his Indian self, Fernández learning a couple of lines of Nahuatl for the role. Zapata's special powers manifested themselves in a profound connection to horses, which would throw their riders at his silent urging. Arau meant to supply a Zapata for the Mexico of the new millennium—and one, incidentally, that would please Subcomandante Marcos. Box office receipts, however, suggested he had not achieved that goal.[86]

The best part of the film was its visual images. Most of it was shot in and around the burned-out shell of Cuahuixtla hacienda, which had taken land from Anenecuilco before the revolution and was destroyed during the decade of war. The celluloid Zapata spent his wedding night there on a bed under the stars with Josefa Espejo, who wore only a mound of Calla lilies when he entered the room.[87] The grove of leafless trees in April at Chinameca was another nice touch. Finally, there was a striking scene at the end of the film in which the camera panned across Zapata's body, buried and, as in Rivera's mural, nourishing the roots of a cornfield, which rose from the corpse like frozen lightning. Moving up from there, the shot reached ground level, where candles burned between the cornstalks, and then, above the corn, the night sky.

Despite the perceived shortcomings of this offering, the urban Zapata lived on. Writing for the *Los Angeles Times* in 2002, Jesse Katz described Los Angeles as "a Zapata city. He runs through L.A.'s veins, through its language, its rhythms, its history, its food. He is a validation of everything Mexican here." He is "a mural, a shrine, a statue, a T-shirt, and a prison tattoo, the namesake of Mi General Zapata Bakery in East L.A. and the Viva Zapata Lock and Key Service in Pico-Union. His credo is recited like biblical verse: 'It is better to die on your feet than to live on your knees.'"[88] One could not say quite the same thing about El Paso, Texas, but there a women's group, La Mujer Obrera (The Woman Worker), adapted Zapata's image to its cause. Consisting largely of former garment workers who had lost their jobs in the aftermath of NAFTA, this organization hung a picture of Zapata on the walls of its offices alongside images of female members of the EZLN.[89] The point seems to have been, in part, that these women on the border shared both the pain caused by NAFTA and the figure of Zapata with their Chiapan counterparts.

Indeed, Zapata was also being newly resurrected in the United States. As in Mexico, this was in some respects a resurrection that dated back to the 1960s, but the revaluing of Indian identity that came somewhat later—and which the EZLN expressed so effectively—occurred in the United States as well, and there too Zapata was a component of the process. It is perhaps not surprising, then, that there was also, coinciding almost perfectly with the Chiapan uprising, a work of Chicano fiction in which an Indian Zapata was reborn: Gary D. Keller's "Zapata Rose in 1992," which was republished two years later as *Zapata Lives!*[90] In this work Zapata emerged from "a long sleep" in a Toltec Indian sepulcher, and contemplated another revolution in interaction with such diverse characters as a son of Díaz Soto y Gama, Miguel Cervantes (author of *Don Quixote*), the sixteenth-century Spanish Saint Theresa de Avila, Lefty Womack, Pedro Martínez, and César Chávez.[91] The story ended as Indians inspired by his presence gathered to march (much, of course, as was then happening every April 10), and realize a peaceful revolution, on the five hundredth anniversary of Columbus's voyage.[92]

Despite Zapata's many travels, Morelos was still his ultimate home and at the dawn of the new century the EZLN took him back there. In an early 2001 march into the center of the country, neo-Zapatistas traced a circle around the capital, "where power lives," and then walked down into Morelos.[93] In Cuernavaca Marcos read a letter ostensibly written by Zapata for the Morelenses.[94] It started with an apology for having been absent for so long and told of Zapata's stay in southeastern Mexico, where he had met "indigenous people like us, peasants like us and Mexicans like us." Zapata wrote that he had told the Chiapans about how the Morelenses had organized to fight, and "how I escaped from the betrayal at Chinameca and traversed the fatherland to see that our ideals were fulfilled." Because they now knew of the Morelos experience the people of Chiapas, he continued, would not give up or sell out or lose, though Fox sought to do as Madero had done and keep everything the same after the end of a dictatorship. Zapata momentarily confused the PRI with Porfirio Díaz—not unintentionally, one imagines—and then quoted from a letter he had written in 1911: "I, since I'm not a politician, don't understand these half-triumphs." He finished by asking that the Morelenses advise the EZLN in its efforts to gain recognition for indigenous rights—an "undertaking that is the same as that for which the Liberating Army of the South [the first Zapatistas] fought." He also requested that his audience listen to "this little boy," Marcos, but that they not "make too much of his jokes because they are very bad. There's a reason that some want to shoot him." Marcos had little to say on his own account but "¡Viva Zapata, cabrones!"

NINE

CONCLUSION

Of Leviathan, Lo Mexicano, *and Zapata on the Border*

In recent decades the possible uses of Zapata's image have become nearly limitless, making generalizations about them risky. He was rebel and media star, macho and mystic, Moses and sex toy as the century turned, but the routine, workaday Zapata was still around too, in classrooms throughout Mexico and abroad, where futures were purportedly being crafted. Serious scholars of Zapatismo published books for children that seemed to intend simply to get the history straight and make it accessible.[1] Students, meanwhile, drew their own conclusions from whatever material they were given. In 1992 at Cuautla a journalist quizzed sixth grader Pedro González as they waited for the president to arrive. Asked what he knew about Zapata, González exclaimed, "Yikes! . . . that he was in the revolution, that he died today." "Today?" the interviewer probed. "Well, [today] a bunch of years ago," came the response. "He said 'Land and Liberty'; in school we even get homework about his life."[2] Two years later a young girl named María de Jesús Ocampo had a watercolor reproduced in a glossy magazine (see Figure 9.1). Maybe it was *her* homework, a picture of Emiliano and Eufemio Zapata in a setting that resembled the Garden of Eden. The brothers wore their crisscrossing cartridge belts, their sombreros, and their big mustaches, but Eufemio's arm, slung around Emiliano's shoulders, qualified the macho trappings. So did the small clouds that floated overhead, the red and yellow birds that flew fearlessly toward them, and the assortment of plants that grew near their feet. For these children Zapata was a chore, or a proponent of peace, brotherhood, and beauty, or both; in neither case did the prevailing political winds seem to have much effect.

Still, the posthumous career of Emiliano Zapata does have a shape. In fact, it is a relatively manageable tool with which we can evaluate the dynamics of state power and national identity over a more extended period of time than historians interested in these issues have generally covered.

FIGURE 9.1
María de Jesús Ocampo, drawing of Zapata with brother Eufemio.
(First published by CISAN-Universidad Nacional Autónoma de México's
Voices of Mexico *27 (April–June 1994): 95.)*

As leader of one among several revolutionary factions, during his lifetime Zapata was a controversial figure. Generally feared and reviled by the ur-banites who controlled the national media, he inspired intense devotion on his home turf—though that devotion was neither as unwavering nor as unanimous as it has been portrayed. His alleged death at the hacienda of Chinameca in 1919 gave his image new dimensions in Morelos, where he quickly became an important ancestor, as leaders so often have throughout human history. Though Zapatismo has not become a religion, there were several religious components in the way he was remembered by the inhabit-ants of the region in which he lived. He became a martyr with millennial trappings, his memory resonating with such earlier mythical interests of central and southern Mexicans as the earth and corn, and with figures such as Santiago, Quetzalcóatl, Moses, Jesus Christ, and the caudillo Morelos.

On the national scene Zapata's passing enabled politicians—once his most obvious enemies were out of the way—to make him one of the found-ing fathers of a conceptually unified revolution, representative in particular of peasant sacrifices and demands. He came to serve official Mexico as a patriarch with a dose of machismo, a mestizo whose Indianness remained near the surface, and most of all as a representative of a land reform that met some campesino aspirations while tying peasants to a single-party system. The state's embrace of Zapata's image was no more unusual than the appearance of the regional cult had been. Given the local sovereignty that had reared its head around Mexico between 1910 and 1920, the state would have to be rebuilt laboriously, as would a sense of national community. And so, in service of the idea of nation, postrevolutionary leaders hammered together cultural offerings from a variety of regions.[3] Zapata was largely borrowed by the national government, not invented—recontextualized, not reconfigured—as a way, first, of recognizing and seeking to incorporate a particular provincial constituency, and second, because he seemed ideal for general peasant consumption. He was a means for the aspiring rulers of Mexico to open negotiations with inhabitants of rural Mexico, to signal their seriousness about reform and to determine what revolutionary rewards campesinos expected. By meeting some of those expectations, politicians hoped to generate a measure of legitimacy for themselves.

In many respects, then, it was a case of the tail wagging the dog, *action* coming from the plebs, *reaction* from the emerging elite; the state was mirroring society, as Knight puts it, not attempting to recast it.[4] Even Zapata's initial adoption by the state, we should recall, relied greatly on the efforts of voceros who were only sporadically rewarded from government coffers. Zapata was not an ambitious element of the cultural project, and, given the concrete rewards of Cardenista land reform, it is hard to calculate the benefits politicians might have received from the use of his memory.

The true test came after 1940, when it became policy to industrialize Mexico at the expense of Zapata's campesino constituency. Could the state's Zapata hold peasant loyalty under such circumstances? Official Mexico now came to operate a broader, blander Zapata, who embraced productivity, progress, national greatness, and the allied cause while being emptied of some of his previous, more specific meaning.[5] In this form he probably became more of a role model than he had been, an image that might help shape Mexicans to some ideal specifications. He also continued to be a tool of negotiation, but of a negotiation that was increasingly ritualized.[6] In a process partially replicated at other locations, Morelenses usually toed the line when national leaders arrived in Cuautla to pontificate about Zapata. They did so to maximize the benefits they might receive, as individuals or as members of local communities, from the state: the pensions, political positions, public works, and agricultural implements that visiting dignitaries distributed. These benefits—or sometimes mere promises of benefits—were usually not elements of such clearly delineated programs as land reform. Rather, they were represented as one-time manifestations of government largesse and were generally personalized—López Mateos himself, for instance, was understood to be bringing electricity to parts of Morelos in 1960.

But Morelenses did not show up at commemorations only for material rewards. Among the benefits, as had been the case since 1920, were the national recognition of the contributions they had made to the revolution and the opportunity to honor Zapata publicly and properly. Benefits such as these, which directly engaged the religious facets of the local and regional myth, were far from negligible. They did not, however, do much to alleviate rural poverty and they cost the state little, so we might argue that it was here, to the extent that people were content with such rewards, that the cultural project was successful. At any rate, the ritual grew ever thicker, replacing public discussion—there was no dialogue at Cuautla commemorations.[7]

That does not mean, though, that Morelenses did not often see this happening, or that they were mute about it. Relatively few joined Rubén Jaramillo's periodic rebellions, but grumbling surrounded the rituals of the Golden Age. The state's manipulation of Zapata was not accepted as something natural, unquestionable; rather, it was perceived and remarked on, and those remarks often found their way into the public record. If there was little open discussion about Zapata at Cuautla, there were multiple public utterances around the country, and there were opportunities for the exchange of impressions, both in formal celebrations distant from Zapata's stomping grounds and in informal encounters around the edges of official ceremonies.

Zapata did, then, bridge the gap between the state and a key constituency, but generated only a thin form of hegemony at best. So exactly how did the government profit from bothering with him? The official Zapata undoubtedly provided the state with some of its coherence, but beyond that the answer seems to lie in the fact that though the hypocrisy of politicians was duly noted, those who expressed their anger about it did not formulate alternative visions of Zapata capable of rallying strong resistance: Zapata, and the nation he represented, were not—maybe *could* not be—turned against the PRI.[8] Why not? In part, it seems, because a small amount of false consciousness was enough. Describing a crowd that assembled on the Zócalo to celebrate Mexican independence, a resident of Mexico City recently told a writer for *National Geographic*, "They may scream at the government all year, but tonight people come out to cheer." The whole point of myths and rituals is precisely that emotional surge, however it manifests itself, which sets rational thinking about concrete interests to the side and thus produces feelings of solidarity among people even in the absence of agreement.[9] The feelings of solidarity produced during a commemoration may last only a few moments, but the residue they leave may still make a heavily ritualized Zapata, for example, a hard image with which to pick a fight. (I may complain incessantly about the current president of the United States, but in the presence of the presidential motorcade I might still sense the power and even some of the dignity the office is supposed to contain, and I might remember the feeling.) In such circumstances agency and false consciousness, both taking less than ideal form, coexist rather than preclude one another. In any event, insofar as it was hard for people to see how to use Zapata against the government, he was an excellent image with which to imply that the status quo, the existing terms of negotiation, no matter how unfair, were better than open conflict. Surely if hegemony existed anywhere in the world in the twentieth century, it existed during Mexico's seventy-one-year period of single-party rule. And in that long story it is most useful as a concept for the period between 1940 and 1968, because it may help explain why political control persisted despite—at least in the countryside—the absence of serious social programs.[10]

Under such circumstances it may take a great deal of complaining before any kind of deconsecration or reconsecration of a mythical figure can occur, but that is precisely what happened with Zapata in the 1960s.[11] That development reinforces the common contention that there was a major turning point in Mexican history at this time, but it also suggests that we be careful about assuming that the massacre at Tlatelolco—and, thereafter, the capital's "Generation of Tlatelolco"—were the only hinges on which that history turned.[12] Decades of accumulating rhetoric, urbanization, and travel changed Zapata in Guerrero, in California, and in Mexico City at roughly the same time. He became more ambiguous, more plastic, even in part the object of play. And of course Zapata the rebel was reborn.

Was this the end of postrevolutionary hegemony, at least as measured by this single myth? It is hard to know. Though we might feel safe in saying legitimacy existed during the miracle years and did not exist during the decade of revolutionary warfare, it seems to me that in many situations in human history—perhaps most of them—one can find it if one wants to, or find it missing if one does not.[13] Given the many variables involved, its presence or absence is often hard to verify convincingly. My hope was that looking only at memories of Zapata over the long term would make measuring hegemony easier, but the history of Zapata's myth suggests that Mexico after the late 1960s is one of those cases about which one could come down on either side. True, the PRI defeated the guerrillas and continued to send functionaries to Zapata's commemorations—more often, in fact, than ever before. On the other hand, it was no longer difficult to turn Zapata into a figure of dissent, opposition, resistance. If hegemony existed, it was razor thin.

But the regime was increasingly wounded by its own devices—or perhaps we should say, hopelessly entangled in webs it had done much to weave. Its continual resurrecting of Zapata, though purely rhetorical, perpetuated messianic elements that were eventually turned against it. A second, closely related irony involves Zapata's renewed Indianness. Anthony D. Smith has persuasively argued that nations are built around preexisting ethnic cores, from which, facing the realities of a multiethnic universe, they tend to expand to include other ethnic groups.[14] Put in those terms, the Mexican state used Zapata to help conceptualize a nation that was mestizo at its core but moved out to include the Indian at its periphery. There were, however, complications. The state acknowledged the Indianness within caudillo and nation in part because that acknowledgment was a necessary step toward resolving the Indian "problem"—assimilating the marginal Indian and thus creating a homogeneous nation. But the official notion that Mexico was of mixed, mestizo, ancestry meant the Indian was within the *core* of the national idea, as well as on its periphery. Under those circumstances, there was no way to make the Indian disappear. The state's Zapata was thus a mestizo, but one in which the power of Rivera's Indian Zapata remained visible. This made him ethnically flexible, a mestizo or an Indian, depending on the interpretation and the interpreter. And that meant the EZLN and other Indian groups could use him to imagine a nation against the state's construct, but one that would not contradict the basic assumptions of most Mexicans. *That* nation, as we saw in Chapter 8, was Indian at its core and moved out to embrace, as Subcomandante Marcos put it, all who lived in misery.

Zapata's myth also turned on national officials when they came to believe that the land reform the regime had linked to Zapata had undermined development by creating an undynamic, unproductive agricultural sector. The discursive trick of holding out the hope of land to pacify the campesinos thus came back to haunt them, creating a Zapata they could not live with but which they would change at their peril. Unwilling to surrender Zapata, they nevertheless began to test the waters, talking about ending land reform and in the process ceasing to shape their rhetoric in ways that would give their Zapata its maximum effect. When Carlos Salinas took the plunge, he was unable to hold Zapata despite considerable efforts. Zapata made a firm commitment to the rebel camp with the 1994 rebellion in Chiapas. The benefits he offered the single-party state were only now, seventy-five years after his supposed death, more or less at an end.

So maybe this says something about hegemony. It supports James Scott's position that hegemony *cannot* take a thick form, while at the same time suggesting how effective a thin form—even an extremely thin form—might be.[15] It may also indicate that discussion of whether a set of power relationships is hegemonic or not is too simplistic. Because what Zapata reveals is a spectrum of hegemonic relationships, with several stops between what is obviously hegemony and what is obviously not. Zapata's story might, then, help us describe several different types of hegemony—something better than thick, thin, thinner, thinnest. But having to slice it so thin suggests that it might be advisable to move beyond the concept, arguing that it is no longer an especially useful tool in helping us explain power relationships and enabling us to compare one case to another.

Leaving aside the issue of hegemony, then, what else might we conclude from Zapata's story about the relationship between Mexican state and society? One thing that jumps to mind is that Zapata's myth suggests the conditions necessary to generate a powerful hero cult in the modern world. Zapata has emerged as a rare kind of hero because of the fine mix of local, national, and international views of his legacy. The most solid presence of Zapata is, of course, in and around Morelos, where he could lead because he convinced people he was capable and trustworthy—that his promises were not empty like those of other politicians. But his presence in locales such as Chiapas has become appreciable too, and it seems likely that his deep roots in Morelos have, ironically, served him well in other places where trustworthiness and "intransigence" are valued. The state, meanwhile, made Zapata a founding father but could not establish control of him—it was unable, for instance, to bring his body to Mexico City in the 1970s. And so Zapata has hung in the balance, the object of varied claims and ever more vital as a result.

Given Mexico's size, ethnic diversity, geographical divisions, and history of local and regional identities, the usefulness of a myth that functions on both national and local scenes is obvious. It seems likely, though, that myths need this kind of flexibility to flourish over the long run in any modern nation. As we have established, one of the crucial functions of myths is to moderate differences between groups of people who, when thinking rationally about their interests, simply do not agree. Without some tension built in, paradoxically, they are unlikely to be of much value. Often, though, hero cults that initially look promising fail to meet this standard. The figure of Francisco Madero was adopted by the postrevolutionary state as a possible source of unity between factions, but it was missing the machismo that might have helped root it in the local scene and has therefore lacked the lasting power of Zapata's cult.[16] On the other hand, the new state wanted nothing to do with Pancho Villa, with the result that his stature at the national level has always been stunted despite his centrality to memories of the revolution in northern Mexico. Moving farther afield, Soviet hero Vladimir Ilyich Lenin was comparable to Zapata in that both died at the end of periods of revolutionary warfare, making it predictable that their memories would be employed in the service of new revolutionary regimes. But Lenin differed from Zapata in having lived in exile for many years, and in being an intellectual who achieved national power before he died. Because of these aspects of culture, class, and career he lacked regional rootedness. The result was that although the Soviet state used its autocratic power to mythify Lenin, embalming and then displaying his body for decades in Red Square, he never inspired great popular loyalty.[17] When the Soviet Union crumbled, so did many of his statues. His body remains on display, but his cult's future in the ex-Soviet world is uncertain.

A related difference between Zapata and Lenin is that the Mexican state did not emerge from the revolutionary process with a well-defined ideology. Rather than complementing ideology, as Lenin's image did, we might argue that Zapata and other symbols of the Mexican Revolution filled in where formal ideology might have been, thus playing a larger role in supplying cultural glue for a postrevolutionary society than did similar images in the Soviet case. And in that there were some advantages, because a symbol is generally more flexible than an ideology. In fact, we might twist Marshall McLuhan to suggest that unlike Lenin's image, which was constrained by its connection to communism, Zapata's image was supple enough to become not only message but medium—a path of communication as much as something to be communicated.[18] The creativity and endurance of the twentieth-century Mexican state may owe a great deal to such message-media.

What kind of state was it? For many years scholars viewed it as an all-powerful "Leviathan," especially during the Golden Age.[19] More recently, scholars such as Alan Knight, Mary Kay Vaughan, and Jeffrey Rubin have argued that the state did not have all the power previously ascribed to it.[20] Mexico's leaders had not been able to impose their policies and projects; in many respects the state was a rickety, uneven structure with limited ability to touch and shape the Mexican people. Hegemony, they generally concluded, had been achieved, but it was thin and the product of constant negotiation. But before we accept that belief in the Mexican state's power was just a fit of false consciousness from which the academic community suffered, we have to account for that state's longevity in a part of the world so frequently rocked by military coups during the twentieth century.

The history of Zapata's myth tends to reinforce the positions of more recent scholars about the dynamics of power and culture, but it also suggests some substantial successes of the state's program. The official Zapata did not broadly fool people or, it appears, do much to reprogram them, but it did help forge relations between campesinos and the new system and contribute to the stability of the regime by forestalling rebelliousness in Zapata's name for many decades. By this measure, the state was no Leviathan, but it was also no paper tiger. Perhaps the strength and success of both the state's Zapata and the broader cultural project lay precisely in the fact that they were not especially overbearing, that the government did not fully control Zapata or even seek, it seems, to produce false consciousness of the thick variety. This might lead, then, to a better appreciation of the nature of Mexican authoritarianism. Though states are inevitably rather decentralized structures, it is also true that the postrevolutionary Mexican state was streamlined by putting a tremendous amount of power into the hands of the chief executive. That office, rather than any individual holding it, gradually became an expression of institutionalized revolutionary charisma. This made other segments of the state little more than rubber-stamping societies, but they were also smokescreens, shielding presidents from much of the blame for their policies. This strong presidentialism within a growing and cumbersome bureaucracy made the state more successful in pursuing certain ends than it might otherwise have been. In combination with rhetoric like that about Zapata, it made it a confusing, Kafkaesque structure to approach, evaluate, or resist. Various observers have called this regime "a perfect dictatorship" or a "*dictablanda*." The latter characterization is usually translated as a "soft dictatorship," but it might also signify a regime that is—to expand on the definition of the word "bland"—featureless, nondescript, or, better yet, inscrutable.[21] Though it was not a massive state possessed of abundant resources, messages synchronized, tentacles everywhere, it was, as reflected in its sometimes mystifying, sometimes numbing use of Zapata, quite effective in increasing and perpetuating its power.

Zapata's value to that kind of state, and his lasting appeal more generally, have ultimately had much to do with what he could say about *lo mexicano*—what it means to be Mexican. As we saw in the Introduction, at the time of independence Mexican intellectuals linked such figures as Hidalgo and Morelos with Cuauhtémoc and the Virgin of Guadalupe to create a history for the emerging nation. Working on a more material plane,

Friedrich Katz has noted that peasant uprisings have been crucial factors in important national transformations. He considers the conquest period—conceptualized not merely as the imposition of Spanish rule but rather as a broad rebellion against the Aztec state by other indigenous groups—and independence as two times when rural revolts shaped watershed events in Mexican history.[22]

We have, therefore, at the birth of independent Mexico the emergence of a set of patriotic heroes whose activities coincided with peasant rebellions and who partially represented those rebellions in national memory. In part because of the peasant uprisings, those patriotic heroes had strong associations with Indian ethnicity: Cuauhtémoc falls into that camp, of course, as do the dark-skinned Virgin of Guadalupe and Hidalgo and Morelos, whose independence forces were heavily Indian. Later in the century Benito Juárez contributed his Zapotec ethnicity to the mix. When he defeated Maximilian in the 1860s, he also established liberalism as a core component of the official tradition.

Katz's third example of the connection between peasant uprisings and national transformation is naturally the Mexican Revolution. In building their following, Zapata and his collaborators appealed to the legacy of the usual ancestors—particularly Juárez, Morelos, and the Virgin of Guadalupe—and in the process constructed Zapata's image, in part, on the pedestal of the heroes that preceded him. Surely the Zapatistas hoped that associating themselves and their cause with these figures would heighten their appeal, but they also seem to have seen them as models of honorable behavior to follow. In other words, they were connected not just by metaphor but also by actions and practices: Zapata's home state was named for the caudillo Morelos, who had enjoyed one of his greatest victories at Cuautla; the Virgin of Guadalupe was a prominent figure in the religious lives of many Zapatistas. The links in the heroic chain thus fit together as follows: independence propagandists utilized the Indianness of Cuauhtémoc and the Virgin of Guadalupe; Juárez reaffirmed Mexican independence; and Zapata chose to remember and honor not only the Virgin of Guadalupe and independence heroes but Juárez too, who was presumably valuable both for his liberalism and for his Indian ethnicity.[23]

But it was only after the revolution that the concept of lo mexicano became a focal point of Mexican thought, the best-known scrutiny of the subject coming from the pen of Octavio Paz in *The Labyrinth of Solitude* (1950). Paz's book is pertinent here both as analysis and as historical event—indeed, it may have been something of a self-fulfilling prophecy to the extent that what it said about Mexican identity was influential enough to help shape that identity. At the center of Paz's treatment of lo mexicano was Zapata, who represented the revolution looking backward toward the sources of Mexicanness. This, Paz thought, was a necessary step: Mexico had to come to terms with its past to find itself and thus become capable of meeting modern exigencies.[24]

Paz's picture of Zapatismo as a backward-looking Indian uprising is debatable. His belief that the Zapata that he and others remembered in 1950, however, might help Mexicans bridge past, present, and future is arresting in that memories of Zapata have been on the point of doing just that since the late 1960s, when Zapata became more meaningful to inhabitants of the modernizing, mestizo worlds of both Mexico City and the Chicano movement. The Internet-wielding Indian rebellion that broke out in Chiapas in 1994—Indians seeking a modernity for themselves different from the modernity emanating from Mexico City, which had always excluded them—might be seen as an effort to build such a bridge. The well-grounded conceptualizations of Zapata and the nation that emerged from Chiapas certainly touched a deep nerve in Mexican life, and it may be that Mexico's rulers and its rebels will someday come to an agreement on what Zapata means for the future, an agreement flexible enough to hold things together in a way that would serve needs on both sides better than the Zapata that was to some extent agreed upon during the miracle period.

In both image and deed, then, Zapata was prefigured. From one perspective the myth of Zapata is, as myths tend to be, about creation, explaining how the world of revolutionary Mexico spun into being. But perhaps surprisingly, given that he was ostensibly a revolutionary, Zapata tapped into an already existing story about Mexicanness rather than marking out a starting point for a new national narrative. He was given meaning and direction by the historically conditioned hopes, expectations, and interests of those who followed him. Something also emerged from him after his death, back into the culture, in terms of what he meant and how he could be used. But what emerged was not precisely what went in, and that is true because of the contingencies of the life that lay between the birth of the hero and the posthumous image: the mustache, the eyes, the horse, what he said, how he died. Though Zapata refracted the national myth rather than recasting it, his symbolic presence was critical in paving the way for new undertakings. Would land reform have played such a large role in Mexico's twentieth century without Zapata? Many have argued it would not have because of his ideological influence on the Constitution of 1917.

Perhaps. What I am suggesting is that it might not have because Mexico would then have missed his mustache and the insistent, intransigent icon that was built around it. In 1989, José Muñoz Cota waxed poetic about a painting by Fernando Alferez that portrayed only Zapata's eyes. "In the sad gaze of Emiliano Zapata," Muñoz Cota wrote, "the tragedy of our history comes to light."[25] Five years later the Chiapan rebels appeared in ski masks that revealed only their eyes. Was that coincidence . . . or not?

Two final thoughts about Zapata's image and the flow of Mexican history. The appearance of the EZLN revealed that there is a larger history of Zapatismo that has continued until the present, though it has often been nearly invisible. Moreover, the persistence of the myth of Zapata and its attendant larger history of Zapatismo indicate that accounts of the death of the revolution have been, in some respects, premature. It has long been conventional to say—because it is in great part true—that revolutionary reform ended with the Cárdenas regime, and that the revolution was little but rhetoric thereafter. More recently, historians have started to find ways to discuss certain issues and periods of twentieth-century Mexican history with limited attention to the revolution, making "modernity," for instance, the focus of their studies and even claiming that for some periods and topics the revolution does not matter.[26] But as I have tried to show, rhetoric—and other facets of culture—matter profoundly. A larger history of Zapatismo exists because people have chosen to call themselves Zapatistas. Broadening slightly, the revolution lives on because its insertion into the national myth has meant Mexicans cannot really leave it alone.

With the dawn of a new century and the end of the single-party system that may be changing, but the prospects for the endurance and development of Zapata's cult seem excellent. Both limitations and prospects are visible along the U.S.-Mexico border, where I observe Zapata's career on a daily basis. In the early twenty-first century, Ciudad Juárez, Chihuahua, is a distant outpost of Zapata's myth. Still, each April 10 the primary schools hold ceremonies for him, and this is particularly true at the school named for Zapata—located in the section of the city of the same name—where local authorities sometimes show up.[27]

City officials also visit the statue of Zapata on anniversaries of his death, or at least they did on April 10, 2005, when I was in attendance as well. Not knowing when the commemoration would begin—or even if there would be one—I arrived at the statue shortly after eight on this, a Sunday morning. The statue is located, ironically, where the streets División del Norte (Northern Division, the official name of Villa's army) and Alvaro Obregón come together. These two streets—and a spur—enclose a small, triangular island of earth, which is planted with young pines and oleander and topped with Zapata's monument. The statue, which reaches considerable height with the help of a substantial pedestal, is not an especially successful work of art. Zapata holds the Plan of Ayala in his left hand and a rifle in his right arm, which he extends, awkwardly, perpendicular to his body. It is not hard for the viewer to position the statue in such a way that she or he can read, over Zapata's left shoulder, a message whitewashed onto a dry mountainside: "*Cd. Juárez, La BIBLIA es la verdad, LEELA*" (Ciudad Juárez, the Bible is the truth, read it). Telephone wires cut across every possible view of the monument.

The neighborhood is working class and has been there a while, sprawling over desert hills. It probably started, decades earlier, as many neighborhoods on both sides of the border do, through the initiative of migrants who had squatted there. It was not a place in 2005, however, where recent migrants from rural areas were likely to come in large numbers, though Juárez, with its assembly plants, attracts many Mexicans coming from farther south in search of opportunity. Buses from three lines stop at the triangle, and there is a church nearby, with a playground. There are also a number of small businesses: the Paletería Patzcuaro, the Farmacía Revolución, a convenience store named Del Rio, and the Panadería La Rosa del Oro among them. And then there is a laundromat named for Zapata, or rather, almost certainly, named for the location—the juncture of streets—that was named for the statue, which was named for Zapata.

Not knowing how long I would have to wait, I parked in front of the *panadería* (bakery). It was a breezy morning under a clear spring sky. It seemed unlikely anything would happen; there was nothing resembling expectation in the behavior of the inhabitants of the neighborhood. Zapata's main company was a young man waiting for a bus on the low brick-and-cement foundation from which the pedestal rose. Vans stuffed with multigenerational families pulled up to the bakery, letting out the women to buy Sunday morning sweetbreads. A few dogs skulked around, as did a truck distributing gas, which played, repeatedly, an electronic version of the first strains of "La Cucaracha." The main event as far as anyone else was concerned was likely the suspicious-looking Anglo sitting in his parked car, taking notes and, after a few minutes, eating pastries. A man came to my window to sell me some gum but settled for a few pesos "to get something to eat."

Finally, around 9:30, two men pulled up in a white pickup loaded with sound equipment and folding chairs. Things started to move quickly. Buses arrived, two of them blocking traffic on one side of the triangle. Soon the municipal band, composed largely of older men, was seated, and other

FIGURE 9.2
Commemorating Zapata's death in Juárez, 2005. Photograph by the author.

groups began to assemble: girls in matching skirts from Emiliano Zapata grade school, the "Band of War and Escort" from Secondary School 3003, and a handful of Boy Scouts. Tuning up and marching practice followed, while a dozen dignitaries were seated in a long row in front of the statue. These included representatives of the governor of Chihuahua, the city government, and the local fire and police departments. A general from the Juárez garrison was also present, and the municipality's coordinator of Civic and Cultural Acts, Eduardo Limón Alonso, presided.

There were two short speeches by politicians, with discussion of the importance of heroes and the respect they deserved. A girl from Emiliano Zapata school presented a history of Zapata's life. The band punctuated the discourse with music, including, of course, the national anthem. Toward the end there was a skit. A man dressed like Zapata but older, taller, and heavier than the caudillo had ever been—and, if possible, with a larger mustache—began by declaiming on Zapata, drawing in part on Armando List Arzubide's corrido. He then became Zapata when an actor playing Guajardo approached him for an *abrazo* (embrace) to seal their deal. Seconds later, Guajardo and two cronies gunned him down. For reasons unexplained, Zapata held a rooster through much of the performance, as did one of his murderers, and the play ended with a brief cockfight. Thankfully, Limón Alonso proclaimed the red one the winner before any noticeable bloodshed occurred. The officials then gathered around the statue to place a wreath, which was lashed to the pedestal with a rope in anticipation of high winds predicted for that afternoon.

It was, in general, a formal process, but a friendly one too. There were few observers—a handful of parents, a couple of passersby. It was clearly an event that was artificially inserted into the neighborhood, as the statue had likely been in the first place. It was not that there was no popular resonance of the Zapata cult in Chihuahua. Ejidos in the state regularly held commemorations, and two years earlier the telephone workers of Nuevo Casas Grandes had chosen the occasion to march on the offices of their mayor to demonstrate support for campesinos, reject a new labor law, and oppose the U.S. war in Iraq.[28] We can only imagine what children took away from Juárez commemorations or from attending a school named for Zapata. Still, the cult has obviously not developed the same force just south of the border that it has in Oaxaca.

A year earlier, in May 2004, I traveled to south Texas to participate in the dedication of Emiliano Zapata Elementary School, part of the La Joya Independent School District, in the town of Palmview. I was invited by librarian Mary Ann Lacey with the request that I explain why a school should be named for Zapata. Such an explanation was needed, she said, because some people in the area questioned the choice, noting that Zapata had been nothing but a bandit. As I was to learn—this was my first extended visit to the area—it was an almost entirely Mexican-American and Mexican part of the world, including the politicians and school officials who attended the dedication. Presumably, then, Zapata's bad press was not coming only from a minute number of Anglos; rather, his legacy was contested within the Mexican community. Given that northeastern Mexico, home to Carranza, Pablo González, and Guajardo, was only a few miles away, this should not, I suppose, have surprised me.

I knew, of course, that to accept the invitation was to step into my own story, and I did it with some discomfort about whether I could find anything to say that was both constructive and honest. Luckily, I was warmly received, and the positive feelings generated by the dynamic community of recent immigrants that surrounded me made me feel better about what I had devised to say. "Some people," I noted, soon after taking the podium, "have called Zapata the cleanest revolutionary who ever lived, but it's pretty hard for a revolutionary to be clean. That kind of view of him is unrealistic." I went on to explain that from my point of view Zapata was particularly admirable for overcoming his limited education to condense campesino demands so effectively in the Plan of Ayala, and then for acting on those demands when he got the chance. "He did what he said he intended to do," I pontificated, "far more than any other revolutionary of the period." After talking not only about his life but about the construction of memories about him, I was ready for the grand finale:

> he increasingly became a symbol of Mexican national identity—that is, he became someone remembered as something positive about Mexico, an image that Mexicans could rally around. And for that reason, it is not at all surprising to me that you have a school named for him here. He's a perfect choice in a place where land has long been important, where education is crucial to deal with a quickly changing world, where Mexico is so significant—just across the river—and where people want to remember and value their Mexican roots, history, and traditions. Inspired by those memories and values, I know that the children who attend this school will go on to do great things.

By the time I finished I could not have been more serious about or committed to what I was saying—however insufficient or unsubtle my words may have been.

School Superintendent Filomena Leo then took the microphone to assure me, and the audience, that they did indeed value their Mexican roots and traditions in south Texas. In that valuing, just outside the reach of the Mexican state on a segment of the border that has boomed during the NAFTA years, lie some of the cult's prospects, but those prospects remain abundant throughout greater Mexico. On both sides of the border, in Mexico City and Chiapas and Morelos too, Zapata rides on.

NOTES

INTRODUCTION

1. An *ejido* is land a village holds collectively—the form in which land was generally distributed after the revolution. A *colonia* is a sector of a city.

2. A *corrido* is a variety of Mexican folk song associated with the revolutionary period.

3. Roger Bartra, *The Cage of Melancholy: Identity and Metamorphosis in the Mexican Character*, trans. Christopher J. Hall (New Brunswick, N.J.: Rutgers University Press, 1992), 164.

4. Manú Dornbierer, *El prinosaurio: La bestia política mexicana* (Mexico City: Grijalbo, 1994), 169–170, 191.

5. *Webster's New Collegiate Dictionary* (Springfield, Mass.: G.&C. Merriam, 1974), 762.

6. Benedict Anderson, *Imagined Communities: Reflections on the Origin and Spread of Nationalism*, rev. ed. (London and New York: Verso, 1991), 6, defines a nation as "an imagined political community—and imagined as both inherently limited and sovereign."

7. Anderson, *Imagined Communities*, 4–12.

8. See David I. Kertzer, *Ritual, Politics, and Power* (New Haven: Yale University Press, 1988), 178.

9. Nora Hamilton, *The Limits of State Autonomy: Post-Revolutionary Mexico* (Princeton, N.J.: Princeton University Press, 1982), 7.

10. Anthony D. Smith, *Myths and Memories of the Nation* (New York: Oxford University Press, 1999), 8–19.

11. For a French example, see Mona Ozouf, *Festivals and the French Revolution* (Cambridge, Mass.: Harvard University Press, 1988); also see Smith, *Myths*, 154.

12. On the workings of myth and ritual in Mexican localities, see William H. Beezley, Cheryl English Martin, and William E. French, "Introduction: Constructing Consent, Inciting Conflict," in *Rituals of Rule, Rituals of Resistance: Public Celebrations and Popular Culture in Mexico*, ed. William H. Beezley, Cheryl English Martin, and William E. French (Wilmington, Del.: SR Books, 1994), xxix; and Mary Kay Vaughan,

"The Construction of the Patriotic Festival in Tecamachalco, Puebla, 1900–1946," in *Rituals of Rule*, 214, 219.

13. Joel S. Migdal, *State in Society: Studying How States and Societies Transform and Constitute One Another* (New York: Cambridge University Press, 2001), especially 259–260.

14. For "web of significance," see Clifford Geertz, *The Interpretation of Cultures* (New York: Basic Books, 1973), 5.

15. Prasenjit Duara, *Rescuing History from the Nation: Questioning Narratives of Modern China* (Chicago: University of Chicago Press, 1995), 9.

16. Adam Kuper, *The Chosen Primate: Human Nature and Cultural Diversity* (Cambridge, Mass.: Harvard University Press, 1994), 81–82; Brian M. Fagan, *World Prehistory: A Brief Introduction* (New York: Longman, 1999), 60–61.

17. Bruce Mazlish, *The Leader, the Led, and the Psyche: Essays in Psychohistory* (Hanover, N.H., and London: Wesleyan University Press, 1990), 5.

18. Max Weber, *On Charisma and Institution Building*, ed. S. N. Eisenstadt (Chicago: University of Chicago Press, 1968), 48; Clifford Geertz, "Centers, Kings, and Charisma: Reflections on the Symbolics of Power," in *Rites of Power: Symbolism, Ritual, and Politics Since the Middle Ages*, ed. Sean Wilentz (Philadelphia: University of Pennsylvania Press, 1985).

19. Mary Miller and Karl Taube, *An Illustrated Dictionary of the Gods and Symbols of Ancient Mexico and the Maya* (London: Thames and Hudson, 1993), 15, 28–29, 141.

20. Miller and Taube, *Illustrated Dictionary*, 141–142. See Serge Gruzinski, *Man-Gods in the Mexican Highlands: Indian Power and Colonial Society, 1520–1800*, trans. Eileen Corrigan (Stanford: Stanford University Press, 1989), 22, 44, for the tendency to mix attributes of gods and humans.

21. Miller and Taube, *Illustrated Dictionary*, 39, 69–70; Gruzinski, *Man-Gods*, 142; Michael E. Smith, *The Aztecs*, 2nd ed. (Malden, Mass.: Blackwell, 2003), 206.

22. Miller and Taube, *Illustrated Dictionary*, 17–18, 20, 32–33, 74–76, 90.

23. David Brading, *The First America: The Spanish Monarchy, Creole Patriots, and the Liberal State, 1492–1867* (New York: Cambridge University Press, 1991), 350; David Brading, *Mexican Phoenix: Our Lady of Guadalupe: Image and Tradition Across Five Centuries* (New York: Cambridge University Press, 2001), 3, 18, 43.

24. Miller and Taube, *Illustrated Dictionary*, 74; William B. Taylor, *Magistrates of the Sacred: Priests and Parishioners in Eighteenth-Century Mexico* (Stanford: Stanford University Press, 1996), 72.

25. Taylor, *Magistrates*, 50–51, 73, 550.

26. Brading, *First America*, 361; Brading, *Mexican Phoenix*, 5, 74.

27. William B. Taylor, "Santiago's Horse: Christianity and Colonial Indian Resistance in the Heartland of New Spain," in *Violence, Resistance, and Survival in the Americas*, ed. William B. Taylor and Franklin Pease (Washington, D.C.: Smithsonian Institution Press, 1994), 157–158, 162; Brading, *Mexican Phoenix*, 19, 41.

28. Eric Van Young, "Millennium on the Northern Marches: The Mad Messiah of Durango and Popular Rebellion in Mexico, 1800–1815," in *Comparative Studies in Society and History* 21 (1986): 393, 402, 405–407.

29. David Brading, *Mito y profecía en la historia de México*, trans. Tomás Segovia (Mexico City: Vuelta, 1988), 17–18; Brading, *First America*, 5, 580–581, 601.

30. Brading, *First America*, 284–285, 363, 583–584; Inga Clendinnen, *Aztecs: An Interpretation* (New York: Cambridge University Press, 1991), 2; Enrique Florescano, "Quetzalcóatl: Un mito hecho de mitos," in *Mitos mexicanos*, ed. Enrique Florescano (Mexico City: Nuevo Siglo, 1995), 114–115.

31. Taylor, *Magistrates*, 26.

32. Enrique Florescano, *Memory, Myth, and Time in Mexico: From the Aztecs to Independence*, trans. Albert G. Bork (Austin: University of Texas Press, 1994), 216–217; Robert H. Duncan, "Embracing a Suitable Past: Independence Celebrations under Mexico's Second Empire," *Journal of Latin American Studies* 30 (1998): 268.

33. Brading, *First America*, 601–602.

34. Claudio Lomnitz-Adler, *Exits from the Labyrinth: Culture and Ideology in the Mexican National Space* (Berkeley and Los Angeles: University of California Press, 1992), 290–292.

35. Brading, *First America*, 662–663.

36. Mauricio Tenorio-Trillo, *Mexico at the World's Fairs: Crafting a Modern Nation* (Berkeley and Los Angeles: University of California Press, 1996), 250–251; Barbara A. Tenenbaum, "Streetwise History: The Paseo de la Reforma and the Porfirian State, 1876–1910," in *Rituals of Rule*, 141.

37. Cited by Arnaldo Córdova, "La mitología de la Revolución Mexicana," in *Mitos mexicanos*, ed. Enrique Florescano (Mexico City: Nuevo Siglo, 1995), 21.

38. Ilene V. O'Malley, *The Myth of the Revolution: Hero Cults and the Institutionalization of the Mexican State, 1920–1940* (New York: Greenwood Press, 1986), 4–8, 130–132, 140.

39. O'Malley, *Myth*, 69, 117.

40. Thomas Benjamin, La Revolución: *Mexico's Great Revolution as Memory, Myth, and History* (Austin: University of Texas Press, 2000), 13, 32, 68, 151.

41. Armando Bartra, *Los herederos de Zapata: Movimientos campesinos posrevolucionarios en México* (Mexico City: Ediciones Era, 1985); Ricardo Pérez Montfort, "La unión de revolucionarios agraristas del sur (unos zapatistas después de la muerte de Emiliano Zapata)," in *Morelos: Cinco siglos de historia regional*, ed. Horacio Crespo (Mexico City: Centro de Estudios Históricos del Agrarismo en México and Universidad Autónoma del Estado de Morelos, 1984), 275–283.

42. For corridos, see Catalina H. de Giménez, *Así cantaban la revolución* (Mexico City: Grijalbo, 1990). See also Alba C. de Rojo, Rafael López Castro, and José Luis Martínez, *Zapata: Iconografía* (Mexico City: Fondo de Cultura Económica, 1979); María Eugenia Arías Gómez, "Algunos cuadernos históricos sobre Emiliano Zapata y el Zapatismo," in *Emiliano Zapata y el movimiento zapatista* (Mexico City: Secretaría

de Educación Pública and the Instituto Nacional de Antropología e Historia, 1980), 181–280; and Dennis Gilbert, "Emiliano Zapata: Textbook Hero," *Mexican Studies/ Estudios Mexicanos* 19 (2003): 127–159.

43. Carlos J. Sierra Brabatta, *Zapata: Señor de la tierra, capitán de los labriegos* (Mexico City: Departamento del Distrito Federal, 1985).

44. See Robert Redfield, *Tepoztlán, a Mexican Village: A Study of Folk Life* (Chicago: University of Chicago Press, 1930); Oscar Lewis, *Life in a Mexican Village: Tepoztlán Restudied* (Urbana: University of Illinois Press, 1951); Arturo Warman, *"We Come to Object": The Peasants of Morelos and the National State*, trans. Stephen K. Ault (Baltimore: Johns Hopkins University Press, 1980); Guillermo de la Peña, *Herederos de promesas: Agricultura, política y ritual en los Altos de Morelos* (Mexico City: Casa Chata, 1980); and JoAnn Martin, *Contesting Authenticity: Battles Over the Representation of History in Morelos, Mexico* (South Bend, Ind.: Helen Kellog Institute for International Studies, University of Notre Dame, 1993).

45. The most significant oral history project is the Programa de Historia Oral, directed by Alicia Olivera and Eugenia Meyer, with the participation of Salvador Rueda, Laura Espejel, Carlos Barreto, et al. Extended interviews include Oscar Lewis, *Pedro Martínez: A Mexican Peasant and His Family* (New York: Vintage Books, 1964); and Luz Jiménez, *Life and Death in Milpa Alta*, trans. and ed. Fernando Horcasitas (Norman: University of Oklahoma Press, 1972).

46. Salvador Rueda Smithers and Laura Espejel López, "El siglo xx: Bajo el signo de Emiliano Zapata," in *Morelos: El estado* (Cuernavaca: Gobierno del Estado de Morelos, 1993). Another general essay is Benjamin Smith, "Emiliano Zapata: Contestation and Construction" (master's thesis, University of Cambridge, 2001). Works on the recent struggle for Zapata include Adriana López Monjardín and Francisco Javier Pineda, "La disputa simbólica por la herencia de Zapata," in *Globalización, deterioro ambiental y reorganización social en el campo*, ed. Hubert Carton de Grammont (Mexico City: Juan Pablos and Universidad Nacional Autónoma de México, 1995), 236–251.

47. Lynn Stephen, *Zapata Lives! Histories and Cultural Politics in Southern Mexico* (Berkeley and Los Angeles: University of California Press, 2002).

48. Lomnitz-Adler, *Exits*, 29–30, 35.

49. Alan Knight, *The Mexican Revolution*, 2 vols. (Cambridge: Cambridge University Press, 1986).

50. See Ramón Eduardo Ruíz, *The Great Rebellion: Mexico 1905–1924* (New York: Norton, 1980).

51. This question is at the center of Kevin J. Middlebrook's *The Paradox of Revolution: Labor, the State, and Authoritarianism in Mexico* (Baltimore: Johns Hopkins University Press, 1995), 1.

52. Alan Knight, "Popular Culture and the Revolutionary State in Mexico, 1910–1940," *Hispanic American Historical Review* 74 (August 1994): 440.

53. Judith Hellman, *Mexico in Crisis*, 2nd ed. (New York: Holmes and Meier, 1983); Middlebrook, *Paradox*, 4–5, 317.

54. Edwin Lieuwen, *Mexican Militarism: The Political Rise and Fall of the Revolutionary Army, 1910–1940* (1968); Hans Werner Tobler, "Peasants and the Shaping of the Revolutionary State, 1910–1940," in *Riot, Rebellion, and Revolution: Rural Social Conflict in Mexico*, ed. Friedrich Katz (Princeton, N.J.: Princeton University Press, 1988), 487–518.

55. Florencia Mallon, *Peasant and Nation: The Making of Postcolonial Mexico and Peru* (Berkeley and Los Angeles: University of California Press, 1995), 220. To be precise, this is Mallon's definition of a *regional* political culture, but it is clearly more broadly applicable.

56. Lomnitz, *Exits*, 29–30, 35, 55–57, 61–62, 76–77, 98, 102, 105–106.

57. Mary Kay Vaughan, *Cultural Politics in Revolution: Teachers, Peasants, and Schools in Mexico, 1930-1940* (Tucson: University of Arizona Press, 1997), 7

58. Alan Knight, "Revolutionary Project, Recalcitrant People: Mexico, 1910–1940," in *The Revolutionary Process in Mexico: Essays on Political and Social Change, 1880–1940*, ed. Jaime Rodríguez O. (Los Angeles: UCLA Latin American Center Publications, University of California, Los Angeles, 1990), 230, 260–263; Alan Knight, "Popular Culture."

59. Antonio Gramsci, *Selections from the Prison Notebooks of Antonio Gramsci*, ed. and trans. Quintin Hoare and Geoffrey Nowell Smith (New York: International Publishers, 1971), 53. Mallon, *Peasant and Nation*, 6–7; Vaughan, *Cultural Politics*, 199.

60. Derek Sayer, "Everyday Forms of State Formation: Some Dissident Remarks on 'Hegemony,'" in *Everyday Forms of State Formation: Revolution and the Negotiation of Rule in Modern Mexico*, ed. Gilbert M. Joseph and Daniel Nugent (Durham, N.C.: Duke University Press, 1994), 369–372.

61. On thick and thin hegemony, see James C. Scott, *Domination and the Arts of Resistance: Hidden Transcripts* (New Haven: Yale University Press, 1990), 72–74.

62. On the gender dimension, see Jean Franco, *Plotting Women: Gender and Representation in Mexico* (New York: Columbia University Press, 1989), 102.

63. Octavio Paz, *The Labyrinth of Solitude: Life and Thought in Mexico*, trans. Lysander Kemp (New York: Grove Press, 1961).

CHAPTER 1

1. A *charro* is a horseman best identified by the manner of dress described here.

2. For the quotations, see the Pact of Xochimilco, in Manuel González Ramírez, *Planes políticos y otros documentos* (Mexico City: Fondo de Cultura Económica, 1954), 113–122. See also Leon Canova to the U.S. Secretary of State, Mexico City, December 8, 1914, Department of State, Records Relating to the Internal Affairs of Mexico, 1910–1929 (hereafter cited as USDS-IAM) 812.00/14048.

3. For the quotation, see Enrique Krauze, *El amor a la tierra: Emiliano Zapata*, Biografía del poder, no. 3 (Mexico City: Fondo de Cultura Económica, 1987), 81. See

also the photographs in Alba C. de Rojo, Rafael López Castro, and José Luis Martínez, *Zapata: Iconografía* (Mexico City: Fondo de Cultura Económica, 1979), 62–68.

4. For the claim that he was no politician, see Zapata to Gildardo Magaña, December 6, 1911, in Gildardo Magaña [and Carlos Pérez Guerrero], *Emiliano Zapata y el agrarismo en México*, 5 vols. (Mexico City: Editorial Ruta, 1951–1952), 2:140–142.

5. Samuel Brunk, *Emiliano Zapata: Revolution and Betrayal in Mexico* (Albuquerque: University of New Mexico Press, 1995), 6–11, 20.

6. John Womack, Jr., *Zapata and the Mexican Revolution* (New York: Vintage Books, 1970), 6; Serafín M. Robles, "Se incorpora Jesus Morales: toma de Chietla, Puebla," *El Campesino* (Mexico City), June 1952.

7. Roberto Melville, *Crecimiento y rebelión: El desarrollo económico de las haciendas azucareras en Morelos (1880–1910)* (Mexico City: Editorial Nueva Imagen, 1979), 22, 34–44; Alicia Hernández Chávez, *Anenecuilco: Memoria y vida de un pueblo* (Mexico City: El Colegio de México, 1991), 109–110, 252–257.

8. For the quotation, see Mario Gill, "Zapata: Su pueblo y sus hijos," *Historia Mexicana* 2 (1952): 305–306. See also Jesús Sotelo Inclán, *Raíz y razón de Zapata* (Mexico City: Editorial Etnos, 1943), 169–214.

9. Womack, *Zapata*, 3–9; Sotelo Inclán, *Raíz*, 172–177.

10. Brunk, *Emiliano Zapata*, 29–31.

11. Eduardo Adame Medina, "De Villa de Ayala a Chinameca, 1909–1919," *El Campesino*, July 1958; Magaña, *Emiliano Zapata*, 1:110–111.

12. Juan Andreu Almazán, "Memorias del General Juan Andreu Almazán," serialized in *El Universal*, 1957–1958, bound photocopy at the Colegio de México, Chapters 17 and 18; Womack, *Zapata*, 79–84.

13. Warman, "*We Come to Object*," 112, 124–125, is excellent on guerrilla warfare. See also "Memorándum de la situación política del Estado de Morelos," Archivo General de la Nación, Mexico City, Archivo de Alfredo Robles Domínguez (hereafter cited as ARD) 7:37:12–18; Antonio Carriles to Juan Pagaza, Cuernavaca, May 23–24, 1911, ARD 6:28:10–11; and "Relación de los sucesos en el Estado de Morelos," Centro de Estudios Sobre la Universidad, Mexico City, Archivo de Gildardo Magaña (hereafter cited as AGM) 12:1:19.

14. Alfredo Robles Domínguez to Emiliano Zapata, June 1, 1911, ARD 4:17:73; Magaña, *Emiliano Zapata*, 1:165–166, 185.

15. *El Imparcial* (Mexico City), June 17, 19, and 20, 1911; "Relación de los sucesos en el estado de Morelos," AGM 12:1:19; Teofanes Jiménez to Francisco de la Barra, August 18, 1911, Mexico City, AGM 6:J–3:35; Sergio Valverde, *Apuntes para la historia de la revolución y de la política en el estado de Morelos* (Mexico City: n.p., 1933), 43–44, 93–94.

16. *El Imparcial*, June 19, 1911.

17. *El Imparcial*, June 20, 1911.

18. Representatives of the Merchants, Professionals, and Agriculturists to Francisco León de la Barra, undated, AGM 12:7:140.

19. For the classic Latin American statement on this theme, see Domingo Faustino Sarmiento, *Life in the Argentine Republic in the Days of the Tyrants; or, Civilization and Barbarism* (New York: Collier Books, 1961). See also Salvador Rueda Smithers, *El paraíso de la caña: Historia de una construcción imaginaria* (Mexico City: INAH, 1998), 173–175.

20. For a fuller discussion of these issues, see Samuel Brunk, "'The Sad Situation of Civilians and Soldiers': The Banditry of Zapatismo in the Mexican Revolution," *American Historical Review* 101 (1996): 331–353, and JoAnn Martin, "Criminal Instabilities: Narrative Interruptions and the Politics of Criminality," in *Crime's Power: Anthropologists and the Ethnography of Crime*, ed. Philip C. Parnell and Stephanie C. Kane (New York: Palgrave Macmillan, 2003), 173–195.

21. *El Imparcial*, June 21, 1911.

22. Brunk, *Emiliano Zapata*, 51–53; Magaña, *Emiliano Zapata*, 1:248.

23. For the Plan of Ayala, see Womack, *Zapata*, 400–404.

24. Giménez, *Así cantaban*, 63; John M. Ingham, *Mary, Michael, and Lucifer: Folk Catholicism in Central Mexico* (Austin: University of Texas Press, 1986), 57–59, 122, 188.

25. See Silva's "Bola de la toma de Cuautla por Zapata," in Giménez, *Así cantaban*, 275–282, as well as pages 130, 136–137 in the same volume. For Silva's sense of service to the cause, see Silva to Zapata, undated, Archivo General de la Nación, Mexico City, Archivo de Zapata (hereafter cited as AZ) 14:20:26. Using corridos as historical sources is tricky because, as elements of popular culture that are meant primarily to be performed rather than written down, they change over time. The first publication of this song in an anthology seems to have been in Merle E. Simmons, *The Mexican Corrido as a Source for Interpretive Study of Modern Mexico, 1870–1950* (Bloomington: Indiana University Press, 1957), but it does appear earlier in a collection of undated broadsides—the flyers on which most corridos were first distributed in written form—by Eduardo Guerrero, entitled *Corridos históricos de la revolución mexicana desde 1910 a 1930 y otros notables de varias epocas* (Mexico City, 1931). It seems likely that the broadside in question was from 1911—that the corrido appeared at that time as "news," as the refutation of *El Imparcial* suggests—but it is not certain.

26. Giménez, *Así cantaban*, 49, considers this a culture of mixed oral and written tradition.

27. Giménez, *Así cantaban*, 49–50, 54–55, and, for examples of these urban corridos, 283–286, 295–296.

28. "Bola de la historia del pronunciamiento del general Emiliano Zapata o la traición de Federico Morales," in Giménez, *Así cantaban*, 289–294.

29. "A la tumba de los héroes," in Baltasar Dromundo, *Emiliano Zapata: Biografía* (Mexico City: Imprenta Mundial, 1934), 276–277. The Reform era (1855–1876) was a crucial period in the formation of the Mexican state, during which Juárez led the Liberal Party in creating a constitution, fighting off a French occupation, and establishing a measure of political stability.

30. "Bola de la toma de Cuautla por Zapata," in Giménez, *Así cantaban*, 275–282.

31. Giménez, *Así cantaban*, 211–212.

32. Interview with Domingo Yedra Islas, conducted by Laura Espejel, Milpa Alta, D.F., October 3 and 21, 1973, as part of the Programa de Historia Oral of the Instituto Nacional de Antropología e Historia and the Instituto de Investigaciones Dr. José María Luis Mora (hereafter cited as PHO) -Z/1/15; Salvador Rueda, "La zona armada de Genovevo de la O," *Cuicuilco* 2 (January 1981): 38–40; and Laura Espejel, "El movimiento campesino en el oriente del estado de México: El caso de Juchitepec," *Cuicuilco*, 2 (January 1981): 36.

33. For examples of the complaints that reached Zapata, see the citizens of San Andrés de la Cal to Zapata, October 14, 1913, Archivo General de la Nación, Mexico City, Archivo de Genovevo de la O (hereafter cited as AO) 13:9:33–34; and Timoteo Sánchez to Zapata, Tepoztlán, March 30, 1914, AO 14:4:28. See also Zapata's circular of December 20, 1911, in Octavio Magaña's "Historia documental de la revolución mexicana," AGM (unnumbered boxes), no. 212, pp. 3–7; and his circular of October 28, 1913, Archivo General de la Nación, Mexico City, Archivo del Cuartel General del Sur (hereafter cited as ACGS) 1:3:22-23.

34. For more on Zapata's urban advisors, see Samuel Brunk, "Zapata and the City Boys: In Search of a Piece of the Revolution," *Hispanic American Historical Review* 73 (1993): 33–65.

35. Salvador Rueda Smithers, "Emiliano Zapata, los signos de un caudillo, biografía de un símbolo," in *Estadistas, caciques y caudillos*, ed. Carlos Martínez Assad (Mexico City: Instituto de Investigaciones Sociales, 1988), 139; Ricardo Pérez Montfort, "Imágenes del zapatismo entre 1911 y 1913," and Francisco Pineda, "Guerra y cultura: el antizapatismo en el gobierno de Madero," both in *Estudios sobre el zapatismo*, ed. Laura Espejel (Mexico City: Instituto de Antropología e Historia, 2000); *La Tribuna*, May 2, 3, and 28, 1913.

36. J. Figueroa Domenech, *Veinte meses de anarquía* (Mexico City: n.p., 1913), cited by Lola Elizabeth Boyd, *Emiliano Zapata en las letras y el folklore mexicano* (Madrid: José Porrua Turanzas, 1979), 103.

37. Antonio D. Melgarejo, *Los crímenes del zapatismo: (Apuntes de un guerrillero)*, 2nd ed. (Mexico City: Editora y Distribuidora Nacional de Publicaciones, 1979), 121 and 78, respectively, for the quotations. See also pp. 108–111 and 117–118 of this volume, as well as Alfonso López Ituarte [Héctor Ribot], *El Atila del sur* (Mexico City: Imprenta 1a de Humboldt, [1913]), and John Rutherford, *Mexican Society During the Revolution: A Literary Approach* (Oxford: Clarendon Press, 1971), 48, 75, 150–151.

38. See the "Reformas al Plan de Ayala," May 30, 1913, in *Emiliano Zapata: Antología*, ed. Laura Espejel, Alicia Olivera, and Salvador Rueda (Mexico City: Instituto Nacional de Estudios Históricos de la Revolución Mexicana, 1988), 133, and the Marciano Silva corridos, "El exterminio de Morelos," and "Danza de Juvencio Robles" in Giménez, *Así cantaban*, 302–309.

39. For the Plan of Guadalupe, see González Ramírez, *Planes*, 137–140. For Carranza and land reform, see Magaña, *Emiliano Zapata*, 4:268–269.

40. For one of Zapata's efforts at instilling discipline in anticipation of entering Mexico City, see his circular, Yautepec, Morelos, July 14, 1914, in Espejel et al., eds., *Emiliano Zapata*, 211. See also Leon Canova to the Secretary of State, Mexico City, December 8, 1914, USDS-IAM 812.00/14048; and John Silliman to the Secretary of State, Mexico City, November 30, 1914, USDS-IAM 812.00/13939. For representative corridos, see "Nuevo corrido suriano dedicado al general Emiliano Zapata" and "Entrada triunfal de las fuerzas revolucionarias a la capital de México el 6 de diciembre de 1914," in Giménez, *Así cantaban*, 334–337 and 340–344, respectively.

41. For the quotation, see Antonio Barona to Evaristo Fuentes, August 17, 1914, AO 4:2:91. See also Alfredo Serratos to Gildardo Magaña, October 1, 1914, AGM 27:7:110; Manuel N. Robles to Zapata, October 12, 1914, AZ 1:21:65; Fernando Solís to Zapata, Mexico City, April 19, 1915, AZ 7:5:76–77; César Prescora Roeves to González Garza, October 24, 1914, AGM 27:7:136; and Castillo to Zapata, April 13, 1915, AZ 7:5:25–28.

42. For the quotation, see Zapata's circular, June 20–21, 1915, AZ 21:6:12. See also Brunk, *Emiliano Zapata*, 139–170.

43. See the Tlaltizapán Festival Commission to [Zapata], AGM 28:5:605; Sabas Piñero to Zapata, Campos de Chinameca, October 12, 1915, AZ 10:5:7; the President of the Junta Patriótica of Cuautla to Zapata, September 6, 1915, AZ 10:1:40; Feliciano Domínguez to Zapata, Villa de Ayala, August 21, 1915, AZ 9:6:3; and Zapata to Pipino L. Valero, Quilamula, September 24, 1914, AO 18:2:47.

44. Augustina Salazar to Zapata, Anenecuilco, October 23, 1915, AZ 10:6:13; Francisca Z. García to Zapata, Cuautla, October 2, 1915, AZ 10:4:14; Lucio Rios to Zapata, Cuautla, August 2, 1914, AO 16:2:43.

45. Circular of February 11, 1914, in Espejel et al., eds., *Emiliano Zapata*, 181–182; and "Decreto de Nacionalización de Bienes," Cuernavaca, September 8, 1914, in Magaña, *Emiliano Zapata*, 5:102–103.

46. See, for instance, Jesús Blancas to Zapata, June 12, 1915, AZ 19:2:85; Modesto Rangel to Zapata, Xochitepec, Morelos, June 27, 1915, AZ 19:2:49; and Zapata to Ricardo Reyes Márquez, Tlaltizapán, Morelos, August 25, 1915, AZ 9:6:36.

47. Zapata to González Garza, Tlaltizapán, June 3, 1915, Universidad Panamericana, Mexico City, Archivo de Roque González Garza (hereafter cited as AGG) 12:291; the citizens of Tixtla, Guerrero to Zapata, August 13, 1914, AO 16:1:99; and Emigdio Martínez to Zapata, Jonacatepec, Morelos, October 1, 1914, AZ 1:21:4.

48. On stealing food, see AGM 31:3 generally, and Gregorio Zúñiga to Timoteo Sánchez, Tlaltizapán, April 22, 1916, AGM 31:3:175. See also Don Leonor of Tepalcingo, Morelos, cited in Elena Azaola Garrido, "Tepalcingo: La dependencia política de un municipio de Morelos," in *Los campesinos de la tierra de Zapata*, Vol. 3, *Política y conflicto*, Elena Azaola Garrido and Esteban Krotz (Mexico City: SEP/INAH, 1976), 42; and the interview with Leopoldo Alquicira Fuentes, conducted by Alicia Olivera, Tepepan, D.F., July 21 and 31, 1973, PHO-Z/1/3, pp. 27–29.

49. Brunk, "'The Sad Situation,'" 346–349.

50. For the quotation, see the Ley de 5 de Marzo de 1917, in Espejel et al., eds., *Emiliano Zapata*, 378–382. See also the citizens of Tepalcingo, Morelos to Zapata, October 6 and 8, 1915, AZ 10:4:36–37 and 19:6:11–12 respectively; Zapata's circular to municipal authorities, May 31, 1916, in Espejel et al, eds., *Emiliano Zapata*, 346–347; and the document of August 29, 1915, in AZ 9:6:51–52.

51. For the quotation, see Zapata to Antonio Díaz Soto y Gama, Tlaltizapán, Morelos, February 8, 1916, ACGS 1:2:54–55. Also see Brunk, *Emiliano Zapata*, 182–185.

52. See the act creating the Asociación Defensora for Tochimilco, Puebla, December 12, 1916, AZ, box 26; acts of the meetings creating the Centro Consultivo, Tlaltizapán, Morelos, January 3–5, 1917, AZ, box 26; and Díaz Soto y Gama, "Bases a que se sujetará el Centro Consultivo de Propaganda y Unificación Revolucionaria," Tlaltizapán, November 28, 1916, AGM 28:2:525.

53. See the fragment of "El asesinato del valiente general Domingo Arenas" in Simmons, *The Mexican Corrido*, 308.

54. Manifiesto al Pueblo Mexicano, January 20, 1917, in Espejel et al., eds., *Emiliano Zapata*, 366–368.

55. Zapata's circular, Tlaltizapán, Morelos, July 10, 1918, AZ 20:13:9.

56. For the letters exchanged by Zapata and Guajardo, see Rafael Sánchez Escobar, *El ocaso de los héroes: Como murieron algunos connotados revolucionarios* (Mexico City: Casa de Orientación para Varones, 1934), 30–32.

57. Salvador Reyes Avilés to Gildardo Magaña, April 10, 1919, in Isidro Fabela and Josefina E. Fabela, eds., *Documentos históricos de la revolución mexicana*, 27 vols. (Mexico City: Editorial Jus, 1970), 21:313–316.

CHAPTER 2

1. Interview with Carmen Aldana, conducted by Laura Espejel, Tepalcingo, Morelos, March 2 and 30, 1974, PHO-Z/1/32.

2. Reyes Avilés to Magaña, April 10, 1919, in Fabela and Fabela, ed., *Documentos históricos*, 21:313–316.

3. For the quotations, see González to Carranza, Cuautla, April 10, 1919, in Centro de Estudios Históricos del Agrarismo en México, *El ejército campesino del sur (ideología, organización y programa)* (Mexico City: Federación Editorial Mexicana, 1982), 218. See also Valentín López González, *La muerte del General Emiliano Zapata*, Cuadernos Zapatistas (Cuernavaca: Comité Coordinador para la Celebración del Primer Centenario del Natalicio del General Emiliano Zapata Salazar, 1979); and *Excélsior* (Mexico City), April 11 and 12, 1919.

4. *Excélsior*, April 11, 1919; see Giménez, *Así cantaban*, 312–315, for a 1913 corrido that records one rumor of Zapata's demise.

5. Sánchez Escobar, *El ocaso*, 54, 152; Domingo Diez, *Bosquejo geográfico histórico de Morelos*, 3rd ed. (Cuernavaca: Summa Morelense, 1982), 201; Gustavo Casasola, *Hechos y hombres de México: Emiliano Zapata* (Mexico City: Casasola, 1994); Porfirio Palacios, *Emiliano Zapata (datos biográficos e históricos)*, 2nd ed. (Mexico City: Centro de Estudios Históricos del Agrarismo en México, 1982), 194; *Excélsior*, March 31, 1965, April 13, 1919; Jesús Silva Herzog, *Una vida en la vida de México*, 2nd ed. (Mexico: Siglo XXI, 1975), 71; *El Nacional* (Mexico City), April 10, 1953.

6. *Excélsior*, April 11, 1919.

7. *El Demócrata*, April 11 and 12, 1919; *Excélsior*, April 12, 1919.

8. *Excélsior*, April 13, 1919.

9. *El Demócrata*, April 13, 1919.

10. *Excélsior*, April 12, 13, 14, and 16, 1919; *El Demócrata*, April 12, 1919.

11. *Excélsior*, April 12, 1919.

12. *Excélsior*, April 13 and 14, 1919; *El Demócrata*, April 13 and 14, 1919.

13. Walter Burkert, *Creation of the Sacred: Tracks of Biology in Early Religions* (Cambridge, Mass.: Harvard University Press, 1996), 31–32; John Eade and Michael J. Sallnow, "Introduction," in *Contesting the Sacred: The Anthropology of Christian Pilgrimage*, ed. John Eade and Michael J. Sallnow (London: Routledge, 1991), 6; Emile Durkheim, *The Elementary Forms of the Religious Life*, trans. Joseph Ward Swain (New York: Free Press, 1965), 56–57.

14. Paz, *Labyrinth*, 54.

15. The popularity of bandits in particular often increases after they die. See Paul J. Vanderwood, *Disorder and Progress: Bandits, Police, and Mexican Development*, rev. ed. (Wilmington, Del.: Scholarly Resources, 1992), 95.

16. Lewis, *Pedro Martínez*, 108.

17. Lewis, *Pedro Martínez*, 101–102.

18. Claudio Lomnitz-Adler, *Deep Mexico, Silent Mexico: An Anthropology of Nationalism* (Minneapolis: University of Minnesota Press, 2001), 280. In an interview with me on June 4, 1996, Marcos González of Oaxaca argued that the way Zapata died proved "that he was right."

19. Jiménez, *Life and Death*, 133, 135, 139.

20. Jiménez, *Life and Death*, 143.

21. Jiménez, *Life and Death*, xvii.

22. Jiménez, *Life and Death*, 173; Frances Karttunen, "The Linguistic Career of Doña Luz Jiménez," *Estudios de Cultura Náhuatl* 30 (1999): 267.

23. Francisco Mendoza et al., "Al Pueblo Mexicano," April 15, 1919, in Espejel et al., eds., *Emiliano Zapata* 447–451.

24. [Genovevo de la O?], circular of May 25, 1919, in Espejel et al., eds., *Emiliano Zapata*, 452–453.

25. "A los Revolucionarios del Sur," September 5, 1919, in Espejel et al., eds., *Emiliano Zapata*, 454–455.

26. For the quotations, see Genovevo de la O's "Manifiesto a la Nación Mexicana," December 1919, in Espejel et al., eds., *Emiliano Zapata*, 458–459. See also de la O to Gabriel Mariaca, December 1919, AO 9:13:17; and Magaña's circular, November 30, 1919, Archivo Histórico de la Defensa Nacional, Mexico City (hereafter cited as AHDN) XI/III/1–105, Magaña, cancelados, 65.

27. Magaña to de la O, undated fragment, AO 10:3:43; Magaña to de la O, Sierra de Puebla, January 31, 1920, AO 9:15:8.

28. Silva, "Historia de la Muerte del Gran General Emiliano Zapata," in Giménez, *Así cantaban*, 378–382.

29. Silva, "Duelo del Gral. Emiliano Zapata," in *Los corridos de Marciano Silva*, ed. Carlos Barreto Mark (Cuernavaca: Gobierno del Estado de Morelos, 1983), 25. Giménez, *Así cantaban*, 55, argues that Silva never extolled Zapata as an individual after his death and that those corridos that did so were at the service of the postrevolutionary government's appropriation of Zapata's memory. This is true of some of them, but the emphasis on Zapata after his death did not necessarily have ulterior motives. For an earlier Zapatista corrido that stressed the individual heroism of those killed in battle at a time when serving a state project could not have been an issue, see "Duelo de Ignacio Maya," in Giménez, *Así cantaban*, 323–326. See also Robert Redfield, *Tepoztlán*, 190, and Simmons, *The Mexican Corrido*, 289, for the importance of the theme of the hero's tragic death.

30. Rosalind Rosoff and Anita Aguilar, *Así firmaron el Plan de Ayala* (Mexico City: Secretaría de Educación Pública, 1976), 91; interview with José Lora Mirasol, conducted by Laura Espejel, Mexico City, October 2 and 4, 1973, PHO-Z/1/14, pp. 46–47.

31. Beatriz Bissio, "'Bienvenidos a la tierra de Zapata,'" *Cuadernos del tercer mundo* (1977), 112.

32. Salvador Rueda Smithers and Laura Espejel López, "El siglo XX: Bajo el signo de Emiliano Zapata," in *Morelos: El estado* (Cuernavaca: Gobierno del Estado de Morelos, 1993), 80.

33. "Importantísimas revelaciones de la familia del extinto Emiliano Zapata," in Giménez, *Así cantaban,* 195, 383–385.

34. Carlos Reyes Avilés, *Cartones Zapatistas* (Mexico City: n.p., 1928), 51–52. For the contention that the myth he did not die was strongest among people in more isolated areas, see *El Universal Gráfico* (Mexico City), April 10, 1934.

35. Redfield, *Tepoztlán*, 204.

36. Redfield, *Tepoztlán*, 202–203.

37. See references to the myth in *El Universal Gráfico*, April 10, 1934, and April 13, 1938; *Novedades* (Mexico City), October 20, 1949, newspaper clipping in Mexico City, Hemeroteca Nacional, Fondo Silvino González (hereafter cited as FSG); Simmons, *The Mexican Corrido*, 559; Gill, "Zapata," 294–295; *Nosotros* (Mexico City), January 25, 1958; *Ultimas Noticias* (Mexico City), January 26, 1960; and *Excélsior*, February 6, 1960.

38. Redfield, *Tepoztlán*, 204

39. *El Universal Gráfico*, April 13, 1938.

40. Gill, "Zapata," 294–295.

41. *El Campesino*, May 13, 1968.

42. Alicia Olivera, "¿Ha muerto Emiliano Zapata? Mitos y leyendas en torno del caudillo," *Boletín del Instituto Nacional de Antropología e Historia*, época II, 13 (1975): 45; interview with Carmen Aldana, PHO-Z/1/32.

43. Interview with Serafín Plasencia Gutiérrez, conducted by Laura Espejel and Salvador Rueda, September 13 and 20, 1974, Mexico City, PHO-Z/1/59. See also interview with Prospero García Aguirre, conducted by Laura Espejel and Salvador Rueda, Tlatenchi, Jojutla, Morelos, August 16, 1975, PHO-Z/1/17, pp. 11–18.

44. Interview with Carmen Aldana, 73; Olivera, "¿Ha Muerto?," 44.

45. *Excélsior*, April 10, 1996.

46. Américo Paredes, ed., *Folktales of Mexico* (Chicago: University of Chicago Press, 1970), xlviii.

47. Redfield, *Tepoztlán*, 202–203; interview with Prospero García Aguirre, 11–18.

48. For the quotation, see O'Malley, *Myth*, 44. See also interview with Carmen Aldana, 70, 73; interview with Agapito Pariente A., conducted by Alicia Olivera, Tepalcingo, Morelos, March 2, 1974, PHO-Z/1/29, pp. 16–19; interview with Andrés Avila Berrera, conducted by Laura Espejel, Atatlahucan, Morelos, May 15, 1973, PHO/1/53, p. 36; Arías Gómez, "Algunos cuadernos," 271.

49. Olivera, "¿Ha muerto?," 50.

50. Rueda and Espejel, *El siglo xx*, 80.

51. *El Universal Gráfico*, April 13, 1938; Redfield, *Tepoztlán*, 204; *Novedades*, October 20, 1949.

52. Interview with Serafín Plasencia Gutiérrez, pp. 87–89.

53. A *ranchero* is a small landowner, roughly middle class in socioeconomic status. Dressing like a ranchero would mean charro attire, as described at the beginning of Chapter 2.

54. Interview with Prospero García Aguirre, pp. 12–14.

55. *Excélsior*, April 10, 1996.

56. Olivera, "¿Ha muerto?," 50.

57. Olivera, "¿Ha muerto?," 45.

58. Frank Tannenbaum, *The Mexican Agrarian Revolution* (New York: Macmillan, 1929; reprint: Archon Books, 1968), 161.

59. *Novedades*, October 20, 1949.

60. Rueda and Espejel, *El siglo xx*, 80.

61. Olivera, "¿Ha muerto?," 46–47.

62. Olivera, "¿Ha muerto?," 51.

63. Arías Gómez, "Algunos cuadernos," 271.

64. Olivera, "¿Ha muerto?," 48.

65. For Quintero, see Bissio, "Bienvenidos," 112. See also interview with Domingo Yedra Islas, pp. 74–75.

66. Carole A. Myscofski, "Messianic Themes in Portuguese and Brazilian Literature in the Sixteenth and Seventeenth Centuries," *Luso-Brazilian Review* 28 (1991): 79–80;

Olivera, "¿Ha muerto?," 48, 51; Paredes, *Folktales*, xlix; Scott, *Domination* (New Haven: Yale University Press), 96–98, 101.

67. Interview with Agapito Pariente A.

68. "El Exterminio de Morelos" and "Duelo del Gral. Emiliano Zapata," in Barreto Mark, ed., *Los corridos*, 13, 25. See also Giménez, *Así cantaban*, 82.

69. Olivera, "¿Ha muerto?, 49.

70. Interview with Leopoldo Alquicira Fuentes, conducted by Alicia Olivera, Tepepan, D.F., July 21 and 31, 1973, PHO-Z/1/3, pp. 42–43.

71. The word *soldadera* is used to designate both female camp followers and female soldiers; here it seems that the former meaning is intended.

72. Beatriz Bissio, "Bienvenidos," 110–112.

73. *Novedades*, May 12, 1951.

74. Interview with José Lora Mirasol, 46.

75. Cited in Rueda and Espejel, "El siglo xx," 80.

76. For discussions of martyrdom and the prefiguring of death in the region, see Ingham, *Mary, Michael, and Lucifer* (Austin: University of Texas Press, 1986), 6, and Gruzinski, *Man-Gods*, 23, 56–57, 102–103.

77. Lewis, *Pedro Martínez*, 90.

78. Interview with Jesús Chávez, conducted by María Alba Pastor, Cuautla, August 31, 1973, PHO/1/99, pp. 39–41.

79. *Universal Gráfico*, April 10, 1934, FSG.

80. Salvador Calderón Ramírez, "'La Bachillera' Madrina de Zapata," in *Todo*, June 20, 1940.

81. Interview with Prospero García Aguirre.

82. Interview with Prospero García Aguirre.

83. Interview with Ana María Zapata, conducted by author, Cuautla, June 29, 1996.

84. Rueda Smithers, "Emiliano Zapata: Los signos," 134, 138.

85. Bissio, "Bienvenidos," 106.

86. Lomnitz, *Deep Mexico*, 7.

87. Interview with José Lora Mirasol, 46–47.

CHAPTER 3

1. For the quotations, see Diego Rivera (with Gladys March), *My Art, My life: An Autobiography* (New York: Citadel Press, 1960), 91. See also Raquel Tibol, *Diego Rivera: Arte y política* (Mexico City: Grijalbo, 1979), 17; and Luis Suárez, *Confesiones de Diego Rivera*, 3d ed. (Mexico City: Editorial Grijalbo, 1975), 111–112, 133.

2. Patrick Marnham, *Dreaming with his Eyes Open: A Life of Diego Rivera* (New York: Knopf, 1999), 76–77.

3. Suárez, *Confesiones*, 111–112; Marnham, *Dreaming*, 115.

4. Suárez, *Confesiones*, 67; Alberto Híjar, "Los Zapatas de Diego Rivera," in *Los Zapatas de Diego Rivera* (Mexico City: Consejo Nacional para la Cultura y las Artes, 1989), 26.

5. Luis Cardoza y Aragón, "Ensayo Crítico," in *Diego Rivera: los murales en la Secretaría de Educación Pública* (Mexico City: Secretaría de Educación Pública, 1986), 13; David Craven, *Diego Rivera as Epic Modernist* (New York: G. K. Hall, 1997), 83; *Los Zapatas*, 62–63.

6. *Los Zapatas*, 66–67.

7. David Alfaro Siqueiros, *Me llamaban el coronelazo: Memorias* (Mexico City: Grijalbo, 1977), 212.

8. For the corrido and the SEP images, see http://www.sep.gob.mx/wb2/sep/sep_1734_recorrido_virtual, May 26, 2003 (accessed January 2, 2005). Also see Híjar, "Los Zapatas," 24. Craven, *Diego Rivera*, 84–89.

9. Cited in Adrián Villagómez L., "Tres Comentarios a los Zapatas de Diego," in *Los Zapatas*, 40.

10. Desmond Rochfort, *Mexican Muralists: Orozco, Rivera, Siqueiros* (San Francisco: Chronicle Books, 1998), 71.

11. Craven, *Diego Rivera*, 112–113.

12. Bertram Wolfe, *The Fabulous Life of Diego Rivera* (New York: Stein and Day, 1963), 264; Híjar, "Los Zapatas," 32, 86–87; Leonard Folgarait, *Mural Painting and Social Revolution in Mexico, 1920–1940* (New York: Cambridge, 1998), 110–111. An agrarista was a proponent of land distribution.

13. Marnham, *Dreaming*, 225–227.

14. *Los Zapatas*, 83; Rojo, et al., *Zapata: Iconografía*, 85. For an analysis of the photograph with which Posada worked, Ariel Arnal, "Construyendo símbolos—fotografía política en México, 1865–1911," *Estudios Interdisciplinarios de América Latina y el Caribe*, 9 (1998). The idea that cartridge belts are part of Zapata's iconography comes from Teresa Avila.

15. Marnham, *Dreaming*, 82.

16. On Galindo, see Gabriela Cano, "Galindo, Hermila," in *Encyclopedia of Mexico: History, Society and Culture*, ed. Michael S. Werner (Chicago: Fitzroy Dearborn, 1997), 549–550.

17. Hermila Galindo, *Un presidenciable* (Mexico City: Talleres Gráficos de la Imprenta Nacional, 1919), 63–67. See also Alvaro Matute, *Historia de la revolución mexicana, 1917–1924*. Vol. 8, *Carrera del caudillo* (Mexico City: El Colegio de México, 1980), 49–51.

18. Luis L. León, *Crónica del poder: En los recuerdos de un político en el México revolucionario* (Mexico City: Fondo de Cultura Económica, 1987), 36, 60.

19. Interview with Vicente Estrada Cajigal, conducted by Eugenia Meyer and Alicia Olivera, Cuernavaca, February 15 and 27, March 5 and 13, 1973, PHO/4/12, p. 47. See also *Campaña política del C. Alvaro Obregón* (Mexico City: n.p., 1923), 1:202.

20. Linda B. Hall, *Alvaro Obregón: Power and Revolution in Mexico* (College Station: Texas A&M University Press, 1981), 203–244.

21. Zapata to Obregón, Tlaltizapán, August 17, 1918, AGM 30:20:354; Magaña to Zapata, August 22, 1918, AGM 30:20:355; Zapata to Obregón, August 24, 1918, AGM 30:20:359; and Octavio Magaña Cerda, *Yo acuso a los responsables: el pueblo que nos juzgue* (Mexico City: B. Costa-Amic, 1961), 26–34.

22. Womack, *Zapata*, 365, 367, 373; Mary Kay Vaughan, *The State, Education, and Social Class in Mexico, 1880-1928* (DeKalb: Northern Illinois Press, 1982), 143; Matute, *La carrera*, 136; Randall George Hansis, "Alvaro Obregón, the Mexican Revolution and the Politics of Consolidation, 1920–1924" (Ph.D. diss., University of New Mexico, 1971), 296–297.

23. Jeffrey Kent Lucas, "Twentieth Century Mexico through the Eyes of Antonio Díaz Soto y Gama" (Ph.D. diss., University of Texas, El Paso, 2006).

24. Díaz Soto y Gama to Jenaro Amezcua, Mexico City, July 23, 1921, Centro de Estudios de Historia de México, Condumex, Mexico City, Archivo de Jenaro Amezcua (hereafter cited as AA) VIII-3, manuscritos, 1:36.

25. Moisés González Navarro, *La Confederación Nacional Campesino (un grupo de presión en la reforma agraria mexicana* (Mexico City: B. Costa-Amic, 1968), 129. See also *Excélsior*, May 31, 1921; and Salvador Díaz Soto Ugalde, "Biografía del Lic. Antonio Díaz Soto y Gama," unpublished manuscript, 73–77.

26. Obregón to Díaz Soto y Gama, Mexico City, July 21, 1923, Archivo General de la Nación, Mexico City, Fondo Presidentes, Alvaro Obregón/Plutarco Elías Calles (hereafter cited as AGN-OC), 725-D-7; Díaz Soto y Gama to Obregón, Mexico City, July 26, 1923, AGN-OC, 226-D-4.

27. Arías Gómez, "Algunos cuadros históricos," 227.

28. Díaz Soto y Gama to Francisco Mendoza, Mexico City, July 1, 1920, AA VIII-2, manuscritos, 5:434; Díaz Soto y Gama to Obregón, Mexico City, June 17, 1921, AGN-OC, 407-D-2; National Agrarian Party to Obregón, Mexico City, August 13, 1923, AGN-OC, 408-S-7; and Comité Pro-Morelos to Calles, Mexico City, April 25, 1925, AGN-OC, 408-M-29.

29. Linda B. Hall, "Alvaro Obregón and the Politics of Mexican Land Reform," *Hispanic American Historical Review* 60 (1980): 213–238.

30. For the quote see *Excélsior*, July 6, 1920; see also *Excélsior*, June 29, 1920, and July 15, 16, 17, 18, 19, 20, 21, and 23, 1920; Matute, *La carrera*, 143; and Pablo González, *El centinela fiel del constitucionalismo* (Saltillo: Textos de Cultura Historiográfica, 1971), 453.

31. Redfield, *Tepoztlán*, 198; Alicia Olivera, "Un trovador zapatista de Morelos," *Boletín INAH* 36 (1969): 29.

32. Lewis, *Life in a Mexican Village*, 109–110; interview with Domingo Yedra Islas, PHO-Z/1/32, p. 38.

33. *Excélsior*, July 19, 1920; González, *El centinela*, 970, 1013, 1030; and, for Rios Zertuche's account, Ignacio A. Richkarday, "Algo más sobre el asesinato de Zapata," *Todo*, September 6, 1951.

34. [Gildardo Magaña, ed.], *Ofrenda a la memoria de Emiliano Zapata* (Mexico City?: n.p., 1938), 103.

35. *El Demócrata*, April 10 and 12, 1921; O'Malley, *The Myth*, 45–46.

36. Francisco Bulnes, "Juárez y Zapata," *El Universal*, April 26, 1921. Villa de Ayala was the head village of the municipality in which Anenecuilco was located. It was the site of many Zapatista events and presumably, in Bulnes's mind, the place where the Plan of Ayala was written, though this was not the case.

37. *Excélsior*, April 11, 1922.

38. José Rivera Castro, "Política Agraria, Organizaciones, Luchas y Resistencias Campesinas entre 1920–1928," in *Historia de la cuestión agraria mexicana*. Vol. 4, *Modernización, lucha agraria y poder político, 1920–1934*, ed. Enrique Montalvo (Mexico City: Siglo XXI and CEHAM, 1988), 35 ff.; *El Universal*, April 10, 1922; *Excélsior*, April 10, 1922; O'Malley, *Myth*, 46; Rueda and Espejel, "El siglo xx," 63. Despite his Communist identification, Ramos Pedrueza was a strong Obregonista in 1920.

39. *El Universal*, April 10, 1922.

40. *El Demócrata*, April 10, 1922.

41. *Excélsior*, April 11, 1923; José G. Parrés to Obregón, Cuernavaca, March 27, 1923, and Obregón to the State Treasurer of Morelos, Mexico City, March 29, 1923, both in AGN-OC, 205-Z-2. On veladas, see Benjamin, *La Revolución*, 108–109.

42. *El Demócrata*, April 11, 1923.

43. For ritual as a method of exchanging resources and thus greasing political wheels, see Claudio Lomnitz, "Ritual, Rumor and Corruption in the Constitution of Polity in Modern Mexico," *Journal of Latin American Anthropology* 1 (1995): 20–47, 39–41.

44. *Excélsior*, April 10, 1924; Obregón's personal secretary to the director of the National Railroads of Mexico, Mexico City, April 8, 1924, AGN-OC, 205-Z-2. See also, in the same file, Rodrigo Gómez to Obregón's personal secretary, Mexico City, April 2, 1924; and Benjamin, *La Revolución*, 72–73.

45. *Excélsior*, April 12, 1924.

46. On symbolic occupation, see Kertzer, *Ritual*, 23, 29.

47. *El Universal*, 11 April 1924. As far as I know, this slogan was not one Zapata used. It may have been coined by the Mexican Liberal Party (PLM)—on the PLM's use of it, see Ricardo Flores Magón, *La revolución mexicana*, 3rd ed. (Mexico City: Editores Mexicanos Unidos, 1985), 108. The painter Dr. Atl associated a similar slogan with the Zapatistas as early as 1915—see Alicia Azuela de la Cueva, *Arte y poder* (Mexico City: Fondo de Cultura Económica, 2005), 40. Thanks to John Lear for this source.

48. *El Universal*, April 11, 1924; *Excélsior*, April 12, 1924.

49. *Excélsior*, April 3, 1924.

50. *El Universal*, April 12 and 14, 1924; O'Malley, *Myth*, 51–52.

51. Luis L. León to Calles, Mexico City, February 23, 1926, AGN-OC, 408-M-29; Gloria Villegas Moreno, "La Soberana Convención y los perfiles del discurso zapatista," in *Estudios sobre el zapatismo*, 358–359; *Excélsior*, April 12, 1926.

52. *Excélsior*, April 11, 1928; O'Malley, *Myth*, 54.

53. Smith, *Myths*, 154.

54. Octavio Rivera, "Emiliano Zapata y el Plan de Ayala," unidentified newspaper clipping, FSG; O'Malley, *Myth*, 59.

55. *La Prensa* (Mexico City), April 10 and 11, 1931.

56. "Importantísimas revelaciones de la familia del extinto Emiliano Zapata," and "El tesoro de Emiliano Zapata," in Giménez, *Así cantaban*, 383–385 and 386–388; see also 195–197.

57. "Corrido del Espectro de Emiliano Zapata," in *Diccionario histórico y biográfico de la revolución mexicana*, 8 vols. (Mexico City: Instituto Nacional de Estudios Históricos de la Revolución Mexicana, 1990–1994), 4: 680; see also Simmons, *Mexican Corrido*, 310. An excerpt from the "Calavera de Emiliano Zapata" appears in Simmons, *Mexican Corrido*, 311.

58. Giménez, *Así cantaban*, 197–198.

59. Dr. Atl [Gerardo Murillo], *Las artes populares en México* (Mexico City: Libreria México, 1921), 15–16.

60. Vicente T. Mendoza, *El corrido mexicano* (Mexico City: Fondo de Cultura Económica, 1954), 81–85; Simmons, *Mexican Corrido*, 313–315.

61. Dromundo to Amezcua, Mexico City, April 7, 1935, AA, VIII-3, manuscritos, 7:611.

62. Dromundo, *Emiliano Zapata*, 255–257.

63. The phrase "romantic visibility" comes from Gabriela Cano, personal communication, based on her impression of another of Dromundo's works, *Francisco Villa y la "Adelita"* (Victoria de Durango, Durango: 1936).

64. Germán List Arzubide, *Emiliano Zapata: Exaltación* (Jalapa: Talleres Gráficos del Gobierno de Veracruz, 1927).

65. List Arzubide, *Emiliano Zapata*, 7.

66. List Arzubide, *Emiliano Zapata*, 7–9. This account first appeared in print in Julio Cuadros Caldas, *México-Soviet* (Puebla: Santiago Loyo, 1926), 140–141. Cuadros Caldas claimed to have heard it from two men who worked for Zapata's father.

67. List Arzubide, *Emiliano Zapata*, 19–20.

68. List Arzubide, *Emiliano Zapata*, 22.

69. List Arzubide, *Emiliano Zapata*, 28–29.

70. List Arzubide, *Emiliano Zapata*, 30–31, 34–35.

71. Reyes Avilés, *Cartones*.

72. Reyes Avilés, *Cartones*, preface.

73. Meyer, Krauze, and Reyes, *Estado y sociedad*, 100.

74. Reyes Avilés, *Cartones*, 9–10.

75. Reyes Avilés, *Cartones*, 40–41.

76. Reyes Avilés, *Cartones*, 45.

77. Reyes Avilés, *Cartones*, 46–47. This story was printed in *El Demócrata*, April 10, 1923, where it was attributed to Gildardo Magaña.

78. Reyes Avilés, *Cartones*, 50.

79. Reyes Avilés, *Cartones*, 54, 58, 61.

80. These articles are collected in Octavio Paz Solórzano, *Hoguera que fue*, ed. Felipe Gálvez (Mexico City: Universidad Autónoma Metropolitana, Unidad Xochimilco, 1986).

81. For the quotation, see Paz Solórzano, *Hoguera*, 164–165. See also 147, 181, 187–189 in the same volume, and *El Universal Gráfico*, April 10, 1934, FSG.

82. Paz Solórzano, *Hoguera*, 143–144. In 1911 Zapata described his economic status much as Paz did—see Alfonso Taracena, *La tragedia zapatista* (Mexico City: Editorial Bolívar, 1931), 16.

83. Paz Solórzano, *Hoguera*, 157–158.

84. Paz Solórzano, *Hoguera*, 335.

85. On voceros see Benjamin, *La Revolución*, 31–32.

86. See Humberto Masacchio, *Diccionario enciclopédico de México*, 4 vols. (Mexico City: A. León, 1989); Paz Solórzano, *Hoguera*, 47 ff.; and, for Dromundo, *Excélsior*, April 11, 1961 and Baltasar Dromundo, *Oración a Emiliano Zapata* (Mexico City: Editorial Ruta, 1952). See also the interview of Germán List Arzubide in James M. Wilkie and Edna Monzón de Wilkie, *Frente a la Revolución Mexicana: 17 protagonistas de la etapa constructiva*, 3 vols. (Mexico City: Universidad Autónoma Metropolitana, 2001), 2: 243–301.

87. On the growth of the state and the opportunities it offered, see Mercedes Blanco, *Empleo público en la administración central mexicana: evoluciones y tendencias (1920–1988)* (Mexico City: CIESAS, 1995), 115; and Roderic A. Camp, *Intellectuals and the State in Twentieth-Century Mexico* (Austin: University of Texas Press, 1985), 23, 67, 114.

88. Enrique Rajchenberg S., "Las figuras heroicas de la revolución en los historiadores protomarxistas," *Secuencia* 28 (1994): 49–64.

89. Dr. Pedro de Alba, "El agrarismo de Zapata y el agrarismo del Gral. Obregón," *El Universal*, May 10, 1924.

90. Marnham, *Dreaming*, 227.

91. Knight, "Racism, Revolution, and *Indigenismo*: Mexico, 1910–1940," in *The Idea of Race in Latin America, 1870–1940*, ed. Richard Graham (Austin: University of Texas Press, 1990), 85–87.

92. Mendoza, *El corrido*, 81–85.

93. See O'Malley, *Myth*, 46, 50, 53, for an emphasis on state/vocero agency in this regard.

94. Lomnitz-Adler, *Deep Mexico*, 53.

95. On the revolutionary family, see Benjamin, *La Revolución*, 68. On the patriarch/macho distinction, see Anne Rubenstein, "Bodies, Cities, Cinema: Pedro Infante's Death as Political Spectacle," in *Fragments of a Golden Age: The Politics of Culture in Mexico Since 1940*, ed. Gilbert Joseph, Anne Rubenstein, and Eric Zolov (Durham, N.C.: Duke University Press, 2001), 226–227.

96. *Excélsior*, 10 April 1931.

97. On the drive for order, see David Lorey, "Postrevolutionary Contexts for Independence Day: The 'Problem' of Order and the Invention of Revolution Day," in *¡Viva México! ¡Viva La Independencia!: Celebrations of September 16*, ed. William H. Beezley and David E. Lorey (Wilmington, Del.: Scholarly Resources, 2000), 234–235.

98. Paz Solórzano, *Hoguera*, 78.

99. Lucino Luna Domínguez and Efraín Escarpulli Limón, *Anenecuilcayotl: Anenecuilco desconocido* (Mexico City: Unidad Regional Morelos de la Dirección General de Culturas Populares, 1997), 266.

100. On the belief that a revolutionary process needs to create a selfless "new man" see Ernesto (Che) Guevara, *Man and Socialism in Cuba*, trans. Margarita Zimmerman (Havana: Book Institute, 1967).

101. See Lomnitz-Adler, *Exits*, 55–56, on the more general appropriation by the nation of the culture of Morelos.

102. *El Demócrata*, 12 April 1921.

103. Teodoro Hernández, "El XXX Aniversario de la Muerte de Zapata," *El Popular* (Mexico City), April 9, 1949, and Teodoro Hernández, "En el Aniversario de la Muerte de Zapata," *La Prensa*, April 10, 1937, both found in FSG.

104. Interview with Mateo Zapata, conducted by the author, Cuautla, June 27, 1996.

105. *Excélsior*, April 11, 1926.

106. Joann Martin, *Contesting Authenticity*, 13.

107. Barreto Mark, *Los corridos*, 33, 35–36.

108. Baltasar Dromundo, *Emiliano Zapata*, 276–277.

109. For the Soviet case, Nina Tumarkin, *Lenin Lives!: The Lenin Cult in Soviet Russia* (Cambridge, Mass.: Harvard University Press, 1983), 6, 84.

CHAPTER 4

1. José G. Parrés, "Zapata y su concepto sobre la lealtad," in *Ofrenda a la memoria de Emiliano Zapata*, [ed. Gildardo Magaña] (Mexico City?: n.p., 1938), 23–34.

2. José G. Parrés, "Aniversario de hoy: El ejemplo de Zapata," *El Nacional*, April 10, 1936, FSG.

3. José G. Parrés to Obregón, Cuernavaca, March 23, 1923, AGN-OC, 205-Z-2.

4. Parrés, "Aniversario."

5. Parrés, "Zapata," 23–34.

6. Emilio Portes Gil, *Quince años de política mexicana* (Mexico City: Ediciones Botas, 1941), 29.

7. Benjamin, *La Revolución*, 94.

8. Cited in Luis González, *Historia de la Revolución Mexicana, 1934–1940*. Vol. 14, *Los artífices del cardenismo* (Mexico City: El Colegio de Mexico, 1979), 81.

9. Alan Knight, "Cardenismo: Juggernaut or Jalopy," *Journal of Latin American Studies* 26 (1994), 73-107.

10. Joy Elizabeth Hayes, *Radio Nation: Communication, Popular Culture, and Nationalism in Mexico, 1920–1950* (Tucson: University of Arizona Press, 2000), 66–67; Benjamin, *La Revolución*, 94.

11. Rueda Smithers, "Emiliano Zapata," 148; José Refugio Bustamante and José Urbán to the Comité Nacional Pro-Homenaje a Emiliano Zapata, Cuernavaca, December 23, 1931, AA VIII-2, impresos, 1:42; A.L. Juárez, secretario of the Comité Nacional Pro-Homenaje Integral a Emiliano Zapata, to Salvador Navarro Aceves, Xochimilco, October 15, 1931, AA VIII-2, impresos, 1:41; Comité Nacional Pro-Homenaje Integral a Emiliano Zapata to congressional deputies, Mexico City, May 5, 1938, AA VIII-2, impresos, 2:104.

12. Jenaro Amezcua and Anastasio Fernández to unknown, Xochimilco, D.F., October 3, 1935, AA VIII-3, manuscritos, 7:659; *Excélsior*, June 27, 1931.

13. *Morelos Nuevo* (Cuernavaca), January 31, 1932. Parrés had declared April 10 a day of mourning in 1921, but now the legislature reinforced it.

14. For the quote, see [Rafael E. Melgar], *Calendario nacionalista y enciclopedia nacional popular* (Mexico City: Talleres Gráficos de la Nación, 1935), 126. See also O'Malley, *Myth*, 65; Imelda de Leon, ed., *Calendario de Fiestas Populares* (Mexico City: SEP, 1988), ix; and *El Porvenir* (Monterrey), April 11, 1939.

15. *Primer congreso de unificación de las organizaciones campesinas de la república* (Puebla: S. Loyo, 1927), 69–73. Thanks to Thomas Benjamin for pointing out this source.

16. Policarpo B. Arellano to Zapata, Tlaltizapán, July 17, 1915, AZ 19:3:56; and Bibiano A. Trejo to Zapata, Tlaltizapán, April 5, 1915, AZ 7:4:33.

17. Benjamin, *La Revolución*, 123.

18. *Excélsior*, March 31, 1965, April 10, 1932; *El Nacional*, April 10, 1932; interview with Vicente Estrada Cajigal, PHO/4/12, pp. 47–48; Benjamin, *La Revolución*, 125–126.

19. *El Universal*, April 11, 1924; Carleton Beals, *Mexican Maze* (New York: Lippincott, 1931), 22; *Polígrafo* (Cuautla), April 18, 1971.

20. *Excélsior*, February 19, 1932.

21. *El Nacional*, April 11, 1932; *Excélsior*, April 10 and 11, 1932; interview with Professor Juventino Pineda, conducted by Carlos Barreto M., August 7, 1974, PHO-Z/1/57, p. 29; interview with Vicente Estrada Cajigal, PHO/4/12.

22. *Homenaje de la Secretaría de Agricultura y Fomento a la memoria del caudillo agrarista Emiliano Zapata en el aniversario de su muerte* (Mexico City: Talleres Gráficos de la Nación, 1934); O'Malley, *Myth*, 63.

23. For Cárdenas's Indian policies see Alan Knight, "Mexico, c. 1930–1946," in *The Cambridge History of Latin America*, ed. Leslie Bethell (New York: Cambridge University Press, 1990), 7:29–30; and Alexander S. Dawson, *Indian and Nation in Revolutionary Mexico* (Tucson: University of Arizona Press, 2004), 85, 104, 152.

24. *Homenaje de la Secretaría de Agricultura*, 5–6.

25. William Cameron Townsend, *Lázaro Cárdenas: Mexican Democrat* (Ann Arbor, Mich.: George Wahr, 1952), 135.

26. Donald Hodges, "The Plan of Cerro Prieto: The Peasant-Worker Movement in Morelos (1942–1962)," *Canadian Journal of Latin American and Caribbean Studies*, 16 (1991): 124, describes the CNC that soon developed as the sole officially recognized bargaining agent for the peasants, as well as a branch of the ruling party whose leaders the party hand-picked. Naturally, this created a substantial conflict of interest.

27. *Excélsior*, April 11, 1939.

28. Vaughan, *The State*, 141; Mary Kay Vaughan, *History Textbooks in Mexico in the 1920s* (Buffalo: Council on International Studies, State University of New York at Buffalo, 1974), 2; José Vasconcelos, *Memorias II: El desastre, el proconsulado* (Mexico City: Fondo de Cultura Económica, 1982), 37–38.

29. Rafael Aguirre Cinta, *Lecciones de historia general de México desde los tiempos primitivos hasta nuestros días* (Mexico City: Franco-Americana, 1924 [sic]). The book I reviewed was ostensibly a 1924 edition but covered events through the late 1920s. See also Vaughan, *History Textbooks*, 5–6.

30. For the quotation, see Aguirre Cinta, *Lecciones*, 1924 [sic], 236; see also 233–234.

31. Rafael Aguirre Cinta, *Lecciones de historia general de México desde los tiempos primitivos hasta nuestros días* (Mexico City: Franco-Americana, 1926), 23–24.

32. On the transfer of sacrality, see Adrian A. Bantjes, "Burning Saints, Molding Minds: Iconoclasm, Civic Ritual, and the Failed Cultural Revolution," in *Rituals of Rule*; and Guillermo Palacios, *La pluma y el arado: los intelectuales pedagogos y la construcción sociocultural del "problema campesino" en México, 1932–1934* (Mexico City: El Colegio de México, 1999), 151.

33. Vaughan, *Cultural Politics*, 29-32; Josefina Vázquez de Knauth, *Nacionalismo y educación en México* (Mexico City: El Colegio de México, 1970), 137–138, 147–148; Benjamin, *La Revolución*, 127, 144; Victoria Lerner, *Historia de la revolución mexicana*. Vol. 17, *La educación socialista* (Mexico City: Colegio de México, 1979), 65.

34. Vázquez de Knauth, *Nacionalismo*, 147–148.

35. Alfonso Teja Zabre, *Breve historia de México* (Mexico City: Secretaría de Educación Pública, 1935), 244–246; Palacios, *La pluma*, 134; Gilbert, "Emiliano Zapata," 139.

36. John A. Britton, *Educación y radicalismo en Mexico*. Vol. 1, *Los años de Bassols (1931–1934)* (Mexico City: Sepsetentas, 1976), 152; Vázquez de Knauth, *Nacionalismo*, 191. The "land for everyone" quotation originated in Zapata's "Manifiesto al Pueblo Mexicano," January 20, 1917, which can be found in Espejel et al., eds., *Emiliano Zapata*, 366–368.

37. Jose M. Bonilla, *Historia Nacional* (Mexico City: Herrero Hermanos, 1939), 324.

38. Palacios, *La pluma*, 137; Britton, *Educación: Años de Bassols*, 56.

39. *El Maestro Rural*, December 15, 1933

40. *El Maestro Rural*, February 15, 1934.

41. *El Maestro Rural*, April 1, 1934.

42. *El Maestro Rural*, November 15, 1934, April 15, 1935.

43. Palacios, *La pluma*, 142; Smith, "Emiliano Zapata," 92.

44. Interview with Marcos González.

45. Dromundo, *Emiliano Zapata*.

46. O'Malley, *Myth*, 62; Arías Gómez, "Algunos cuadros," 259; Dromundo, *Emiliano Zapata*, 260; Dromundo to Amezcua, Mexico City, April 7, 1935, AA VIII-3, manuscritos, 7:611.

47. Magaña, *Emiliano Zapata*; Alfonso Taracena, *La revolucion desvirtuada: Continuación de la verdadera revolución mexicana*, 6 vols. (Mexico City: B. Costa-Amic, [1966–1969]), 3:322, 336.

48. Alicia Hernández Chávez, *Historia de la Revolución Mexicana, periódo 1934–1940*. Vol. 16, *La mecánica cardenista* (Mexico City: El Colegio de México, 1979), 94; Arías Gómez, "Algunos cuadros," 254.

49. *Gildardo Magaña: Breves datos biográficos* (n.p.: Secretaría General del Centro Nacional Orientador Pro-Magaña, [1939]), 61.

50. Magaña, *Emiliano Zapata*, 1:254–259, 2:37, 114, 174.

51. Magaña, *Emiliano Zapata*, 1:158–161.

52. Magaña, *Emiliano Zapata*, 1:xii–ix.

53. Magaña, *Emiliano Zapata*, 1:105, 206, 262–263, 303, 2:102.

54. Magaña, *Emiliano Zapata*, 1:106, 108.

55. Magaña, *Emiliano Zapata*, 1:189, 197–199, 221, 281, 293, 302, 2:27, 63, 86, 112, 311, 318–319.

56. Magaña, *Emiliano Zapata*, 2:267.

57. Magaña to Jenaro Amezcua, Morelia, January 19, 1938, AA VIII-3, manuscritos, 11:948; *Ofrenda*, 9–13.

58. Gildardo Magaña, "Perfil del Reformador," in *Ofrenda*, 17.

59. Fortina Ayaquica, "Continuación de la Lucha," in *Ofrenda*, 45–46; Juan Torices Mercado, "Ecce Homo Emiliano Zapata," in *Ofrenda*, 120.

60. Rafael Ramos Pedrueza, "Emiliano Zapata," in *Ofrenda*, 50–53.

61. Boyd, "Zapata," 903.

62. Mauricio Magdaleno, *Teatro revolucionario mexicano* (Madrid: Editorial Cenit, 1933). Magdaleno enjoyed a number of political posts from the mid-1930s until the 1950s—see Humberto Masacchio, *Diccionario*.

63. Magdaleno, *Teatro*, 106–107

64. Magdaleno, *Teatro*, 104–105.

65. Magdaleno, *Teatro*, 109, 112.

66. Magdaleno, *Teatro*, 116–118.

67. Magdaleno, *Teatro*, 121–122.

68. Magdaleno, *Teatro*, 125, 126, 142, 145.

69. Magdaleno, *Teatro*, 150–151, 156.

70. Magdaleno, *Teatro*, 161–164.

71. Fernando Carlos Vevia Romero, *Teatro y revolución mexicana* (Guadalajara: Universidad de Guadalajara, 1991), 51.

72. Magdaleno to Jenaro Amezcua, Mexico City, December 6, 1939, AA VIII-3, manuscritos, 13:1087; Magdaleno, "Escaparate," *El Nacional*, April 10, 1935, FSG.

73. Gregorio López y Fuentes, *Tierra* (Mexico City: Grijalbo, 1986), 88–89.

74. López y Fuentes, *Tierra*, 102.

75. López y Fuentes, *Tierra*, 109.

76. López y Fuentes, *Tierra*, 111.

77. Armando List Arzubide, "El asesinato del Gral. Emiliano Zapata," in *Teatro histórico escolar* (Mexico City?: 1938).

78. John W. Sherman, *The Mexican Right: The End of Revolutionary Reform, 1929–1940* (Westport, Conn.: Praeger, 1997), 122–123.

79. Diego Arenas Guzmán, "Cuando Transigió Zapata," *El Universal*, August 26, 1933; Francisco S. Mancilla, "Zapata no Transigió," *El Universal*, October 2, 1933, FSG.

80. *El Mundo* (Mexico City), September 5, 1933, FSG; *El Universal*, September 6, 1933, August 7, 1933, FSG.

81. *El Universal*, September 23, 1933, FSG.

82. Gregorio Torres Quintero, *La patria mexicana: elementos de historia nacional, segundo ciclo*, 7th ed. (Mexico City: Gómez Cárdenas, 1939), 371, 376.

83. Dromundo to Jenaro Amezcua, Mexico City, February 6, 1935, AA VIII-3, manuscritos, 7:594.

84. For the quotation, see Salvador Novo, *La vida en México en el períódo presidencial de Lázaro Cárdenas* (Mexico City: Empresas Editoriales, 1964), 158. See also [Pablo González], *Recopilación de documentos y de algunas publicaciones de importancia* (Monterrey: n.p., 1923); O'Malley, *Myth*, 48; Sherman, *Mexican Right*, 107; and E. Tamez, Consul of Mexico at Eagle Pass, Texas to Obregón, June 24, 1921, AGN-OC, 101-R1-A-1.

85. L. F. Bustamante, "Dizque Don Pablo no Autorizó la Muerte de Emiliano Zapata," *El Universal Gráfico,* November 10, 1937.

86. Senator Agustín del Castillo, Jenaro Amezcua et al. to Cárdenas, Mexico City, December 26, 1937, Archivo General de la Nación, Mexico City, Fondo Presidentes, Lázaro Cárdenas (hereafter cited as AGN-LC), 562.2/22; *Novedades* (Mexico City), November 16, 1937, FSG.

87. *La Prensa*, November 13, 1937, FSG.

88. Example of a constitutive act from San Miguel (Canoas), Puebla, September 26, 1935, AA VIII-2, impresos, 2:64; Amezcua circular to federal deputies, December 30, 1936, AA VIII-3, manuscritos, 9:877.

89. Pérez Montfort, "La Unión," 276–282; Gabriel Baldovinos de la Peña, *Emigdio Marmolejo León: vigencia de un liderazgo agrario morelense* (Mexico City: Centro de Estudios Históricos del Agrarismo en México and Confederación Nacional Campesina, 1991), 41.

90. *La Prensa*, November 15, 1937, FSG.

91. Act of formation of Comité Reivindicador Pro-Emiliano Zapata, November 17, 1937, Mexico City, AA VIII-3, manuscritos, 10:940; Senator Agustín del Castillo, Jenaro Amezcua et al. to Cárdenas, Mexico City, December 26, 1937, AGN-LC 562.2/22. For the original context of the Spartacus quote see Emiliano Zapata to Pascual Orozco, April 7, 1913, in Centro de Estudios Históricos del Agrarismo en México, *El ejército*, 65–68.

92. For the quotation, see *Excélsior*, November 12, 1937; see also the same newspaper, November 11 and 17, 1937, and Novo, *La vida*, 158–159. Despite González's assertion, the contention that he had destroyed Morelos was not new; see, for instance, Ernest Gruening, *Mexico and Its Heritage* (London: Stanley Paul, 1928), 310–311.

93. President Isaias Pérez of Sociedad Cooperativa Agricola "Pequeños Agricultores" of Puente de Ixtla, Morelos, to Cárdenas, November 15, 1937, AGN-LC, 549.5/70.

94. Antonino L. Topete to Cárdenas, Rosario, Sinaloa, January 23, 1938, AGN-LC, 549.5/70; Romeo León Orantes of the Procuraduria General to the Oficial Mayor de la Presidencia de la República, Mexico City, November 19, 1937, AGN-LC, 549.5/70; González, *El centinela*, 617, 973–978.

95. Jenaro Amezcua to the President of the Cámara de Diputados, Mexico City, December 18, 1937, AA VIII-3, manuscritos, 10:943; Comité Nacional Pro-Homenaje Integral a Emiliano Zapata to diputados, Mexico City, May 5, 1938, AA VIII-2, impresos, 2:104 and 2:105.

96. Amezcua and Casals form letter, Mexico City, April 1, 1939, AA VIII-3, manuscritos, 13:1078; AA VIII-3, manuscritos, 13:1078 bis; and record of the assembly of the URAS on November 26, 1938, AA VIII-3, manuscritos, 12:1053.

97. Adrian A. Bantjes, *As if Jesus Walked on Earth: Cardenismo, Sonora, and the Mexican Revolution* (Wilmington, Del.: Scholarly Resources, 1998), 183–184; Marjorie Becker, *Setting the Virgin on Fire: Lázaro Cárdenas, Michoacán Peasants, and the Redemption of the Mexican Revolution* (Berkeley and Los Angeles: University of California Press, 1995), 144–145.

98. *Gildardo Magaña*, 13.

99. Almazán, "Memorias," chapters 17 and 18; Serafín M. Robles, "El jefe suriano combate en Amayuca, Morelos," *El Campesino*, May 1952; Juan Angel Andonegui, "Cuando imperaba el zapatismo," *El Universal*, April 18, 1948.

100. Huerta to de la Barra, Chietla, September 20, 1911, AGM 20:1:116; Huerta to de la Barra, Chiautla, September 26, 1911, AGM 21:2:111 and 12:1:29; Huerta to de la Barra, Piaxtla, October 5, 1911, AGM 21:4:320; David Lorey, "Almazán, Juan Andreu," in *Encyclopedia of Mexico*.

101. Brunk, *Emiliano Zapata*, 139–140.

102. Lorey, "Almazán, Juan Andreu."

103. Enrique Lumen, *Almazán: Vida de un caudillo y metabolismo de una revolución* (Mexico: Editorial Claridad, 1940), 54–55, 75–76, 79, 109, 112, 133.

104. Albert L. Michaels, *The Mexican Election of 1940* (Buffalo: State University of New York at Buffalo, 1971), 43.

105. Dromundo, *Emiliano Zapata*, 56-57; Octavio Paz Solórzano, "Juan Andrew Almazán y el corazón de Aquiles Serdán," in *Hoguera*, 208–217.

106. Michaels, *Mexican Election*, 40; Lumen, *Almazán*, 228–229.

107. Díaz Soto Ugalde, "Biografía," 132–133.

108. Interview with Enriqueta, Magdalena, and Salvador Díaz Soto Ugalde, Mexico City, July 1994.

109. Díaz Soto y Gama, "El pensamiento agrario del sur," *El Universal*, August 2, 1938, FSG. See also Michaels, *Mexican Election*, 43, 48, and the interview of Díaz Soto y Gama in *Novedades*, May 9, 1940.

110. José G. Parrés, "Aniversario de hoy: El ejemplo de Zapata," *El Nacional*, April 10, 1936, FSG.

111. Amezcua to Avila Camacho, Mexico City, September 6, 1940, AA VIII-3, manuscritos, 13:1140; González Navarro, *La Confederación*, 159; Ricardo Pérez Montfort, *Guía del archivo del General Jenaro Amezcua, 1909–1947* (Mexico City: CEHAM and Condumex, 1982).

112. Miguel A. Velasco, *Liquidación del latifundismo* (Mexico City: Editorial Popular, 1939), 7. Thanks are due the late Joseph Cotter for telling me about this pamphlet.

113. Cited in Brabatta, *Zapata*, 79.

114. Alfredo Castillo, "Presencia de Zapata," *Novedades*, October 20, 1949, FSG.

115. See Weeks, *Juárez Myth*, 37, for the elements of a commemoration for Benito Juárez in 1887; on the routinization of charisma, see Weber, *On Charisma*, 48–65.

116. Inés Aguilar and José Hernández Zúñiga, Mexico City, April 1, 1933, to Abelardo Rodríguez, Archivo General de la Nación, Mexico City, Fondo Presidentes, Abelardo Rodríguez (hereafter cited as AGN-AR), exped. 330/343. For more on Aguilar, see Chapter 8.

CHAPTER 5

1. Sotelo Inclán, *Raíz*, 9.
2. The following paragraphs are based on Sotelo Inclán, *Raíz*, 10–18, except where otherwise noted.
3. Alicia Olivera de Bonfil and Eugenia Meyer, *Jesús Sotelo Inclán y sus conceptos sobre el movimiento zapatista (entrevista)* (Mexico City: Instituto Nacional de Antropología e Historia, 1970), 9–10.
4. Olivera and Meyer, *Jesús Sotelo Inclán*, 23.
5. Sotelo Inclán, *Raíz*, 208.
6. *Excélsior*, April 12, 1944, November 29, 1960.
7. Olivera and Meyer, *Jesús Sotelo Inclán*, 16.
8. Olivera and Meyer, *Jesús Sotelo Inclán*, 15; Sotelo Inclán, *Raíz*, 28, 192–194.
9. Sotelo Inclán, *Raíz*, 144–152.
10. Sotelo Inclán, *Raíz*, 175–176, 197, 199.
11. Paredes, ed., *Folktales*, xlvi–xlvii; Oscar Lewis, *Tepoztlán: Village in Mexico* (New York: Holt, Rinehart and Winston, 1960), 44.
12. Amezcua to Felipe Zepeda et al., Mexico City, November 1, 1942, AA VIII-2, impresos, 2:112; Jenaro Amezcua, *Defensa y confesión* (Mexico City: URAS, 1944), 16.
13. Prudencio Casals R. to Avila Camacho, Mexico City, March 31, 1941, Archivo General de la Nación, Mexico City, Fondo Presidentes, Manuel Avila Camacho (here-

after cited as AGN-AC), exped. 135.21/21; Declaración de Principios, Plan de Acción y Estatutos del "Frente Zapatista de la República," Mexico City, July 1941 (approved in assembly in Cuautla, June 23, 1940), AGN-AC, 437.1/121; and Pérez Montfort, *Guía*.

14. Wilfrido Cajigal C. and Prudencio Casals to Avila Camacho, Mexico City, May 12, 1945, AGN-AC, 437.1/121.

15. Manifesto of the Zapatista Front, Mexico City, December 17, 1941, AGN-AC, 556.1/115. This text was printed on December 27 in both *El Universal* and *La Prensa*. For the document from which the Front drew, see Magaña, *Emiliano Zapata*, 3:312–317.

16. Record of the velada at the Teatro Hidalgo, Mexico City, April 10, 1942, AGN-AC, 710.1/101–102.

17. Record of the twenty-fifth anniversary of Zapata's death, Mexico City, AGN-AC, 710.1/101–102.

18. *Excélsior*, April 11, 1941; Brabatta, *Zapata*, 80–84.

19. *Excélsior*, April 11, 1949; *El Campesino*, May 1, 1954.

20. Brabatta, *Zapata*, 100.

21. *El Campesino*, May 1, 1950; *Excélsior*, April 11, 1950, February 6, 1960, May 12, 1962; *El Eco del Sur* (Cuautla), April 10, 1966; Roderic Ai Camp, *Mexican Political Biographies, 1935–1993*, 3rd ed. (Austin: University of Texas Press, 1995), 399–400. For the assertion that Castrejón was not at Chinameca, see Mario Huacuja, "Que Zapata Tenía Fe Ciega en la Lealtad de Guajardo," *Novedades*, May 12, 1951.

22. *El Campesino*, May 1, 1950.

23. Joseph L. Arbena, "Sport, Development, and Mexican Nationalism, 1920–1970," *Journal of Sport History* 18 (1991): 350, 354–355.

24. *Presente* (Cuernavaca), April 5, 1959.

25. For the quotation, see Gill, "Zapata," 309–310. See also Ana María Zapata to the state legislature of Morelos, Mexico City, September 7, 1935, AA VIII-3, manuscritos, 7:641; Act forming the Union of Morelos Women, September 29, 1935, AA VIII-3, manuscritos, 7:654; Ana María Zapata to Cárdenas, Cuautla, October 23, 1935, AGN-LC, 201.5/33; and Lerner, *La educación socialista*, 98.

26. Thomas F. Walsch, *Katherine Anne Porter and Mexico: The Illusion of Eden* (Austin: University of Texas Press, 1992), 128.

27. Anne Rubenstein, *Bad Language, Naked Ladies, and Other Threats to the Nation: A Political History of Comic Books in Mexico* (Durham, N.C.: Duke University Press, 1998), 46–49; Michael Nelson Miller, *Red, White, and Green: The Maturing of Mexicanidad, 1940–1946* (El Paso: Texas Western Press, 1998), 141–177.

28. Anna Macias, *Against All Odds: The Feminist Movement in Mexico to 1940* (Westport, Conn.: Greenwood Press, 1982), 104–146.

29. Porfirio Palacios, Secretary General of the Frente Zapatista et al., Cuernavaca, July 16, 1950, Archivo General de la Nación, Mexico City, Fondo Presidentes, Miguel Alemán (hereafter cited as AGN-MA), exped. 003.11/10534.

30. Gill, "Zapata," 306–307; *El Campesino*, May 1, 1955.

31. Teodoro Hernández, "El XXX Aniversario de la Muerte de Zapata," *El Popular*, April 9, 1949, FSG.

32. Amezcua to Adolfo López Mateos, December 28, 1959, Archivo General de la Nación, Mexico City, Fondo Presidentes, Adolfo López Mateos (hereafter cited as AGN-LM), exped. 133.2/77; *El Campesino*, January 1960.

33. Secretaría de Educación Pública, *La Revolución Mexicana* (Mexico City: SEP, 1954), 33.

34. SEP, *La Revolución*, 33; Jesús Cárabes Pedroza, *Mi libro de tercer año: Historia y civismo* (Mexico City: Comisión Nacional de los Libros de Texto Gratuitos, 1966), 115–122; Vázquez de Knauth, *Nacionalismo y educación*, 200–201, 210–216.

35. Eduardo Blanquel, *Mi libro de sexto año: Historia y civismo* (Mexico City: Comisión Nacional de los Libros de Texto Gratuitos, 1966), 226–228.

36. Francisco Javier Carranza, *Fiestas escolares: enciclopedia lírico-literaria* (Mexico City: Editorial Avante, 1957), 211–212.

37. SEP, *La Revolución*, 65–67.

38. Adrián Castrejón et al. to Avila Camacho, Mexico City, March 23, 1946, AGN-AC, 704/807; José Parrés to Avila Camacho, April 26, 1946, AGN-AC, 704/807; Presidential Secretary Jesús González to Parrés, April 29, 1946, AGN-AC, 704/807.

39. *El Campesino*, February 1, 1952.

40. Magaña, *Emiliano Zapata*, 3:4, 23, 208; 4:66, 253 ff.

41. Magaña, *Emiliano Zapata*, 3:197, 4:257; 5:57.

42. Magaña, *Emiliano Zapata*, 4:194.

43. Serafín M. Robles to Miguel Alemán, Mexico City, October 9, 1950, AGN-MA, 050/8732.

44. See *El Campesino*, October 1949, November 1949, December 1949, December 1950, and January 1952.

45. Serafín M. Robles, "10 de Abril de 1919," *El Campesino*, April 1, 1950.

46. Serafín M. Robles, "10 de Abril de 1953," *El Campesino*, April 1, 1953.

47. Díaz Soto y Gama to Miguel Mendoza López Schwerdtfeger, Mexico City, December 6, 1954, Biblioteca Manuel Orozco y Berra, Mexico City, Papeles de Familia, Archivo Miguel Mendoza López Schwerdtfeger (hereafter cited as AMLS), exped. 27.

48. SEP, *La Revolución*, 28–32.

49. *Cuadernos del Senado: XLIV legislatura del Congreso de la Unión* (Mexico City: n.p., 1958); *El Universal*, October 11, 1958; *Excélsior*, October 8, 1958.

50. Díaz Soto y Gama, *La revolución agraria del sur y Emiliano Zapata, su caudillo* (Mexico City: Policromia, 1960), 217–219, 237.

51. Díaz Soto y Gama, *La revolución*, 87.

52. Díaz Soto y Gama, *La revolución*, 251; see also 243–247.

53. Díaz Soto y Gama, *La revolución*, 254, 258-260, 273–274.

54. Díaz Soto y Gama, *La revolución*, 116, 160–161.

55. Díaz Soto y Gama, *La revolución*, 225; Díaz Soto y Gama, "El Pensamiento Agrario del Sur," 1938, Archivo General de la Nación, Mexico City, Archivo Díaz Soto y Gama, microfilm roll 2; *Excélsior*, December 4, 1960.

56. *Novedades*, July 15, 1961; *El Universal*, September 6, 1961. See also Alfonso Taracena, *Zapata: Fantasía y realidad*, 2nd ed. (Mexico City: B. Costa Amic, 1974)—the first edition was published in 1970.

57. Octavio Paz and Luis Mario Schneider, *México en la obra de Octavio Paz*, 3 vols. (Mexico City: Fondo de Cultura Económica, 1987), 1:234–235, 361.

58. Paz, *The Labyrinth*, 20, 31, 54, 142–144, 148, 205.

59. *Excélsior*, April 10, 1999.

60. Dawn Ades, *Art in Latin America: The Modern Era, 1820–1980* (New Haven: Yale University Press, 1989), 181–188; de Rojo et al., *Zapata: Iconografía*; *¡Viva Zapata! 20 grabados* (Mexico City: Taller de Gráfica Popular, 1970).

61. *El Campesino*, April 1, 1950.

62. Quirico Michelena y Llaguna to Manuel Avila Camacho, Mexico City, December 10, 1943, AGN-AC, 523.3/60.

63. Serafín Robles and Porfirio Palacios to Alemán, March 6, 1950, AGN-MA, 369/2985; Miller, *Red, White, and Green*, 87–99.

64. Undated, unsigned Informe sobre el Proyecto de Filmación de una Película del Frente Zapatista sobre la Vida de Zapata, AGN-MA, 369/2985.

65. *El Campesino*, May 1, 1951. For the Henríquez Guzmán campaign's references to Zapata, see Elisa Servín, *Ruptura y oposición: El movimiento henriquista, 1945–1954* (Mexico City: Cal y Arena, 2001), 290, 317

66. *El Campesino*, May 1, 1952.

67. *El Campesino*, November 1, 1952 for the quotation; see also Tanalís Padilla, "'*Por las buenas no se puede*': Rubén Jaramillo's Campaigns for Governor of Morelos, 1946 and 1952," *Journal of Iberian and Latin American Studies* 7 (2001): 37.

68. José Velasco Toro, *Política y legislación agraria en México: De la desamortización civil a la reforma campesina* (Xalapa: Universidad Veracruzana, 1993), 100–101; Jesús Silva Herzog, *El agrarismo mexicano y la reforma agraria* (Mexico City: Fondo de Cultura Económica, 1959), 489–493.

69. Francisco A. Gómezjara, *El movimiento campesino en México* (Mexico City: Editorial Campesina, 1970), 207–208; Francisco A. Gómezjara, *Bonapartismo y lucha campesina en la costa grande de Guerrero* (Mexico City: Posada, 1979), 286–288; Miguel Aroche Parra, *El Che, Jenaro y las guerrillas: Estrategía y táctica de la revolución en México* (Mexico City: Federación Editorial Mexicana, 1974), 38, 85–87; Antonio Sotelo Pérez, *Breve historia de la Asociación Cívica Guerrerense* (Chilpancingo: Universidad Autónoma de Guerrero, 1991), 62, 73, 83, 112–120.

70. Rubén Salido Orcillo, "Zapata y sus Generales," *Novedades*, February 24, 1960; Rubén Salido Orcillo, "Don Emiliano, Enciclopedista," *Novedades*, May 11, 1962, both in FSG.

71. Alvaro D. Bórquez Almendez, "Zapata fue un caudillo, pero no un patricio," *La Prensa*, October 15, 1940, FSG; Rubén Salazar Mallen, "Emiliano Zapata," *Excélsior*, April 2, 1951; Fernando Díez de Urdanivia, "Zapata y Garrido," *Excélsior*, April 14, 1949; Eugenio Martínez Nuñez, "Zapata y el Zapatismo," *El Universal*, June 22, 1955, FSG.

72. José P. Saldaña Treviño, *Del triunfo al destierro* (Monterrey: Gobierno del Estado de Nuevo León, 1987), 35; *El Campesino*, December 1, 1953.

73. *El Nacional*, April 11, 1949, FSG.

74. Record of the Cuautla ceremony, April 10, 1941, AGN-AC, 710.1/101-2; Brunk, *Emiliano Zapata*, 122–127.

75. *El Campesino*, February 1, 1951.

76. On Díaz, see Barry Carr, *Marxism and Communism in Twentieth Century Mexico* (Lincoln: University of Nebraska Press, 1992), 32.

77. Record of the Communist Party velada, Mexico City, April 8, 1942, AGN-AC, 710.1/101–102.

78. *La Voz de Mexico*, February 21, 1958, in AMLS.

79. *El Campesino*, November 1, 1951.

80. Lomnitz-Adler, *Exits*, 117.

81. Sotelo Inclán, *Raíz*, 211–214; Guillermo Liera B., Secretary General of the Department of Indigenous Affairs, to Presidential Secretary Jesús González, Mexico City, April 12, 1946, AGN-AC, 135.21/21; Albino Sánchez et al. to Alemán, Cuautla, June 14, 1948, AGN-MA, 404.1/2979; Womack, *Zapata*, 379–382.

82. Comisariado Ejidal Joaquín Quintero et al. to Alemán, Anenecuilco, April 1952, AGN-MA, 404.1/2979.

83. Jesús Corona y Navarro to Alemán, Mexico City, September 24, 1952, AGN-MA 404.1/2979.

84. Interview with Ana María Zapata, Cuautla, July 29, 1996; Ana María Zapata to Alemán, Cuautla, March 31, 1952, AGN-MA, 514/34132.

85. Ana María Zapata to Alemán, Cuautla, March 31, 1952, AGN-MA, 514/34132.

86. González Navarro, *La Confederación*, 214; *El Eco del Sur*, April 10, 1966; Womack, *Zapata*, 82–83.

87. Elpidio Perdomo to Avila Camacho, Cuernavaca, February 23, 1942, AGN-AC, 534.1/780; Gill, "Zapata," 309.

88. Luis Gutiérrez y González, "Hoy visita a la viuda de Zapata!," *Hoy*, March 28, 1953.

89. Gill, "Zapata," 295.

90. *El Informador* (Cuernavaca), April 9, 1950.

91. *Presente*, April 12, 1959.

92. *El Eco del Sur*, April 10, 1966.

93. *Presente*, April 15, 1962.

94. *Polígrafo*, April 10 and 13, 1966.

95. *Polígrafo*, April 11, 1967.

96. Rubén M. Jaramillo, *Autobiografía* (Mexico City: Editorial Nuestro Tiempo, 1967), 15–16.

97. Plutarco García Jiménez, "El movimiento jaramillista: Una experiencia de lucha campesina y popular del período post-revolucionario en México, in *Morelos: Cinco siglos de historia regional*, ed. Horacio Crespo (Mexico City: Centro de Estudios Históricos del Agrarismo en México, 1984), 304–308; Donald Hodges, "Plan of Cerro

Prieto," 127–129; Neil Harvey, "Jaramillo, Rubén," in *Encyclopedia of Mexico*, 715–716; Pablo Cerdán to Avila Camacho, Jonacatepec, Morelos, July 12, 1944, AGN-AC, 559.1/51; Padilla, "'*Por las buenas*,'" 23.

98. Renato Ravelo Lecuona, *Los jaramillistas* (Mexico City: Editorial Nuestro Tiempo, 1978), 204. Ravelo Lecuona's informants are not identified. See also Raul Macín, *Rubén Jaramillo, profeta olvidado* (Mexico City: Diogenes, 1984), 29.

99. Ravelo Lecuona, *Los jaramillistas*, 159.

100. For the quotations, see Ravelo Lecuona, *Los jaramillistas*, 210–212, and Macín, *Rubén Jaramillo*, 13. See also Donald C. Hodges, *Mexican Anarchism After the Revolution* (Austin: University of Texas Press, 1995), 67.

101. Michael C. Meyer and William L. Sherman, *The Course of Mexican History*, 5th ed. (New York: Oxford University Press, 1995), 651–662.

102. Adolfo López Mateos, *José María Morelos, Ponciano Arriaga y Emiliano Zapata, en la reforma agraria de México* (Mexico City: Editorial la Justicia, 1958), 12–14, 19.

103. *Excélsior*, April 11, 1960; *El Informador*, April 17, 1960.

104. *Excélsior*, April 11, 1962, April 12, 1963.

105. Susan R. Walsch Sanderson, *Land Reform in Mexico: 1910–1980* (Orlando: Academic Press, 1984), 90–95.

106. *Excélsior*, April 11, 1966.

107. *El Campesino*, May 31, 1968.

108. Román Badillo, "La Comida del Pobre: fué el ideal de Zapata," *El Universal*, April 21, 1961; *El Campesino*, April 15, 1967.

109. *Excélsior*, April 11, 1953.

110. On the government's control of the media, see John Mraz, "Today, Tomorrow and Always: The Golden Age of Illustrated Magazines in Mexico, 1937–1960," in Joseph, Rubenstein, and Zolov, eds., *Fragments of a Golden Age*, 122–123. For the bomb, see *Excélsior*, April 10, 1954.

CHAPTER 6

1. *El Campesino*, May 31, 1968. I know nothing more about Ortega than is reported in this passage.

2. Paz, *Labyrinth*, 142, 148.

3. *Excélsior*, November 20, 1931.

4. Report from the "Primera Comisión de Gobernación," Mexico City, November 17, 1936, to Honorable Asamblea, AA, VIII-3, manuscritos, 9:852.

5. Ayudante Municipal of Chinameca, Ignacio González et al., to Cárdenas, Chinameca, March 2, 1940, AGN-LC, 562.2/22; Oficial Mayor, Encargado de la Secretaria General de Gobierno, José Urbán to Juan Gallardo Moreno, Oficial Mayor de la Secretaria Particular de la Presidencia de la República, Cuernavaca, May 22, 1940, AGN-LC, 562.2/22.

6. Manifesto of the Frente Revolucionaria de Chinameca, Morelos y Pueblos Circunvecinos Pro-Estatua de Emiliano Zapata, Chinameca, March 14, 1941, AGN-AC, 135.21/21; Secretary General Jesús Flores López of the Frente Revolucionaria de Chinameca, Morelos y Pueblos Circunvecinos Pro-Estatua de Emiliano Zapata to Avila Camacho, Chinameca, March 11, 1942, AGN-AC, 135.21/21; Sierra Brabatta, *Zapata*, 89.

7. *Excélsior*, April 11, 1959.

8. Boyd, *Emiliano Zapata*, 100; de Rojo et al., *Zapata*, 135.

9. *Excélsior*, March 31, 1965; *Periódico Oficial de Morelos* (Cuernavaca), March 10, 1965.

10. *El Eco del Sur*, April 11, 1965.

11. *El Demócrata*, April 12, 1919.

12. Diputado Miguel H. Zúñiga to Cárdenas, Cuernavaca, February 18, 1939, AGN-LC, 562.2/22; Presidente Municipal Ausensio Barreto et al. to Cárdenas, Jonacatepec, Morelos, February 20, 1939, AGN-LC, 562.2/22; Lic. Juan Gallardo Moreno to Manuel Moreno, March 21, 1939, AGN-LC, 562.2/22; Valverde, *Apuntes*, 175–176.

13. President of the Municipal Committee of the Zapatista Front Gregorio Castañeda Domínguez et al. to Avila Camacho, Tlaltizapán, July 25, 1944, AGN-AC, 135.21/134.

14. Secretary General de Gobierno, Ernesto Escobar Muñoz to Luis Viñals Carsi, Sub-Jefe del Estado Mayor Presidencial, Cuernavaca, August 2, 1944, AGN-AC, 562.4/321; *El Campesino*, September 1, 1949, January 1, 1955, August 31, 1969; Sierra Brabatta, *Zapata*, 98.

15. For the first quotation, see Ramón García Ruiz of the SEP to the governor of Morelos, Cuernavaca, August 15, 1931, AA, VIII-3, manuscritos, 3:210; for the second, Luna Domínguez and Escarpulli Limón, *Anenecuilcayotl*, 247.

16. Sotelo Inclán, *Raíz*, 209–210; Gill, "Zapata," 303, 311–312; Governor Rodolfo López de Nava to Ruiz Cortines, Cuernavaca, April 10, 1955, AGN-ARC, 135.21/35-16; the invitation to the Plan of Ayala commemoration in Anenecuilco, November 1960, AGN-ALM, 135.21/205; and *Excélsior*, November 29, 1960.

17. Taracena, *La revolución desvirtuada*, 2:326.

18. Governor Rodolfo López de Nava to Ruiz Cortines, Cuernavaca, March 27, 1954, AGN-ARC, 515.1/355; *El Campesino*, May 1, 1954, September 1, 1954.

19. José Saldivar to Amezcua, Colonia Dr. José G. Parres, Morelos, April 12, 1937, AA, VIII-3, manuscritos, 10:905.

20. *El Campesino*, May 1, 1955.

21. *El Informador*, April 18, 1954; Lewis, *Tepoztlán*, 45; Ramón Vergara Flores et al. to López Mateos, Colonia Lázaro Cárdenas, Zacatepec, Morelos, December 12, 1961, AGN-ALM, 562.2/66; Rueda, "Emiliano Zapata," 138.

22. Judith Friedlander, *Being Indian in Hueyapan: A Study of Forced Identity in Contemporary Mexico* (New York: St. Martin's Press, 1975), 153, 155, 159.

23. Tenorio-Trillo, *Mexico at the World's Fairs*, 250–251; Tenenbaum, "Streetwise History."

24. José G. Parrés, Secretary General of the Zapatista Front, to Avila Camacho, Mexico City, April 6, 1946, AGN-AC, 562.2/67; Secretary Jesús González for Avila Camacho to Parrés, April 23, 1946, AGN-AC, 562.2/67; González Navarro, *La Confederación*, 200.

25. *El Campesino*, September 1, 1949, December 1, 1949.

26. AGN-MA, 101/66-A; *El Campesino*, April 1, 1950; *Ignacio Asúnsolo* (Mexico City: Museo Nacional de Arte, 1985), 35, 50, 62, 124–125.

27. Alemán to the Secretary of Hacienda y Crédito Público, Mexico City, February 12, 1952, AGN-MA, 934/32124; *Ignacio Asúnsolo*, 66.

28. *El Campesino*, September 1, 1952; J. de D. Bojórquez for the Bloque de Obreros Intelectuales to Ruiz Cortines, Mexico City, February 2, 1953, AGN-RC 562.2/7. An association of leftish writers and artists, the block was founded in 1922.

29. *El Campesino*, March 1, 1953; Porfirio Palacios, *Emiliano Zapata: datos biográfico-históricos* (Mexico City: Libro Mex, 1960), 306–307.

30. *El Campesino*, May 1, 1953.

31. Ayudante Municipal Pedro Benito Sánchez and others to Ruiz Cortines, San Miguel Anenecuilco, January 18, 1958, AGN-RC 562.2/93.

32. President of the Zapatista Front Benigno Abúndez et al. to Ruiz Cortines, Mexico City, February 11, 1956, AGN-RC, 1235.21/35; Miguel Hidalgo Salazar to Ruiz Cortines, Mexico City, September 20, 1956, AGN-RC, 562.2/93.

33. Palacios, *Emiliano Zapata*, 307; Sierra Brabatta, *Zapata*, 121–122.

34. *Excélsior*, June 14, 1953. For El Caballito, see Chapter 4.

35. Benjamin, *La Revolución*, 117–136.

36. Sierra Brabatta, *Zapata*, 84.

37. Oficial Mayor Robert Amorós G. to Higinio Peña Ch., Mexico City, January 24, 1946, AGN-AC 562.2/67.

38. *Excélsior*, April 11, 1953; Sierra Brabatta, *Zapata*, 112–120.

39. *El Maestro Rural*, April 1, 1934; Becker, *Setting the Virgin*, 82. Amezcua's initiatives also helped spread the cult. See AA VIII-3, manuscritos, 3:203, 3:209, 3:220.

40. Cárdenas to Governor of Aguascalientes Juan G. Alvarado, Mexico City, December 1, 1937, AGN-LC, 704/215; *El Nacional*, November 20, 1933.

41. *El Campesino*, March 1, 1953.

42. See for instance *Excélsior*, April 10, 1959; *El Campesino*, July 1959.

43. *Excélsior*, April 11, 1964.

44. Víctor Raúl Martínez Vásquez, ed., *La revolución en Oaxaca, 1900–1930* (Oaxaca: Instituto de Administración Pública de Oaxaca, 1985).

45. *El Zancudo* (Oaxaca), April 6, 1923.

46. Enrique Othon Díaz, *Madre tierra: Poemas al ejido* (Oaxaca: n.p., 1933), 173–174, 180.

47. *Libertad* (Oaxaca), [April 1934?].

48. Stephen, *Zapata Lives!*, 233–235.

49. Lynn Stephen, *Viva Zapata!: Generation, Gender, and Historical Consciousness in the Reception of Ejido Reform in Oaxaca* (San Diego: Center for US-Mexican Studies, 1994), 18.

50. Stephen, *Zapata Lives!*, 254–256.

51. Stephen, *Viva Zapata!*, 19.

52. Stephen, *Zapata Lives!*, 256–258, 260–261.

53. For the quotation, see Stephen, *Zapata Lives!*, 282; see also pp. 8, 259, 284.

54. Stephen, *Zapata Lives!*, 57, 268–269.

55. Stephen, *Zapata Lives!*, 256–258, 232–233; *Oaxaca Nuevo* (Oaxaca), April 12, 1937.

56. *Oaxaca Nuevo*, April 9, 1938.

57. *Oaxaca Nuevo*, April 10 and 11, 1938.

58. *Oaxaca Nuevo*, April 10, 1938.

59. *Oaxaca Nuevo*, April 9, 1938.

60. Ismael Flores to Cárdenas, Oaxaca, August 28, 1940, AGN-LC, 433/480.

61. *Oaxaca Nuevo*, April 10 and 11, 1940.

62. *Oaxaca Gráfico* (Oaxaca), April 10, 1964; "Episodios Oaxaqueños: ¿David Rodríguez Zapatista?," in *Oaxaca en México* (May 1965): 30.

63. *La Voz de Oaxaca* (Oaxaca), April 10, 1945.

64. *El Campesino*, June 1, 1955. A municipality (*municipio*) is comparable to a county in the United States.

65. *El Campesino*, June 1, 1955.

66. *El Campesino*, April 1957; *El Imparcial* (Oaxaca), April 11, 1957.

67. *Oaxaca Gráfico*, April 11, 1965.

68. *Oaxaca Gráfico*, April 12, 1966.

69. *Oaxaca Gráfico*, April 10 and 11, 1962. On Pérez Gasga, see *Presente*, April 15, 1962.

70. *Oaxaca en México* (April-May, 1964): 6.

71. For the isthmus, see *El Campesino*, May 31, 1968.

72. *El Campesino*, June 1, 1951.

73. *El Campesino*, May 1, 1952, July 1, 1953, May 1, 1955.

74. José Castro López of the Vanguardia Universitaria Hidalguense et al. to Ruiz Cortines, Mexico City, April 14, 1957, AGN-ARC 562.4/112.

75. Citizens of Texcalyacac, Mexico to Avila Camacho, April 22, 1941, AA VIII-3, manuscritos, 14:1161.

76. For commemorative rituals in Ciudad Juárez, Chihuahua, see *El Continental* (El Paso, Texas), April 11, 1933, April 10, 1938, April 11, 1940.

77. Luis Morett Alatorre, *La lucha por la tierra en los valles del yaqui y mayo: Historia oral del sur de Sonora* (Mexico City: Universidad Autónoma Chapingo, 1989), 45–46.

78. See the Liga Femenil, Ejido de Tepehuaje, Ciudad Jiménez, Nuevo León to Avila Camacho, June 8, 1943, AGN-AC, 562.2/67; González Navarro, *La Confederación*, 237–238; Pedro Magallanes, President of Ejido Emiliano Zapata, San Pedro, Coahuila to Ruiz Cortines, March 30, 1954, AGN-RC, 562.2/47; and Comisariado Ejidal José Rangel to Ruiz Cortines, Monterrey, November 21, 1954, AGN-ARC, 505.1/72.

79. *El Campesino*, May 1, 1950.

80. *El Campesino*, April 30, 1970.

81. *Diccionario Histórico y Biográfico*, 4:676–677.

82. Tannenbaum, *Mexican Agrarian Revolution*; Frank Tannenbaum, *Peace by Revolution: Mexico After 1910* (New York: Columbia University Press, 1933).

83. Tannenbaum, *Mexican Agrarian Revolution*, 159–162; Tannenbaum, *Peace*, 155, 161, 176–177, quotation on 180.

84. Tannenbaum, *Peace*, 176–179.

85. Tannenbaum, *Mexican Agrarian Revolution*, 161–162; Tannenbaum, *Peace*, 88, 179–180.

86. Deborah Gronich Tate, "The Image of Emiliano Zapata in the United States, 1911–1988" (master's thesis, College of William and Mary, 1989), 50, 52–54; Beals, *Mexican Maze*, 22–23.

87. Edgcumb Pinchon, *Zapata the Unconquerable* (New York: Doubleday, Doran, 1941), vi; Tate, "The Image," 66–67; Paul J. Vanderwood, "An American Cold Warrior: *Viva Zapata!*," in *American History/American Film: Interpreting the Hollywood Image*, ed. John E. O'Connor and Martin A. Jackson (New York: Frederick Ungar, 1979), 185; Jesse Katz, "The Curse of Zapata," *Los Angeles Magazine* 47:12 (December 2002): 102–105, 176–179. Thanks to Pedro Santoni for providing me with a copy of the Katz article.

88. Pinchon, *Zapata*, 12, 84–85.

89. There was probably such a woman in Morelos at the time—Pinchon got the name, but not the romance, from Rosa E. King, *Tempest over Mexico: A Personal Chronicle* (Boston: Little, Brown, 1935; reprint: New York: Arno Press, 1970), 142–144, 158–162.

90. Pinchon, *Zapata*, 48–54, 280–281, 277–289, 325.

91. The word *pocho* is often used as a slur against "Americanized" people of Mexican ancestry, but here it seems more analogous to the word "gringo." The pocho in question may have been director-producer Irving Allen, who was of Polish background.

92. Record of twenty-fifth anniversary of April 10, Mexico City, AGN-AC, 710.1/101-2.

93. Undated, unsigned Informe sobre el Proyecto de Filmación de una Película del Frente Zapatista sobre la Vida de Zapata," AGN-MA 369/2985; *El Compadre Mendoza*, dir. Fernando de Fuentes, 1934.

94. Thomas H. Pauly, *An American Odyssey: Elia Kazan and American Culture* (Philadelphia: Temple University Press, 1983), 144–145.

95. Lester Cole, *Hollywood Red: The Autobiography of Lester Cole* (Palo Alto, Calif.: Ramparts, 1981), 259–263.

96. For the quotation, see Peter Biskind, "Ripping off Zapata: Revolution Hollywood Style," *Cineaste* 7 (1976), no. 2: 11–15. See also Pauly, *American Odyssey*, 146; Tate, "The Image," 76; Deborah E. Mistron, "The Institutional Revolution: Images of the Mexican Revolution in the Cinema" (Ph.D. diss., Indiana University, 1982), 81–89; and Katz, "Curse of Zapata."

97. For the quote see Steinbeck's first script, "Zapata: A Narrative, in Dramatic Form, of the Life of Emiliano Zapata," in *Zapata*, ed. Robert Morsberger (New York:

Penguin, 1993), 140. See also Robert Morsberger, "Emiliano Zapata: The Man, the Myth, and the Mexican Revolution," in *Zapata*, John Steinbeck (New York: Penguin, 1993), 4–5; Arthur G. Pettit, *Images of the Mexican American in Fiction and Film*, ed. Dennis E. Showalter (College Station: Texas A&M University Press, 1980), 224; Elia Kazan, *Elia Kazan, A Life* (New York: Knopf, 1988), 427.

98. Kazan, *Elia Kazan*, 397–398 for Kazan's quotes; also see 399–401, 418–420 in the same work, and Cole, *Hollywood Red*, 261–263. For Figueroa, see Alberto Isaac, *Conversaciones con Gabriel Figueroa* (Guadalajara: Universidad de Guadalajara, 1993), 42–44.

99. See Elia Kazan's letter to the editor in the *Saturday Review of Literature*, April 5, 1952, 22–23; Kazan, *Elia Kazan*, 254.

100. Steinbeck, "Zapata: A Narrative," 53.

101. Steinbeck, "Zapata: A Narrative," 47, 141.

102. Vanderwood, "American Cold Warrior," 191–195; Kazan, *Elia Kazan*, 395–396, 420.

103. Steinbeck, "Zapata: A Narrative," 141, 145; Morsberger, "Emiliano Zapata," 6; Robert E. Morsberger, "Steinbeck's Zapata: Rebel Versus Revolutionary," in *Zapata*, John Steinbeck (New York: Penguin, 1993), 215; John Steinbeck, "*Viva Zapata!*: The Screenplay," in *Zapata*, ed. Robert Morsberger (New York: Penguin, 1993), 275.

104. Morsberger, "Emiliano Zapata," 11–12; Pettit, *Images*, 225; Steinbeck, "Viva Zapata!," 246.

105. Steinbeck, "Zapata: A Narrative," 168; Elia Kazan, *Viva Zapata!*, Twentieth Century Fox, 1952.

106. Morsberger, "Emiliano Zapata," 11–12; Morsberger, "Steinbeck's Zapata," 213.

107. See Kazan, *Elia Kazan*, 395 for the quote; also see Steinbeck, "Viva Zapata!," 325–330.

108. Kazan, *Elia Kazan*, 387; Pettit, *Images*, 230.

109. Pauly, *American Odyssey*, 156; Isaac, *Conversaciones*, 44.

110. Elia Kazan, *Kazan: The Master Director Discusses His Films*, interviewed by Jeff Young (New York: Newmarket Press, 1999), 93; Morsberger, "Steinbeck's Zapata," 214.

111. Steinbeck, "Viva Zapata!," 250.

112. Morsberger, "Emiliano Zapata," 15.

113. Vanderwood, "American Cold Warrior," 188–189.

114. See Hollis Alpert's review in the *Saturday Review of Literature*, February 9, 1952.

115. Carleton Beals, letter to the editor of the *Saturday Review of Literature*, May 24, 1952, 25–28.

116. Salamón de la Selva to Alemán, Mexico City, February 12, 1952, AGN-MA 369/2985.

117. Telegram of President Adrián Castrejón and Porfirio Palacios for the Zapatista Front to Ruiz Cortines, December 8, 1952, AGN-ARC, 562.2/7.

118. Steinbeck, "Zapata: A Narrative," 46–47.

119. John Hutton, "'If I am to Die Tomorrow': Roots and Meanings of Orozco's *Zapata Entering a Peasant's Hut," Museum Studies* 11 (1984): 48; Rochfort, *Mexican Muralists*, 99–111.

120. Alma Reed, *Orozco* (New York: Oxford University Press, 1956), 13–14.

121. On these dynamics, see David G. Gutiérrez, "Migration, Emergent Ethnicity, and the 'Third Space': The Shifting Politics of Nationalism in Greater Mexico," *Journal of American History* 86 (1999): 485.

122. Hutton, "'If I am to die,'" 37–51.

123. José Eduardo Limón, *American Encounters: Greater Mexico, the United States, and the Erotics of Culture* (Boston: Beacon Press, 1998), 102; Douglas Monroy, *Rebirth: Mexican Los Angeles from the Great Migration to the Great Depression* (Berkeley and Los Angeles: University of California Press, 1999), 38–39; Gutiérrez, "Migration," 482.

124. Felipe Salazar, "Como Murió El General Zapata," *La Prensa* (San Antonio, Texas), September 18, 1932, FSG.

125. *El Continental*, April 10, 1938.

126. People of Mexican ancestry in the United States referred to themselves as Mexicans, Mexican-Americans, Hispanics, and Chicanos, depending on historical period, region, allegiance, and ideology. In the following paragraphs I use Mexican when discussing those in the process of migrating, Mexican-American as a generic designation for established communities in the United States, and Chicano to describe people who referred to themselves as such.

127. *El Continental*, March 22 and 23, 1952.

128. Morsberger, "Emiliano Zapata," 13; *New York Times*, June 17, 1951; and personal communications, May 8, 2004, in the vicinity of La Joya and Edinburgh, Texas.

129. Linda Chávez, "Anthony Quinn Had Charisma," *El Paso Times*, June 10, 2001.

130. Alex Avila, "Does Jesse Jackson Mean Business?" *Hispanic* 10:11 (November 1997).

131. Edward Rivera, *Family Installments: Memories of Growing Up Hispanic* (New York: William Morrow, 1982), 222.

132. This organization had several different names during the 1960s; for the sake of simplicity I refer to it as the United Farm Workers.

133. Ronald B. Taylor, *Chavez and the Farm Workers* (Boston: Beacon Press, 1975), 126–127, 131; quotation at 180–181.

134. Peter Matthiessen, *Sal Si Puedes: Cesar Chavez and the New American Revolution* (New York: Random House, 1969), 40.

135. John Gregory Dunne, *Delano: The Story of the California Grape Strike* (New York: Farrar, Straus and Giroux, 1967), 95.

136. Richard Griswold del Castillo and Richard A. García, *César Chávez : A Triumph of Spirit* (Norman: University of Oklahoma Press, 1995), 51–52.

137. Shifra M. Goldman, "How, Why, Where, and When It All Happened: Chicano Murals of California," in *Signs From the Heart: California Chicano Murals*, ed.

Eva Sperling Cockcroft and Holly Barnet-Sánchez (Social and Public Resource Center, Venice, Calif., 1990), 26.

138. Rodolfo Gonzales, *I Am Joaquín/Yo Soy Joaquín* (New York: Bantam, 1972), 34–36; Luis Leal, "Beyond Myths and Borders in Mexican and North American Literature," in *Common Border, Uncommon Paths: Race, Culture, and National Identity in U.S.-Mexican Relations*, ed. Jaime E. Rodriguez O. (Wilmington, Del.: SR books, 1997), 160–162; Marín, *Social Protest*, 43.

139. Rafael Perez-Torres, *Movements in Chicano Poetry: Against Myths, Against Margins* (New York: Cambridge, 1995), 73–74.

140. Ruben Salazar, *Border Correspondent: Selected Writings, 1955–1970*, ed. Mario T. Garcia (Berkeley and Los Angeles: University of California Press, 1998), 195–196, 205; Roberto Rodriguez and Patrisia Gonzales, "Zapata Lives on Both Sides of the Border" (accessed October 10, 2003).

141. Matthiessen, *Sal Si Puedes*, 73.

142. Vanderwood, "American Cold Warrior," 188–189, 196; Elia Kazan, *Kazan on Kazan*, interview by Michel Ciment (New York: Viking, 1974), 94. Especially influential after the Second World War, existentialism is a philosophical position that stresses individual responsibility in a world viewed as alienating. Simon Blackburn, *The Oxford Dictionary of Philosophy* (New York: Oxford University Press, 1996).

143. *El Campesino*, May 1, 1953.

144. Lewis, *Pedro Martínez*, 288.

145. For the image of the pyramid, see Octavio Paz, *The Other Mexico: Critique of the Pyramid*, trans. Lysander Kemp (New York: Grove, 1972).

CHAPTER 7

1. Sandra Cisneros, "Eyes of Zapata," in *Women Hollering Creek and Other Stories* (New York: Random House, 1991), 85.

2. Cisneros, "Eyes," 85–86, 101.

3. Cisneros, "Eyes," 94, 98.

4. Cisneros, "Eyes," 100.

5. Cisneros, "Eyes," 105.

6. Cisneros, "Eyes," 94.

7. Cisneros, "Eyes," 102, 88–89, 95.

8. Cisneros, "Eyes," 87, 99. The italics indicate a quotation from a source Cisneros consulted, probably Díaz Soto y Gama, *La revolución*.

9. Cisneros, "Eyes," 105.

10. Cisneros, "Eyes," 104, 111; Barbara Brinson Curiel, "The General's Pants: A Chicana Feminist (Re)vision of the Mexican Revolution in Sandra Cisneros's 'Eyes of Zapata,'" *Western American Literature* 35 (2001): 405–406, 418–419.

11. Cisneros, "Eyes," 107.

12. Cisneros, "Eyes," 99.

13. Cisneros, "Eyes," 97–99, 112. "Mexicano" here refers to the Aztec language, Nahuatl.

14. *La Prensa*, February 18, 1964; interview with Leonor Alfaro, conducted by Ximena Sepúlveda and María Isabel Souza, Cuautla, August 31, 1973, PHO/1/100; interview with Miguel Espejo, conducted by Carlos Barreto M., Villa de Ayala, September 21, 1974, PHO-Z/CRMG/1/65; Gill, "Zapata," 307.

15. For Torre y Mier's homosexuality, and the implication he liked what he saw in Zapata, see Carlos Tello Díaz, *El exilio: un relato de familia* (Mexico City: Cal y Arena, 1993). Thanks to Victor Macias for this source. See also *Excélsior*, April 10, 1995.

16. Krista Comer, *Landscapes of the New West: Gender and Geography in Contemporary Women's Writing* (Chapel Hill: University of North Carolina Press, 1999), 176; Brinson Curiel, "The General's Pants," 405–406.

17. Comer, *Landscapes*, 180.

18. See, for instance, Adolfo López Mateos, *José Maria Morelos*, 19.

19. *Excélsior*, April 11, 1951.

20. For an overview of these processes, see Anne Rubenstein, "Mass Media and Popular Culture in the Twentieth Century," in *The Oxford History of Mexico*, ed. William Beezley and Michael Meyer (New York: Oxford University Press, 2000), 637–670.

21. Paco Ignacio Taibo II, *'68* (Mexico City: Joaquin Moritz, 1991), 22–23.

22. For the quotation, see Elena Poniatowska, *Massacre in Mexico*, trans. Helen R. Lane (New York: Viking, 1975; reprint, Columbia: University of Missouri Press, 1984), 31. See Eric Zolov, *Refried Elvis: The Rise of the Mexican Counterculture* (Berkeley and Los Angeles: University of California Press, 1999), 59–60, on the legislation.

23. For the quotations, see Poniatowska, *Massacre*, 41, 47. See also Bruce Campbell, *Mexican Murals in Times of Crisis* (Tucson: University of Arizona Press, 2003), 340; and Daniel Cazés, ed., *Memorial del 68: Relato a muchas voces* (Mexico City: La Jornada, 1993), 39.

24. Julio Scherer García and Carlos Monsiváis, *Parte de Guerra: Tlatelolco 1968* (Mexico City: Nuevo Siglo, 1999), 186–187, 207.

25. Daniel Cazés, *Crónica 1968* (Mexico City: Plaza y Valdés, 1993), 92.

26. Zolov, *Refried*, 138, 167, 175–180, 186, 189.

27. José Agustín, *Tragicomedia mexicana 2: La vida en México de 1970 a 1988* (Mexico City: Planeta, 1992), 30; Amparo Ochoa, "Bola Suriana de la Muerte de Emiliano Zapata," in *El Cancionero Popular*, vol. I (Mexico City: Fonarte Latino/IODA, 1975).

28. Eric Zolov, "Discovering a Land 'Mysterious and Obvious': The Renarrativizing of Postrevolutionary Mexico," in Joseph, Rubenstein, and Zolov, eds., *Fragments of a Golden Age*, 257, and, for Mexico's "onda Chicana," Zolov, *Refried Elvis*, 175–176.

29. Hodges, *Mexican Anarchism*, 129.

30. *El Campesino*, October 2 and 31, 1971.

31. For the photograph and the quotations, see Juan Miguel de Mora, *Las guerrillas en México y Jenaro Vázquez Rojas (su personalidad, su vida y su muerte)* (Mexico City: Editora Latino Americana, 1972), front matter, 361, 388–391, 395–403. See also Jaime López, *10 años de guerrillas en México, 1964–1974* (Mexico City: Posada, 1974), 99–100.

32. López, *10 años*, 34–38, 44–45; also Bartra, *Los herederos*, 89.

33. de Mora, *Las guerrillas*, 35–39.

34. de Mora, *Las guerrillas*, 127–129, 141, 154–156, 159–161, 172–178.

35. de Mora, *Las guerrillas*, 248–249; José Luis Orbe Diego et al., *Lucio Cabañas y el Partido de los Pobres: Una experiencia guerrillera en México* (Mexico City: Nuestra América, 1987), 31.

36. de Mora, *Las guerrillas*, 305–309.

37. For the quote, see Luis Suárez, *Lucio Cabañas: el guerrillero sin esperanza*, 4th ed. (Mexico City: Roca, 1976), 278–280; also see p. 199.

38. Orbe Diego, *Lucio Cabañas*, 263–264.

39. Juan Miguel de Mora, *Lucio Cabañas: su vida y su muerte* (Mexico City: Editores Asociados, 1974), 88–89.

40. Suárez, *Lucio Cabañas*, 299–301.

41. de Mora, *Lucio Cabañas*, 10.

42. Suárez, *Lucio Cabañas*, 27.

43. Francisco José Ruiz Cervantes, "La lucha de clases en Oaxaca: 1971–1977 (segunda parte)," in René Bustamante V. et al., *Oaxaca una lucha reciente: 1960–1978* (Mexico City: Ediciones Nueva Sociología, 1978); Hugo Esteve Díaz, *Las armas de la utopía: La tercera ola de los movimientos guerrilleros en México* (Mexico City: Instituto de Proposiciones Estratégicas, 1996), 79.

44. Peter Schweizer, *Reagan's War: The Epic Story of His Forty Year Struggle and Final Triumph Over Communism* (New York: Doubleday, 2002), 53.

45. For the quotation, see Womack, *Zapata*, 205. See also pp. 94, 96, 108, 210, 215, 219, 222, 224, 240, 379, and, on *Viva Zapata!*, 420.

46. Womack, *Zapata*, 323.

47. Womack, *Zapata*, x.

48. Cecilia Greaves, "La Secretaría de Educación Pública y la lectura, 1960–1985," in *Historia de la lectura en México* (Mexico City: Colegio de Mexico, 1988), 369.

49. *El Campesino*, May 31, 1969.

50. Taracena, *Zapata*, 7.

51. Mauricio Tenorio-Trillo, "*Liaisons dangereuses*: Memoria y olvido historiográfico," in *Cincuenta años de investigación histórica en México*, ed. Gisela von Wobeser (Mexico City: UNAM, 1998), 36.

52. Felipe Cazals, *Emiliano Zapata*, Producciones Aguila, 1970; Mistron, "Institutional Revolution," 93–94; Emilio García Riera, *Breve historia del cine mexicano: Primer siglo, 1897–1997* (Mexico City: Ediciones Mapa, 1998), 257; Raquel Peguero, "Zapata aún no cabalga por los senderos del cine mexicano," *La Jornada*, April 10, 1999; Felipe Soto Viterbo, "Máquina del tiempo: cine zapateado," in *Expansión*, December 11, 2002.

53. O'Malley, *Myth*, 143.

54. Jorge Carlos Barberi, "Comentarios Fílmicos: 'Emiliano Zapata,'" *El Nacional*, November 26, 1970, FSG.

55. *La Jornada*, April 10, 1999.

56. *La Jornada*, April 10, 1999; Mistron, "Institutional Revolution," 94.

57. *La Jornada*, April 10, 1999.

58. *El Campesino*, April 30, 1971.

59. Stanley Meisler, "Mexican Hero Zapata Center of New Dispute," *Los Angeles Times*, April 14, 1974.

60. *El Campesino*, March 31, 1974.

61. Meisler, "Mexican Hero."

62. *La Jornada*, April 10, 1999.

63. For the images, see *Alberto Gironella: exposición antológica* (Mexico City: Museo Rufino Tamayo, 1984). See also Juan Acha in *Excélsior*, December 31, 1972.

64. "Alberto Gironella: 'Lo mio es el loco intento de pintar el tiempo' (conversación con José de la Colina)," in *Alberto Gironella: Exposición antológica* (Mexico City: Museo Rufino Tamayo, 1984), 74 ff.; Rita Eder, *Gironella* (UNAM, 1981), 62.

65. Eder, *Gironella*, 49–50.

66. *Excélsior*, November 10, 1972.

67. Juan Acha, "El ambientalismo de Gironella: Vulgurización de la gran pintura," *Excélsior*, November 19, 1972; Raquel Tibol, "No hay cementerios en los enterramientos de Gironella," *Excélsior*, November 19, 1972; Eder, *Gironella*, 53–54, 96, 98.

68. *Excélsior*, November 10, 1972.

69. *El Campesino*, March 31, 1969; *El Campesino*, February 28, 1969.

70. *Oaxaca Gráfico*, April 9 and 11, 1969; *Excélsior*, April 10 and 11, 1969.

71. See *El Campesino*, January 31, 1971, Rubén Salazar, *Border Correspondent*, 254, and Bartra, *Los herederos*, 119, for claims of Zapatista stature.

72. *El Campesino*, April 30, 1973. See also *Excélsior*, April 10, 1969.

73. *Excélsior*, April 11, 1970.

74. *Excélsior*, April 11, 1975; *El Renovador* (Cuernavaca), April 13, 1975.

75. Bartra, *Los herederos*, 95–99, 102.

76. *Excélsior*, April 11, 1969; Sanderson, *Land Reform*, 58, 117.

77. *Excélsior*, April 11, 1974.

78. Bartra, *Los herederos*, 89, 103–106.

79. Enrique Astorga Lira and Clarisa Hardy Raskovan, *Organización, lucha y dependencia económica: La Unión de Ejidos Emiliano Zapata* (Mexico City: Nueva Imagen, 1978), 14; Marcel Morales Ibarra, *Morelos agrario: la construcción de una alternativa* (Mexico City: Plaza y Valdés, 1994), 84, 89; Victor Raúl Martínez Vásquez, *Movimiento popular y política en Oaxaca (1968–1986)* (Mexico City: Consejo Nacional Para la Cultura y las Artes, 1990), 138, 142–143.

80. *Excélsior*, April 10, 1975.

81. Bartra, *Los herederos*, 127–136.

82. *Excélsior*, April 11, 1977.

83. *Excélsior*, April 10, 1977. For more unhappiness with Palacios, see *El Campesino*, August 31, 1971. *El Campesino*, naturally, refuted the charges.

84. *Excélsior*, April 11, 1978.

85. *Nexos*, September 1979; Graciela Flores Lúa, Luisa Paré, and Sergio Sarmiento Silva, *Las voces del campo: movimiento campesino y política agraria, 1976–1984* (Mexico City: Siglo Veintiuno, 1988), 74. On the UCEZ, see Luis Vázquez León, *Ser indio otra vez: La purepechización de los tarascos serranos* (Mexico City: Consejo Nacional para la Cultura y las Artes, 1992), 90, 124–125.

86. Bartra, *Los herederos*, 148.

87. On the CNPA, see Ana María Prieto, "Mexico's National *Coordinadoras* in a Context of Economic Crisis," trans. Sandra del Castillo, in *The Mexican Left, The Popular Movements, and the Politics of Austerity*, ed. Barry Carr and Ricardo Anzaldúa Montoya (San Diego: Center for U.S.-Mexican Studies, University of California, San Diego, 1986), 75–94, espec. 84–87.

88. *El Campesino*, April 30, 1971; *Excélsior*, April 11, 1971.

89. *El Nacional*, April 14, 1971.

90. *El Día* (Mexico City), April 18, 1971.

91. *El Campesino*, April 20, 1971.

92. *Polígrafo*, April 18, 1971.

93. *Polígrafo*, April 23, 1971.

94. *El Campesino*, April 20, 1972.

95. *Excélsior*, April 1978, 11, 1979.

96. *Excélsior*, August 9, 1979.

97. *El Nacional*, August 25, 1979, FSG; Lúa et al., *Las voces*, 75.

98. *Excélsior*, October 15, 1979.

99. *Excélsior*, October 16, 1979.

100. *Excélsior*, October 17, 1979.

101. *Excélsior*, October 15, 1979; Lúa et al., *Las voces*, 76.

102. Lúa et al., *Las voces*, 71.

103. *Excélsior*, November 21, 1979. See also Rueda and Espejel, *El siglo xx*, 88; Neil Harvey, *The Chiapas Rebellion: The Struggle for Land and Democracy* (Durham, N.C.: Duke University Press, 1998), 131–132.

104. *Excélsior*, April 10 and 11, 1978; Rubio, *Resistencia campesina*, 27.

105. See *Chinameca: 10 de Abril de 1979* (Cuernavaca: Cuadernos Zapatistas, 1979), 5, for the second quotation; for the first, see *Villa de Ayala y Chinameca* (Cuernavaca: Cuadernos Zapatistas, 1979), 21–22.

106. *Nexos*, June 1979.

107. *Excélsior*, April 10, 1979

108. *Polígrafo*, April 10, 1979.

109. *Homenaje a Emiliano Zapata* (Cuernavaca: Cuadernos Zapatistas, 1979), 11, 13–15; *Homenaje del pueblo a Emiliano Zapata Salazar* (Cuernavaca: Cuadernos Zapatistas, 1979), 19.

110. *Chinameca: 10 de Abril de 1979*, 5.

111. Enrique Ochoa, *Feeding Mexico: The Political Uses of Food Since 1910* (Wilmington, Del.: SR Books, 2000), 188–191.

112. Harvey, *Rebellion*, 133, 137.

113. Bartra, *Los herederos*, 153–154.

114. *Excélsior*, April 11, 1985; *Noticias* (Oaxaca), April 11, 1985.

115. *Noticias*, April 11, 1988.

116. *Noticias*, April 11, 1987.

117. *Excélsior*, April 11, 1988.

118. Alan Knight, "Weapons and Arches in the Mexican Revolutionary Landscape," in *Everyday Forms of State Formation: Revolution and the Negotiation of Rule in Modern Mexico*, ed. Gilbert M. Joseph and Daniel Nugent (Durham, N.C.: Duke University Press, 1994), 64.

119. *La SEMIP en el 65° aniversario de la muerte de Emiliano Zapata* (Mexico City: SEMIP, 1984).

120. *Diario de Morelos* (Cuernavaca), April 10, 1986.

121. *Noticias*, April 11, 1985, April 11, 1987.

CHAPTER 8

1. The source for this passage, except where otherwise indicated, is my interview with Ana María Zapata, Cuautla, June 29, 1996.

2. Gustavo Baz was a physician who joined the Zapatistas after Huerta's coup and later had a successful political career.

3. *Excélsior*, June 9, 1970.

4. It had not been legal, since the revolution, for campesinos to sell the ejidal land they had been granted, the idea being to keep land from falling back into the hands of large landholders.

5. *Excélsior*, April 11, 1988.

6. *Excélsior*, April 11, 1988. Salinas's dissertation was published as *Producción y participación política en el campo* (Mexico City: UNAM, 1980).

7. The PAN would win its first governorship in 1989.

8. *Excélsior*, April 11, 1988.

9. Adolfo Gilly, ed., *Cartas a Cuauhtémoc Cárdenas* (Mexico City: Ediciones Era, 1989), 79.

10. For the quotation, *Diario de Morelos*, April 11, 1989. Also see *Excélsior*, April 10 and 11, 1989.

11. *Diario de Morelos*, April 11, 1990; *Excélsior*, April 11, 1990.

12. *Excélsior*, August 9, 1991. Warman's book is entitled *Y venimos a contradecir: Los campesinos de Morelos y el estado nacional* (Mexico City: INAH, 1976).

13. Pamela Kilian, *Barbara Bush: Matriarch of a Dynasty* (New York: St. Martin's Press, 2003), 40.

14. For this announcement, see *The Americas*, Part 3, *Continent on the Move*, executive producer Judith Vecchione, 57 minutes, WGBH Boston and Central Television Enterprises for Channel 4, UK, 1993, video recording.

15. Heather L. Williams, *Social Movements and Economic Transition: Markets and Distributive Conflict in Mexico* (New York: Cambridge University Press, 2001), 72. This is the event that Ana María Zapata refers to in the opening passage of this chapter.

16. See, for example, Stephen, *Zapata Lives!*, 153–154; and Guiomar Rovira, *¡Zapata vive!: La rebelión indígena de Chiapas contada por sus protagonistas* (Barcelona: Virus, 1994), 200.

17. *Excélsior*, April 11, 1992; *Diario de Morelos*, April 11, 1992; and, for the quotation, *Noticias*, April 11, 1992.

18. Gilbert, "Emiliano Zapata," 148 ff.

19. *Excélsior*, April 11, 1990.

20. *Excélsior*, April 10, 1991.

21. *Excélsior*, April 11, 1992.

22. Comandancia General del EZLN, "Declaración de la Selva Lacandona," January 2, 1994, in *EZLN: Documentos y comunicados*, 2 vols. (Mexico City: Era, 1994–1995), 1:33–35.

23. *New York Times*, January 4, 1994.

24. Luis Antonio Nájera Muñoz to López Mateos, Tuzantán, Chiapas, April 17, 1962, AGN-ALM, 135.21/380.

25. *Excélsior*, April 11, 1981.

26. *Excélsior*, April 11, 1985.

27. Stephen, *Zapata Lives!*, 50–61; George A. Collier, "Zapatismo Resurgent: Land and Autonomy in Chiapas," in NACLA: *Report on the Americas* 33 (2000): 22.

28. For the quotation, see "Estatutos de las Fuerzas de Liberación Nacional," in *Rebellion in Chiapas: An Historical Reader*, ed. John Womack, Jr. (New York: New Press, 1999), 196. See also in the same volume pp. 174–175, 187, 190–192; Stephen, *Zapata Lives!*, 151–152; Neil Harvey, "Peasant Strategies and Corporatism in Chiapas," in *Popular Movements and Political Change in Mexico*, ed. Joe Foweraker and Ann Craig (Boulder, Colo.: Lynn Rienner Publishers, 1990); and Donald Hodges and Ross Handy, *Mexico Under Siege: Popular Resistance to Presidential Despotism* (New York: Zed Books, 2002), 195.

29. Subcomandante Marcos, "Chiapas: El sureste en dos vientos, una tormenta y una profecía," August 1992, in EZLN, 1:65; Stephen, *Zapata Lives!*, 137–139.

30. For the quotation, see Dornbierer, *El Prinosaurio*, 169–171. Also see Enrique Rajchenberg S. and Catherine Héau-Lambert, "Historia y simbolismo en el movimiento zapatista," in *Chiapas* (Mexico City: Instituto de Investigaciones Económicas, Universidad Autónoma de México, 1996), 46.

31. Comité Clandestino Revoluciónario Indígena—Comandancia General (hereafter CCRI-CG) del EZLN, "Composición del EZLN y condiciones para el diálogo," January 6, 1994, EZLN, 1:73–74.

32. CCRI-CG to the Coordinadora Nacional de Pueblos Indios, February 8, 1994, in *EZLN*, 1:133.

33. ["Dicen algunos miembros del EZLN"], January 26, 1994, in *EZLN*, 1:107. The Tzeltal are one of several Mayan groups, distinguished from each other by language and other cultural attributes.

34. Rubio, *Resistencia*, 32–34; *Emiliano Zapata en la provincia mexicana* (Cuernavaca: Cuadernos Zapatistas, 1979), 77 ff. Tlatoani was a title for the Aztec emperor.

35. Miguel León-Portilla, *Los manifiestos en nahuatl de Emiliano Zapata* (Mexico City: Universidad Nacional Autónoma de México, Instituto de Investigaciones Históricas, 1978). See also the same author's third-grade social science text: Miguel León-Portilla, ed., *Mexico: Su evolución cultural*, vol. 2 (Mexico City: SEP and Editorial Porrua , 1981), 101, 198, for the Indian Zapata. The comic book history is Armando Bartra and Angel Mora, *México: Historia de un pueblo*. Vol. 18, *Tierra y libertad* (Mexico City: SEP and Nueva Imagen, 1982), 54.

36. Mark Taylor, "Votán-Zapata: Theological Discourse in Zapatista Political Struggle," in *Converging on Culture: Theologians in Dialogue with Cultural Analysis and Criticism*, ed. Delwin Brown, Sheila Greeve Davaney, and Kathryn Tanner (New York: Oxford University Press, 2001), 183–186; Gary Gossen, *Telling Maya Tales: Tzotzil Identities in Modern Mexico* (New York: Routledge, 1999), 259; Lynn Stephen, "Pro-Zapatista and Pro-PRI: Resolving the Contradictions of Zapatismo in Rural Oaxaca," *Latin American Research Review* 32 (1997): 60.

37. Marcos's letter of December 13, 1994, in *EZLN*, 2:159–163; Stephen, *Zapata Lives!*, 162–164.

38. CCRI-CG del EZLN to the Mexican People, World People and Governments, and National and International Press, April 10, 1994, in *EZLN*, 1:210–213.

39. CCRI-CG del EZLN to the Mexican People, World People and Governments, and National and International Press, April 10, 1994, in *EZLN*, 1:208–210; Rovira, *¡Zapata vive!*, 282–284.

40. CCRI-CG del EZLN, "Votán-Zapata se levantó de nuevo," April 10, 1995, in *EZLN*, 2:306–309.

41. CCRI-CG del EZLN to Zapata, Jefe Máximo del Ejército Zapatista de Liberación Nacional, in *La Jornada*, April 12, 1997.

42. Doris Sommer, "Taking a Life: Hot Pursuit and Cold Rewards in a Mexican Testimonial Novel," in *The Seductions of Biography*, ed. Mary Rhiel and David Suchoff (New York: Routledge, 1996), 147, 166; Elena Poniatowska, *Here's to You, Jesusa!*, trans. Deanna Heikkinen (New York: Farrar, Straus and Giroux, 2001), 73–76. The original edition was published in 1969. Thanks to Gabriela Cano for the insight about sexual violence.

43. JoAnn Martin, "When the People Were Strong and United: Stories of the Past and the Transformation of Politics in a Mexican Community, in *The Paths to Domination, Resistance, and Terror*, ed. Carolyn Nordstrom and JoAnn Martin (Berkeley and Los Angeles: University of California Press, 1992), 181; for Margarita Zapata, see *The Last Zapatistas: Forgotten Heroes*, producer Manuel Peñafiel, dir. Francesco Taboada Tabone, 2001, video recording.

44. Jeannette Rodda, *Go Ye and Study the Beehive: The Making of a Western Working Class* (New York: Garland, 2000), 156–157.

45. For the campus Zapata, see Alma M. García, *Narratives of Mexican American Women: Emergent Identities of the Second Generation* (New York: Rowman and Littlefield, 2004), 165–166.

46. *La Jornada*, April 11, 1996, for the first quotation; Rovira, *¡Zapata vive!*, 227, for the second.

47. Guiomar Rovira, *Mujeres de maíz* (Mexico City: Ediciones Era, 1997), 109.

48. For the text of the "Ley Revolucionaria de Mujeres," see Rosa Rojas, ed., *Chiapas ¿y las mujeres qué?* (Mexico City: Ediciones la Correa Feminista, 1994), 21–22.

49. Stephen, *Zapata Lives!*, 176–215; Brunk, *Emiliano Zapata!*, 185.

50. For the first quotation, see Cimacnoticias, "El asunto del agua no sólo es abrir una llave: Mazahuas," http://www.cimacnoticias.com/noticias/04oct/04100407.html, October 4, 2004 (accessed April 11, 2007); for the second, from the Programa de las Naciones Unidas para el Medio Ambiente, "México: Crece el frente mazahua," http://www.pnuma.org/informacion/noticias/2004-09/29sep04e.doc, September 29, 2004 (accessed April 11, 2007). See also the press release from the Comisión Nacional para el Desarrollo de los Pueblos Indígenas, http://www.cdi.gob.mx/index.php?id_seccion=1899, Mexico City, October 12, 2006 (accessed April 11, 2007); *La Jornada*, February 9, 2005; and Cimacnoticias, "Constituyen su ejército las Mazahuas del Cutzamala," http://www.cimacnoticias.com/noticias/04sep/04092702.html, Mexico City, September 27, 2004 (accessed April 11, 2007). Thanks to María Teresa Fernández Aceves for calling this group to my attention.

51. *La Jornada*, April 11, 1999.

52. *Wall Street Journal*, January 12, 1994; for Mateo's lasting unhappiness with the EZLN, see "La Revolución vista desde el 2003," univision.com (accessed November 24, 2003).

53. Interview with Alfonso Arroyo Méndez, conducted by the author, Oaxaca, June 4, 1996.

54. *Wall Street Journal*, January 21, 1994.

55. The quotation on liberty comes from my interview with Jorge Ortega Atristaín, Oaxaca, June 3, 1996, See also *Uno Más Uno*, June 25, 1994.

56. Comunicado del Subcomandante Insurgente Marcos, August/September 1999, http://ezln.org/documentos/1999/19990900a.es.htm (accessed March 27, 2004).

57. *El Bravo* (Matamoros), March 15, 1998. Thanks to Aaron Mahr for this source. See also Kathleen Bruhn, "Antonio Gramsci and the Palabra Verdadera: The Political Discourse of Mexico's Guerrilla Forces," *Journal of Interamerican Studies and World Affairs* 41 (1999): 41.

58. *La Jornada*, April 11, 2002.

59. *Noticias*, April 11, 1993.

60. The conviction was overturned in 2005.

61. *Diario de Morelos*, April 10 and 11, 1995; *Noticias*, April 11, 1995; "Palabras del Presidente Ernesto Zedillo," Chinameca, Morelos, April 10, 1995, http://www .quicklink.com/mexico/gobfed/zedill67.htm; and *La Jornada*, April 11, 1995.

62. *Noticias*, April 10 and 11, 1995.

63. *Noticias*, April 10, 1995.

64. *Noticias*, April 10 and 11, 1995.

65. *Noticias*, April 11, 1995.

66. *Excélsior*, April 11, 1985, April 11, 1989, April 11, 1997, April 11, 1998; *El Norte* (Monterrey) April 11, 1998, April 11, 2003.

67. Carlos Monsiváis, "Crónica de Tepoztlán," *La Jornada*, April 15, 1996; María Rosas, *Tepoztlán: Crónica de desacatos y resistencia* (Mexico City: Ediciones Era, 1997), 102–107.

68. *Excélsior*, August 9, 1996.

69. *La Jornada*, April 11, 2000.

70. *Excélsior*, April 11, 1998.

71. For the quotation, see *Excélsior*, January 10, 1972; see also Michael J. Ard, *An Eternal Struggle: How the National Action Party Transformed Mexican Politics* (Westport, Conn.: Praeger, 2003), 100–101.

72. *Unión de Morelos* (Cuernavaca), April 10, 2001.

73. *Unión de Morelos*, April 11, 2001. For doubts about the authenticity of the clothing displayed in this museum, see *Excélsior*, April 10, 1995, and *La Jornada*, April 10, 1999.

74. He was grandson of Vicente Estrada Cajigal, the governor who pushed for Zapata's first Cuautla statue in 1932.

75. *Unión de Morelos*, April 11, 2001.

76. For the first quotation, see *La Jornada*, April 11, 2001; for the second, *Unión de Morelos*, April 11, 2001.

77. Though the case of Marcos Olmedo demonstrates that representatives of the state were not always cautious.

78. *La Jornada*, April 8–10, 1995.

79. Alfonso Arau, *Zapata: El sueño del héroe*, prod. Alfonso Arau and Javier Rodríguez Borgio, Latin Arts LLC, Comala Films, Rita Rusic, 2004.

80. Katz, "The Curse"; Felipe Soto Viterbo, "Máquina del tiempo: Cine zapateado," *Expansión*, December 11–25, 2002.

81. John Hecht, "Filmmaker Has Revolutionary Idea," *The Hollywood Reporter* (Los Angeles), October 14, 2003.

82. Diego Cevallos, "Revolutionary Zapata Reinvented," Interpress Service News Agency, http://www.ipsnews.net/interna.asp?idnews=23585 (accessed February 27, 2005); Hecht, "Filmmaker has Revolutionary Idea."

83. *La Jornada*, April 10, 1999; *El Norte*, November 19, 2002.

84. *Seattle Times*, October 29, 2003.

85. See the *Seattle Times*, October 29, 2003, for the quotation; see also *The Guardian* (London), August 28, 2003.

86. Diego Cevallos, "Zapata, the Revolutionary, as the Subject of Fantasy," IPS-Inter Press Service, May 6, 2004; Womack, *Zapata*, 286; *Austin American-Statesman*, September 28, 2003.

87. This is surely a reference to Diego Rivera, who painted Indian women with Calla lilies several times.

88. Katz, "The Curse."

89. Sharon A. Navarro, "Las Voces de Esperanza/Voices of Hope: La Mujer Obrera, Transnationalism, and NAFTA-Displaced Women Workers in the U.S.-Mexico Borderlands," in *Globalization on the Line: Culture, Capital, and Citizenship at U.S. Borders*, ed., Claudia Sadowski-Smith (New York: Palgrave, 2002), 190; Sharon A. Navarro, *"Las Mujeres Invisibles/*The Invisible Women," in *Women's Activism and Globalization*, ed. Nancy A. Naples and Manisha Desai (New York: Routledge, 2002), 94.

90. Gary D. Keller, "Zapata Rose in 1992," in the short story collection *Zapata Rose in 1992 and Other Tales* (Tempe, Ariz.: Maize Press, 1992); idem, *Zapata Lives!* (Tempe, Ariz.: Maize Press, 1994).

91. Keller, *Zapata Rose*, 243–245. The Toltecs were the rulers of a central Mexican empire during the tenth through twelfth centuries.

92. Keller, *Zapata Rose*, 299–326.

93. CCRI-CG del EZLN, "Mensaje del SubComandante Insurgente Marcos," Puebla, February 27, 2001, in *La marcha del color de la tierra: Comunicados, cartas y mensajes del Ejército Zapatista de Liberación Nacional del 2 de diciembre del 2000 al 2 de abril del 2001* (Mexico: Rizoma, 2001), 126–131.

94. CCRI-CG del EZLN, "Mensaje del SubComandante Insurgente Marcos," Cuernavaca, March 6, 2001, in *La marcha del color*, 197–200.

CHAPTER 9

1. See, for example, Laura Espejel and Ruth Solís Vicarte, *Emiliano Zapata* (Mexico City: Instituto Nacional de Estudios Históricos de la Revolución Mexicana, 1992).

2. *Diario de Morelos*, April 11, 1992.

3. Ana María Alonso, "The Effects of Truth: Re-Presentations of the Past and the Imagining of Community," *Journal of Historical Sociology* 1 (1988): 43.

4. Alan Knight, "Historical Continuities in Social Movements," in *Popular Movements and Political Change in Mexico*, ed. Joe Foweraker and Ann Craig (Boulder, Colo.: Lynn Rienner Publishers, 1990), 96.

5. See Alonso, "The Effects of Truth," 45, for a discussion of emptying symbols of their meanings.

6. See Lomnitz "Ritual, Rumor and Corruption," 20–47, on the workings of ritual.

7. Lomnitz, "Ritual, Rumor and Corruption," 32–33, takes a broader look at this trend.

8. This is a qualified example of what Philip Corrigan and Derek Sayer, *The Great Arch: English State Formation as Cultural Revolution* (New York: Blackwell, 1985), 198, mean when they note the importance of rendering subordinate classes speechless.

9. Michael Parfit, "Mexico City: Pushing the Limits," *National Geographic*, August 1996, 24; Kertzer, *Ritual, Politics, and Power*, 66–68.

10. Thanks to University of Texas-El Paso doctoral student Antonio López for helping me clarify my thinking in this paragraph.

11. The argument by James C. Scott, *Domination and the Arts of Resistance: Hidden Transcripts* (New Haven: Yale University Press, 1990), 227, that a prehistory of "hidden transcripts" precedes clear expressions of oppositional goals, is useful here, though the "transcripts" in this case were not hidden.

12. See Knight, "Historical Continuities," for a discussion of this issue from a different angle.

13. I find evidence for this conclusion in the comparisons about hegemony made in Mallon, *Peasant and Nation*, and Vaughan, *Cultural Politics in Revolution*, as well as Jeffrey L. Gould's discovery of decades of hegemony even in Somocista Nicaragua— see *To Lead as Equals: Rural Protest and Political Consciousness in Chinandega, Nicaragua, 1912–1979* (Chapel Hill: University of North Carolina Press, 1990).

14. Smith, *Myths*, 12–14.

15. Scott, *Domination*, 66–72.

16. O'Malley, *Myth*, 38.

17. Tumarkin, *Lenin Lives!*, 197.

18. McLuhan is famous, of course, for writing that "the medium is the message." Marshall McLuhan, *Understanding Media: The Extensions of Man* (New York: McGraw-Hill, 1964), 7–21.

19. For this characterization, see Thomas Benjamin, "The Leviathan on the Zócalo: Recent Historiography of the Postrevolutionary Mexican State," *Latin American Historical Review* 20 (1985): 195–217.

20. For the first two, see the Introduction. See also Jeffrey W. Rubin, *Decentering the Regime: Ethnicity, Radicalism, and Democracy in Juchitán, Mexico* (Durham, N.C.: Duke University Press, 1997).

21. For "dictablanda," see Guillermo O'Donnell and Philippe C. Schmitter, *Transitions from Authoritarian Rule: Tentative Conclusions about Uncertain Democracies* (Baltimore: Johns Hopkins University Press, 1986), 9. See also Mario Vargas Llosa, "Mexico: The Perfect Dictatorship," *New Perspectives Quarterly* 8 (1991): 23.

22. Friedrich Katz, "Introduction: Rural Revolts in Mexico," in *Riot, Rebellion, and Revolution: Rural Social Conflict in Mexico,* ed. Friedrich Katz (Princeton, N.J.: Princeton University Press, 1988), 16–17.

23. See Samuel Brunk and Ben Fallaw, "Conclusion: Rethinking Latin American Heroes," in *Heroes and Hero Cults in Latin America*, ed. Samuel Brunk and Ben Fallaw

(Austin: University of Texas Press, 1996), 272–275, for a slightly extended version of this analysis.

24. Paz, *Labyrinth*, 142–145.

25. José Muñoz Cota, "Los Ojos de Emiliano Zapata," *Novedades*, May 30, 1989, FSG.

26. This applies, for example, to some of the chapters in Joseph et al., eds., *Fragments of a Golden Age*. Anne Rubenstein questioned whether the revolution was important for some topics later in the century in her remarks at the roundtable, "The State of Mexican History in the Twenty-First Century: New Questions, Old Problems," at the annual meeting of the American Historical Association, Seattle, January 7, 2005.

27. *El Diario* (Ciudad Juárez), April 11, 2003.

28. *El Diario*, April 11, 2003.

BIBLIOGRAPHY

PRIMARY SOURCES

Archival Collections: Mexico City

Archivo General de la Nación
    Archivo de Alfredo Robles Domínguez (ARD).
    Archivo de Antonio Díaz Soto y Gama.
    Archivo de Emiliano Zapata (AZ).
    Archivo de Genovevo de la O (AO).
    Archivo del Cuartel General del Sur (ACGS).
    Fondo Presidentes
        Adolfo López Mateos (AGN-LM).
        Alvaro Obregón/Plutarco Elías Calles (AGN-OC).
        Lázaro Cárdenas (AGN-LC).
        Manuel Avila Camacho (AGN-AC).
        Miguel Alemán (AGN-MA).
Archivo Histórico de la Defensa Nacional (AHDN).
Biblioteca Manuel Orozco y Berra. Papeles de Familia, Archivo Miguel Mendoza Ló-
    pez Schwerdtfeger (AMLS).
Centro de Estudios de Historia de México, Condumex. Archivo de Jenaro Amezcua
    (AA).
Instituto de Investigaciones Sobre la Universidad y la Educación, Archivo Histórico de
    la UNAM, Mexico City, Archivo de Gildardo Magaña (AGM).
Universidad Panamericana. Archivo de Roque González Garza (AGG).

Archival Collections: United States

United States Department of State. Records Relating to the Internal Affairs of Mexico,
    1910–1929 (USDS-IAM).

Interviews

CONDUCTED BY AUTHOR

Arroyo Méndez, Alfonso, Oaxaca, June 4, 1996.

Díaz Soto Ugalde, Enriqueta; Magdalena Díaz Soto Ugalde; and Salvador Díaz Soto Ugalde, Mexico City, July 1994.

González, Marcos, Oaxaca, June 4, 1996.

Ortega Atristaín, Jorge, Oaxaca, June 3, 1996.

Zapata, Ana María, Cuautla, Morelos, June 29, 1996.

Zapata, Mateo, Cuautla, Morelos, June 27, 1996.

PROGRAMA DE HISTORIA ORAL. INSTITUTO NACIONAL DE ANTROPOLOGÍA E HISTORIA AND INSTITUTO DE INVESTIGACIONES DR. JOSÉ MARÍA LUIS MORA, MEXICO CITY.

Aldana, Carmen. PHO-Z/1/32.

Alfaro, Leonor. PHO/1/100.

Alquicira Fuentes, Leopoldo. PHO-Z/1/3.

Avila Berrera, Andrés. PHO/1/53.

Chávez, Jesús. PHO/1/99.

Espejo, Miguel. PHO-Z/CRMG/1/65.

Estrada Cajigal, Vicente. PHO/4/12.

García Aguirre, Prospero. PHO-Z/1/117.

Lora Mirasol, José. PHO-Z/1/14.

Pariente A., Agapito. PHO-Z/1/29.

Pineda, Juventino. PHO-Z/1/57.

Plasencia Gutiérrez, Serafín. PHO-Z/1/59.

Yedra Islas, Domingo. PHO-Z/1/15.

Periodicals and Electronic News Sources

Austin American-Statesman. Austin, Texas. 2003.

El Bravo. Matamoros, Tamaulipas. 1998.

El Campesino. Mexico City. 1949–1974.

Cimacnoticias. 2004.

El Día. Mexico City. 1971.

El Diario. Ciudad Juárez, Chihuahua. 2003.

Diario de Morelos. Cuernavaca, Morelos. 1986–1995.

El Eco del Sur. Cuautla, Morelos. 1965–1966.

El Paso Times. 2001.

Excélsior. Mexico City. 1919–1998.

The Guardian. London. 2003.

The Hollywood Reporter. Los Angeles. 2003.

El Imparcial. Mexico City. 1911.

El Imparcial. Oaxaca. 1957.

El Informador. Cuernavaca, Morelos. 1950–1960.

La Jornada. Mexico City. 1994–2002.

Libertad. Oaxaca. 1934?

El Maestro Rural. Mexico City. 1933–1935.

Morelos Nuevo. Cuernavaca, Morelos. 1932.

El Mundo. Mexico City. 1933.

New York Times. 1951, 1974, 1994.

El Norte. Monterrey, Nuevo León. 1998, 2003.

Nosotros. Mexico City. 1958.

Noticias. Oaxaca. 1985–1995.

Novedades. Mexico City. 1937–1962.

Oaxaca Gráfico. 1962–1969.

Oaxaca Nuevo. 1937–1940.

Periódico Oficial de Morelos. Cuernavaca, Morelos. 1965.

Polígrafo. Cuautla, Morelos. 1966–1979.

El Popular. Mexico City. 1949.

El Porvenir. Monterrey, Nuevo León. 1939.

La Prensa. Mexico City. 1931–1941.

La Prensa. San Antonio, Texas. 1932.

Presente. Cuernavaca, Morelos. 1959–1962.

El Pueblo. Mexico City. 1917.

El Renovador. Cuernavaca. 1975.

Seattle Times. 2003.

La Tribuna. Mexico City. 1913.

Ultimas Noticias. Mexico City. 1960.

Unión de Morelos. Cuernavaca, Morelos. 2001.

El Universal. Mexico City. 1917–1961.

El Universal Gráfico. Mexico City. 1934–1938.

Univision.com. 2003.

Uno Más Uno. Mexico City. 1994.

La Voz de Mexico. 1958.

La Voz de Oaxaca. 1945.

Wall Street Journal. 1994.

El Zancudo. Oaxaca. 1923.

NEWPAPER CLIPPINGS

Mexico City. Hemeroteca Nacional. Fondo Silvino González (FSG).

BOOKS, ARTICLES, AND INTERNET SOURCES

Ades, Dawn. *Art in Latin America: The Modern Era, 1820–1980.* New Haven: Yale University Press, 1989.

Aguirre Cinta, Rafael. *Lecciones de historia general de México desde los tiempos primitivos hasta nuestros días*. Mexico City: Franco-Americana, 1926.

————. *Lecciones de historia general de México desde los tiempos primitivos hasta nuestros días*. Mexico City: Franco-Americana, 1930?.

Agustín, José. *Tragicomedia mexicana*. Vol. 2, *La vida en México de 1970 a 1988*. Mexico City: Planeta, 1992.

Alberto Gironella: Exposición antológica. Mexico City: Museo Rufino Tamayo, 1984.

"Alberto Gironella: 'Lo mio es el loco intento de pintar el tiempo' (conversación con José de la Colina)." In *Alberto Gironella: Exposición antológica*. Mexico City: Museo Rufino Tamayo, 1984.

Almazán, Juan Andreu. "Memorias del General Juan Andreu Almazán." Serialized in *El Universal*, 1957–1958. Bound photocopy at the Colegio de México.

Alonso, Ana María. "The Effects of Truth: Re-Presentations of the Past and the Imagining of Community." *Journal of Historical Sociology* 1 (1988): 33–57.

Alpert, Hollis. Review of *Viva Zapata! Saturday Review of Literature*, February 9, 1952, 25–26.

Amezcua, Jenaro. *Defensa y confesión*. Mexico City: URAS, 1944.

Anderson, Benedict. *Imagined Communities: Reflections on the Origin and Spread of Nationalism*. Rev. ed. London and New York: Verso, 1991.

Arbena, Joseph L. "Sport, Development, and Mexican Nationalism, 1920–1970." *Journal of Sport History* 18 (1991): 350–364.

Ard, Michael J. *An Eternal Struggle: How the National Action Party Transformed Mexican Politics*. Westport, Conn.: Praeger, 2003.

Arías Gómez, María Eugenia. "Algunos cuadernos históricos sobre Emiliano Zapata y el Zapatismo." In *Emiliano Zapata y el movimiento zapatista*, 181–280. Mexico City: Secretaría de Educación Pública and the Instituto Nacional de Antropología e Historia, 1980.

Arnal, Ariel. "Construyendo simbolos: Fotografía política en México, 1865–1911." *Estudios Interdisciplinarios de América Latina y el Caribe* 9 (1998).

Aroche Parra, Miguel. *El Che, Jenaro y las guerrillas: Estrategia y táctica de la revolución en México*. Mexico City: Federación Editorial Mexicana, 1974.

Astorga Lira, Enrique, and Clarisa Hardy Raskovan. *Organización, lucha y dependencia económica: La Unión de Ejidos Emiliano Zapata*. Mexico City: Nueva Imagen, 1978.

Avila, Alex. "Does Jesse Jackson Mean Business?" *Hispanic*, November 1997.

Ayaquica, Fortino. "Continuación de la Lucha." In *Ofrenda a la memoria de Emiliano Zapata*, [edited by Gildardo Magaña], 45–46. Mexico City?: n.p., 1938.

Azaola Garrido, Elena. "Tepalcingo: La dependencia política de un municipio de Morelos." In *Los campesinos de la tierra de Zapata*, Vol. 3, *Política y conflicto*, Elena Azaola Garrido and Esteban Krotz, eds. 13–186. Mexico City: Secretaría de Educación Pública and Instituto Nacional de Antropología e Historia, 1976.

Azuela de la Cueva, Alicia. *Arte y poder*. Mexico City: Fondo de Cultura Económica, 2005.

Baldovinos de la Peña, Gabriel. *Emigdio Marmolejo León: Vigencia de un liderazgo agrario morelense*. Mexico City: Centro de Estudios Históricos del Agrarismo en México and Confederación Nacional Campesina, 1991.

Bantjes, Adrian A. *As if Jesus Walked on Earth: Cardenismo, Sonora, and the Mexican Revolution*. Wilmington, Del.: Scholarly Resources, 1998.

———. "Burning Saints, Molding Minds: Iconoclasm, Civic Ritual, and the Failed Cultural Revolution." In *Rituals of Rule, Rituals of Resistance: Public Celebrations and Popular Culture in Mexico*, edited by William H. Beezley, Cheryl E. Martin, and William E. French, 261–284. Wilmington, Del.: Scholarly Resources, 1994.

Barreto Mark, Carlos, ed. *Los corridos de Marciano Silva*. Cuernavaca: Gobierno del Estado de Morelos, 1983.

Bartra, Armando. *Los herederos de Zapata: Movimientos campesinos posrevolucionarios en México*. Mexico City: Ediciones Era, 1985.

Bartra, Armando, and Angel Mora. *México: Historia de un pueblo*. Vol. 18, *Tierra y libertad*. Mexico City: SEP and Nueva Imagen, 1982.

Bartra, Roger. *The Cage of Melancholy: Identity and Metamorphosis in the Mexican Character*, translated by Christopher J. Hall. New Brunswick, N.J.: Rutgers University Press, 1992.

Beals, Carleton. Letter to the editor. *Saturday Review of Literature*, May 24, 1952, 25–28.

———. *Mexican Maze*. New York: Lippincott, 1931.

Beane, Wendell C., and William G. Doty, eds. *Myths, Rites, Symbols: A Mircea Eliade Reader*. New York: Harper and Row, 1975.

Becker, Marjorie. *Setting the Virgin on Fire: Lázaro Cárdenas, Michoacán Peasants, and the Redemption of the Mexican Revolution*. Berkeley and Los Angeles: University of California Press, 1995.

Beezley, William H., Cheryl English Martin, and William E. French, eds. *Rituals of Rule, Rituals of Resistance: Public Celebrations and Popular Culture in Mexico*. Wilmington, Del.: SR Books, 1994.

Benjamin, Thomas. *La Revolución: Mexico's Great Revolution as Memory, Myth, and History*. Austin: University of Texas Press, 2000.

———. "The Leviathan on the Zócalo: Recent Historiography of the Postrevolutionary Mexican State." *Latin American Historical Review* 20 (1985): 195–217.

Biskind, Peter. "Ripping off Zapata: Revolution Hollywood Style." *Cineaste* 7, no. 2 (1976): 11–15.

Bissio, Beatriz. "'Bienvenidos a la tierra de Zapata.'" *Cuadernos del tercer mundo* (1977): 102–112.

Blackburn, Simon. *The Oxford Dictionary of Philosophy*. New York: Oxford University Press, 1996.

Blanco, Mercedes. *Empleo público en la administración central mexicana: Evoluciones y tendencia (1920–1988)*. Mexico City: CIESAS, 1995.

Blanquel, Eduardo. *Mi libro de sexto año: historia y civismo*. Mexico City: Comisión Nacional de los Libros de Texto Gratuitos, 1966.

Bonilla, José M. *Historia Nacional.* Mexico City: Herrero Hermanos, 1939.

Boyd, Lola Elizabeth. *Emiliano Zapata en las letras y el folklore mexicano.* Madrid: José Porrua Turanzas, 1979.

Brading, David. *The First America: The Spanish Monarchy, Creole Patriots, and the Liberal State, 1492–1867.* New York: Cambridge University Press, 1991.

———. *Mexican Phoenix: Our Lady of Guadalupe: Image and Tradition Across Five Centuries.* New York: Cambridge University Press, 2001.

———. *Mito y profecía en la historia de México,* translated by Tomás Segovia. Mexico: Vuelta, 1988.

Britton, John A. *Educación y radicalismo en Mexico.* Vol. 1, *Los años de Bassols (1931–1934).* Mexico City: Sepsetentas, 1976.

Brunk, Samuel. *Emiliano Zapata: Revolution and Betrayal in Mexico.* Albuquerque: University of New Mexico Press, 1995.

———. "'The Sad Situation of Civilians and Soldiers': The Banditry of Zapatismo in the Mexican Revolution." *American Historical Review* 101 (1996): 331–353.

———. "Zapata and the City Boys: In Search of a Piece of the Revolution." *Hispanic American Historical Review* 73 (1993): 33–65.

Brunk, Samuel, and Ben Fallaw, eds. *Heroes and Hero Cults in Latin America.* Austin: University of Texas Press, 2006.

Bruhn, Kathleen. "Antonio Gramsci and the Palabra Verdadera: The Political Discourse of Mexico's Guerrilla Forces." *Journal of Interamerican Studies and World Affairs* 41 (1999): 29–55.

Burkert, Walter. *Creation of the Sacred: Tracks of Biology in Early Religions.* Cambridge, Mass.: Harvard University Press, 1996.

Calderón Ramírez, Salvador. "'La Bachillera' Madrina de Zapata." *Todo,* June 20, 1940.

Cano, Gabriela. "Galindo, Hermila." In *Encyclopedia of Mexico: History, Society and Culture,* edited by Michael S. Werner. Chicago: Fitzroy Dearborn, 1997.

Camp, Roderic Ai. *Intellectuals and the State in Twentieth-Century Mexico.* Austin: University of Texas Press, 1985.

———. *Mexican Political Biographies, 1935–1993.* 3rd ed. Austin: University of Texas Press, 1995.

Campaña política del C. Alvaro Obregón. Mexico City: n.p., 1923.

Campbell, Bruce. *Mexican Murals in Times of Crisis.* Tucson: University of Arizona Press, 2003.

Cárabes Pedroza, Jesús. *Mi libro de tercer año: historia y civismo.* Mexico City: Comisión Nacional de los Libros de Texto Gratuitos, 1966.

Cardoza y Aragón, Luis. "Ensayo Crítico." In *Diego Rivera: Los murales en la Secretaría de Educación Pública,* 9–18. Mexico City: Secretaría de Educación Pública, 1986.

Carr, Barry. *Marxism and Communism in Twentieth Century Mexico.* Lincoln: University of Nebraska Press, 1992.

Carranza, Francisco Javier. *Fiestas escolares: Enciclopedia lírico-literaria.* Mexico City: Editorial Avante, 1957.

Casasola, Gustavo. *Hechos y Hombres de México: Emiliano Zapata*. Mexico City: Casasola, 1994.

Cazés, Daniel. *Crónica 1968*. Mexico City: Plaza y Valdés, 1993.

———, ed. *Memorial del 68: Relato a muchas voces*. Mexico City: La Jornada, 1993.

Centro de Estudios Históricos del Agrarismo en México. *El ejército campesino del sur (ideología, organización y programa)*. Mexico City: CEHAM, 1982.

Cevallos, Diego. "Revolutionary Zapata Reinvented." IPS-InterPress Service. http://www.ipsnews.net/interna.asp?idnews=23585, May 8, 2004 (accessed February 27, 2005).

———. "Zapata, the Revolutionary, as the Subject of Fantasy." IPS-Inter Press Service, May 6, 2004 (accessed September 20, 2004).

Chinameca: 10 de Abril de 1979. Cuernavaca: Cuadernos Zapatistas, 1979.

Cisneros, Sandra. "Eyes of Zapata." In *Women Hollering Creek and Other Stories*. New York: Random House, 1991.

Clendinnen, Inga. *Aztecs: An Interpretation*. New York: Cambridge University Press, 1991.

Cole, Lester. *Hollywood Red: The Autobiography of Lester Cole*. Palo Alto, Calif.: Ramparts, 1981.

Collier, George A. "Zapatismo Resurgent: Land and Autonomy in Chiapas." In *NACLA: Report on the Americas* 33 (2000): 20–25.

Comer, Krista. *Landscapes of the New West: Gender and Geography in Contemporary Women's Writing*. Chapel Hill: University of North Carolina Press, 1999.

Comisión Nacional para el Desarrollo de los Pueblos Indígenas. Press release. http://www.cdi.gob.mx/index.php?id_seccion=1899, Mexico City, October 12, 2006 (accessed April 11, 2007).

Córdova, Arnaldo. "La mitología de la Revolución Mexicana." In *Mitos mexicanos*, edited by Enrique Florescano, 21–25. Mexico City: Nuevo Siglo, 1995.

Corrigan, Philip, and Derek Sayer. *The Great Arch: English State Formation as Cultural Revolution*. New York: Blackwell, 1985.

Craven, David. *Diego Rivera as Epic Modernist*. New York: G. K. Hall, 1997.

Cuadernos del Senado: XLIV legislatura del Congreso de la Unión. Mexico City: n.p., 1958.

Cuadros Caldas, Julio. *México-Soviet*. Puebla: Santiago Loyo, 1926.

Curiel, Barbara Brinson. "The General's Pants: A Chicana Feminist (Re)vision of the Mexican Revolution in Sandra Cisneros's 'Eyes of Zapata.'" *Western American Literature* 35 (2001): 403–427.

Dawson, Alexander S. *Indian and Nation in Revolutionary Mexico*. Tucson: University of Arizona Press, 2004.

de la Peña, Guillermo. *Herederos de promesas: Agricultura, política y ritual en los Altos de Morelos*. Mexico City: Casa Chata, 1980.

de Leon, Imelda, ed. *Calendario de Fiestas Populares*. Mexico City: SEP, 1988.

de Mora, Juan Miguel. *Las guerrillas en México y Jenaro Vázquez Rojas (su personalidad, su vida y su muerte)*. Mexico City: Editora Latino Americana, 1972.

———. *Lucio Cabañas: Su vida y su muerte*. Mexico City: Editores Asociados, 1974.

de Rojo, Alba C., Rafael López Castro, and José Luis Martínez. *Zapata: Iconografía*. Mexico City: Fondo de Cultura Económica, 1979.

Díaz Soto Ugalde, Salvador. "Biografía del Lic. Antonio Díaz Soto y Gama." Unpublished manuscript in hands of the author.

Díaz Soto y Gama, Antonio. *La revolución agraria del sur y Emiliano Zapata, su caudillo*. Mexico City: Imprenta Policromia, 1960.

Diccionario histórico y biográfico de la revolución mexicana. 8 vols. Mexico City: Instituto Nacional de Estudios Históricos de la Revolución Mexicana, 1990–1994.

Domenech, J. Figueroa. *Veinte meses de anarquía*. Mexico City: n.p., 1913.

Dornbierer, Manú. *El prinosaurio: La bestia política mexicana*. Mexico City: Grijalbo, 1994.

Dr. Atl [Gerardo Murillo]. *Las artes populares en México*. Mexico City: Libreria México, 1921).

Dromundo, Baltasar. *Emiliano Zapata: Biografía*. Mexico City: Imprenta Mundial, 1934.

———. *Francisco Villa y la "Adelita"*. Victoria de Durango, Durango, 1936.

———. *Oración a Emiliano Zapata*. Mexico: Editorial Ruta, 1952.

Duara, Prasenjit. *Rescuing History from the Nation: Questioning Narratives of Modern China*. Chicago: University of Chicago Press, 1995.

Duncan, Robert H. "Embracing a Suitable Past: Independence Celebrations under Mexico's Second Empire." *Journal of Latin American Studies* 30 (1998): 249–277.

Dunne, John Gregory. *Delano: The Story of the California Grape Strike*. New York: Farrar, Straus and Giroux, 1967.

Durkheim, Emile. *The Elementary Forms of the Religious Life*, translated by Joseph Ward Swain. New York: Free Press, 1965.

Eade, John, and Michael J. Sallnow. Introduction. In *Contesting the Sacred: The Anthropology of Christian Pilgrimage*. London: Routledge, 1991.

Eder, Rita. *Gironella*. Mexico City: Universidad Nacional Autónoma de México, 1981.

Emiliano Zapata en la provincia mexicana. Cuernavaca: Cuadernos Zapatistas, 1979.

"Episodios Oaxaqueños: ¡David Rodríguez Zapatista!" In *Oaxaca en México*, May 1965.

Espejel, Laura. "El movimiento campesino en el oriente del estado de Mexico: El caso de Juchitepec." *Cuicuilco* 2 (1981): 33–37.

Espejel, Laura, Alicia Olivera, and Salvador Rueda, eds. *Emiliano Zapata: Antología*. Mexico City: Instituto Nacional de Estudios Históricos de la Revolución Mexicana, 1988.

Esteve Díaz, Hugo. *Las armas de la utopía: La* tercera ola *de los movimientos guerrilleros en México*. Mexico City: Instituto de Proposiciones Estratégicas, 1996.

EZLN: *Documentos y comunicados*. 2 vols. Mexico City: Era, 1994, 1995.

Fabela, Isidro, and Josefina E. Fabela, eds. *Documentos históricos de la revolución mexicana*. Vol. 21, *Emiliano Zapata, el Plan de Ayala, y su política agraria*. Mexico City: Editorial Jus, 1970.

Fagan, Brian M. *World Prehistory: A Brief Introduction*. New York: Longman, 1999.

Flores Lúa, Graciela, Luisa Paré, and Sergio Sarmiento Silva. *Las voces del campo: Movimiento campesino y política agraria, 1976–1984.* Mexico City: Siglo Veintiuno, 1988.

Flores Magón, Ricardo. *La revolución mexicana.* 3rd ed. Mexico City: Editores Mexicanos Unidos, 1985.

Florescano, Enrique. *Memory, Myth, and Time in Mexico: From the Aztecs to Independence,* translated by Albert G. Bork. Austin: University of Texas Press, 1994.

———. "Quetzalcóatl: Un mito hecho de mitos." In *Mitos mexicanos.* Mexico City: Nuevo Siglo, 1995.

Folgarait, Leonard. *Mural Painting and Social Revolution in Mexico, 1920–1940.* New York: Cambridge University Press, 1998.

Franco, Jean. *Plotting Women: Gender and Representation in Mexico.* New York: Columbia University Press, 1989.

Friedlander, Judith. *Being Indian in Hueyapan: A Study of Forced Identity in Contemporary Mexico.* New York: St. Martin's Press, 1975.

Galindo, Hermila. *Un presidenciable.* Mexico City: Talleres Gráficos de la Imprenta Nacional, 1919.

García Jiménez, Plutarco. "El movimiento jaramillista: Una experiencia de lucha campesina y popular del periodo post-revolucionario en México." In *Morelos: Cinco siglos de historia regional,* edited by Horacio Crespo, 301–310. Mexico City: Centro de Estudios Históricos del Agrarismo en México, 1984.

Geertz, Clifford. "Centers, Kings, and Charisma: Reflections on the Symbolics of Power." In *Rites of Power: Symbolism, Ritual, and Politics Since the Middle Ages,* edited by Sean Wilentz, 13–38. Philadelphia: University of Pennsylvania Press, 1985.

———. *The Interpretation of Cultures.* New York: Basic Books, 1973.

Gilbert, Dennis. "Emiliano Zapata: Textbook Hero." *Mexican Studies/Estudios Mexicanos* 19 (2003): 127–159.

Gildardo Magaña: Breves datos biográficos. N.p.: Secretaría General del Centro Nacional Orientador Pro-Magaña, 1939.

Gill, Mario. "Zapata: Su pueblo y sus hijos." *Historia Mexicana* 2 (1952): 294–312.

Gilly, Adolfo, ed. *Cartas a Cuauhtémoc Cárdenas.* Mexico City: Ediciones Era, 1989.

Goldman, Shifra M. "How, Why, Where, and When It All Happened: Chicano Murals of California." In *Signs from the Heart: California Chicano Murals,* edited by Eva Sperling Cockcroft and Holly Barnet-Sánchez, 23–53. Venice, Calif.: Social and Public Resource Center, 1990.

Gómezjara, Francisco A. *Bonapartismo y lucha campesina en la costa grande de Guerrero.* Mexico City: Posada, 1979.

———. *El movimiento campesino en México.* Mexico City: Editorial Campesina, 1970.

Gonzales, Rodolfo. *I Am Joaquín/Yo Soy Joaquín.* New York: Bantam, 1972.

[González, Pablo]. *Recopilación de documentos y de algunas publicaciones de importancia.* Monterrey: n.p., 1923.

González, Pablo, Jr. *El centinela fiel del constitucionalismo.* Saltillo: Textos de Cultura Historiográfica, 1971.

González Navarro, Moisés. *La Confederación Nacional Campesino (un grupo de presión en la reforma agraria mexicana)*. Mexico City: B. Costa-Amic, 1968.

González Ramírez, Manuel. *Planes políticos y otros documentos*. Mexico City: Fondo de Cultura Económica, 1954.

González y González, Luis. *Historia de la revolución mexicana, 1934-1940*. Vol. 14, *Los artífices del cardenismo*. Mexico City: El Colegio de Mexico, 1979.

Gossen, Gary. *Telling Maya Tales: Tzotzil Identities in Modern Mexico*. New York: Routledge, 1999.

Gould, Jeffrey L. *To Lead as Equals: Rural Protest and Political Consciousness in Chinandega, Nicaragua, 1912–1979*. Chapel Hill: University of North Carolina Press, 1990.

Gramsci, Antonio. *Selections from the Prison Notebooks of Antonio Gramsci*. Edited and translated by Quintin Hoare and Geoffrey Nowell Smith. New York: International Publishers, 1971.

Greaves, Cecilia. "La Secretaría de Educación Pública y la lectura, 1960–1985." In *Historia de la lectura en México*, 338–372. Mexico City: El Colegio de Mexico, 1988.

Griswold del Castillo, Richard, and Richard A. García. *César Chávez: A Triumph of Spirit*. Norman: University of Oklahoma Press, 1995.

Gruening, Ernest. *Mexico and Its Heritage*. London: Stanley Paul, 1928.

Gruzinski, Serge. *Man-Gods in the Mexican Highlands: Indian Power and Colonial Society, 1520–1800*, translated by Eileen Corrigan. Stanford, Calif.: Stanford University Press, 1989.

Guevara, Ernesto "Che." *Man and Socialism in Cuba*, translated by Margarita Zimmerman. Havana: Book Institute, 1967.

Gutiérrez, David G. "Migration, Emergent Ethnicity, and the 'Third Space': The Shifting Politics of Nationalism in Greater Mexico." *Journal of American History* 86 (1999): 481–517.

Gutiérrez y González, Luis. "Hoy visita a la viuda de Zapata!" *Hoy*, March 28, 1953.

H. de Giménez, Catalina. *Así cantaban la revolución*. Mexico City: Grijalbo, 1990.

Hall, Linda B. "Alvaro Obregón and the Politics of Mexican Land Reform." *Hispanic American Historical Review* 60 (1980): 213–238.

———. *Alvaro Obregón: Power and Revolution in Mexico*. College Station: Texas A&M University Press, 1981.

Hamilton, Nora. *The Limits of State Autonomy: Post-Revolutionary Mexico*. Princeton, N.J.: Princeton University Press, 1982.

Hansis, Randall George. "Alvaro Obregón, the Mexican Revolution and the Politics of Consolidation, 1920–1924." Ph.D. diss., University of New Mexico, 1971.

Harvey, Neil. *The Chiapas Rebellion: The Struggle for Land and Democracy*. Durham, N.C.: Duke University Press, 1998.

———. "Jaramillo, Rubén." In *Encyclopedia of Mexico: History, Society and Culture*, edited by Michael S. Werner, 715–716. Chicago: Fitzroy Dearborn, 1997.

———. "Peasant Strategies and Corporatism in Chiapas." In *Popular Movements and Political Change in Mexico*, edited by Joe Foweraker and Ann Craig, 183–198. Boulder, Colo.: Lynn Rienner Publishers, 1990.

Hayes, Joy Elizabeth. *Radio Nation: Communication, Popular Culture, and Nationalism in Mexico, 1920–1950*. Tucson: University of Arizona Press, 2000.

Hecht, John. "Filmmaker Has Revolutionary Idea," *The Hollywood Reporter*. October 14, 2003.

Hernández Chávez, Alicia. *Anenecuilco: Memoria y vida de un pueblo*. Mexico City: El Colegio de México, 1991.

———. *Historia de la Revolución Mexicana, periódo 1934–1940*. Vol. 16, *La mecánica cardenista*. Mexico City: El Colegio de México, 1979.

Híjar, Alberto. "Los Zapatas de Diego Rivera." In *Los Zapatas de Diego Rivera*, 21–32. Mexico City: Consejo Nacional para la Cultura y las Artes, 1989.

Hodges, Donald C. *Mexican Anarchism After the Revolution*. Austin: University of Texas Press, 1995.

———. "The Plan of Cerro Prieto: The Peasant-Worker Movement in Morelos (1942-1962)." *Canadian Journal of Latin American and Caribbean Studies* 16 (1991): 123–143.

Hodges, Donald C., and Ross Handy. *Mexico Under Siege: Popular Resistance to Presidential Despotism*. New York: Zed Books, 2002.

Homenaje a Emiliano Zapata. Cuernavaca: Cuadernos Zapatistas, 1979.

Homenaje de la Secretaría de Agricultura y Fomento a la Memoria del Caudillo Agrarista Emiliano Zapata en el aniversario de su muerte. Mexico City: Talleres Gráficos de la Nación, 1934.

Homenaje del pueblo a Emiliano Zapata Salazar. Cuernavaca: Cuadernos Zapatistas, 1979.

Hutton, John. "'If I am to Die Tomorrow': Roots and Meanings of Orozco's *Zapata Entering a Peasant's Hut*." *Museum Studies* 11 (1984): 38–51.

Ignacio Asúnsolo. Mexico City: Museo Nacional de Arte, 1985.

Ingham, John M. *Mary, Michael, and Lucifer: Folk Catholicism in Central Mexico*. Austin: University of Texas Press, 1986.

Isaac, Alberto. *Conversaciones con Gabriel Figueroa*. Guadalajara: Universidad de Guadalajara, 1993.

Jaramillo, Rubén M. *Autobiografía*. Mexico City: Editorial Nuestro Tiempo, 1967.

Jiménez, Luz. *Life and Death in Milpa Alta*, translated and edited by Fernando Horcasitas. Norman: University of Oklahoma Press, 1972.

Joseph, Gilbert M., and Daniel Nugent, ed. *Everyday Forms of State Formation: Revolution and the Negotiation of Rule in Modern Mexico*. Durham, N.C.: Duke University Press, 1994.

Joseph, Gilbert M., Anne Rubenstein, and Eric Zolov, eds. *Fragments of a Golden Age: The Politics of Culture in Mexico Since 1940*. Durham, N.C.: Duke University Press, 2001.

Karttunen, Frances. "The Linguistic Career of Doña Luz Jiménez." *Estudios de Cultura Náhuatl* 30 (1999): 267–274.

Katz, Friedrich. "Introduction: Rural Revolts in Mexico." In *Riot, Rebellion, and Revo-

lution: Rural Social Conflict in Mexico, 3–17. Princeton, N.J.: Princeton University Press, 1988.

Katz, Jesse. "The Curse of Zapata." *Los Angeles Magazine*, December 2002, 102–105, 176–179.

Kazan, Elia. Letter to the editor. *Saturday Review of Literature*, April 5, 1952, 22–23.

Kazan, Elia. *Elia Kazan: A Life*. New York: Knopf, 1988.

——. *Kazan on Kazan*. Interview by Michel Ciment. New York: Viking, 1974.

——. *Kazan: The Master Director Discusses His Films*. Interview by Jeff Young. New York: Newmarket Press, 1999.

Keller, Gary D. "Zapata Rose in 1992." In *Zapata Rose in 1992 and Other Tales*. Tempe, Ariz.: Maize Press, 1992.

Kertzer, David I. *Ritual, Politics, and Power*. New Haven: Yale University Press, 1988.

Kilian, Pamela. *Barbara Bush: Matriarch of a Dynasty*. New York: St. Martin's Press, 2003.

King, Rosa E. *Tempest over Mexico: A Personal Chronicle*. Boston: Little, Brown, 1935; reprint: New York: Arno Press, 1970.

Knight, Alan. "Cardenismo: Juggernaut or Jalopy." *Journal of Latin American Studies* 26 (1994): 73–107.

——. "Historical Continuities in Social Movements." In *Popular Movements and Political Change in Mexico*, edited by Joe Foweraker and Ann Craig, 78–102. Boulder, Colo.: Lynn Rienner, 1990.

——. *The Mexican Revolution*. 2 vols. Cambridge: Cambridge University Press, 1986.

——. "Mexico, c. 1930-1946." In *The Cambridge History of Latin America*, edited by Leslie Bethell, 3–82. New York: Cambridge University Press, 1990.

——. "Popular Culture and the Revolutionary State in Mexico, 1910–1940." *Hispanic American Historical Review* 74 (1994): 393–444.

——. "Racism, Revolution, and *Indigenismo*: Mexico, 1910–1940." In *The Idea of Race in Latin America, 1870–1940*, edited by Richard Graham, 71–113. Austin: University of Texas Press, 1990.

——. "Revolutionary Project, Recalcitrant People: Mexico, 1910–1940." In *The Revolutionary Process in Mexico: Essays on Political and Social Change, 1880–1940*, edited by Jaime Rodríguez O., 227–264. Los Angeles: UCLA Latin American Center Publications, University of California, Los Angeles, 1990.

——. "Salinas and Social Liberalism in Historical Context." In *Dismantling the Mexican State?* edited by Rob Aitken, Nikki Craske, Gareth A. Jones, and David E. Stansfield, 1–23. New York: St. Martin's Press, 1996.

——. "Weapons and Arches in the Mexican Revolutionary Landscape." In *Everyday Forms of State Formation: Revolution and the Negotiation of Rule in Modern Mexico*, edited by Gilbert M. Joseph and Daniel Nugent, 24–66. Durham, N.C.: Duke University Press, 1994.

Krauze, Enrique. *El amor a la tierra: Emiliano Zapata*. Biografía del poder, no. 3. Mexico City: Fondo de Cultura Económica, 1987.

Kuper, Adam. *The Chosen Primate: Human Nature and Cultural Diversity*. Cambridge, Mass.: Harvard University Press, 1994.

Leal, Luis. "Beyond Myths and Borders in Mexican and North American Literature." In *Common Border, Uncommon Paths: Race, Culture, and National Identity in U.S.-Mexican Relations*, edited by Jaime E. Rodriguez O., 143–165. Wilmington, Del.: SR Books, 1997.

León-Portilla, Miguel. *Los manifiestos en nahuatl de Emiliano Zapata*. Mexico City: Universidad Nacional Autónoma de México, Instituto de Investigaciónes Históricas, 1978.

———, ed. *México: Su evolución cultural*. Vol. 2. Mexico City: SEP and Editorial Porrua, 1981.

Lerner, Victoria. *Historia de la revolución mexicana*. Vol. 17, *La educación socialista*. Mexico City: Colegio de México, 1979.

Lewis, Oscar. *Life in a Mexican Village: Tepoztlán Restudied*. Urbana: University of Illinois Press, 1951.

———. *Pedro Martínez: A Mexican Peasant and His Family*. New York: Vintage Books, 1964.

———. *Tepoztlán: Village in Mexico*. New York: Holt, Rinehart and Winston, 1960.

Lieuwen, Edwin. *Mexican Militarism: The Political Rise and Fall of the Revolutionary Army, 1910–1940*. Albuquerque: University of New Mexico Press, 1968.

Limón, José Eduardo. *American Encounters: Greater Mexico, the United States, and the Erotics of Culture*. Boston: Beacon Press, 1998.

List Arzubide, Armando. "El asesinato del Gral. Emiliano Zapata." In *Teatro histórico escolar*. Mexico City?: n.p., 1938.

List Arzubide, Germán. *Emiliano Zapata: exaltación*. Jalapa: Talleres Gráficos del Gobierno de Veracruz, 1927.

Lomnitz-Adler, Claudio. *Deep Mexico, Silent Mexico: An Anthropology of Nationalism*. Minneapolis: University of Minnesota Press, 2001.

———. *Exits from the Labyrinth: Culture and Ideology in the Mexican National Space*. Berkeley and Los Angeles: University of California Press, 1992.

———. "Ritual, Rumor and Corruption in the Constitution of Polity in Modern Mexico." *Journal of Latin American Anthropology* 1 (1995): 20–47.

López, Jaime. *10 años de guerrillas en México, 1964–1974*. Mexico City: Posada, 1974.

López González, Valentín. *La muerte del General Emiliano Zapata*. Cuernavaca: Comité Coordinador para la Celebración del Primer Centenario del Natalicio del General Emiliano Zapata Salazar, 1979.

López Ituarte, Alfonso [Héctor Ribot]. *El Atila del sur*. Mexico City: Imprenta 1a de Humboldt, [1913].

López Mateos, Adolfo. *José María Morelos, Ponciano Arriaga y Emiliano Zapata, en la reforma agraria de México*. Mexico City: Editorial la Justicia, 1958.

López Monjardín, Adriana, and Francisco Javier Pineda. "La disputa simbólica por la herencia de Zapata." In *Globalización, deterioro ambiental y reorganización social en el campo*, edited by Hubert Carton de Grammont, 236–251. Mexico City: Juan Pablos and Universidad Nacional Autónoma de México, 1995.

López y Fuentes, Gregorio. *Tierra*. Mexico City: Grijalbo, 1986.

Lorey, David. "Almazán, Juan Andreu." In *Encyclopedia of Mexico: History, Society and Culture*, edited by Michael S. Werner, 40–42. Chicago: Fitzroy Dearborn, 1997.

———. "Postrevolutionary Contexts for Independence Day: The 'Problem' of Order and the Invention of Revolution Day." In *¡Viva México! ¡Viva La Independencia! Celebrations of September 16*, edited by William H. Beezley and David E. Lorey, 233–248. Wilmington, Del.: Scholarly Resources, 2000.

Lucas, Jeffrey Kent. "Twentieth Century Mexico through the Eyes of Antonio Díaz Soto y Gama." Ph.D. diss., University of Texas, El Paso, 2006.

Lumen, Enrique. *Almazán: Vida de un caudillo y metabolismo de una revolución*. Mexico City: Editorial Claridad, 1940.

Luna Domínguez, Lucino, and Efraín Escarpulli Limón. *Anenecuilcayotl: Anenecuilco desconocido*. Mexico City: Unidad Regional Morelos de la Dirección General de Culturas Populares, 1997.

Macias, Anna. *Against All Odds: The Feminist Movement in Mexico to 1940*. Westport, Conn.: Greenwood Press, 1982.

Macín, Raul. *Rubén Jaramillo, profeta olvidado*. Mexico City: Diogenes, 1984.

Magaña, Gildardo [and Carlos Pérez Guerrero]. *Emiliano Zapata y el agrarismo en México*. 5 vols. Mexico City: Editorial Ruta, 1951–1952.

Magaña, Gildardo. "Perfil del Reformador." In *Ofrenda a la memoria de Emiliano Zapata*. Mexico City?: n.p., 1938.

Magaña Cerda, Octavio. *Yo acuso a los responsables: El pueblo que nos juzgue*. Mexico City: B. Costa-Amic, 1961.

Magdaleno, Mauricio. *Teatro revolucionario mexicano*. Madrid: Editorial Cenit, 1933.

Mallon, Florencia. *Peasant and Nation: The Making of Postcolonial Mexico and Peru*. Berkeley and Los Angeles: University of California Press, 1995.

La marcha del color de la tierra: Comunicados, cartas y mensajes del Ejército Zapatista de Liberación Nacional del 2 de diciembre del 2000 al 2 de abril del 2001. Mexico: Rizoma, 2001.

Marcos, Subcomandante. "Comunicado del Subcomandante Insurgente Marcos." http://ezln.org.mx/documentos/1999/19990900a.es.htm, August/September 1999 (accessed March 27, 2004).

Marnham, Patrick. *Dreaming with His Eyes Open: A Life of Diego Rivera*. New York: Knopf, 1999.

Martin, JoAnn. *Contesting Authenticity: Battles Over the Representation of History in Morelos, Mexico*. South Bend, Ind.: Helen Kellog Institute for International Studies, University of Notre Dame, 1993.

———. "Criminal Instabilities: Narrative Interruptions and the Politics of Criminality." In *Crime's Power: Anthropologists and the Ethnography of Crime*, edited by Philip C. Parnell and Stephanie C. Kane, 173–195. New York: Palgrave Macmillan, 2003.

————. "When the People Were Strong and United: Stories of the Past and the Transformation of Politics in a Mexican Community." In *The Paths to Domination, Resistance, and Terror*, edited by Carolyn Nordstrom and JoAnn Martin, 177–189. Berkeley and Los Angeles: University of California Press, 1992.

Martínez Vásquez, Víctor Raúl. *Movimiento popular y política en Oaxaca (1968–1986)*. Mexico City: Consejo Nacional Para la Cultura y las Artes, 1990.

————. *La revolución en Oaxaca, 1900–1930*. Oaxaca: Instituto de Administración Pública de Oaxaca, 1985.

Masacchio, Humberto. *Diccionario enciclopédico de México*. 4 vols. Mexico City: A. León, 1989.

Matthiessen, Peter. *Sal Si Puedes: Cesar Chavez and the New American Revolution*. New York: Random House, 1969.

Matute, Alvaro. *Historia de la revolución mexicana, 1917–1924*. Vol. 8, *La carrera del caudillo*. Mexico City: El Colegio de México, 1980.

Mazlish, Bruce. *The Leader, the Led, and the Psyche: Essays in Psychohistory*. Hanover, N.H., and London: Wesleyan University Press, 1990.

McLuhan, Marshall. *Understanding Media: The Extensions of Man*. New York: McGraw-Hill, 1964.

[Melgar, Rafael E.]. *Calendario nacionalista y enciclopedia nacional popular*. Mexico City: Talleres Gráficos de la Nación, 1935.

Melgarejo, Antonio D. *Los crímenes del zapatismo: (apuntes de un guerrillero)*. 2nd ed. Mexico City: Editora y Distribuidora Nacional de Publicaciones, 1979.

Melville, Roberto. *Crecimiento y rebelión: El desarrollo económico de las haciendas azucareras en Morelos (1880–1910)*. Mexico City: Editorial Nueva Imagen, 1979.

Mendoza, Vicente T. *El corrido mexicano*. Mexico City: Fondo de Cultura Económica, 1954.

Michaels, Albert L. *The Mexican Election of 1940*. Buffalo: State University of New York at Buffalo, 1971.

Middlebrook, Kevin J. *The Paradox of Revolution: Labor, the State, and Authoritarianism in Mexico*. Baltimore: Johns Hopkins University Press, 1995.

Migdal, Joel S. *State in Society: Studying How States and Societies Transform and Constitute One Another*. New York: Cambridge University Press, 2001.

Miller, Mary, and Karl Taube. *An Illustrated Dictionary of the Gods and Symbols of Ancient Mexico and the Maya*. London: Thames and Hudson, 1993.

Miller, Michael Nelson. *Red, White, and Green: The Maturing of Mexicanidad, 1940–1946*. El Paso: Texas Western Press, 1998.

Mistron, Deborah E. "The Institutional Revolution: Images of the Mexican Revolution in the Cinema." Ph.D. diss., Indiana University, 1982.

Monroy, Douglas. *Rebirth: Mexican Los Angeles from the Great Migration to the Great Depression*. Berkeley and Los Angeles: University of California Press, 1999.

Monsiváis, Carlos. "On Civic Monuments and Their Spectators," translated by Elena C. Murray. In *Mexican Monuments: Strange Encounters*, edited by Helen Escobedo, 105–128. New York: Abbeville Press, 1989.

Morales Ibarra, Marcel. *Morelos agrario: La construcción de una alternativa*. Mexico: Plaza y Valdés, 1994.

Morett Alatorre, Luis. *La lucha por la tierra en los valles del yaqui y mayo: Historia oral del sur de sonora*. Mexico City: Universidad Autónoma Chapingo, 1989.

Morsberger, Robert E. "Emiliano Zapata: The Man, the Myth, and the Mexican Revolution." In *Zapata*, John Steinbeck, 3–15. New York: Penguin, 1993.

———. "Steinbeck's Zapata: Rebel Versus Revolutionary." In *Zapata*, John Steinbeck, 203–223. New York: Penguin, 1993.

Mraz, John. "Today, Tomorrow and Always: The Golden Age of Illustrated Magazines in Mexico, 1937–1960." In *Fragments of a Golden Age: The Politics of Culture in Mexico Since 1940*, edited by Gilbert Joseph, Anne Rubenstein, and Eric Zolov, 116–157. Durham, N.C.: Duke University Press, 2001.

Myscofski, Carole A. "Messianic Themes in Portuguese and Brazilian Literature in the Sixteenth and Seventeenth Centuries." *Luso-Brazilian Review*, 28 (1991): 77–94.

Navarro, Sharon A. "Las Mujeres Invisibles/The Invisible Women." In *Women's Activism and Globalization*, edited by Nancy A. Naples and Manisha Desai, 83–98. New York: Routledge, 2002.

———. "Las Voces de Esperanza/Voices of Hope: La Mujer Obrera, Transnationalism, and NAFTA-Displaced Women Workers in the U.S.-Mexico Borderlands." In *Globalization on the Line: Culture, Capital, Citizenship at U.S. Borders*, edited by Claudia Sadowski-Smith, 183–200. New York: Palgrave, 2002.

Novo, Salvador. *La vida en México en el período presidencial de Lázaro Cárdenas*. Mexico City: Empresas Editoriales, 1964.

O'Donnell, Guillermo and Philippe C. Schmitter. *Transitions from Authoritarian Rule: Tentative Conclusions about Uncertain Democracies*. Baltimore: Johns Hopkins University Press, 1986.

Olivera, Alicia. "¿Ha muerto Emiliano Zapata? Mitos y leyendas en torno del caudillo." *Boletín del Instituto Nacional de Antropología e Historia*, época II, 13 (1975): 43–52.

———. "Un trovador zapatista de Morelos." *Boletín del Instituto Nacional de Antropología e Historia* 36 (1969): 28–33.

Olivera de Bonfil, Alicia, and Eugenia Meyer. *Jesús Sotelo Inclán y sus conceptos sobre el movimiento zapatista (entrevista)*. Mexico City: Instituto Nacional de Antropología e Historia, 1970.

O'Malley, Ilene V. *The Myth of the Revolution: Hero Cults and the Institutionalization of the Mexican State, 1920–1940*. New York: Greenwood Press, 1986.

Orbe Diego, José Luis, et al. *Lucio Cabañas y el Partido de los Pobres: Una experiencia guerrillera en México*. Mexico City: Nuestra América, 1987.

Othon Díaz, Enrique. *Madre tierra: Poemas al ejido*. Oaxaca: n.p., 1933.

Ozouf, Mona. *Festivals and the French Revolution*. Cambridge, Mass.: Harvard University Press, 1988.

Padilla, Tanalís, "'*Por las buenas no se puede*': Rubén Jaramillo's Campaigns for Governor of Morelos, 1946 and 1952." *Journal of Iberian and Latin American Studies* 7 (2001): 21–47.

Palacios, Guillermo. *La pluma y el arado: Los intelectuales pedagogos y la construcción sociocultural del "problema campesino" en México, 1932–1934*. Mexico City: El Colegio de México, 1999.

Palacios, Porfirio. *Emiliano Zapata: Datos biográfico-históricos*. Mexico City: Libro Mex, 1960.

———. *Emiliano Zapata (datos biográficos e históricos)*. 2nd ed. Mexico City: Centro de Estudio Históricos del Agrarismo en México, 1982.

Paredes, Américo, ed. *Folktales of Mexico*. Chicago: University of Chicago Press, 1970.

Parfit, Michael. "Mexico City: Pushing the Limits." *National Geographic*, August 1996, 24–43.

Parrés, José G. "Zapata y su concepto sobre la lealtad." *Ofrenda a la memoria de Emiliano Zapata*, [edited by Gildardo Magaña], 23–34. Mexico City?: n.p., 1938.

Pauly, Thomas H. *An American Odyssey: Elia Kazan and American Culture*. Philadelphia: Temple University Press, 1983.

Paz, Octavio. *The Labyrinth of Solitude: Life and Thought in Mexico*, translated by Lysander Kemp. New York: Grove Press, 1961.

———. *The Other Mexico: Critique of the Pyramid*, translated by Lysander Kemp. New York: Grove Press, 1972.

Paz, Octavio, and Luis Mario Schneider. *México en la obra de Octavio Paz*. 3 vols. Mexico City: Fondo de Cultura Económica, 1987.

Paz Solórzano, Octavio. *Hoguera que fue*. Edited by Felipe Gálvez. Mexico City: Universidad Autónoma Metropolitana, Unidad Xochimilco, 1986.

Pérez Montfort, Ricardo. *Guía del archivo del General Jenaro Amezcua, 1909-1947*. Mexico City: CEHAM and Condumex, 1982.

———. "Imágenes del zapatismo entre 1911 y 1913." In *Estudios sobre el zapatismo*, edited by Laura Espejel, 163–208. Mexico City: Instituto de Antropología e Historia, 2000.

———. "La unión de revolucionarios agraristas del sur (unos zapatistas después de la muerte de Emiliano Zapata)." In *Morelos: Cinco siglos de historia regional*, edited by Horacio Crespo, 275–283. Mexico City: Centro de Estudios Históricos del Agrarismo en México and Universidad Autónoma del Estado de Morelos, 1984.

Perez-Torres, Rafael. *Movements in Chicano Poetry: Against Myths, Against Margins*. New York: Cambridge University Press, 1995.

Pettit, Arthur G. *Images of the Mexican American in Fiction and Film*. Edited by Dennis E. Showalter. College Station: Texas A&M University Press, 1980.

Pinchon, Edgcumb. *Zapata the Unconquerable*. New York: Doubleday, Doran, 1941.

Pineda, Francisco. "Guerra y cultura: El antizapatismo en el gobierno de Madero." In *Estudios sobre el zapatismo*, edited by Laura Espejel, 209–233. Mexico City: Instituto de Antropología e Historia, 2000.

Poniatowska, Elena. *Here's to You, Jesusa!*, translated by Deanna Heikkinen. New York: Farrar, Straus and Giroux, 2001.

———. *Massacre in Mexico*, translated by Helen R. Lane. New York: Viking, 1975; reprint, Columbia: University of Missouri Press, 1984.

Portes Gil, Emilio. *Quince años de política mexicana*. Mexico City: Ediciones Botas, 1941.

Prieto, Ana María. "Mexico's National *Coordinadoras* in a Context of Economic Crisis," translated by Sandra del Castillo. In *The Mexican Left, the Popular Movements, and the Politics of Austerity*, edited by Barry Carr and Ricardo Anzaldúa Montoya, 75–94. San Diego: Center for U.S.-Mexican Studies, University of California, San Diego, 1986.

Primer congreso de unificación de las organizaciones campesinas de la república. Puebla: S. Loyo, 1927.

Rajchenberg S., Enrique. "Las figuras heroicas de la revolución en los historiadores protomarxistas." *Secuencia* 28 (1994): 49–64.

Programa de las Naciones Unidas para el Medio Ambiente. "México: crece el frente maza-hua." http://www.pnuma.org/informacion/noticias/2004-09/29sep04e.doc, September 29, 2004 (accessed April 11, 2007).

Rajchenberg S., Enrique, and Catherine Héau-Lambert. "Historia y simbolismo en el movimiento zapatista." In *Chiapas*, 41–57. Mexico City: Instituto de Investigaciones Económicas, Universidad Autónoma de México, 1996.

Ramos Pedrueza, Rafael. "Emiliano Zapata." In *Ofrenda a la memoria de Emiliano Zapata*, [edited by Gildardo Magaña], 49–55. Mexico City?: n.p., 1938.

Ravelo Lecuona, Renato. *Los jaramillistas*. Mexico City: Editorial Nuestro Tiempo, 1978.

Redfield, Robert. *Tepoztlán, a Mexican Village: A Study of Folk Life*. Chicago: University of Chicago Press, 1930.

Reed, Alma. *Orozco*. New York: Oxford University Press, 1956.

Reyes Avilés, Carlos. *Cartones Zapatistas*. Mexico City: n.p., 1928.

Rivera, Diego (with Gladys March). *My Art, My life: An Autobiography*. New York: Citadel Press, 1960.

Rivera, Edward. *Family Installments: Memories of Growing Up Hispanic*. New York: William Morrow, 1982.

Rivera Castro, José. "Política agraria, organizaciones, luchas y resistencias campesinas entre 1920–1928." In *Historia de la cuestión agraria mexicana*. Vol. 4, *Modernización, lucha agraria y poder político, 1920-1934*, edited by Enrique Montalvo, 21–149. Mexico City: Siglo XXI and CEHAM, 1988.

Rochfort, Desmond. *Mexican Muralists: Orozco, Rivera, Siqueiros*. San Francisco: Chronicle Books, 1998.

Rodda, Jeannette. *Go Ye and Study the Beehive: The Making of a Western Working Class*. New York: Garland Press, 2000.

Rodriguez, Roberto, and Patrisia Gonzales. "Zapata Lives on Both Sides of the Border" http://www.eco.utexas.edu/~archive/chiapas95/1995.02/msg00280.html (accessed October 10, 2003).

Rojas, Rosa, ed. *Chiapas ¿y la mujeres qué?* Mexico City: Ediciones la Correa Feminista, 1994.

Rosas, María. *Tepoztlán: crónica de desacatos y resistencia.* Mexico City: Ediciones Era, 1997.

Rosoff, Rosalind, and Anita Aguilar. *Así firmaron el Plan de Ayala.* Mexico City: Secretaría de Educación Pública, 1976.

Rovira, Guiomar. *Mujeres de maíz.* Mexico City: Ediciones Era, 1997.

———. *¡Zapata vive!: La rebelión indígena de Chiapas contada por sus protagonistas.* Barcelona: Virus, 1994.

Rubenstein, Anne. *Bad Language, Naked Ladies, and Other Threats to the Nation: A Political History of Comic Books in Mexico.* Durham, N.C.: Duke University Press, 1998.

———. "Bodies, Cities, Cinema: Pedro Infante's Death as Political Spectacle." In *Fragments of a Golden Age: The Politics of Culture in Mexico Since 1940*, edited by Gilbert Joseph, Anne Rubenstein, and Eric Zolov, 199–233. Durham, N.C.: Duke University Press, 2001.

———. "Mass Media and Popular Culture in the Twentieth Century." In *The Oxford History of Mexico*, edited by William Beezley and Michael Meyer, 637–670. New York: Oxford University Press, 2000.

———. Remarks at roundtable, "The State of Mexican History in the Twenty-First Century: New Questions, Old Problems." Presented at the annual meeting of the American Historical Association, Seattle, January 7, 2005.

Rubin, Jeffrey W. *Decentering the Regime: Ethnicity, Radicalism, and Democracy in Juchitán, Mexico.* Durham, N.C.: Duke University Press, 1997.

Rueda Smithers, Salvador. "Emiliano Zapata, los signos de un caudillo, biografía de un símbolo." In *Estadistas, caciques y caudillos*, edited by Carlos Martínez Assad, 133–151. Mexico City: Instituto de Investigaciones Sociales, 1988.

———. *El paraíso de la caña: historia de una construcción imaginaria.* Mexico City: Instituto Nacional de Antropología e Historia, 1998.

———. "La zona armada de Genovevo de la O." *Cuicuilco* 2 (1981): 38–43.

Rueda Smithers, Salvador, and Laura Espejel López. "El siglo xx: Bajo el signo de Emiliano Zapata." In *Morelos: El estado*, 63–89. Cuernavaca: Gobierno del Estado de Morelos, 1993.

Ruíz, Ramón Eduardo. *The Great Rebellion: Mexico 1905–1924.* New York: Norton, 1980.

Ruiz Cervantes, Francisco José. "La lucha de clases en Oaxaca: 1971–1977 (segunda parte)." In *Oaxaca una lucha reciente: 1960–1978*, edited by René Bustamante V. et al., 43–69. Mexico City: Ediciones Nueva Sociología, 1978.

Rutherford, John. *Mexican Society During the Revolution: A Literary Approach.* Oxford: Clarendon Press, 1971.

Salazar, Ruben. *Border Correspondent: Selected Writings, 1955–1970.* Edited by Mario T. Garcia. Berkeley and Los Angeles: University of California Press, 1998.

Saldaña Treviño, José P. *Del triunfo al destierro*. Monterrey: Gobierno del Estado de Nuevo León, 1987.

Sánchez Escobar, Rafael. *El ocaso de los héroes: Como murieron algunos connotados revolucionarios*. Mexico City: Casa de Orientación para Varones, 1934.

Sanderson, Susan R. Walsch. *Land Reform in Mexico: 1910–1980*. Orlando, Fla.: Academic Press, 1984.

Sarmiento, Domingo Faustino. *Life in the Argentine Republic in the Days of the Tyrants; or, Civilization and Barbarism*. New York: Collier Books, 1961.

Sayer, Derek. "Everyday Forms of State Formation: Some Dissident Remarks on 'Hegemony.'" In *Everyday Forms of State Formation: Revolution and the Negotiation of Rule in Modern Mexico*, edited by Gilbert M. Joseph and Daniel Nugent, 367–377. Durham, N.C.: Duke University Press, 1994.

Scherer García, Julio, and Carlos Monsiváis. *Parte de Guerra: Tlatelolco 1968*. Mexico City: Nuevo Siglo, 1999.

Schweizer, Peter. *Reagan's War: The Epic Story of His Forty Year Struggle and Final Triumph Over Communism*. New York: Doubleday, 2002.

Scott, James C. *Domination and the Arts of Resistance: Hidden Transcripts*. New Haven: Yale University Press, 1990.

Secretaría de Educación Pública. *La Revolución Mexicana*. Mexico City: Secretaría de Educación Pública, 1954.

La SEMIP en el 65° aniversario de la muerte de Emiliano Zapata. Mexico City: Secretaría de Energía, Minas e Industria Paraestatal, 1984.

Servín, Elisa. *Ruptura y oposición: El movimiento henriquista, 1945–1954*. Mexico City: Cal y Arena, 2001.

Sherman, John W. *The Mexican Right: The End of Revolutionary Reform, 1929–1940*. Westport, Conn.: Praeger, 1997.

Sierra Brabatta, Carlos J. *Zapata: Señor de la tierra, capitán de los labriegos*. Mexico City: Departamento del Distrito Federal, 1985.

Silva Herzog, Jesús. *El agrarismo mexicano y la reforma agaria*. Mexico City: Fondo de Cultura Económica, 1959.

———. *Una vida en la vida de México*. 2nd ed. Mexico City: Siglo XXI, 1975.

Simmons, Merle E. *The Mexican Corrido as a Source for Interpretive Study of Modern Mexico, 1870–1950*. Bloomington: Indiana University Press, 1957.

Siqueiros, David Alfaro, *Me llamaban el coronelazo: Memorias*. Mexico City: Grijalbo, 1977.

Smith, Anthony D. *Myths and Memories of the Nation*. New York: Oxford University Press, 1999.

Smith, Benjamin. "Emiliano Zapata: Contestation and Construction." Master's thesis, University of Cambridge, 2001.

Smith, Michael E. *The Aztecs*. 2nd ed. Malden, Mass.: Blackwell, 2003.

Sommer, Doris. "Taking a Life: Hot Pursuit and Cold Rewards in a Mexican Testimonial Novel." In *The Seductions of Biography*, edited by Mary Rhiel and David Suchoff, 147–172. New York: Routledge, 1996.

Sotelo Inclán, Jesús. *Raíz y razón de Zapata*. Mexico City: Editorial Etnos, 1943.

Sotelo Pérez, Antonio. *Breve historia de la Asociación Cívica Guerrerense*. Chilpancingo: Universidad Autónoma de Guerrero, 1991.

Soto Viterbo, Felipe. "Máquina del Tiempo: Cine zapateado." *Expansión*, December 11–25, 2002.

Steinbeck, John. *Zapata*. Edited by Robert Morsberger. New York: Penguin, 1993.

Stephen, Lynn. "Pro-Zapatista and Pro-PRI: Resolving the Contradictions of Zapatismo in Rural Oaxaca." *Latin American Research Review* 32 (1997): 41–70.

———. *Viva Zapata!: Generation, Gender, and Historical Consciousness in the Reception of Ejido Reform in Oaxaca*. San Diego: Center for US-Mexican Studies, 1994.

———. *Zapata Lives! Histories and Cultural Politics in Southern Mexico*. Berkeley and Los Angeles: University of California Press, 2002.

Suárez, Luis. *Confesiones de Diego Rivera*. 3rd ed. Mexico City: Editorial Grijalbo, 1975.

———. *Lucio Cabañas: el guerrillero sin esperanza*, 4th ed. Mexico City: Roca, 1976.

Taibo II, Paco Ignacio. *'68*. Mexico City: Joaquin Moritz, 1991.

Tannenbaum, Frank. *The Mexican Agrarian Revolution*. New York: Macmillan, 1929; reprint: Archon Books, 1968.

———. *Peace by Revolution: Mexico After 1910*. New York: Columbia University Press, 1933.

Taracena, Alfonso. *La revolución desvirtuada: Continuación de la verdadera revolución mexicana*. 6 vols. Mexico City: B. Costa-Amic, 1966–1969.

———. *La tragedia zapatista*. Mexico City: Editorial Bolívar, 1931.

———. *Zapata: Fantasía y realidad*. 2nd ed. Mexico City: B. Costa-Amic, 1974.

Tate, Deborah Gronich. "The Image of Emiliano Zapata in the United States, 1911–1988." Master's thesis, College of William and Mary, 1989.

Taylor, Mark. "Votán-Zapata: Theological Discourse in Zapatista Political Struggle." In *Converging on Culture: Theologians in Dialogue with Cultural Analysis and Criticism*, edited by Delwin Brown, Sheila Greeve Davaney, and Kathryn Tanner, 176–195. New York: Oxford University Press, 2001.

Taylor, Ronald B. *Chávez and the Farm Workers*. Boston: Beacon Press, 1975.

Taylor, William B. *Magistrates of the Sacred: Priests and Parishioners in Eighteenth-Century Mexico*. Stanford, Calif.: Stanford University Press, 1996.

———. "Santiago's Horse: Christianity and Colonial Indian Resistance in the Heartland of New Spain." In *Violence, Resistance, and Survival in the Americas*, edited by William B. Taylor and Franklin Pease, 153–189. Washington, D.C.: Smithsonian Institution Press, 1994.

Teja Zabre, Alfonso. *Breve historia de México*. Mexico City: Secretaría de Educación Pública, 1935.

Tello Díaz, Carlos. *El exilio: Un relato de familia*. Mexico City: Cal y Arena, 1993.

Tenenbaum, Barbara A. "Streetwise History: The Paseo de la Reforma and the Porfirian State, 1876–1910." In *Rituals of Rule, Rituals of Resistance: Public Celebrations and Popular Culture in Mexico*, edited by William H. Beezley, Cheryl English Martin, and William E. French, 127–150. Wilmington, Del.: SR Books, 1994.

Tenorio-Trillo, Mauricio. "Liaisons dangereuses: Memoria y olvido historiográfico." In *Cincuenta años de investigación histórica en México*, edited by Gisela von Wobeser, 31–44. Mexico City: Universidad Nacional Autónoma de México, 1998.

———. *Mexico at the World's Fairs: Crafting a Modern Nation*. Berkeley and Los Angeles: University of California Press, 1996.

Tibol, Raquel. *Diego Rivera: Arte y política*. Mexico City: Grijalbo, 1979.

Tobler, Hans Werner. "Peasants and the Shaping of the Revolutionary State, 1910–1940." In *Riot, Rebellion, and Revolution: Rural Social Conflict in Mexico*, edited by Friedrich Katz, 487–518. Princeton, N.J.: Princeton University Press, 1988.

Torices Mercado, Juan. "Ecce Homo Emiliano Zapata." In *Ofrenda a la memoria de Emiliano Zapata*, [edited by Gildardo Magaña], 119–126. Mexico City?: n.p., 1938.

Torres Quintero, Gregorio. *La patria mexicana: Elementos de historia nacional, segundo ciclo*. 7th ed. Mexico City: Gómez Cárdenas, 1939.

Townsend, William Cameron. *Lázaro Cárdenas: Mexican Democrat*. Ann Arbor, Mich.: George Wahr, 1952.

Tumarkin, Nina. *Lenin Lives! The Lenin Cult in Soviet Russia*. Cambridge, Mass.: Harvard University Press, 1983.

Valverde, Sergio. *Apuntes para la historia de la revolución y de la política en el estado de Morelos*. Mexico City: n.p., 1933.

Van Young, Eric. "Millenium on the Northern Marches: The Mad Messiah of Durango and Popular Rebellion in Mexico, 1800–1815." *Comparative Studies in Society and History* 21 (1986): 386–413.

Vanderwood, Paul J. "An American Cold Warrior: *Viva Zapata!*" In *American History/American Film: Interpreting the Hollywood Image*, edited by John E. O'Connor and Martin A. Jackson, 183–201. New York: Frederick Ungar, 1979.

———. *Disorder and Progress: Bandits, Police, and Mexican Development*. Rev. ed. Wilmington, Del.: Scholarly Resources, 1992.

Vargas Llosa, Mario. "Mexico: The Perfect Dictatorship." *New Perspectives Quarterly* 8 (1991): 23–24.

Vasconcelos, José. *Memorias II: El desastre, el proconsulado*. Mexico City: Fondo de Cultura Económica, 1982.

Vaughan, Mary Kay. "The Construction of the Patriotic Festival in Tecamachalco, Puebla, 1900–1946." In *Rituals of Rule, Rituals of Resistance: Public Celebrations and Popular Culture in Mexico*, edited by William H. Beezley, Cheryl English Martin, and William E. French, 213–245. Wilmington, Del.: SR Books, 1994.

———. *Cultural Politics in Revolution: Teachers, Peasants, and Schools in Mexico, 1930–1940*. Tucson: University of Arizona Press, 1997.

———. *History Textbooks in Mexico in the 1920s*. Buffalo: Council on International Studies, State University of New York at Buffalo, 1974.

———. *The State, Education, and Social Class in Mexico, 1880–1928*. DeKalb: Northern Illinois Press, 1982.

Vázquez de Knauth, Josefina. *Nacionalismo y educación en México*. Mexico City: El Colegio de México, 1970.

Vázquez León, Luis. *Ser indio otra vez: La purepechización de los tarascos serranos*. Mexico City: Consejo Nacional para la Cultura y las Artes, 1992.

Velasco, Miguel A. *Liquidación del latifundismo*. Mexico City: Editorial Popular, 1939.

Velasco Toro, José. *Política y legislación agraria en México: De la desamortización civil a la reforma campesina*. Xalapa: Universidad Veracruzana, 1993.

Vevia Romero, Fernando Carlos. *Teatro y revolución mexicana*. Guadalajara: Universidad de Guadalajara, 1991.

Villa de Ayala y Chinameca. Cuernavaca: Cuadernos Zapatistas, 1979.

Villagómez L., Adrián. "Tres Comentarios a los Zapatas de Diego." In *Los Zapatas de Diego Rivera*. Mexico City: Consejo Nacional para la Cultura y las Artes, 1989.

¡Viva Zapata! 20 grabados. Mexico City: Taller de Gráfica Popular, 1970.

Warman, Arturo. *"We Come to Object": The Peasants of Morelos and the National State*. Translated by Stephen K. Ault. Baltimore: Johns Hopkins University Press, 1980.

Weber, Max. *On Charisma and Institution Building*. Edited by S.N. Eisenstadt. Chicago: University of Chicago Press, 1968.

Webster's New Collegiate Dictionary. Springfield, Mass.: G. C. Merriam, 1974.

Wilkie, James M., and Edna Monzón de Wilkie. *Frente a la Revolución Mexicana: 17 protagonistas de la etapa constructiva*. 3 vols. Mexico City: Universidad Autónoma Metropolitana, 2001.

Williams, Heather L. *Social Movements and Economic Transition: Markets and Distributive Conflict in Mexico*. New York: Cambridge University Press, 2001.

Wolfe, Bertram. *The Fabulous Life of Diego Rivera*. New York: Stein and Day, 1963.

Womack, John Jr. *Zapata and the Mexican Revolution*. New York: Vintage Books, 1970.

Los Zapatas de Diego Rivera. Mexico City: Consejo Nacional para la Cultura y las Artes, 1989.

Zedillo, Ernesto. "Palabras del Presidente Ernesto Zedillo." http://www.quicklink.com/mexico/gobfed/zedill67.htm, April 10, 1995.

Zolov, Eric. "Discovering a Land 'Mysterious and Obvious': The Renarrativizing of Postrevolutionary Mexico." In *Fragments of a Golden Age: The Politics of Culture in Mexico since 1940*, edited by Gilbert Joseph, Anne Rubenstein, and Eric Zolov, 234–272. Durham, N.C.: Duke University Press, 2001.

———. *Refried Elvis: The Rise of the Mexican Counterculture*. Berkeley and Los Angeles: University of California Press, 1999.

AUDIOVISUAL MEDIA

Music

Ochoa, Amparo. "Bola Suriana de la Muerte de Emiliano Zapata." In *El Cancionero Popular*, vol. I. Fonarte Latino/IODA, 1975.

Film and Videotape

The Americas. Part 3, *Continent on the Move.* Executive producer Judith Vecchione. 57 minutes. WGBH Boston and Central Television Enterprises for Channel 4, U.K., 1993. Video recording.

Arau, Alfonso. *Zapata: El sueño del héroe.* Produced by Alfonso Arau and Javier Rodríguez Borgio. Latin Arts LLC, Comala Films, Rita Rusic, 2004. Feature Film.

Cazals, Felipe. *Emiliano Zapata.* Producciones Aguila, 1970. Feature Film.

de Fuentes, Fernando. *El Compadre Mendoza.* 1933. Feature Film.

Kazan, Elia. *Viva Zapata!* Twentieth Century Fox, 1952. Feature Film.

Taboada Tabone, Francisco, and Sarah Perrig. *The Last Zapatistas: Forgotten Heroes.* Produced by Manuel Peñafiel, 2001. Video recording.

INDEX

Abúndez, Angel, 57
Acapulco, Guerrero, 54
Agrarian Labor Party of Morelos, 146
Aguascalientes, 2–3
Aguilar, Antonio, 198–200, 205, 245
Aguilar, Inés, 118, 187–189
Aguilar Camín, Héctor, 227
Aguirre, Vicente, 123
Aguirre Cinta, Rafael, 99
Albuquerque, New Mexico, 181
Aldana, Carmen, 41, 52, 55
Alemán, Miguel, 125–127, 129, 132,
    138–140, 142–143, 146, 158–160, 169,
    172, 177, 243
Alencaster, José, 35
Alfaro, Inés. See Inés Aguilar
Alferez, Fernando, 260
Almazán, Juan Andreu, 25, 114–116, 133
Alpert, Hollis, 177
Alvarez Amaya, Jesús, 136
Amacuzac, Morelos, 155
Amezcua, Jenaro, 92, 111–113, 116, 122,
    128, 138
ancestor worship, 5–9, 12
Anderson, Benedict, 5
Anenecuilco, Morelos, 1, 24–25, 30, 36,
    42, 55, 57, 69, 77, 120, 132, 142–143,
    154, 160, 221, 223, 225, 232, 241, 247;
    museum at, 121, 156–157, 209, 224;
    and Zapata's birthday, 81, 85, 156, 224
Apango, Guerrero, 168

Arabia, 53–54, 152
Arau, Alfonso, 245–247
Arizona, 234
Armendáriz, Pedro, 138, 175
Army of Zapatista Women in Defense of
    Water, 235
Arriaga, Guillermo, 135
Article 27, Constitution of 1917, 2, 100,
    139, 225–226, 228, 233, 241
Asúnsolo, Enrique, 159
Asúnsolo, Ignacio, 159, 168
Atlixco, Puebla, 170, 184
Avila Camacho, Manuel, 114, 116,
    121–126, 132, 136, 142, 154, 158, 161, 169
Ayaquica, Fortino, 106
Azompa, Oaxaca, 165
Aztecs, 8–10, 12, 71, 95, 171, 223, 258
Aztlán, 183

Bacum, Sonora, 169
Banderas, Antonio, 245
banditry, 28–29, 38, 120, 162
Bárcenas, Victoriano, 49, 56, 109
Barraza Allande, Luciano, 206
Barrios, Roberto, 125–127
Bartra, Roger, 1
Bassols, Narciso, 99
Baz, Gustavo, 220
Beals, Carleton, 171, 177, 183
Benjamin, Thomas, 13–14, 16
Bernal, Antonio, 182

Bi-National Indigenous Front of Oaxaca, 240

Bird Jaguar, 8

Blanco Sánchez, Javier, 212

Blanquel, Eduardo, 131

Bobadilla, Rosa, 128

Bonilla, José M., 100

Bonillas, Ignacio, 63–64

Bórquez Alméndrez, Alvaro D., 140

Bracero Program, 123, 128, 130

Bracho, Angel, 136

Brando, Marlon, 1, 175, 177, 181–182, 199

Browder, Earl, 141

Bucharest, Romania, 135

Bulnes, Francisco, 68, 139

Bush, George H. W., 225

Cabañas, Lucio, 195–197

Cabrera Rojas, Miguel, 54

Cacahuananche, Guerrero, 170

California, 183, 193, 253

Calles, Plutarco Elías, 64, 73, 78, 80–81, 83, 86, 89–91, 94–95, 97, 99, 105, 115–116, 161, 243; at 1924 commemoration, 70–72

Caloca, Lauro G., 71, 73

Campobello, Nellie, 128

Capistrán, Jesús, 53, 243

Cárabes Pedroza, J. Jesús, 130–131

Cárdenas, Cuauhtémoc, 223–224, 227, 240

Cárdenas, Lázaro, 15, 89, 91–92, 95, 97–99, 103, 109–111, 113–118, 122, 124, 128, 130, 141, 143, 146–147, 150, 154–156, 161–164, 167–169, 181, 211–212, 220, 223–224, 243, 251, 260

Cardenista Peasant Central (Central Campesina Cardenista, CCC), 227

Carrancistas. See Constitutionalists

Carranza, Venustiano, 2–3, 21, 32, 34–35, 37, 39, 42, 49, 63–67, 69, 74, 76, 80, 92, 110–112, 120, 130–132, 141, 161, 192, 197, 212, 230, 237, 264

Carrasco Altamirano, Diódoro, 239–240

Carrillo Olea, Jorge, 239

Carrillo Puerto, Felipe, 61

Casasano, Morelos, 148

Castañeda, Leopoldo, 85

Castillo, Heberto, 223

Castrejón, Adrián, 126, 159, 169, 178

Castro, Fidel, 194

Catholicism, 9–10, 89, 111, 128, 158, 242

caudillos, 11

Cazals, Felipe, 198–200, 205, 246

Celaya, Battle of, 37

Center for Revolutionary Propaganda and Unification, 38

Cervantes, Miguel, 248

Cervera Pacheco, Víctor, 224–225

Chamilpa, Morelos, 206

charisma, 7, 117, 257

Chávez, César, 182–183, 189, 248

Chávez, Jesús, 200

Chávez, Linda, 181

Chiapas, state of, 2, 14, 133, 215, 228, 230–241, 244–245, 247–248, 255, 259–260, 265

Chicano Movement, 19, 182–183, 185, 193, 227, 245, 248, 259

Chihuahua, state of, 21, 25–26, 169, 181, 196, 205, 263

Chinameca, Morelos, 2, 31, 40–43, 49–58, 69, 75, 80, 94, 98, 107, 109, 117, 120–121, 126, 133, 137, 140, 152, 156–157, 176, 181, 195, 203, 205–206, 221, 230, 232, 239, 241, 242–244, 248, 250; statue of Zapata, 154, 214; and Zapata's remains, 153–155

Cholula, Puebla, 8

Cisneros, Sandra, 187–189, 207, 234

Ciudad Jiménez, Nuevo León, 169

Ciudad Juárez, Chihuahua, 181, 260–261

Ciudad Obregón, Sonora, 169

Coacalco, Mexico state, 231

Coahuila, state of, 24, 34, 190

Cocoyoc, Morelos, 53
Cole, Lester, 173–174
Colosio, Luis Donaldo, 238
Comandante Susan, 235
commemorations, 75, 84, 86–87, 93–99,
    103, 116–117, 124–130, 142, 144–145,
    148–152, 154–157, 162–171, 173, 184–185,
    206, 210, 214, 217, 221, 228, 239,
    251–254, 260, 263; beginning of, for
    Zapata, 67–70; and ritual protest,
    207–209, 215–216, 227, 244
communism, 66, 80, 97, 99, 110, 116,
    126, 132, 134, 139, 141–142, 173–174,
    176–177, 183, 190–191, 198, 256
Confederation of Mexican Workers
    (Confederación de Trabajadores de
    México, CTM), 117
Confederation of Precursors and Vet-
    erans of the Liberating Army of the
    South (Confederación de Precursores
    y Veteranos del Ejército Liberator del
    Sur), 142
Constitution of 1857, 12, 23
Constitution of 1917, 2, 15, 38–39, 64, 72,
    91, 130, 139, 225, 233, 259
Constitutionalists, 32, 34–35, 37–43,
    45–47, 49–50, 52, 54, 56, 66, 69, 72,
    76, 80, 107, 111–112, 114, 126, 134,
    140–141, 155, 195, 203, 236
Convention government, 2–3, 35–38, 65
Coria, Miguel, 54
corridos, 1, 14, 32, 39, 49–51, 55–56, 85–86,
    101, 109, 147; as cultural unifier,
    30–31; urban, 31, 35, 60, 73–76, 83,
    107, 193
Cortés, Agustín, 41, 53
Cortés, Hernán, 61, 77, 183
Cortés, Joaquín, 53
Cortés González, Claudia, 191
Cortés Juárez, Erasto, 136–137
Covián Pérez, Miguel, 149
Coyuca de Benítez, Guerrero, 184

Creelman, James, 24
Crisóstomo, Iris, 235
Cristero Rebellion, 89, 98
Crusade for Justice, 182
Cuadros Caldas, Julio, 133
Cuatro Caminos, Michoacán, 162, 227
Cuauhtémoc, 10–12, 46, 82, 130, 183, 196,
    223, 231, 246, 257–258
Cuautla, Morelos, 22, 26, 28–32, 42–43,
    45, 50, 53, 57, 108, 143, 155–157, 211–212,
    258; commemorations at, 68–71, 73,
    78, 85–86, 117–118, 124–130, 138, 142,
    145, 148–152, 154, 162, 166–168, 171,
    184–185, 207, 210, 214, 217, 241, 243,
    249, 251–252; Zapata's statue at, 93–
    94, 115–116, 153, 158, 161, 212–213, 226
Cuba, 227
Cuban Revolution, 139, 191, 206
Cuernavaca, Morelos, 26, 28, 35, 61, 63,
    81, 83, 92, 113, 144, 148, 157, 159, 174,
    180, 195, 214, 239, 248
Culiacán, Sinaloa, 223

Dance of the Christians and Moors, 10
Dávalos de Montero, María Elena
    Hortensia, 194, 234
Day of the Dead, 9, 12, 55, 204
de Alba, Pedro, 80–81
death, 8, 46, 135
de Avila, Theresa, 248
de Castillo, Agustín G., 112
de Jesús Ocampo, María, 249–250
de la Huerta, Adolfo, 65–67
de la Madrid, Miguel, 216, 219, 222
Delano, California, 182–183
de la O, Genovevo, 48–49, 64–65, 67, 70
de la Torre y Mier, Ignacio, 189
Delgado, Jesús, 52, 56, 58
Del Rey, California, 182
del Rio, Dolores, 138
Denver, Colorado, 182
Díaz, Félix, 114

Díaz, José, 141
Díaz, Porfirio, 1–2, 12, 23–24, 26, 32, 59, 65, 114, 120, 130, 158, 176, 189, 212, 228, 248
Díaz Ordaz, Gustavo, 131, 149–150, 167, 191–192, 199, 205
Díaz Soto y Gama, Antonio, 65–66, 68, 70, 72–73, 78, 80, 86, 89, 100, 113, 115–117, 120, 133–135, 150, 171, 248
Dispoto, Bruno, 183
Doctorow, E. L., 245
Domenech, J. Figueroa, 33
Domínguez, Belisario, 133
Dr. Atl (Gerardo Murillo), 75
Dromundo, Baltasar, 75–76, 80–81, 103, 107, 111, 113, 115, 160, 211
Dunn, H. H., 172
Durango, state of, 80, 169, 221

Echeverría Alvarez, Luis, 205–206, 208, 210, 216, 221
education, 38, 90–91, 98–101, 190, 227–228, 249, 264
Egypt, 55
El Atravezaño, Jalisco, 170
El Campesino, 127, 132, 138, 158–159, 168, 170, 199, 205, 210
El Continental, 181
El Demócrata, 42–43, 45, 68–69, 84, 86
El Eco del Sur, 144, 155
El Greco, 201, 204
Elías, Francisco S., 95
El Imparcial, 28–30
El Informador, 144
El Maestro Rural, 100–101, 161, 194
El Nacional, 94, 103, 210
El Paso, Texas, 181, 247
El Universal, 69, 72, 79
Emiliano Zapata Agrarian League of the South, 139, 151
Emiliano Zapata Eastern Mexico Democratic Front (Frente Democrática Oriental de México, FDOMEZ), 227

Emiliano Zapata Elementary School, 263
Emiliano Zapata Guerrilla Nucleus, 229
Emiliano Zapata Independent National Peasant Alliance (Alianza Nacional Campesina Independiente Emiliano Zapata, ANCIEZ), 230
Emiliano Zapata Peasant Organization (Organización Campesina Emiliano Zapata, OCEZ), 227, 229
Emiliano Zapata Revolutionary Brigade, 196
Emiliano Zapata Union of Communal Landholders (Union de Comuneros Emiliano Zapata, UCEZ), 209
Emiliano Zapata Union of Ejidos, 208
Emiliano Zapata Unit, 196
Emiliano Zapata Worker-Peasant Union (Unión de Obreros y Campesinos Emiliano Zapata, UOCEZ), 227
Esparza, Silerio, 221
Espejel, Laura, 14
Espejo, Josefa, 54, 127, 129, 175–176, 187, 198, 247
Espinoza, Arturo, 73–74
Estrada Cajigal, Sergio, 243–244
Estrada Cajigal, Vicente, 64, 94
estridentismo, 76
Etla, Oaxaca, 165, 205
Excélsior, 42–43, 45, 52, 67–68, 72, 94, 97, 149, 151, 160, 190, 206, 208, 212–213, 227–228, 241

Federal District, 21, 32, 47, 71, 75, 80, 85, 120, 149, 160, 169, 210, 223, 242
Félix, María, 128, 138
Fernández, Alejandro, 245–247
Fernández, Emilio "El Indio," 138
Fernández Ledesma, Gabriel, 136
Figueroa, Ambrosio, 25
Figueroa, Gabriel, 174, 176
Figueroa, Rubén, 195

Figueroa, Ruffo, 141
Florescano, Enrique, 227
Fox, Vicente, 11, 20, 242, 244, 248
Franco, Francisco, 55, 120, 142, 146

Galindo, Hermila, 63–64, 83, 234
Galís, Pioquinto, 243
Gamio, Manuel, 82–83
Gandhi, Mahatma, 182
García Aguirre, Prospero, 52, 57
García Bustos, Arturo, 136
García Sánchez, Pedro, 164, 168
Gill, Mario, 129, 144
Gironella, Alberto, 200–205, 207, 237
Gironella, Emiliano, 204
Gómez, Carlos, 164
Gómez, Marte, 134
Gonzales, Rodolfo "Corky," 182–183
González, Mario, 163
González, Pablo, 40, 42–43, 45–46,
   49–51, 63–64, 66–67, 69, 77–78, 93,
   105, 107, 109, 111–113, 116, 132, 140,
   203, 264
González, Pedro, 249
González, Roque, 206
Great Britain, 121
Guadalupe Tepeyac, Chiapas, 235
Guajardo, Jesús, 40–45, 49, 51–52, 56–57,
   66–67, 69, 75–76, 78, 107, 109, 115,
   126, 140, 172, 181, 197, 200, 263–264
Guajardo, José Juan, 200
Guanajuato, state of, 242
Guerreran Civic Association, 194
Guerrero, Eduardo, 74–75, 101
Guerrero, state of, 19, 25, 32, 43, 46–47,
   71, 101, 114, 139, 141, 151, 154, 168, 170,
   185, 194–196, 239, 241, 253
Guerrero, Vicente, 148, 231
guerrillas, 194–197, 205, 229–230,
   241–242, 253
Guevara, Ernesto "Che," 191–192, 194
Guilá, Oaxaca, 166, 168
Guzmán Araujo, Roberto, 145

Havana, Cuba, 59
Hebrews, 55
hegemony, 16–18, 252–256
Henríquez Guzmán, Miguel, 138, 146, 151
Hernández, Teodoro, 130
Hernández y Hernández, Francisco, 167
Hernández Zúñiga, José, 118
hero cults, 5–6, 11, 52, 117, 131, 148, 191,
   212, 227, 236, 243, 255, 257–258
Herrera Tello, María Teresa, 244
Hidalgo, Miguel, 10–11, 31, 46, 48, 63, 71,
   84, 86, 121, 140, 147–148, 166, 183, 192,
   231, 233, 257–258
hidden imam, 55
Hirschfeld Almada, Julio, 194
Hitler, Adolf, 122
Horcasitas, Fernando, 47
House of the Indigenous Student, 72
House of the World Worker (Casa del
   Obrero Mundial, COM), 65
House Un-American Activities Commis-
   sion (HUAC), 173, 176
Huautla, Morelos, 79
Huautla de Jiménez, Oaxaca, 241
Huerta, Victoriano, 21, 29, 32–34, 65,
   104, 114, 120, 130–134, 197–198, 201
Hueyapan, Morelos, 158
Huipulco, 160, 208
Huitzilac, Morelos, 159
Hungary, 53

Ibáñez, Crisóforo, 71
independence celebrations, 84, 92
Independent Central of Agricultural
   Workers and Peasants (Central
   Independiente de Obreros Agrícolas y
   Campesinos, CIOAC), 225
Indians, 28, 32, 51, 54, 60, 81–82, 94, 101,
   162, 168, 175, 216, 228–229, 235, 242,
   258
indígenismo, 82
industrialization, 124–126, 190, 226, 251
Iñigo, Alejandro, 206

Institutional Revolutionary Party
  (Partido Revolucionario Institucional,
  PRI), 2–3, 15, 19–20, 125–126, 138–139,
  144, 147–149, 191, 196–197, 208, 212,
  220, 222–223, 226, 229, 231, 237,
  240–242, 244, 248, 252–255, 260
intellectual advisors of Zapata, 33–35, 65,
  87, 134
Intellectual Workers' Block, 159
Isthmus of Tehuantepec, 167, 240
"It is better to die on your feet than live
  on your knees," 234, 247
Itzmatitlán, Morelos, 148

Jalisco, state of, 71, 141, 170, 180
Jaramillo, Rubén, 146–147, 151, 190, 193,
  195, 252
Jáuregui, Eusebio, 45, 51–52
Jesus Christ, 9, 11, 46, 50, 55–57, 77, 93,
  132, 147, 177, 201, 246, 250
Jiménez, Luz, 47–48, 108
Jiménez Sánchez, Francisco, 231
Jojutla, Morelos, 29
Jonacatepec, Morelos, 40, 56, 155
Jones, Jennifer, 138
Juárez, Benito, 11–12, 31, 63, 147–148, 167,
  182–183, 192, 233, 258
Juchitán, Oaxaca, 240
Judas, 49, 67, 105
Juxtlahuaca, Oaxaca, 240

Kahlo, Frida, 128, 136
Katz, Friedrich, 258
Katz, Jesse, 247
Kazan, Elia, 104, 173–177, 185, 197, 246
Keller, Gary D., 248
King Arthur, 55
Knight, Alan, 14–16, 18, 256

Labastida Ochoa, Francisco, 217, 222
labor, 38, 72, 79, 81, 89, 117, 191
Lacey, Mary Ann, 263
Laguna region, 115

La Mujer Obrera, 247
"Land and Liberty," 61, 93, 118, 135, 143,
  226, 236, 238–239, 246, 249
land reform, 1, 21–22, 29, 34, 36, 38, 66,
  68–69, 81, 86–87, 90–92, 99–100,
  109–110, 111, 113–117, 123, 132, 134,
  141–143, 147, 149–150, 153, 161, 163,
  168–169, 176, 197, 205–208, 211,
  215–216, 219, 223, 229, 250–251, 254,
  259; end of, 209, 213, 217, 224–226,
  228, 242
La Onda Chicana, 193
La Palma, Michoacán, 170
La Prensa, 111
La Revolución de Emiliano Zapata,
  193–194
Las Lomas, Jalisco, 170
Leigh, Vivien, 138
Lenin, V. I., 163, 256
Leo, Filomena, 265
León, Battle of, 37
León, Luis L., 64
León Bejarano, Armando, 212–214
León de la Barra, Francisco, 26, 29, 114
León-Portilla, Miguel, 231
Lewis, Oscar, 46–47
Limón Alonso, Eduardo, 263
List Arzubide, Armando, 75–76, 83, 99,
  107, 109–110, 193, 263
List Arzubide, Germán, 76–82, 84, 99,
  101, 107, 133
Loma Bonita, Oaxaca, 239–240
Lombardo Toledano, Vicente, 117
lo mexicano, 134, 257–259. See also
  nationalism
Lomnitz, Claudio, 14, 16, 18
López Avelar, Norberto, 126, 143, 146
López Ituarte, Alfonso (Héctor Ribot), 33
López Mateos, Adolfo, 146–150, 154, 158,
  162, 167, 191, 205, 220, 222, 252
López Portillo, José, 208–209, 212–216,
  228–229
López y Fuentes, Gregorio, 108–109

Los Angeles, California, 183, 246–247
Los Angeles Times, 200, 247
Los Lobos del Ritmo, 193
Los Reyes, Michoacán, 170

machismo, 21, 31, 82–84, 200, 246, 256
Macuilxóchitl, Oaxaca, 166
Madero, Francisco, 24–26, 28–34, 46, 65, 92, 99–100, 103–105, 114, 120, 130–132, 134, 161, 175–176, 183, 197, 212, 227, 248, 255
Magaña, Gildardo, 39, 48–49, 65, 69, 71, 103–106, 109–113, 115, 117, 122, 131, 134, 162, 172
Magdalena Ocotlán, Oaxaca, 238
Magdaleno, Mauricio, 106–108, 138, 160
Major Ana María, 235
Mallon, Florencia, 16
Mancisidor, José, 140–141
Maoism, 230
Marmolejo, Emigdio, 94, 243
Martínez, Abraham, 34
Martínez, Pedro, 46–48, 50, 57, 67, 109, 248
Martínez Villacaña, Luis, 217
Martino, César, 97–98, 117
Maximato, 90–91, 94–95, 97
Maximilian, 11, 258
Maya, 8
McLuhan, Marshall, 256
Melgarejo, Antonio, 34
Méndez, Elvira Bautista, 164
Mendivi, Rodolfo, 165
Mendoza, Francisco, 52
Mendoza L. Schwerdtfeger, Miguel, 65, 141–142
messianism, 55–57, 67, 77–78, 117–118, 132, 163
Mexican Food System (Sistema Alimentario Mexicano, SAM), 215
Mexican Liberal Party (Partido Liberal Mexicano, PLM), 65
Mexico, state of, 32, 43, 71, 75, 231, 235

Mexico City, 2–3, 21, 25, 28, 31, 33–35, 37–38, 42, 46, 57, 61, 63–64, 69, 80, 85, 87, 97, 103, 106, 120, 135–136, 148, 153, 177, 190–191, 193–194, 201, 207, 214, 224, 235, 253, 259, 265; and body of Zapata, 160–161, 210–213, 255; commemorations in, 72–73, 123, 129, 141, 149, 173, 208–209, 216, 227, 233; statue of Zapata, 92, 113, 158–160, 215
Michelena y Llaguna, Quirico, 136–137
Michoacán, state of, 71, 103, 113, 162, 170, 209, 227
Milpa Alta, Federal District, 47, 210, 212–213
Ministry of Public Education (Secretaría de Educación Pública, SEP), 60, 80, 98, 100, 130, 132–133, 161, 165, 173, 198, 200, 205
Mixquiahuala de Juárez, Hidalgo, 168, 170
Moctezuma, 9
Mohammed, 119
Molina Enríquez, Andrés, 82–83
Monsiváis, Carlos, 192, 204, 241
Montaño, Otilio, 2, 30, 61, 100, 106–107, 112, 199
Monterrey, Nuevo León, 229
Monument to the Revolution, 160–161, 210–213, 216
Morelia, Michoacán, 227
Morelos, José María, 10–11, 36, 48, 104, 121, 141, 148, 159, 166, 192, 196, 231, 233, 250, 257
Morrow, Dwight, 61
Moses, 55, 217, 249–250
Moya Palencia, Mario, 207
Múgica, Francisco, 69, 114
Muñoz Cota, José, 131, 260
Muñoz Zapata, Gil, 155
Murrieta, Joaquín, 182
myth, defined, 4–5; general nature of, 6–7, 12–13, 108; history of, in Mexico, 9–12, 14

NAFTA (North American Free Trade
Agreement), 225, 227–228, 230, 234,
241, 247, 265
National Action Party (Partido de Acción Nacional, PAN), 11, 142–143, 223,
242–243
National Agrarian Confederation (Confederación Nacional Agraria, CNA),
69, 71–72, 78
National Agrarian Party (Partido Nacional Agrarista, PNA), 65–66, 68–71, 73,
79, 115
National Agricultural School at
Chapingo, 61, 136, 143
National Autonomous University of
Mexico (Universidad Nacional Autónoma de Mexico, UNAM), 115, 120,
159, 190–192, 223, 237
National Committee for Integral Homage to Emiliano Zapata, 92
National Coordinating Committee of Indian Peoples (Coordinadora Nacional
de Pueblos Indios, CNPI), 216, 231
National Institute of Anthropology
and History (Instituto Nacional de
Antropología e Historia, INAH), 51–52,
54, 57
nationalism, 5, 10–11, 13, 72, 82–83,
86–87, 97–98, 110, 118, 126, 130, 141,
149, 151, 170, 180–181, 196, 230, 236,
260. See also lo mexicano
National Palace, 22, 61, 100, 130
National Peasant Confederation (Confederación Nacional Campesina,
CNC), 97, 112, 123, 125–126, 138, 143,
157, 161, 163–164, 166–167, 205–208,
210, 216, 240, 244
National Peasant League (Liga Nacional
Campesina), 93
National Plan of Ayala Coordinating
Committee (Coordinadora Nacional
Plan de Ayala, CNPA), 210, 212–213,
215, 219

National Plan of Ayala Movement (Mo-
vimiento Nacional Plan de Ayala),
209
National Polytechnic Institute, 190–191
National Revolutionary Party (Partido
Nacional Revolucionario, PNR), 90,
92, 97, 103, 116, 162, 220
Nava, Gregorio, 245
Navajoa, Sonora, 169
Neruda, Pablo, 170
New York, 180–181
newspapers, Mexico City, 28, 30–31, 35,
42–43, 46, 140, 200, 206–207, 210,
250
newspapers, Morelos, 144, 151, 206
Niños Héroes, 57
Northern Baja California, state of, 103
Noticias, 216
Nuevo Casas Grandes, Chihuahua, 263
Nuevo León, state of, 66, 169

Oacalco, Morelos, 148
Oaxaca, city of, 164–166, 205, 215, 240
Oaxaca, state of, 9, 14, 23, 43, 54, 71, 138,
162–169, 184, 196, 206, 210, 216, 219,
229, 237, 239–241, 245, 263
Oaxaca en México, 167
Oaxaca Gráfico, 167
Oaxaca Nuevo, 164–165
Oaxtepec, Morelos, 148
Obregón, Alvaro, 32, 37, 49, 52, 60,
63–73, 77–80, 86, 89–90, 100, 105,
114–115, 122, 131, 150, 171
Obregonistas, 66, 68, 77–78
Ochoa, Amparo, 193
Ochoa Campos, Moisés, 160
Ocosingo, Chiapas, 230
Olmecs, 8–9
Olmedo, Marcos, 241
O'Malley, Ilene, 13–14, 16
Orozco, José Clemente, 178–181
Orozco, Pascual, 21, 110
Ortega, Agustín N., 152–153, 155

Ortega, Alfredo, 70
Ortega, Lauro, 222
Ortiz Rubio, Pascual, 94
Othón Díaz, Enrique, 163

Palacios, Porfirio, 137–138, 140, 178, 200,
    209, 214
Palafox, Manuel, 36, 110, 116
Palancares, Jesusa, 234
Pantaleón, Emeterio, 52–53
Pariente, Agapito, 55
Parrés, José G., 65, 68–69, 88–89, 116,
    122, 132, 158, 162
Party of the Democratic Revolu-
    tion (Partido de la Revolución
    Democrática, PRD), 240
Party of the Mexican Revolution
    (Partido de la Revolución Mexicana,
    PRM), 91, 98
Paseo de la Reforma, 12, 92, 158–160
Paz, Octavio, 19, 46, 78, 134–135, 153,
    258–259
Paz Solórzano, Octavio, 78–80, 82,
    84–85, 115, 134
Peasant Justice Brigade of the Party of
    the Poor (Brigada Campesina de
    Ajusticiamiento del Partido de los
    Pobres), 195–196
Perdomo, Elpidio, 122, 143, 155
Pérez, Andrés, 94
Pérez, María Dolores, 72
Pérez Baños, Guadalupe, 166
Pérez Gasca, Alfonso, 166
Pérez Guerrero, Carlos, 103–104, 111–112,
    131–132, 142
Peters, Jean, 181
Picasso, Pablo, 60, 204
Pinchon, Edgcumb, 172–173, 175
Plan of Anenecuilco, 225
Plan of Ayala, 2, 29–30, 32, 36, 57, 61, 77,
    81, 89, 100, 106, 113, 115, 122, 141, 146,
    158, 160, 182, 199, 205, 213, 217, 237,
    239, 261, 264

Plan of Cerro Prieto, 146
Plan of Delano, 182
Plan of Guadalupe, 34
Plan of San Luis Potosí, 24, 29
Plasencia Gutiérrez, Serafín, 53
Polígrafo, 145, 211, 214
Poniatowska, Elena, 234
Pontipirani, Helène, 172
Popular Revolutionary Army (Ejército
    Popular Revolucionario, EPR), 241
Porfiriato, 24, 36, 82, 98, 111, 141, 164, 230
Portes Gil, Emilio, 97
Portugal, 55
Posada, José Guadalupe, 61, 135
Presente, 144
Prestes, Carlos, 141
Program for the Certification of Ejido
    Land Rights and the Titling of
    Urban House Plots (Programa de
    Certificación de Derechos Ejidales
    y Titulación de Solares Urbanos,
    PROCEDE), 239
Puebla, state of, 25, 30, 43, 65, 71, 138,
    170, 207
Puente de Ixtla, Morelos, 113

Quetzalcóatl, 8, 10, 55, 231–232, 246, 250
Quilamula, Morelos, 53
Quinn, Anthony, 175, 177
Quintero, Constancio, 50, 55–56
Quintero, Joaquín, 143
Quiroz, Moisés, 94
Quiroz Medina, Matías, 243

Radical Socialist Party of Tabasco, 72
radio, 91, 109, 128, 136
Rage Against the Machine, 1
Ramírez Arriaga, Manuel, 101
Ramos Pedrueza, Rafael, 69, 82, 99, 106,
    109–110, 141
reactionaries, 105, 109–110, 149, 195
Reagan, Ronald, 196
Redfield, Robert, 51, 67

Reed, Alma, 180
Reform Era, 11
Regional Mexican Labor Confederation
    (Confederación Regional Obrera
    Mexicana, CROM), 72–73, 117
Revolutionary Armed Forces of the
    People, 242
revolutionary family, 83, 90, 105, 110–112,
    123, 129, 132, 196–197
Revolution Day (November 20), 92, 101,
    212
Revolution of Agua Prieta, 64
Reyes Avilés, Carlos, 50, 77–80
Reyes Avilés, Salvador, 40, 42, 45, 50, 78,
    90, 106, 113, 134
Reyes Estrada, Jaime, 206
Ríos Zertuche, Antonio, 67
Riva Palacio, Emilio, 154
Rivera, Diego, 47, 59–63, 71, 73, 76,
    80–83, 86, 93, 100–101, 109, 113,
    135–136, 143, 178, 180, 204, 247, 254
Rivera, Edward, 182
Robles, Serafín M., 132–133
Rodríguez, Abelardo, 118
Rodríguez, José Guadalupe, 61
Roma, Texas, 181
Román, Fina, 234
Romero, Salvador, 136
Rubin, Jeffrey, 256
Rueda, Salvador, 14
Ruiz Cortines, Adolfo, 127, 130, 138, 147,
    151, 159–160, 178
Ruiz Massieu, José Francisco, 238–239
Ruiz Vasconcelos, Ramón, 166

Sacramento, California, 182
Saénz, Moisés, 99
Saint Thomas, 10
saints, cults of, 6, 9, 12
Salazar Solís, Facundo, 210
Salido Orcillo, Rubén, 139–140
Salinas de Gortari, Carlos, 2, 198, 221–
    227, 230–231, 233, 237–239, 244, 254

Salinas de Gortari, Raúl, 238–239
San Andrés Accords, 241
San Antonio, Texas, 24, 111, 181
San Baltazar Chichicápam, Oaxaca, 166,
    168
Sánchez, Graciano, 97, 117
San Cristóbal de las Casas, Chiapas,
    228
San Francisco, California, 196
San Juan Chapultepec, Oaxaca, 165
San Lucas, Federal District, 120
San Luis Potosí, state of, 71
San Nicolás Yaxé, Oaxaca, 166, 168
San Pablo Oxtotepec, Federal District,
    169, 185
Santa María del Tule, Oaxaca, 163
Santa Marta Acatitla, Federal Dis-
    trict, 85
Santiago, 9–11, 19, 56, 250
Scott, James, 255
Sebastiao, Portugal's "hidden king," 55
Serra Rojas, Andrés, 149
Silva, Marciano, 30–32, 49–50, 55–56, 77,
    82, 86, 109, 113, 234
Silva Herzog, Jesús, 13
Simon, Paul, 245
Sinaloa, state of, 112, 215, 223
Sinarquismo, 110, 121
Siqueiros, David Alfaro, 60
Smith, Anthony D., 6, 254
Sonora, state of, 64–65, 71, 95, 169, 196
Sotelo Inclán, Jesús, 119–121, 142, 156–157,
    217, 222, 224
Soviet Union, 87, 115–116
Spanish, 9–12, 31–32, 82–83, 86, 174, 201,
    220, 236
Stalin, Joseph, 116, 174
Steinbeck, John, 173–178
Stephen, Lynn, 14
Stockholm, Sweden, 140
student movement of 1968, 19, 190–195,
    230. See also Tlatelolco
Suárez Téllez, José María, 139, 185, 194

Subcomandante Marcos, 3, 230–232, 237, 245, 247–248, 254
Superbarrio Gómez, 3

Tabasco, state of, 72, 169
Taibo II, Paco Ignacio, 191
Taller de Gráfica Popular (Popular Graphics Workshop), 135–136
Tannenbaum, Frank, 54, 171–172
Tapia, Estanislao, 237
Taracena, Alfonso, 134, 198
Tehuantepec, Oaxaca, 240
Teja Zabre, Alfonso, 100
Temixco, Morelos, 157
Teotihuacán, 8
Tepalcingo, Morelos, 41, 56, 69
Tepepa, Gabriel, 25, 28–29, 79
Tepoztlán, Morelos, 46–47, 51, 53–54, 67, 157, 241, 244
Tetecala, Morelos, 155
Texas, 175, 183, 225, 265
Texcalyacac, Mexico state, 169
textbooks, 14, 98–101, 110–111, 117, 130–131, 226
"the land belongs to he who works it," 71, 76, 122, 125, 164, 167, 183
Tijuana, Baja California Norte, 238
Tlacochahuaya, Oaxaca, 166
Tlalchapa, Guerrero, 184
Tlalnepantla, Morelos, 148
Tlaltizapán, Morelos, 36, 69, 134, 197; commemorations at, 152–153, 157, 222, 241; mausoleum at, 93, 155–156, 224; and Zapata's remains, 155–156, 224, 243
Tlaquiltenango, Morelos, 25, 155
Tlatelolco, 192–195, 205, 229, 253. *See also* student movement of 1968
Tlaxcala, state of, 71, 207
Tlayacapan, Morelos, 148
Toledo Corro, Antonio, 209
Tolsa, Manuel, 92, 160
Toluca, Mexico State, 37

Tonantzin, 9
Topete, Ricardo, 77
Torices Mercado, Juan, 106
Torres Burgos, Pablo, 25, 29, 79
Torres Quintero, Gregorio, 110–111
Totolapan, Morelos, 148
transfer of sacrality, 99, 117–118, 236
Treaty of Ciudad Juárez, 26
Tulancingo de Bravo, Hidalgo, 208
Tuxtepec, Oaxaca, 216
Tuxtla Gutiérrez, Chiapas, 229
Tuzantán, Chiapas, 228

Union of Agrarista Revolutionaries of the South (La Unión de Revolucionarios Agraristas del Sur, URAS), 111–113, 122
Union of Morelos Women, 115, 128
Unión Zapata, Oaxaca, 164, 168
United Farm Workers Union, 182
United States, 11, 19, 26, 37, 57, 78–79, 110, 121, 132, 138, 141, 171–183, 185–186, 193, 196–198, 225, 227, 245, 247, 253, 263
Uranga López, Francisco, 194
Urbán Aguirre, José, 94, 117
Urban Zapatista Front, 194, 234

Vallejo, Demetrio, 192
Vargas, Alberto, 164
Vasconcelos, José, 60–61, 82, 98
Vaughan, Mary Kay, 16, 18, 256
Vázquez Rojas, Genaro, 139, 194–196
Velasco, Miguel A., 116
Venustiano Carranza, Chiapas, 229
Veracruz, state of, 34, 37, 65, 71, 132, 209
Vietnam, 197
Villa, Francisco "Pancho," 2–3, 21–22, 32, 34–35, 37, 100, 106, 111, 127, 131–132, 141, 161, 169, 172, 181–182, 192, 195, 201, 223, 228, 231, 233, 246, 256
Villa de Ayala, Morelos, 25, 42, 68, 142–143, 243–244

Villarreal, Antonio I., 67–68, 141
Villaseñor, Cástulo, 125
Villistas, 38, 127
Virgin Mary, 9, 201
Virgin of Guadalupe, 9–11, 13, 157, 178, 257–258
Viva Zapata!, 104, 174–178, 181, 183, 185, 198–199, 225, 246
voceros of the revolution, 13–14, 79–80, 83, 85, 251
Votán, 231–232
Votán–Zapata, 232–234

Wall Street Journal, 237
Warman, Arturo, 225, 239, 242
Weber, Max, 7
Welch, Raquel, 204
Wilson, Woodrow, 34
Womack, John, 197–198, 205, 222–224, 231, 246, 248
women, 60, 83, 109, 143, 187–189, 220–221, 247; at commemorations, 86, 127–129, 166; courted by Zapata, 97, 103, 129; in fighting, 84; and sexual violence, 63, 130, 188, 234–235; tell Zapata of ambush, 52, 56, 75–76, 82
Worker-Peasant Coalition of the Isthmus (Coalición Obrera Campesina Estudiantil del Istmo, COCEI), 240
World War II, 110, 121, 123, 191

Xochimilco, Federal District, 21, 120, 223, 242
Xochitepec, Morelos, 157

Yampolsky, Mariana, 135
Yautepec, Morelos, 51, 148
Yaxchilan, Chiapas, 8
Yedra Islas, Domingo, 55
Yodohino, Oaxaca, 166
Yucatán, state of, 23

Zacatecas, state of, 71
Zacatepec, Morelos, 146, 156–157, 244
Zanuck, Darryl, 175–176
Zapata, Ana María, 58, 115, 128, 143, 148, 212, 220–222, 226, 237
Zapata, Diego, 122, 143, 212, 214, 226
Zapata, Emiliano, adopted at national level, 59–87; appropriated by national government, 88–118, 242; as bandit, 28–29, 33, 43, 67, 72, 74, 78, 87, 98, 107, 111, 114, 119–120, 141, 162–163, 181, 195, 199–200, 242, 264; body of, 41, 45, 50–52, 80–81, 93–95, 108, 127, 136, 153–156, 160–161, 168, 184, 187, 203–204, 210–213, 217, 224, 243, 247, 255; and the border, 260–265; as charro, 21–22, 60, 63, 79, 82, 84, 132, 141, 159, 187, 246; as conscience of the revolution, 136, 150, 177, 181, 197, 236; death of, 18, 24, 40–58, 64, 75, 80–81, 107–109, 111, 119, 132, 134–136, 154–155, 181, 195, 199, 204, 221, 250; did not die, 50–54, 75–77, 117, 120, 144, 152–153, 171, 196, 204, 221; as father figure, 47, 50, 108; as founding father, 19, 83, 87, 127, 150, 255; geographical spread of cult, 152–186; and "Golden Age," 119–151; as homosexual, 189, 246; horse of, 41, 55, 61, 166; incorruptibility, 105, 126, 129, 132, 148, 177, 196–197; as Indian, 18, 61, 68, 81–84, 95–97, 101, 109, 121, 131, 135, 168, 171, 180, 231–234, 236, 246–248, 250, 254, 259; as macho, 21, 24, 31, 82–84, 94, 97, 103, 105, 107–108, 116, 118, 129–130, 188–189, 198, 234, 246, 249–250; as mestizo, 18, 82, 100, 141, 231, 246, 250; and nationalism, 13, 72, 79, 82, 86–87, 97, 118, 130, 132, 141–142, 149, 161, 170, 196, 233–234, 236, 244, 257–260; and order, 84, 127, 207; as patriarch, 13, 18, 77, 83–84, 94, 129–130,

159, 198, 217, 250; and progress and productivity, 124–125, 127, 129, 131, 163, 180, 207, 251; as rebel, 19, 185–219, 253–254; regional cult of, 41–58; and revolutionary fighting, 21–40; statues and monuments of, 73, 92–95, 115, 126, 129, 154, 157–162, 168–169, 184, 204–205, 208, 212–215, 217, 222–223, 226, 239–240, 243, 261–263; and women, 63, 82–84, 97, 103, 107–109, 127–130, 187–189, 234–235

Zapata, Eufemio, 87, 107, 175, 249

Zapata, Margarita, 234

Zapata, María Elena, 105

Zapata, Mateo, 86, 122, 143–144, 209–213, 217, 225, 237, 246

Zapata, Nicolás, 53, 58, 122, 126, 143, 162, 188, 210, 212–213

Zapata Petroleum Corporation, 225

Zapatista Army of National Liberation (Ejército Zapatista de Liberación Nacional, EZLN), 2, 19, 228–238, 241–242, 245, 247–248, 254, 260

Zapatista Front, 122, 126–127, 129, 131, 133, 136–139, 142, 148–150, 156–162, 165, 168–169, 172–173, 175, 178, 184–185, 194, 198–200, 209–211

Zapotecs, 9

Zedillo, Ernesto, 226–227, 238–239, 241–242

Zedong, Mao, 191

Zicuicho, Michoacán, 170

Zimatlan, Oaxaca, 207

Zotoltitlán, Guerrero, 168

Zúñiga, Gregoria, 53